Elizabeth Jenkins, in this classic biography of Jane Austen, has realised not only a sensitive portrait of the novelist but also a superb landscape of family life in London, Bath and Chawton during the Napoleonic Wars. Miss Jenkins has written many novels, which include *Virginia Water*, *The Winters*, *Robert and Helen*, *Young Enthusiasts* and *The Tortoise and The Hare*, and her studies of *Elizabeth The Great*, *Jane Austen* and *Lady Caroline Lamb* have been recognised as classics in the art of biography.

ACKNOWLEDGEMENTS

I have to acknowledge the kindness of the Clarendon Press in allowing me to make use of Dr. Chapman's editions, Jane Austen's novels and letters.

Also of Sir F. D. Mackinnon in allowing me to quote his opinion expressed in his work *Grand Larceny* on the trial of Mrs. Leigh Perrot.

Thanks are also due to Messrs. John Lane for permission to quote a letter of Captain Frank Austen from *Jane Austen and Her Sailor Brothers*.

JANE AUSTEN

Elizabeth Jenkins

CARDINAL edition published in 1973
by Sphere Books Ltd
30/32 Gray's Inn Road, London WC1X 8JL

First published in Great Britain by
Victor Gollancz Ltd 1938
Copyright © Elizabeth Jenkins 1938, 1972
Sphere Books edition published 1972

Set in Linotype Plantin

Printed in Great Britain by
Hazell Watson & Viney Ltd,
Aylesbury, Bucks

ISBN 0 351 16938 5

CHAPTER ONE

The eighteenth century was an age such as our imagination can barely comprehend; weltering as we do in a slough of habitual ugliness, ranging from the dreary horrors of Victorian sham gothic to the more lively hideousness of modern jerry-building, with advertisements defacing any space that might be left unoffendingly blank, and the tourist scattering his trail of chocolate paper, cigarette ends and film cartons, we catch sight every now and again of a house-front, plain and graceful, with a fanlight like the half of a spider's web and a slip of iron balcony; among the florid or stark disfigurements of a graveyard we discover a tombstone with elegant letters composing, in a single sentence, a well-turned epitaph. Among a bunch of furnishing fabrics, we come upon a traditional eighteenth-century chintz, formal and exquisitely gay; a print shows us the vista of a London street, with two rows of blond, porticoed houses closing in a view of trees and fields. The ghost of that vanished loveliness haunts us in every memorial that survives the age: a house in its park, a tea-cup, the type and binding of a book.

Ill fares the land, to hastening ills a prey
Where wealth accumulates and men decay.

The words greet us from the lid of a china patch box, a pale, bright yellow, a trivial little object devoted to a silly purpose, but it is stamped with a sentiment from *The Deserted Village*. We find it almost impossible to realize that the fleeting vision with which our eyes are occasionally blessed was to the eighteenth-century man or woman the common sight of daily life; plain elegance, uncompromising good taste, surrounded them with an almost monotonous completeness.

But if we are in danger of breaking our hearts over this spirit of beauty which has vanished from the earth, it is our duty to remember that there existed with it, ignored or tolerated, a state of squalor and wretchedness which, to this relatively humane and hygienic age, is nearly as difficult to visualize as its heavenly obverse. The state of English prisons as revealed by Howard's survey published in 1777, the London slums, in which Dr. Johnson roughly computed that one thousand people starved to death every year, the conditions of the Army and Navy, on active service, and when thrown crippled and destitute,

5

without pension and without charity, on a heedless world, the savage callousness of the officials entrusted with the administration of Poor Relief, the manifold horrors, already springing into existence, of the Industrial Revolution—all these things very wholesomely temper our regret, our feeling that, as Dr. Johnson would have said: 'It is a melancholy thing to be reserved to these times,' and very nearly resign us to an age of mob mentality and mass production. None the less, when we are considering that age, the last of those in English history which produced works of great art, we must consider too the texture of the daily experience of the ordinary seeing, hearing, feeling individual; vulgarity they had in plenty, but it was the vulgarity of Gilray and Rowlandson's cartoons, with their bulbous calves and hectic noses; ghastly realism, but in the medium of Hogarth's *Gin Lane* and *The Rake's Progress*; the girl of to-day who can see life only in terms of the cinema, had her counterpart in the eighteenth century, and she spoke in the accents of Lydia Languish. Could there be drawn a more vivid, a more compendious comparison?

That there was no cheap, sophisticated entertainment for the masses was part of a state of things in which thousands and thousands of people were less comfortable, less well dressed, less entertained, less informed than they are to-day; but it also meant that there was not a vast majority which by its very numbers imposed its ideas, its prepossessions and its tastes on the world in which the educated person must now exist; the lower middle class, as it is the most considerable among consumers, dictates the canons of a taste which, by its preponderating bulk, has corrupted and destroyed the standards of language, of architecture, of entertainment and of literature, which once prevailed. This development has brought in its train a great increase in human happiness, and it has annihilated something so precious that its very absence has taken away from us the power to estimate its value. One may find an apt illustration of our gain and loss in the bear-ward who was Tony Lumpkin's companion at The Three Pigeons: he led a dancing bear, something of which we hate to think, but the tunes to which it danced were Dr. Arne's 'Water Parted' and Handel's minuet from 'Ariadne.'

If it be permissible to dwell on the beauty of the eighteenth century without perpetually reminding oneself of its horrors, it is surely so in relation to life in the country. The countryside had then a two-fold loveliness; not only were the roads unspoiled, often unpaved, it is true, but bordered with copse and meadow, orchard and stream, but such buildings as there were adorned the landscape instead of defacing it.

6

Hampshire, in the district about the village of Steventon, had, standing back among the timbered meadows, houses of many ages, from the Elizabethan half-manor, half-farmhouse, of rosy, saffron brick, nestling in the shelter of its hill, to the gentleman's seat, a classical stone erection with concealed roof and stone-garlanded, pillared front, planned with an eye to views and crowning a gentle, tree-covered slope. Of the soil itself, Gilbert White said that it was composed of: 'a kind of white land, neither chalk nor clay, neither fit for pasture nor for the plough.' 'This white soil,' he added, 'produces the brightest hops.'

The village of Steventon itself was little more than a row of cottages, the important families of the neighbourhood living at some distance on their various estates. The Rectory stood on one side of a lane, which had the breadth of a good road, but the weak places in whose unpaved surface were filled up by a man with some shovelsful of stones whenever an unusual amount of company was expected at the houses beyond it. On one side of the lane stood a spacious barn, on the other, surrounded by meadows sprinkled with elm and chestnut trees, was the Rectory, a house with a flat façade and narrow roof, square sashed windows and a trellised porch; the ground in front had a wide, curving drive and to the right of it a plantation of elm, chestnut and fir. At the back, a bow window looked out on to a garden where an alley of turf, bordered by strawberry beds, ended in a sundial; a terrace of turf, shaded by elm trees, ran between the garden and the open meadows, and led to a copse, visible from the house's upper windows.

The bow window belonged to the Rector's study. The Reverend George Austen was a very handsome man with bright hazel eyes and finely curling hair, prematurely white; he was a distinguished classical scholar, and he was also acutely sensitive to the construction of an English sentence. He taught all his own children in their early years, and one of his sons till the latter became of university age, and he augmented his income by taking pupils into the house, three and four at a time until his own family grew too large for them to be accommodated. The Rector enjoyed a state of rational, almost ideal happiness. He lived the life of a scholar, devoting the greater portion of the time that was left over from his parish duties to his books, and at the same time he preserved a simplicity complete enough for perfect freedom yet compatible with every reasonable comfort. He had his strawberry beds, his elm walk, his home meadows, his position in a pleasant neighbourhood as a much-respected country gentleman; but though he kept his carriage, the interior of the Rectory had in some respects the plainness of a cottage; the walls and ceiling were joined without any cornice,

7

and some of the walls were whitewashed; the sunlight which struck through the plantation or the fire and candlelight at night brought out nothing rich, merely the essentials of a living-room in an age that made nothing crude or mean; chairs and a table, a pier glass, a glass-fronted cupboard with a gilt china tea service behind its panes. In a small front parlour at the right of the front door, Mrs. Austen with her aristocratic nose was usually to be found, darning the family stockings whether visitors were there or not. She might, strong in the consciousness of her own, be 'amusingly particular' about other people's noses, but with a growing family on her hands, she had no idea of giving in to fine lady-ism, and people were welcome to call provided they did not expect her to put away the mending. She always said that she was no beauty: her sister Jane was beautiful, but she was merely good-looking and sensible; but she had a distinguished air and a decisive, epigrammatic turn of speech. It was thought that she had perhaps inherited this from her uncle, Dr. Theophilus Leigh, the Master of Balliol, whose *bons mots* were famous. When an acquaintance was described as having been 'egged on' to matrimony, Dr. Leigh had observed: 'Let us hope the yoke will sit lightly on him.'

Mrs. Austen's early married life, however she might bring to it a shrewd and intellectual mind, was domestic to the exclusion of every other interest; she bore four sons in little more than four years, and when she was not tied to her own house, on one occasion at least she went to London to nurse a sister-in-law in her confinement. The lady whom she nursed in town was Mrs. Walter, the wife of George Austen's half-brother; to Mr. and Mrs. Walter some very amusing letters were written by their country relatives at Steventon, and in later years, a few containing little pieces of information about the younger daughter of the Rectory. Mrs. Austen much preferred her own country existence, and said of her stay in London: "Tis a sad place. I would not live in it on any account, one has not time to do one's duty either to God or man.' Of Mrs. Austen's first four children, the third, George, was subject to fits and was never able to live with the family, and the temperament of the Austens is nowhere better shown than by the fact that, affectionate and forthright as they were, beyond the statement of his death in 1838, not a single word in reference to him is discoverable in any of their printed memoirs and correspondence.

The three other little boys, James, Edward and Henry, were splendidly healthy and high-spirited; then a daughter was born, called Cassandra after her mother. Like her brothers, she was put out to nurse for the first months, and when she was brought home, Mrs. Austen wrote and begged Mr. and Mrs. Walter to pay a visit, saying:

8

'I want to show you my Henry and my Cassy, who are both reckoned very fine children.' Presently she wrote: 'My little girl is almost ready to run away!' The child had an aquiline nose, and her eyes were black. Mrs. Austen did not say that she was pretty, but when the baby was two, she wrote to Mrs. Walter: 'My little girl talks all day long, and, in my opinion, is a very entertaining companion.' By this time there was another boy, Francis, also doing well; as his mother said: 'My last boy is very stout'; and again, their friends in London were expecting to hear of a confinement; until on December 17th, 1775, Mr. Austen wrote to Mrs. Walter:

'DEAR SISTER,
'You have doubtless been for some time in expectation of hearing from Hampshire, and perhaps wondered a little we were in our old age grown such bad reckoners, but so it was, for Cassy certainly expected to have been brought to bed a month ago, however, last night the time came, and without a great deal of warning, everything was soon happily over. We have now another girl, a present plaything for her sister Cassy, and a future companion. She is to be Jenny, and seems to me as if she would be as like Harry as Cassy is to Neddy. Your sister, thank God, is pure well after it.'

Among so many brothers, it must have been a delight to little Cassandra to have a sister to look after and to play with, and with a good share of her father's affectionate nature and her mother's practical good sense, she soon became, young as she was, the most important figure in her little sister's world. Mrs. Austen had her last child soon after, a sixth son, christened Charles, and with a new baby and a large young family, she was only too glad that Cassandra took upon herself so much of the care of Jane. The younger child repaid her sister's affection a hundredfold, and Mrs. Austen said that if Cassandra were to have her head cut off, she believed Jane would insist on having hers cut off too.

Life in the Rectory was pleasant for a large party of children; for one thing, the Austens, though very lively, were unusually good tempered. Family disagreements, to say nothing of family quarrels, were unknown to them, and besides being fond of each other, they were very friendly with the pupils their father took into the house. Mr. Austen was careful as to whom he accepted, taking only 'a few youths of chosen friends and acquaintances,' and there are several references to the comfortable way the boys settled in with the family. 'Jemmy and Neddy' were 'very happy in a new playfellow, Lord Lymington.' He

9

was between five and six years old; then there was Master Vander-stegen; *he* was nearly fourteen, and backward, but 'very good tempered and well disposed.' Another reason for the general pleasantness of a family which, living in somewhat close quarters, might have been expected to get in each other's way, was that the boys had vigorous interests of their own. Intelligent as they all were, their father's teaching was at least not irksome to them, and James and Henry had a strong academic bent; but all of them were wildly eager sportsmen. From their earliest years they hunted and shot, and Francis displayed not only the sporting enthusiasm of the family, but a keen business capacity into the bargain. At the age of seven he bought a pony for one pound, eleven shillings and sixpence. It was a bright chestnut and he called it Squirrel. He rode to hounds on it for two years, jumping 'everything that the pony could get his nose over,' and then sold it for two pounds, twelve and six.

For the little girls who could not hunt and shoot, the range of interests was smaller. They did not ride as they might have done. Mrs. Austen had been a horsewoman, and in her trousseau there had been a scarlet riding-habit, but this had long been cut up into coats and trousers for the boys when very little; but there were amusements to get the girls out of doors. When the weather was good, the walks about Steventon were very beautiful; the lanes were full of primroses and violets in the spring, and the neighbourhood had the beauty of Hampshire woodland. Jane said many years afterwards that she thought beauty of landscape must be one of the joys of heaven. There was a home farm also, where Mrs. Austen's dairy was supplied by five Alderney cows; and though Mr. Edward Austen Leigh says that his aunts would never have taken a hand in the actual brewing and baking of the Rectory, yet a household which has its own dairy, bakes its own bread, brews its own ale and does its own laundering on the premises, has always something going on of interest to two eager little girls.

When Cassandra was about ten and Jane seven years old, the Rev. George Austen seems to have felt that for his daughters, at least, his own teaching was not sufficient. Mrs. Austen's sister, the beautiful Jane, had married Dr. Cooper, a clergyman living near Bath, and Dr. Cooper had a sister, Mrs. Cawley, who, the widow of a master of Brasenose, undertook the care of a few children at her house in Oxford. Jane was thought to be too young to benefit very much from any educational advantages Mrs. Cawley might bestow, but it was already taken for granted by the family that where Cassandra went, there, if humanly possible, she must go also. With them went their cousin Jane Cooper. Perhaps the three of them together were happy enough, but Mrs. Cawley was somewhat unsympathetic and very formal in her manners, and coming from such a home as Steventon, Cassandra and Jane felt the change very much. One may imagine Jane, a small, slender child with a round face and big black eyes, following Cassandra like a shadow, shy, but ready at once to be friendly and merry with anyone who was kind. After a while Mrs. Cawley moved to Southampton, and was allowed to take the children with her. Here, however, Cassandra and Jane fell ill of what was called at the time a putrid fever, which was perhaps diphtheria. Jane Cooper longed for her mother and aunt, but Mrs. Cawley would not allow her to write to them; at last, however, her cousin Jane became so very ill that the homesick, frightened child could bear it no longer and wrote to her mother, who, with Mrs. Austen, came down to Southampton immediately. Jane nearly died. She recovered with her mother's nursing, but Mrs. Cooper, who took her daughter away, and went back to Bath with her, had caught the infection, and shortly after died herself.

This severe early illness does not seem to have made the Austens unduly anxious about their younger daughter, and quite soon another boarding-school experiment was tried, this time with much more success. The Abbey School at Reading where Jane and Cassandra were sent was kept by an elderly lady called Mrs. Latournelle. It was a simple sort of place, and Mrs. Sherwood, who went to the Abbey School about five years later than the Austens, has left a vivid account of it in her autobiography.

Mrs. Latournelle was far removed from the severity of Mrs. Cawley. It was true that her cap and neckerchief were always starched and spotless, that her parlour was hung round with pictures of urns and weeping willows embroidered in chenille; but she was at the same time stout and very active, although she had a cork leg, and Mrs. Sherwood estimated her capacity as fit for nothing but giving out clothes for the wash, ordering dinner and making tea. She added that so far as she could remember, Mrs. Latournelle's conversation was never so fluent as upon the topic of plays and play-acting, green-room anecdotes and the private lives of actors.

The school buildings were romantic, formed in part as they were of the old gatehouse of the Abbey, and surrounded by a spacious, shady garden, very delightful to the girls in hot summer evenings. The régime was easy-going in the extreme. Provided the girls appeared in the tutor's study for a few hours each morning, they could spend the rest of the day gossiping in the turrets, lounging in the garden or out of the window above the gateway, quite undeterred by the jovial old lady of the cork leg. At the same time the domestic arrangements were

11

admirably clean and comfortable. Altogether it seems to have been a school in a thousand.

The Austens' stay, however, was not a lengthy one. When Jane was nine they returned home, and from that time they never left it. Mr. Austen had sent his daughters away for the benefit of a young lady's education, and they may indeed have 'scrambled themselves' into the rudiments of one, for if Mrs. Latournelle did not arduously promote a girl's education, at least she did not, like some schoolmistresses, go out of her way to obstruct it; but there can be no doubt that Jane Austen's real education was gained in the years between nine and sixteen which she spent under her father's care. When Henry Austen prefixed a short biographical notice of his sister to the posthumous edition of *Northanger Abbey* and *Persuasion*, he dwelt on what the Rector had done for his brilliant child. 'Being not only a profound scholar, but possessing a most exquisite taste in every species of literature, it is not wonderful that his daughter Jane should at a very early age have become sensible to the charms of style and enthusiastic in the cultivation of her own language.' Whether she joined her brothers' lessons in the Rector's study, or whether Mr. Austen gave her what time he could spare apart from them, we do not know. His attention was not now so fully occupied by his sons. James, who was twelve years older than Jane, had already obtained an Oxford degree and was a Fellow of St. John's. He was the most scholarly of all the brothers, and Jane very much admired his gifts; he was the least lively of the family, with a thin face and dark melancholy eyes; very much in sympathy with the dawning Romantic Revival, and fond of Cowper's poetry. The second brother, Edward, had been removed from the family circle by what was, from a worldly point of view, a stroke of fantastical good fortune. A distant connection of Mr. Austen's, Mr. Thomas Knight of Chawton House in Hampshire and Godmersham Park in Kent, had no children of his own. His family had always been kindly disposed to the Austens and he and his wife had taken a great fancy to Edward and often had him for visits at Chawton or Godmersham, so much so that Mr. Austen began at last to protest and say Edward was getting too far behind with his Latin grammar; but Mrs. Austen said: 'I think, my dear, you had better oblige your cousins and let the child go'; and in due course Mr. Knight adopted Edward and made him the heir to his property. The impression given by Edward's portrait is not that of a clever man, but of an eminently sound and capable one. Mr. and Mrs. Knight chose the one among the Austen boys most suited to the career of a country gentleman; they brought him up with that end perpetually in view, and instead of putting him to the University, as

12

his father would probably have done, they sent him to make the Grand Tour; thus he was abroad when his sisters came home from Reading.

Widely different from James or Edward, was the eldest brother now living at home, Henry, the handsomest, most fascinating, least stable of all the family. Henry inherited his father's bright hazel eyes, and the gaiety and good humour which were family characteristics were concentrated in him with an effect of positive brilliance. He was not profound, but he learned so readily, and executed everything he did with such elegance and dash, that his father's affection for him somewhat overpowered his judgement, and he thought Henry the cleverest of all his children. High spirits and a flow of stimulating conversation made him a delight in a household where the inmates were all prepared to enjoy each other's company, and though people not under the spell of his immediate presence, and writing of him a generation or so later, could point out his weaknesses—how, unlike his brothers, he could not decide on a career and pursue it without looking back, but was first a soldier, then a banker and last a clergyman; how he made a marriage that was not to the family's taste; and that when he wrote on a serious subject his sense of humour could not save him from being pompous and jejune—none the less, he has an infinite claim on our attention and gratitude; he was Jane Austen's favourite brother, and it was he who left the short but invaluable account of her.

The two youngest brothers were also at home, though Francis, a year older than Jane, was soon, at the age of twelve, to enter the Naval Academy at Portsmouth. Francis, as might be expected of the infant horse-dealer, was a 'self-contained' child, and remarkably clever with his hands. When he grew up he made toys for his children which were carefully handed down to generations of descendants. He had a mop of curly hair, and when he had been told to keep out of a room which he wanted to enter, the door would gradually open and the curls would make their appearance. He was resolute and dauntless in the pursuit of his own way, and never frightened of anything, except the sudden braying of a donkey.

The baby, Charles, was very much the property and plaything of his little sisters; when he was a man he was still to Cassandra and Jane 'our own little brother.' It was a very full and well-balanced family life for Jane; parents differing widely but perfectly in sympathy, older brothers to amuse and interest her, a younger brother to take care of, and, more important than all the rest, a sister.

CHAPTER TWO

Beside the immediate family, there was a relation who, from Jane's seventh year or so onwards, occupied a most important place in the Austens' attention; whose cleverness, elegance and fashion made her fascinating to Jane as the latter grew up. Jane was very early able to be amused by people's unconscious humour, but she also delighted in positive wit and sparkle, and her father's niece, Eliza Hancock, besides commanding her admiration and affection, is one of the very few people who are pointed out as having inspired a character in one of Jane Austen's novels.

Eliza, or Betsy as she was called at first, was the child of Mr. Austen's sister Philadelphia and a Dr. Hancock who was known to the great Warren Hastings. Betsy was born in India; she was small, very pretty, with a brown complexion and large black eyes, and like many Anglo-Indian children she grew up imperious and spoilt, with a conviction of her own importance that even the Austen good sense could never entirely subdue. Her mother doted on her; and it was to her mother's friendship with a Mrs. Buchanan that Betsy owed a piece of remarkable good fortune. Mrs. Buchanan, the widow of an officer who had perished in the Black Hole, became Warren Hastings' first wife, and when, a few years later she died at the birth of a daughter, leaving a boy of three years old, Hastings, anxious to send his son away from the baneful effects of the Indian climate, was only too thankful to hear of Mrs. Hancock's brother, the Rev. George Austen, as a guardian for little George. The latter thus became one of Mr. Austen's earliest pupils, though, as he was little more than a baby, he was more in Mrs. Austen's care than the Rector's; and when he died at the age of six of 'a putrid sore throat,' Mrs. Austen was almost as much in grief as if he had been a child of her own. In the meantime, the Governor-General, a domestic man and very fond of children, was grateful for the kindness which Mrs. Hancock showed him in his misery, and when her own daughter was born he stood godfather to the baby and gave her the name he had meant to give his own.

It was Dr. Hancock's intention to make a comfortable fortune and come home to spend it; but when he had settled in England, he found that his means were less adequate than he had thought, and that he himself was obliged to go out to India once more and rebuild his fortune. Left in England, Mrs. Hancock relied completely on her brother's protection and advice, and Betsy quite fell in love with her handsome, kindly uncle. Mr. Austen, with his fondness for intelligent and lively children, was less critical in his affection than Mrs. Austen was likely to be, and was perhaps more agreeable to Miss Betsy as an uncle than Mrs. Austen as an aunt.

Before he could return to his family, Dr. Hancock died in India, leaving his affairs in a much-embarrassed state, but the generosity of Warren Hastings came to the relief of his goddaughter and her mother. He settled ten thousand pounds upon them.

Having lost her husband, and being at the same time comfortably provided for, Mrs. Hancock now had nothing in the world to think of but giving Betsy every advantage and every pleasure that she could possibly obtain for her. She decided that her education should be finished abroad, and in 1780, when Jane was a child of five, Betsy, now known as Eliza, removed with her mother to Paris.

The first mutterings of the Revolution could be heard by those who had ears to hear, but such people did not include Mrs. Hancock and her gay, excitable, pretty daughter. Within the narrow sphere of Parisian society it was possible to be as elegant, as dissipated, as self-centred, as blind and deaf, as seems scarcely credible to those living in a later age, to whom, on looking back, nine years seems but a moment in time before the avalanche of that gigantic disruption. To the eager debutante the social structure in which she moved seemed as solid, as important, as immovable, as the palace of Versailles; in salons and in parks, at *fêtes champêtres,* at before-breakfast concerts and at midnight balls, life passed from day to day in as small a circle, with as heightened a brilliance, as if it were the reflection in a convex mirror.

In the midst of her distractions, Eliza did not forget her Steventon relations; she had a miniature painted for her uncle, which showed her with her face narrow and large-eyed, beneath a very full coiffure, lightly powdered, and wearing a white dress trimmed with blue. She wrote to him: 'It is reckoned like what I am at present. The dress is quite the present fashion of what I usually wear.' Mr. Austen might be pleased with the portrait and the attention, but the next thing he heard about his niece filled him with dismay; she had become engaged to a wealthy Frenchman, Jean Capotte, the Comte de Feuillide. Mr. Austen had not, of course, seen the Comte de Feuillide, but he expressed himself as 'much concerned' at the proposed connection, which would lead, he was afraid, to his sister and her daughter 'giving up their friends, their country and their religion.' But what did it matter what he was afraid of? Eliza loved her uncle dearly and had a great respect for his opinion, but it could hardly be supposed that on such

15

a matter as this she would do otherwise than please herself. Besides, her mother approved of the match. The wedding was celebrated, and shortly afterwards Eliza wrote in glowing terms to her cousin, Phila Walter, of her happiness and importance. Her husband was everything that was handsome and agreeable; to say that he loved her was scarcely to do justice to either of them, 'since he literally adores me.' She enumerated her blessings: her wealth, her rank, her 'numerous and brilliant acquaintance.' It would have been mere hypocrisy to disguise the fact that Eliza de Feuillide was a most sought-after and dazzling young lady; nor was the Comtesse guilty of such affectation.

In 1786 she was expecting a baby, and as she and the Comte wished it to be born in England, she and her mother came to London and took a house in Orchard Street. Here a son was born, and called after his mother's godfather, Hastings de Feuillide. For some time the party moved between England and France. In both countries Eliza was unremitting in the discharge of her social duties. While in London she wrote to Phila Walter describing her mode of life: 'I have been for some time past the greatest rake imaginable, and really wonder how such a meagre creature as I am can support so much fatigue.' She had stood for two hours in the Drawing Room, 'loaded' with the great hoop of her court dress; had gone on to the Duchess of Cumberland's, and from there to Almack's, where she had stayed till five in the morning. It was exhausting, but it was obligatory; but in the midst of these functions there was one which claimed her attention, of a very different nature. In 1788 the trial of Warren Hastings opened in Westminster Hall. The proceedings, of which Macaulay has left so solemn and magnificent a picture, were on a scale so different from anything in our experience that even with his assistance we can hardly conceive them; such were the magnitude of the interests involved and the stupendous eloquence of the orators who inveighed against them. Macaulay's enchantment evokes the scene as no first-hand information can; but the accounts of eye-witnesses, taking for once a second place, provide, as it were, an interesting footnote to the historian. Fanny Burney attended many days of the trial, and with feelings quite as violently party to Hastings as Eliza de Feuillide's could be. She commented on the paleness of Hastings' face and its immovable expression of distress. The gentlemen in the green benches who looked like a pack of hairdressers were really the Commons.

In August, Eliza made a visit to Oxford, where James and Henry were delighted to do the honours to their attractive cousin. Eliza was charmed by the garden of St. John's and 'longed to be a Fellow,' that she 'might walk in it every day.' She was also much taken with academic

16

dress; she thought the square cap 'mighty becoming,' and, as if from an instinctive association of ideas, she added that Henry had grown so tall, he was now taller than his father, and that he wore his hair powdered 'in a very *tonish* style.' There had been 'a coolness' between the writer and Henry, but after Henry's confessing himself to be quite in the wrong, this had been done away with, and they were now on what Eliza described as 'very proper, relation-like terms,' but which were perhaps, if anything, slightly more interesting than the terms between most relations.

Eliza had also a passion for the theatre; in the summer of 1787 she had gone with her mother and Phila Walter to Tunbridge Wells, and had 'bespoken' two comedies at the local theatre; Garrick's *Bon Ton* and Mrs. Cowley's *Which is the Man*, and in the Christmas of that year which she and Mrs. Hancock spent at Steventon, Eliza inspired a burst of amateur theatricals in her cousins and their friends. The fact that *Bon Ton* and *Which is the Man* were the plays decided on shows who was the ruling spirit. The big barn on the other side of the lane was fitted up as a theatre, and meantime the Rectory itself was filled to overflowing. The Austens could only have house-parties at Christmas and Midsummer, when the pupils went home for their holidays; and this Christmas, with the theatricals as an attraction, the fullest advantage was taken of the opportunity. Word was, however, sent to Phila Walter that room could be found for her, provided she would take a part in the plays, but that Mrs. Austen had no room 'for any idle young people.' Phila Walter was sure she could not act and did not mean to try, and remained steadfast to her objection in spite of entreaties from Eliza, who was really very fond of her. ('My Aunt Austen can only promise you "a hole to hide your head in," but I think you will not mind this inconvenience; I am sure I should not— to be with you.') In vain did the Comtesse hold out the promise of 'a most brilliant party and a great deal of amusement, the house full of company, frequent balls.' Phila stood firm and would not come. Otherwise, all was gaiety and enthusiasm. The Austens were not new to amateur theatricals. Three years ago they had given a performance of *The Rivals*. From time to time they had given plays in their own dining-room, though it could scarcely have accommodated more than a row of spectators along the wall. The proceedings this Christmas were on a much handsomer scale; as befitted their respective temperaments, James wrote the prologue and Henry and Eliza acted the chief parts, and one may imagine how very exciting a child of twelve, who had never been inside a real theatre, found the goings-on in the great barn.

17

The Comtesse de Feuillide was naturally an important person at Steventon; her uncle was fond of her and proud of her, James and Henry were fascinated by her, and to her little cousin Jane she was, with her fashion, her liveliness, her assurance, her *savoir vivre*, an object of wonder and admiration. Then something happened which gave her the deepest possible claim on their imaginations, their sympathy and interest. The Revolution had broken out. The Comte de Feuillide, who had come to London to be with his wife because her mother had just died, had taken her to Bath, but Eliza was too unhappy to enjoy it; they returned therefore to town, to be met by letters announcing to the Comte de Feuillide that if he did not return to France immediately, he would be proscribed as an *émigré* and his estates would be confiscated.

Not realizing, perhaps, how acutely dangerous a return would prove, or perhaps realizing too well but deciding on it none the less, he said good-bye to his wife and crossed to France; but the reign of Terror was already established. The travesty of legal process, with which the Committee of Public Safety amused itself, was seldom better exhibited than in the case of a friend of the Comte de Feuillide, the Marquise de Marlboeuf. The Committee having discovered that certain fields on Madame de Marlboeuf's estate were under hay and sanfoin for her cattle, instead of wheat, pronounced the charge that she had purposely allowed arable land to run to waste with the object of creating a famine. The Comte de Feuillide should have realized that death, without the possibility of reprieve, awaited Madame de Marlboeuf, and that all a friend could do was to encourage her meet it with fortitude. Instead, he made an effort both futile and disastrous. Knowing that whatever the nature of the evidence it would be sufficient to convict the prisoner, he attempted to bribe the witnesses into bringing none at all. To take the Count's money and expose him to the Committee in the name of the Republic was equally the duty and the pleasure of loyal citizens, and on February 12th, 1794, Madame de Marlboeuf and the Comte de Feuillide were executed on one scaffold.

A sudden death in the family circle is a shock affecting every member in a different manner. This one was made dreadful by every circumstance of terror, distance, the completeness of bereavement. The death of the Comte de Feuillide was a trifle in that slaughter-house; it was not of great significance when compared with those ages of callous wickedness which had, in their turn, produced the Revolution; but in the Rectory at Steventon the single death was felt as the whole causes and consequences of the Revolution could never be; and to the end of her life Jane had a horror of France. Within a year of her death, she described someone's coming back from France 'thinking of the French as one could wish, disappointed in everything.'*

Poor Eliza, an orphan and a widow, was doubly dear to them now.

* Letter 133.

CHAPTER THREE

The susceptible child was surrounded by scenes and people to love, and poured out her affections on family and home, relations, friends, books, fields, and woods. In the neighbouring parish of Ashe, the Rector's wife, Mrs. Lefroy, was a great friend of Mr. and Mrs. Austen and very kind to Jane, who admired and loved her passionately. Mrs. Lefroy, to her eyes, seemed to present the unusual combination of being at the same time very amusing and very good. Her manners were most attractive—enthusiastic and sweet; she was also elegant and graceful; with so many charms, Jane thought it wonderfully kind of her to be so encouraging to someone so much younger than herself; she was touched and delighted by Mrs. Lefroy's affection for her, and a long time afterwards, among Mrs. Lefroy's many attractions, she remembered with an aching heart 'her looks of eager love.'

Mrs. Lefroy's husband had a nephew, Tom Lefroy, who often stayed with them, with whom Jane got on most successfully in a flirtatious and light-hearted manner; but, as was natural at this time, her chief friends were girls of her own age; there were Elizabeth, Catherine and Alethea Bigg, who lived with their father and their brother Harrison at Manydown Park. When Jane was old enough to go to subscription balls in Basingstoke, she used to be driven over to Manydown to dine, dress and sleep the night. Still more intimate were Martha and Mary Lloyd, the daughters of a widowed lady who rented a house of Mr. Austen's in the next village. Martha and Mary were quiet and pleasant, and to look at them no one would suppose that there had been anything sensational in their family history; actually it contained in the person of their grandmother one of those figures rare in personal experience, a truly wicked and terrifying woman. Mrs. Craven, referred to by her descendants as the cruel Mrs. C., was very beautiful and moved in the first circles, and no one who met her there ever imagined the state of things she had left behind her at home. Her three daughters aroused a streak of morbid cruelty in her, and were subject to shocking ill-treatment: beaten, starved and locked up. When Mrs. Craven was on her round of visits, one of them accompanied her as her maid; but on one occasion their mother left them all at home, and, profiting by this brief respite, the desperate creatures ran away. With two of them the flight was something in the nature of an elopement; they married a farmer and a horse-dealer respectively;

20

the third was taken in by hospitable relations, and subsequently became the wife of the Rev. Mr. Lloyd; on his death she and her daughters came to Deane, and, after a few years, moved some twenty miles away to Ibthorp. On the occasion of this move, Jane made Mary a parting present, which is still in existence. It is described as a very small chintz housewife, furnished with the finest possible variety of needles and thread, the whole rolled up and protected by a little gingham bag. In the housewife 'a tiny pocket' contains a scrap of paper, on which is written with a crow quill:

> *This little bag I hope will prove*
> *To be not vainly made,*
> *For should you thread and needle want*
> *It will afford you aid.*

One of the aspects of Jane Austen's character most frequently dwelt on with surprise and admiration by people who knew her as a woman in the height of her achievement, was her unpretending, exquisite simplicity; but though the simplicity was artless, it was a development, a quality that grew with the growth of her perfect taste. A child, conscious of unusual powers, cannot but be a little awkward with them, it has not discovered the natural outlet for its energy, and will amuse itself with the mere stuff of daily life: will be now one person and now another. Jane was apt to be disconcerting in her behaviour at these years, and it was unfortunate that it was just now she should make the first acquaintance with her cousin Phila Walter. Jane and Cassandra, with Mr. and Mrs. Austen, stayed a few days with the Walters on their way home from a visit in Kent. Phila thought Cassandra very agreeable; she 'kept up' the conversation in a very pleasant manner, and they all thought her very pretty. Jane, said Phila decidedly, was not pretty at all, very much like her brother Henry. (So the likeness noticed by her father the night she was born still persisted.) But as most people thought Henry a very handsome man, this might not, in eyes less severely critical than Phila's, have been a disadvantage. Jane was far from making a good impression altogether; Phila said first that she was 'very prim; unlike a girl of twelve'; but in a letter written the next day she said, 'Jane is whimsical and affected.' In short, one is forced to conclude that on this visit she did not behave as she should. But how much reason she had to appear unlike a girl of twelve may be judged from a glance at something she was writing two years later. Writing was, indeed, her favourite amusement. Cassandra drew and painted, Jane wrote. She practised the art with such unremitting enthusiasm that, on looking back, she said she wished she had written less and read more between the ages of twelve and sixteen. Of what she read, not many titles are known, though a good deal may be gathered as to the type. She read simple works in Italian and French as she was learning both those languages, and had a copy of Berquin's *Ami des Enfants*: a collection of moral tales for children told in vigorous outline and perspicuous style, of which the one most familiar in English translation is 'The Three Cakes,' in which the characters of three schoolboys are displayed by the way in which each treated the present of a large, frosted plum cake. Her bent of mind showed itself in her fondness for history, taught as it then was with the emphasis laid upon the doings of men and women, their characters and influence, rather than upon its economic aspects, but a copy of Goldsmith's *History of England* is preserved in which, on the page where he tells of a man and his wife driven to suicide by the horrors of destitution, she has written in the margin: 'How much the poor are to be pitied and the Rich to be Blamed.'

Besides these serious studies there went on in the Rectory a quantity of play- and novel-reading; nor was this confined to the masterpieces of the age.

The best known of her childish works, and the one which is frequently considered the best, is a satire on a popular type of novel, written when she was fourteen years old, entitled *Love and Friendship*. Since novels began, there has always existed, in a highly thriving state, that kind of novel which is responsible for the idea held by so many people, that novel-reading is a pernicious waste of time. It varies in outward form from generation to generation, but its fundamental characteristics are always the same, and writers of it exist in heretofore unequalled numbers at the present time, though politeness and discretion forbid our pointing any of them out. The surface differences between these books and their eighteenth-century counterparts are great, but the qualities of grotesque and feeble character-drawing, futile conversation and, above all, a pretentious earnestness in the author are strikingly common to both.

Jane Austen had taken the measure of such writers before she could spell, and she fell upon them with an enthusiastic delight, and with a command of language, an ear for the balance of a sentence, an incisive clarity of expression, of such an order that they invest the child's exercise-books with a touch of immortality.

The tearing high spirits which sweep through this sketch of the Adventures of Laura and Sophia, and their lovers Edward and Augustus, communicate the writer's enjoyment to the reader in an intoxicating manner: ' "My father," said Edward, "seduced by the false glare of Fortune and the Deluding Pomp of Title, insisted on my giving my hand to Lady Dorothea. No never exclaimed I. Lady Dorothea is lovely and Engaging; I prefer no woman to her; but know, Sir, that I scorn to marry her in compliance with your Wishes. No! Never shall it be said that I obliged my Father!" ' The heroine's friend Sophia died from the results of a chill caught by fainting too continuously on damp grass, and expired with the parting caution: ' "One fatal swoon has cost me my Life . . . Beware of swoons, dear Laura . . . a frenzy fit is not one quarter so pernicious; it is an exercise to the Body and if not too violent, is I daresay, conducive to health in its consequences— Run mad as often as you choose, but do not faint—" '

Eliza had said, in describing the attractiveness of Cassandra and Jane: 'My heart still gives the preference to Jane, whose kind partiality to me indeed requires a return of the same nature,' and this brilliant piece of nonsense is inscribed: 'To Madame la Comtesse de Feuillide.'

In the published collection of fragments written between the ages of fourteen and sixteen are the first scenes of two comedies, one of them dedicated to The Reverend George Austen, and *Lesley Castle*, an unfinished novel in letters, dedicated to Henry; underneath this dedication is a note: Messrs. Demand and Co.—please to pay Jane Austen Spinster the sum of one hundred guineas on account of your humble Servant. H. T. Austen.

Love and Friendship is perhaps the most remarkable of the extremely youthful pieces; but for sheer wit the first place is held by *The History of England, from the reign of Henry the 4th to the death of Charles the 1st, by a partial, prejudiced and ignorant historian*; the historian being aged fifteen. This work was dedicated to Cassandra and illustrated by her with water-colour sketches.

Of Henry the 6th, the author observes:

'I cannot say much for this Monarch's sense. Nor would I if I could, for he was a Lancastrian. I suppose you know all about the Wars between him and the Duke of York, who was on the right side; if you do not, you had better read some other History, for I shall not be very diffuse in this, meaning by it only to vent my spleen *against*, and show my Hatred *to* all those people and persons whose parties or principles do not suit with mine, and not to give information.'

It is not only that she succeeds, where a child almost never succeeds, in being genuinely witty; but besides having acquired a grasp of the subject itself, she shows in these short paragraphs applied to the various reigns a completely disillusioned attitude to the practice of writing history, at a time when, an ardent schoolgirl, she was passionately

23

interested in the study of it. Henry the 8th's reign might have presented the historian with a tiresome amount of labour, but she says: 'It would be an affront to my Readers were I to suppose that they were not as well acquainted with the particulars of this King's reign as I am myself. It will therefore be saving *them* the task of reading again what they have read before, and *myself* the trouble of writing what I do not perfectly recollect, by giving only a slight sketch of the principal Events which marked his reign.' She asserts that Anne Boleyn's beauty and elegance, taken in conjunction with the King's character, were sufficient proofs of her innocence; and concludes that nothing can be urged in Henry's vindication, except that 'his abolishing Religious Houses and leaving them to the ruinous depredations of time, has been of infinite use to the landscape of England in general.'

If one had been asked to say with what Queen Jane Austen would have found herself most in sympathy, one would have hazarded Queen Elizabeth. It is interesting, therefore, to discover that her heroine was, on the contrary, Mary Queen of Scots. Whether in real life, Jane Austen, even at fifteen, would have had any patience with the lovely but exasperating Mary Stuart, is another question; in imagination, Mary's 'beauty and elegance,' qualities which always fascinated Jane, and her long-drawn-out distress, made her in Jane's mind an object of devotion, and the passage dealing with her misfortunes—by far the longest in the History—is extraordinary in the unchild-like combination of emotion and detachment.

'O what must this bewitching Princess whose only friend was then the Duke of Norfolk, and whose only ones now Mr. Whitaker, Mrs. Lefroy, Mrs. Knight and myself, who was abandoned by her son, confined by her Cousin, abused, reproached and vilified by all, what must not her noble mind have suffered when informed that Elizabeth had given orders for her death? Yet she bore it with a most unshaken fortitude, firm in her mind; constant in her Religion; and prepared herself to meet the cruel fate to which she was doomed, with a magnanimity that would alone proceed from conscious Innocence. And yet could you Reader have believed it possible that some hardened and zealous Protestants have even abused her for that steadfastness in the Catholic Religion which reflected on her so much credit? It may not be unnecessary,' she adds, 'before I entirely conclude my account of this ill-fated Queen, to observe that she had been accused of several crimes during the time of her reigning in Scotland, of which I now most seriously do assure my Reader that she was entirely innocent; having never been guilty of anything more than Imprudencies into which she was betrayed by the openness of her Heart, her Youth and her Education.

24

Having I trust by this assurance entirely done away every Suspicion and every doubt which might have arisen in the Reader's mind, from what other Historians have written of her, I shall proceed to mention the remaining events that marked Elizabeth's reign.'

To read these sketches is sometimes to forget that they were written by a child in an exercise-book, but one passage recalls the family milieu in which they were produced. In writing of Sir Francis Drake, the sister of Francis Austen observes: 'Yet great as he was and justly celebrated as a sailor, I cannot help foreseeing that he will be equalled in this or the next century by one who, tho' now but young, already promises to answer all the ardent and sanguine expectations of his Relations and Friends; among whom I class the amiable lady to whom this work is dedicated and my no less amiable self.'

A Collection of Letters dedicated to Jane Cooper, written at the age of sixteen, contain a 'Letter from a Young Lady in Humble Circumstances to her Friend,' which though less extraordinarily taking and brilliant in childish charm, shows, naturally enough, the most matured power of anything among the schoolroom pieces, and judged from a purely technical standpoint is perhaps the most astonishing item of the whole.

The writer of the letter, Maria Williams, living in a humble manner with her mother, is taken to the ball in the coach of the odious Lady Greville, who is not only a brutal snob, but takes a perverse pleasure in unkindness, as is seen by her going out of her way to get Maria to the house by a quite unnecessary invitation, merely that she may continue her baiting of a humble acquaintance. Short as the letter is, it is sufficient to display with trenchant clarity the character of the bloated, brazen Lady Greville, her elder daughter, who took after her, the younger daughter, who was gentle and kind, the sensitive but independent little heroine, and her mother, who sympathized with Maria's sufferings at the hands of Lady Greville, but thought the connection too valuable to be allowed to drop. After describing Lady Greville's treatment of her at the ball, Maria says: 'The next day while we were at dinner, Lady Greville's Coach stopped at the door, for that is the time of day she generally contrives it should. She sent in a message by the servant to say that "she should not get out but that Miss Maria must come to the Coach door as she wanted to speak to her, and that she must make haste and come immediately——" "What an impertinent Message, Mama!" said I—"Go, Maria," replied she. Accordingly I went and was obliged to stand there at her Ladyship's pleasure, though the wind was extremely high and very cold.

' "Why, I think, Miss Maria, you are not quite so smart as you were last night—But I did not come to examine your dress; but to tell you that you may dine with us the day after to-morrow—not to-morrow, remember, do not come to-morrow, for we expect Lord and Lady Clermont and Sir Thomas Stanley's family—There will be no occasion for your being very fine, for I shan't send the Carriage. If it rains you may take an umbrella—" I could hardly help laughing at hearing her give me leave to keep myself dry—"And pray remember to be in time, for I shan't wait—I hate my Victuals overdone—But you need not come before the time—How does your Mother do? She is at dinner, is not she?" "Yes Ma'am, we were in the middle of dinner when your Ladyship came." "I am afraid you find it very cold Maria," said Ellen. "Yes, it is an horrible east wind," said her Mother—"I assure you I can hardly bear the windows down—But you are used to be blown about by the wind, Miss Maria, and that is what has made your complexion so rudely and coarse. You young ladies who cannot often ride in a Carriage never mind what weather you trudge in, or how the wind shows your legs. I would not have my girls stand out of doors as you do in such a day as this. But some people have no feelings either of cold or delicacy." '

Lady Greville is drawn in the harshest possible outline, and her character, like that of certain figures in the old drama, is revealed by her saying some things which in real life even she would scarcely say. But she is not a caricature. One recognizes immediately the type of person whom she represents, and admits the truth of the presentation. Children who are fond of writing almost always expend themselves on description, or on the adventures of some character with whom they can identify themselves; not one in a thousand takes a theme like this. At sixteen Jane Austen could choose at random a handful of people, to whom no extraneous interest whatever attached itself, either of beauty, character or circumstance, and breathe such life into them that while we are occupied with them we are not conscious of what they are without. It is in such a fragment as this that one can perceive the beginnings of her extraordinary genius. The agonized pity we feel for Macbeth makes us suppose that if we had Shakespeare's intuition, we should regard every criminal with sympathy rather than abhorrence; and the absorbing interest with which Jane Austen can invest a commonplace or tiresome person reminds us that no human being would seem dull to us if we had eyes to see.

If we may take the published *Juvenalia* as representative of what she wrote at this time, we feel it altogether natural that, in her case, the written self-expression showed none of the ordinary symptoms of adolescence, the glooms and gleams of half-formulated thought:

26

Blank misgivings of a creature
Moving about in worlds not realized.

We feel convinced that she never kept a diary or a commonplace book. She had no energy, no time for vague, subjective outpourings; all her growing mental resources, her brilliant vitality, her vigorous imagination, were devoted to the preoccupation, unconscious but absorbing, of studying human beings as she saw them and as her intuition told her that they were.

Know thou thyself, presume not God to scan;
The proper study of mankind is Man.

Pope's great fame was by 1790 suffering eclipse in the Steventon household, devoted to books and keenly interested in the latest literary fashions. There is reason to suppose that he was admired 'no more than was proper.' Jane Austen may never have read the *Essay on Man*; if she had, it is more than probable that she never applied this aphorism to her unassuming self; but it would be difficult to find, in the range of English poetry, words more expressive of the inspiration of her art.

In examining the early pieces, it is interesting to notice their dedications; they show how conscious she was of an audience, warmly partial it is true, but by nature critical and exacting. Her powers of mind, the strength of her creative imagination, her genius for perception and intuition, were gifts no human influence could enhance or take away; but of the style, so integral a feature of her work, who can say how much of its beauty, its finely tempered strength, its dazzling lucidity, is owed to the fact that she was daughter and sister of the Rev. George Austen's family?

27

CHAPTER FOUR

In a world of undistracted leisure, the amusement of novel-reading ranked high.

The circulating library, severely disapproved of by Sir Antony Absolute, was an important feature of every country town by the middle of the eighteenth century. The usual form for a novel was three or four small volumes, bound in calf with a spine elegantly starred and flowered in gilt; as the price of the set was anything from one to three guineas, the purchasing of novels was restricted either to the well-to-do who put their names down on the subscription list of a fashionable author because it was the thing, or to those whose interest was so great that they were prepared to spend a considerable sum to gratify it.

It is always a nice point to decide how far the genius forms the trend of his time, and how far he is formed by it. In his review of *Emma* in the Quarterly of 1816, Sir Walter Scott placed Jane Austen in the foremost rank of innovators. He said of her novels: 'They belong to a class of fiction which has arisen almost in our own times and which draws the characters and incidents introduced more immediately from the current of ordinary life than was permitted by the former rules of the novel.' At the same time, no one who reads the great novels of the mid-eighteenth century, which were to Jane Austen in roughly the same relationship that Dickens and Thackeray are to us, can fail to see that, unique as is her personal contribution to the art of novel-writing, she was also in direct descent from the masters of fiction who preceded her. She is like them in that she abounded in wit, and that her style, with all its individual brilliance and grace, is founded, as on a rock, upon that of the essayists, historians and novelists of the eighteenth century.

Modern English prose has been fathered with good reason on Dryden, who died in 1700; and though our own prose has lost his inimitable blend of vigour and elegance, yet if we compare one of Milton's pamphlets with a single paragraph of Dryden's, we recognize that though Milton and he were contemporaries, the former belongs to the antique world and the latter to our own. To the clarity and raciness of Dryden was added, with a clarity yet more luminous, the exquisite simplicity of Addison; and by the time Addison had made the *Spectator* a popular newspaper, the fundamental characteristics of eighteenth-century prose were so firmly established that everyone who wrote at all, wrote, however lacking in the strength and spirit of the great originals, in a manner that was formed to imitate and embody the salient features of their style. Indeed, it is the miracle of that time, and one conceivable only in an age when the reading public was so small that the influence of one man could be paramount. When Addison said that by the amusement offered in his paper he was going to redeem the folly and grossness of post-Restoration society, and to show that morality was inseparable from good taste, one may doubt how far he was successful in daily life; how widely he influenced the world of letters, a century of almost perfect writing remains to show. Naturally he would not have succeeded so completely had he not been an embodiment in human form of the tendencies of the age; his immediate fame shows how truly he interpreted the public taste; what is remarkable in his achievement is his very early position in the century. He died in 1719, and a hundred years later not novels and histories only, but newspapers, publishers' puffs and advertisements for rouge and face powder were being written in sentences that did credit to their models in the *Spectator*.

Henry Austen said that his sister loved to read the volumes of the *Spectator*, and though her only known comment upon them appears to be a disparagement, one must remember the context in which it was made. She criticized the attitude of girls who, if discovered reading a novel, put it hurriedly aside, or said they were merely skimming it for lack of something better to do; whereas had they been found with the *Spectator* in their hands, they would have displayed it proudly, although the chances were that they would be reading in it something either fantastic, or relating to people and scenes in which no one now took any interest, or something which was frankly indecent. No one can judge the truth of this criticism who knows the *Spectator* only by its best pieces. It was not directed to such essays as those embodying the adventures of Sir Roger de Coverley, the Vision of Mirza or the Trial of the Petticoat.

The implied contrast, to the great advantage of the novel, shows how seriously she admired the masterpieces of this art, and it may throw some light on the furniture of her mind to consider a little the novels to which she so constantly referred. Henry said that much as she admired Fielding, she did not award him the very highest praise, because though she was devoid of mock modesty, she shrank from what was gross. 'Neither nature, wit nor humour could make her amends for so very low a scale of morals.'

At the same time, like the rest of her family, she was quite at home

29

in *Tom Jones*. Writing to her sister in 1791, she said that Tom Lefroy had but one fault: his morning coat was too light; but she supposed that, as an admirer of Tom Jones, Mr. Lefroy copied the colour of his coat, which, as its colour was white, showed very visibly the streams of blood which had flowed down it.

Jane Austen's implied praise of Fielding's nature, wit and humour is especially interesting, because it is in his work that one sees, more clearly than in that of Sterne or Richardson, those qualities of robust gracefulness, of ultra-vivid but harmonious colouring, and a vigorous humanity of outlook which, as it were, pierces through the accretions of commonplace and tedium, and reveals the ordinary man and woman as the wonderful creatures that they are. It is this capacity to illuminate the normal, which cannot exist without the kindred qualities of humour and strong common sense, that she shares with her great predecessor.

Jane Austen's own manner of writing being what it is, the most interesting consideration connected with her reading is perhaps that she had in the background of her consciousness such work as Sterne's, so wild, elusive and, above all, so trembling with sensitive humanity, as is that passage from *A Sentimental Journey* which occurred to her in *Mansfield Park* when Maria Bertram, looking through the iron gates, exclaims: ' "I cannot get out, as the starling said." ' It is Sterne's attempt to reason away the horrors of imprisonment. 'As for the Bastille, the terror is in the word—Make the most of it if you can, I said to myself. The Bastille is but another word for a tower:—and a tower is but another word for a house you can't get out of. . . . I was interrupted in the heyday of this soliloquy with a voice which I took to be that of a child, which complained: "it could not get out," . . . and looking up, I saw it was a starling hung up in a little cage. I stood looking at the bird, and to every person who came through the passage, it ran fluttering towards the side which they approached it, with the same lamentation of its captivity—"I can't get out," said the starling. God help thee!— said I—but I'll let thee out, cost what it will; so I turned the cage about to get at the door; it was twisted and double twisted so fast with wire, there was no getting it open without pulling the cage to pieces. . . . The bird flew to the place where I was attempting his deliverance, and thrusting his head through the trellis, pressed his breast against it as if impatient.—I fear, poor creature, said I, I cannot set thee at liberty. —"No," said the starling; "I can't get out—I can't get out."

'I vow I never had any affections more tenderly awakened. . . . Mechanical as the notes were . . . in one moment they overthrew all

30

my systematic reasonings upon the Bastille, and I heavily walked upstairs, unsaying every word I had said in going down them.'

The novelist of whom Jane Austen was personally the fondest has faded most in popular esteem. The extreme length of Richardson's novels, and the particular nature of his sensibility, which, unlike Sterne's, does not expend itself on objects which human nature will always think worthy of it, but upon characters of a restricted interest, placed in romantic rather than ordinary circumstances, are sufficient reasons for the decline of his once-resplendent popularity. Of his three novels—*Pamela, Clarissa* and *Sir Charles Grandison*, we have no evidence that Jane Austen ever read *Pamela*; but from a reference in *Sanditon* to the hero of *Clarissa*, and to 'such Authors as have since appeared to tread in Richardson's steps, so far as Man's determined pursuit of Woman, in defiance of every opposition of feeling and convenience is concerned,' it seems probable that she had read the second novel; considering her passion for *Sir Charles Grandison*, she was unlikely not to have read the author's previous work, which many people considered the finer of the two; after all, she was allowed, from a very early age, to read what she liked; and as the Rev. George Austen had *Tom Jones* on his shelves, he was not likely to have drawn the line at *Clarissa*; though one is tolerably convinced that that clear-headed and sensible gentleman would have preferred the hearty rudeness of Fielding to the hot-house sensibility of Richardson.

In a synopsis the story of *Clarissa* carries little conviction, but to the reader who has reached the conclusion through the preceding volumes with their long tale of distress, loneliness, trouble, persecution, terror and delirium, the heroine's death following on what would now be described as an acute nervous breakdown seems only too credible. It is necessary to read the novel as a whole to appreciate its cumulative effect and surrender to Richardson's spell. Could it be read as slowly now as it was by its original admirers, in a world which received no emotional excitement from cinemas and journalism, no doubt each separate portion would stand out in its own right; as it is, certain of them emerge with terrible distinctness: the house to which Lovelace carried Clarissa under the pretence that it was a respectable lodging, and Lovelace's own letter to his friend, in which he says that he always put on mourning for such of his mistresses as died in childbed by him, and that his promise to do so was of great comfort to them in their last agonies.

It is perhaps worthwhile to consider *Clarissa*, since its story may help to dispel the delusion, under which some persons appear to labour, that living in a country parsonage at the end of the eighteenth century

31

was like living fifty years later in a novel by Charlotte Yonge. At its worst the society of eighteenth-century England was gross and disgusting; at its best it embodied a beautiful frankness, an honest acceptance of the facts of existence, and it differed from the unhealthy period of the mid and late nineteenth century in that the innocence and elegance of its women were not based on ignorance.

How eagerly Jane Austen received the impression of Richardson's genius, how she 'lived' among his characters, is shown by her frequent references to *Sir Charles Grandison*. Judged by impersonal standards, this novel, the latest of the three, is also the weakest; it contains hardly any of Richardson's alarming excitement and no character to compare with Clarissa in beauty or with Lovelace in interest and conviction. On the other hand, it is entirely proper. True, the heroine, Harriet Byron, is abducted on her way home from a masquerade by a particularly brutal libertine, Sir Hargrave Pollexfen; and as readers of *Clarissa* had realized that Richardson by no means considered a happy ending necessary to a heroine's story, the reader's alarm and that of Harriet's doting relations is extremely high until it is learned that she has been rescued by Sir Charles Grandison, whose entrance into the story at this heaven-sent moment is quite the best thing about him. The other six volumes deal with Harriet's friendship and gratitude to Sir Charles and his very lively and audacious sister, Miss Grandison, and her rapidly falling in love with the former, and with the good that Sir Charles does to a vast number of people. The happy conclusion is scarcely a climax, it is so gently led up to; and the charm of the story is in fact almost all meditative, retrospective, in earnest conversations in which all the chief characters are shown to be virtuous and deserving of happiness, though, as frequently occurs in real life, some can gain it only at the expense of others. The hold the story with its multitudinous figures took on Jane Austen's imagination was extraordinary. Henry Austen said that she remembered and would speak of any date throughout the year on which any episode of the book was said to have taken place; on one occasion she was to wear a cap of white satin and lace, 'with a little flower perking out of the left ear, like Harriet Byron's feather,' because Harriet's costume for the fatal masquerade included 'a white, Paris sort of cap, glittering with spangles and encircled by a chaplet of artificial flowers, with a little white feather perking from the left ear.'

Catherine Morland, the enthusiastic, unsophisticated heroine of *Northanger Abbey*, makes her first acquaintance with fashionable novels under the guidance of her stylish friend Isabella Thorpe, who says:

' "It is so odd to me that you should never have read *Udolpho* before, but I suppose Mrs. Morland objects to novels.'

' "No, she does not. She very often reads *Sir Charles Grandison* herself; but new books do not fall in our way."

' "*Sir Charles Grandison!* That is an amazing horrid book, is it not? I remember Miss Andrews could not get through the first volume."

' "It is not like *Udolpho* at all, but yet I think it is very entertaining."

' "Do you indeed? You surprise me; I thought it had not been readable." '

It would be amusing to speculate which novel of the present century has made so strong an impression on its readers that in a hundred years' time the character of two people in a then contemporary novel could be estimated by their respective attitudes towards it.

CHAPTER FIVE

The young ladies of Steventon Rectory were two very pretty girls. They were rather above middle height. Jane especially was very slender and lightly moving; her hair was dark brown and curled naturally, her large dark eyes were widely opened and expressive. Sir Egerton Brydges, who had admired her when she was a schoolgirl, said that then her cheeks were too full, but a portrait of her as a young woman suggests that she outgrew this defect. She had a clear brown skin and blushed so brightly and so readily that Henry applied Donne's lines to her:

> Her pure and eloquent blood
> Spake in her cheeks and so distinctly wrought
> That you had almost said her body thought.

Her voice was charming—sweet and clear and of exquisite articulation —and though her behaviour was quiet, her unconsidered, spontaneous remarks impressed themselves on the hearer's mind; her conversation was very pleasant when she had to make it in company, and brilliantly lively when she was in the freedom and safety of the home circle. Of the two girls, she was the immediately striking one, though she sometimes kept deliberately behind Cassandra. As the older sister to such a younger, Cassandra was an ideal being. She was very intelligent— indeed, she had their mother's shrewdness—at the same time her outward appearance was completely tranquil; there was a gentle sweetness in her manner which was the more remarkable because it did not bespeak an uncritical or easy-going nature. It is needless to say that she had not Jane's powers of intuition, but, as an ordinary human being, she possessed extremely good judgement and at the same time the tendency to like people and excuse them, and that other unusual combination of great gentleness and undeviating firmness in doing what she considered to be right. The family said of them that Cassandra had the merit of having her temper always under control, and Jane had the happiness of a temper that needed no control.

The sisters slept together, and out of their bedroom opened a good-sized dressing-room, plainly furnished but containing their personal possessions. The carpet had flowers on a brown ground; an oval looking-glass hung between the two windows; there was a chest of drawers of painted wood, with a book-case over it; Cassandra's drawing

34

materials, and Jane's piano; also a writing-desk, a box with a sloping lid.

The part of her life which Jane lived in this room, where she spent so many absorbed and happy hours, with Cassandra beside her, whose presence interrupted her not at all, did not interfere with her life below stairs. At this time Eliza de Feuillide said that Jane and Cassandra were both very pretty and breaking hearts by the dozen, and though the second part of the sentence could perhaps be explained as Eliza's way of putting things, the Austen family, during Jane's late 'teens, were all alive with love-making and getting married. James, who had become the curate of a neighbouring parish, had married the daughter of the great house, Ann Matthew, who was five years older than he was, but for whose discrepancy in age James' seriousness well made up. General Matthew allowed the couple £100 a year, and James had £200 of his own. On this it was possible to live in the country districts of eighteenth-century England very comfortably; Mrs. James Austen had her carriage, and, the Austen passion for sport being shared even by the pensive James, a pack of harriers was kept for the curate.

The marriage of Edward was also about to take place. Edward, the heir to Mr. Knight's great fortune and his estates of Godmersham and Chawton, was marrying in circumstances widely different from his brother's. He had become engaged to the beautiful Elizabeth Bridges, whose father, Sir Brooke Bridges, owned a considerable property. His wife's miniature by Cosway remains to show that Edward Austen's extraordinary good fortune was constant to him in marriage as well as in worldly prosperity.

Edward remained warmly fond of his relations and interested in their affairs, and though he was not so intimate with the family as a whole as he would have been if he had been brought up with them, he claimed Cassandra as his own special sister, and from the time of his marriage she was constantly staying with him. Cassandra in the meantime was becoming very happy on her own account. Martha and Mary Lloyd's kinsman, Lord Craven, another descendant of the Cruel Mrs. C., had a young cousin named Thomas Fowle. As a visitor in the Lloyds' household the latter made the acquaintance of the Austens, and he fell in love with Cassandra Austen. With her parents' consent, the two became engaged. Fowle had just been ordained, and it was confidently hoped that Lord Craven, who was very kind to him, would give him one of the several valuable livings in his gift. A certain Shropshire living, perhaps because it was about to fall vacant, was the one which everybody supposed would be given to Fowle. Because of the present slight uncertainty of his prospects and possibly because Cas-

35

sandra disliked a bustle about herself, the engagement was not publicly announced.

In the meantime there was a wedding actually in their midst. Jane Cooper had accompanied her father, Dr. Cooper, on a cruise for his health, in the course of which she met Lieutenant Thomas Williams, and became engaged to him. Unhappily Dr. Cooper died before the wedding could be arranged, and after the period of mourning, Jane Cooper, having neither father nor mother, came to Steventon to be married from the house of her uncle and aunt.

Jane herself, whose only sister was already engaged, could 'come out' as soon as she liked, even if the Austens rigidly observed the etiquette of not bringing forward the younger girls till the elder were disposed of, but so far her only romantic interest had been a standing flirtation with Mr. Lefroy's nephew, Tom, renewed whenever he came to Ashe, and not considered as very serious at present by anybody.

Of this group of marriages which occupied so much of the family attention, James', the earliest made, was the shortest lived. His wife died while their daughter was so young that all she could remember of her mother was 'a tall and slender lady dressed in white.' The poor young widower was left with a child who asked continually for 'Mama,' and, unable to bear it, or to make any suitable arrangement for the little Anna in his own house, he sent her to Steventon to be 'mothered' by her two young aunts. It is to the recollections of this child, remarkably intelligent for her age, that we owe the descriptions of the dressing-room, and of something else very interesting. Jane, who began to be the perfect aunt long before she was twenty, would tell Anna stories that went on from day to day, and when Anna made up stories for herself, she dictated them to Jane, who wrote them down. But Jane was also writing a story of her own; it was called *First Impressions*, and while Anna played quietly in the dressing-room, Jane would read aloud the completed chapters of this story to Cassandra, who always burst out laughing. Anna heard so much of the story that she grew quite familiar with the names of the people, and at last she began to talk about them downstairs; but no sooner did Cassandra and Jane hear her doing this than they both asked her to be very careful not to say another word about the story to anybody, becauses it was quite private, and a secret that Anna had with them.

First Impressions was not the only story Jane had produced. *Elinor and Marianne*, a novel in which the events were related in letters, she had either sketched out or completed; but though she loved to write, and when actually at work proceeded with complete and unerring self-confidence, as soon as she laid down the pen she became once

36

more the modest, self-distrustful tyro. To their acquaintances at large she would not be known to write for anything. The contemporary novelist whom she admired most was a woman, Madame D'Arblay, who as Fanny Burney had startled the literary world with *Evelina*, published in 1778, when she was a girl of twenty and Jane a child of three. Fanny Burney had followed her first success with *Cecilia*; at last in 1796, in Jane's twenty-first year, it was announced that she was about to bring out her third novel, *Camilla*. The public were, of course, invited to subscribe; several pages of the first of the five volumes are occupied with an imposing subscription list in alphabetical order, and among the A's is found the entry: Miss J. Austen, Steventon.

According to family tradition, the Rev. George Austen paid the money to give his daughter this extreme delight. The anticipation, the eagerness and excitement with which the five thick, small volumes, with their elegant large print, were received and carried off to the dressing-room can be understood when we think of our pleasure in getting hold of a book we have wanted very much to read, and multiply that many hundred times, by imagining ourselves without a cinema, without a wireless set, without a gramophone, without a daily newspaper. Nor were these anticipations disappointed, and if Jane Austen's high opinion of Fanny Burney—or it might possibly be more accurate to say, the immense pleasure she took in Miss Burney's work—should surprise us, considering the immeasurable distance between them in their rank as novelists, we must remember that if Jane Austen were to take pleasure in a contemporary novelist at all before 1815, when, three years before her death, Scott published *Guy Mannering*, it had of necessity to be in someone whose work was inferior to her own.

It must be agreed that despite her virtues, Fanny Burney's faults as a writer are too serious for people who have available for their delight the whole range of nineteenth-century novelists to consider her as more than an excellent but very unequal writer. *Evelina*, *Cecilia* and *Camilla*, and the first especially, contain scenes of a sharpness and gaiety approaching those of Sheridan, but they also contain noble characters who are intolerably priggish and verbose, and long stretches of moralizing through which the reader flounders in despair. These drawbacks are much more pronounced in the second two books. For *Evelina*, written in deadly secrecy, by a girl whose stepmother didn't approve of scribbling, has the true stamp of the first novel: written to please nobody but the writer, unmodified by any idea of public taste, but the instant and overwhelming success of *Evelina* transformed its author from the retiring young lady who could not help sometimes going upstairs to scribble, though she had been told, and had agreed,

37

that she ought not, into the famous Miss Burney, who had become a writer conscious of an eager audience. She was not strong enough to withstand the sensation; the rage for moralizing and sentiment which beset the latter end of the eighteenth century, from whose hampering cerements started forth the true sensibility of the Romantic Revival, is most dutifully pandered to in *Cecilia* and *Camilla*.

Jane Austen already knew *Evelina* and *Cecilia*. One of her nieces remembered, as a very young child, hearing her read a part out of *Evelina*, one of the chapters concerning the Branghtons and Mr. Smith, and she thought it sounded like a play. The scheme of *Evelina*, in which the lovely, country-bred girl of seventeen is brought to town by some very well-bred and charming friends, but has to spend part of her time with a shocking old grandmother, Madame Duval, and her vulgar relations, the Branghtons, who very seriously interfere with the progress of her acquaintance with Lord Orville, which she made under the auspices of her friends the Mirvans, is excellently framed to bring in a wide variety of contrasts among scenes and people. The comic, the vulgar, the embarrassing parts of the story are brilliantly done. The serious love interest is much less successful, and years later, when Jane Austen was reading and commenting upon a story of the then grown-up Anna, she said: 'I do not like a lover's speaking in the third person; it is too much like the formal parts of Lord Orville, and I think is not natural.'

Cecilia, the story of an heiress, with a doleful plot and a set of principal characters each one more tiresome and long-winded than the last, has nevertheless a crowd of incidental figures who do full justice to Fanny Burney's power of vigorous observation and wit.

One of the most successful is Miss Larolles, a young and pretty little creature, a perfect humming-top of fashionable nonsense. Miss Larolles in the theatre explained to Cecilia her disappointment at being unable to attract the attention of a much-sought-after young man, and said: 'I sat on the outside on purpose to speak to a person or two that I knew would be strolling about; for if one sits on the inside there is no speaking to a creature, you know, so I never do it, at the Opera, nor in the boxes at Ranelagh nor anywhere. It's the shockingest thing you can conceive, to be made sit in the middle of those forms; one might as well be at home, for nobody can speak to one.' Nearly twenty years later, when she wrote *Persuasion*, Jane Austen's mind reverted to this speech. Anne Elliot, when she begins tremblingly to hope that Captain Wentworth is becoming reconciled to her, finds herself present at a concert with him in the Assembly Rooms of Bath. She is obliged to talk to her neighbour during the pauses between the songs, but at the

38

interval he leaves her for the bench behind, and Anne, seeing Captain Wentworth standing near, changes her seat to one much nearer the end of the row: 'She could not do so without comparing herself with Miss Larolles, the inimitable Miss Larolles, but still she did it, and not with much happier effect.'

It is at the end of *Cecilia*, however, that one receives a start of surprise and recognition. The physician and family friend, Dr. Lyster, is reviewing the progress of Cecilia's affair with young Delville. 'The whole of this unfortunate business,' said Dr. Lyster, 'has been the result of PRIDE and PREJUDICE . . . yet this, however, remember; that if to PRIDE and PREJUDICE you owe your miseries, so wonderfully are good and evil balanced, that to PRIDE and PREJUDICE you owe also their termination.'

But it is with *Camilla* that we approach Jane Austen most nearly. At the time of its publication, the enthusiasm of Edmund Burke, who put his name down for five sets, probably gave Madame D'Arblay the most pleasure. If she had been asked to say whose name she valued next, she could have made her choice from amongst the most distinguished figures in society; she perhaps never even noticed that of the quite unknown young lady living in a Hampshire parsonage. The wheel has come full circle, and whatever the intrinsic merits of *Camilla*, we read it now because we know it pleased Jane Austen.

The merits are considerable; the book has not the young gaiety of *Evelina*, but it has much more depth and the interest is more continuously sustained; the aridity of *Cecilia* it avoids altogether, and though its length would prevent its being reprinted now, at the time of *Camilla's* publication a good novel in five volumes was better by two-thirds than a good novel in three.

Camilla was clearly destined, by her family's wishes and the author's, for a Mr. Edgar Mandlebert; but though they were mutually attracted and there was no reason why they should not marry immediately, the union was postponed for five volumes by Edgar's sage friend Dr. Marchmont, who, preying on the young man's reflective turn of mind, put this diabolical idea into his head: he was not henceforth to admire Camilla's gaiety and enthusiasm as a mere spectator, but every time she said or did anything, he was to say to himself: 'How should I like this, were she *mine*?' Unhappily for the satisfaction of the female sex, Madame D'Arblay did not see fit to provide Camilla with a female confidante who would encourage her in a similar line of conduct. Dr. Marchmont's interference is, like the irresolution of Hamlet, the mainspring of the action; but the feelings we entertain for Edgar Mandlebert and his affairs are the most tepid to which the book gives rise; and

39

the enjoyment of the novel consists in the solid, brightly coloured secondary characters and the scenes which have a nominal connection with the story but are really there on their own merits.

The most famous of these is the celebrated episode of Mr. Dubster's summer-house. In all Madame D'Arblay's novels there is a strain of extremely vigorous horse-play, supplied by mischievous young men: in *Camilla*, by the heroine's brother Lionel. Mr. Dubster was a self-made man, uncouth and bumptious to the verge of farce. He had been attracted to Camilla at a village assembly, and had no idea that his attentions might be unacceptable. Lionel, having seen as much, drove his unsuspecting sisters out to a bare, flat country district where Mr. Dubster was building a staring villa; the latter, delighted at the interest in his work he supposed Camilla to feel, insisted on taking her and her sister Euphemia up to his summer-house, which overhung the lane and was reached by a single ladder. When the party were inside, they looked out of the window to see Lionel joyously riding off down the lane, and realized that he had taken away the ladder. It was the builders' dinner hour, and Mr. Dubster was particularly annoyed that he could not go after them to see they didn't waste the time for which he was paying them. Camilla in acute dismay tried to attract the attention of people passing in the lane, and the party were finally rescued by a passing troop of huntsmen. This is the episode to which Jane Austen referred when she said that she was obliged to stay with Edward and Elizabeth at their house at Rowling until the end of the month, because her brother Frank, who was to take her home, was going away till then. 'Tomorrow I shall be just like Camilla in Mr. Dubster's summer-house; for my Lionel will have taken away the ladder by which I came here, or at least by which I intended to get away; and here I must stay till his return. My situation, however, is somewhat preferable to hers, for I am very happy here, though I should be glad to get home by the end of the month.'

While Camilla was on a visit to Tunbridge Wells, she was in the awkward position of staying with a good-natured but unperceptive hostess much richer than herself. She accompanied a party to a toyshop and selected some little objects which she thought would cost a few shillings, and when she was told their alarming price, was too nervous not to take them. When the heroine of *Sanditon* was standing in the village library which sold trinkets as well as hiring out books, she felt she had spent enough money for her first evening and turned away from 'all the useless things in the world that could not be done without.' . . . 'She took up a Book; it happened to be a volume of *Camilla*. She had not Camilla's Youth, and had no intention of having her Distress—so she turned from the Drawer of rings and Brooches, repressed further solicitations and paid for what she had bought.'

The exertions of Dr. Marchmont in keeping Edgar and Camilla so long apart provided the reader with many hours in entertainment, but Jane Austen, who might reasonably have been expected to approve of him on this account, was not at all magnanimous. In the September of 1796, when she herself was at Rowling, she wrote to Cassandra: 'Give my love to Mary Harrison, and tell her I wish, whenever she is attached to a young Man, some *respectable* Dr. Marchmont will keep them apart for five volumes'; and at the end of her edition of *Camilla* there is a note in her handwriting, which has been encroached upon by the re-binding of the book: 'Since this work went to the Press a Circumstance of some Importance to the happiness of Camilla has taken place, namely that Dr. Marchmont has at last . . .' Dr. Chapman suggests that Jane Austen had devised Dr. Marchmont's death.

The references to Camilla in *Sanditon*, written in the year of her death, are a proof of Jane Austen's constant affection for the book, but the most brilliant use she makes of it is, naturally enough, a very few years after its publication. In *Northanger Abbey*, Isabella Thorpe's brother John has just arrived in Bath, and Catherine Morland, engrossed with *The Mysteries of Udolpho*, cannot resist talking of them even in such unpromising company. John Thorpe swore at once that he didn't read novels, and that if he did, they should be those of Mrs. Radcliffe; Catherine reminded him gently that *Udolpho* was written by Mrs. Radcliffe, whereupon he exclaimed: ' "So it was. I was thinking of that other stupid book, written by that woman they make such a fuss about; she who married the French emigrant."

' "I suppose you mean *Camilla*?"

' " Yes, that's the book; such unnatural stuff! An old man playing at seesaw; I took up the first volume once and looked it over, but I soon found it would not do; indeed, I guessed what sort of stuff it must be before I saw it; as soon as I heard she had married an emigrant, I was sure I should never be able to get through it."

' "I have never read it."

' "You had no loss, I assure you; it is the horridest nonsense you can imagine; there is nothing in the world in it but an old man's playing at seesaw and learning Latin upon my word, there is not." '

This critique, the justice of which was unfortunately lost on poor Catherine, brought them to the door of Mrs. Thorpe's lodging, and the feelings of the discerning and unprejudiced reader of *Camilla* gave way to the feelings of the dutiful and affectionate son, as they met Mrs. Thorpe, who had descried them from above, in the passage. ' "Ah, mother, how do you do?" said he, giving her a hearty shake of the hand; "where did you get that quiz of a hat, it makes you look like an old witch?" '

In reading and writing, in dancing and visiting, with friends and relations falling in love and marrying, in household occupations and country walks, the time went on with much present enjoyment and a great deal of hope.

Jane was twenty-one in December 1796. In the January of that year Tom Lefroy was with his uncle and aunt at Ashe, and was invited with the rest of the neighbourhood to the ball given by Mr. Bigge for his daughters at Manydown Park. Cassandra was on a visit to a member of the Fowle family, and had perhaps thought that Jane was getting too lively on the subject of Mr. Lefroy, seeing that the affair was not expected to end in a marriage. Jane wrote to her, saying: 'You scold me so much in the nice long letter which I have this moment received from you, that I am almost ashamed to tell you how my Irish friend and I behaved. Imagine to yourself everything most profligate and shocking in the way of dancing and sitting down together. I *can* expose myself, however, *only once* more, because he leaves the country soon after next Friday, on which day we *are* to have a dance at Ashe, after all.'

Their profligacy began to attract general attention, and Tom Lefroy seemed to feel that he had gone far enough. Jane said, in trying to make Cassandra think lightly of the matter, that they really had not met except at the balls. 'He is so excessively laughed at about me at Ashe that he is ashamed of coming to Steventon, and ran away when we called on Mrs. Lefroy a few days ago.' The day before Mrs. Lefroy's ball she wrote: 'I look forward with great impatience to it, as I rather expect to receive an offer from my friend in the course of the evening. I shall refuse him, however, unless he promises to give away his white coat.' Cassandra was to have bought some silk stockings for her, but as she had said nothing about them in her last letter, Jane hoped they had not been bought after all, because she had spent all her money now on white gloves and some pink figured silk.

Invitations for balls and evening parties in the country, at a time when roads between towns and villages lay silent and unlighted between meadows and woods, were always issued for the moonlight nights of the month, and Bottom's cry: 'Look in the almanac; find out moonshine, find out moonshine,' was echoed by every intending hostess. In the Rectory at Ashe they made room for dancing by opening the folding doors between the drawing-room and the morning-room; the windows of the latter looked out on to the lawn, on one side of which was a great yew hedge. The yews, black under the brilliant moon of winter, and the gravel that crackled and glistened under carriage wheels, were exchanged as the guests jumped out of their carriages and ran into the house, for the warmth of high-piled fires, the magic radiance of candlelight, the tuning up of violins and the welcoming, gracious gaiety of Mrs. Lefroy. Jane in her rose-coloured silk dress had a reason besides her love of dancing for being excited; whether Tom Lefroy saw her first on the stairs or in the hall or in one of the halves of the ballroom; how soon they danced together, how much Mrs. Lefroy, in the midst of her cares as hostess, had leisure to keep an eye on them, can never now be known. Tom Lefroy lived to be Lord Chief Justice of Ireland, and as an exceedingly old man he said that he had once been in love with the great Jane Austen; 'but it was a boy's love,' he added.

It has sometimes been noticed that the most disconsolate widowers make the speediest remarriages, and James Austen's was a case in point. His second choice was Mary Lloyd. Eliza de Feuillide did not hesitate to point out for the benefit of her correspondents that Mary was neither handsome nor rich, but she admitted her to be sensible and good-humoured, and added: 'Jane seems much pleased with the match, and it is natural she should, having long known and liked the lady.' Mrs. Austen's pleasure was great; she wrote to Mary in the warmest terms. 'Had the selection been mine, you, my dear Mary, are the person I should have chosen for James's wife, Anna's mother and my daughter, being as certain as I can be of anything in this uncertain world, that you will greatly increase and promote the happiness of each of the three. . . . I look forward to you as a real comfort to me in my old age when Cassandra is gone into Shropshire and Jane the Lord knows where.'

The Shropshire living for Thomas Fowle was looked upon almost as a certainty, but it was not yet vacant, and in the meantime, Lord Craven, anxious to do something for his cousin, took him as chaplain to his own regiment, which had been ordered to the West Indies. The parting between Thomas Fowle and Cassandra was in one sense not so painful as it would be to-day, despite the fact that sea voyages then were so lengthy and posts uncertain; for lovers unless very much favoured by circumstances were frequently as much cut off from each other within the confines of England as they would feel to-day if they were in separate countries. Long absences, still longer engagements, might be avoided, but they had often to be borne; but such a nature as Cassandra's looked forward to the future and, however irksome she found the present, she would not let her friends feel depressed on her

43

account. Mrs. Austen had no idea of what Jane's destination was to be, and Jane at present had a preoccupation quite other than marriage. *First Impressions* was finished in 1797, her twenty-second year. Before its actual publication sixteen years later she renamed it *Pride and Prejudice*, and she rewrote it to such an extent that it is impossible to say how little or how much of the final story was found in the original. But now that it was finished in its first form she did what she had always done with her writings, and showed it to her father.

Whatever it was that met the Reverend George Austen's eye in the three volumes of exquisitely regular and legible handwriting, he thought very well of it. He was prepared to be pleased, naturally; she had afforded him too much amusement from childhood for him not to have a high expectation of it now; but he was not the sort of man to be blinded by fatherly partiality, and he would have been very chary of anything's being published, even anonymously, that was not likely to do her justice. As it was, he had no hesitation in thinking that it should be offered to a publisher; he wrote to Cadell, saying: 'I have in my possession a manuscript novel, comprising 3 vols., about the length of Miss Burney's *Evelina*.' His letter indicated that if Messrs. Cadell thought well of the novel, it could be published at the author's own expense (in other words, at his), and he ended by saying: 'Should you give any encouragement, I will send you the work.'

Messrs. Cadell declined to inspect the work, by return of post. Though they acted stupidly and carelessly, and, for themselves, most unfortunately, they acted altogether in the interests of English literature. However good *First Impressions* may have been, and however readily they themselves might have offered to publish it had they taken the trouble of reading it, it cannot be supposed to have been more than a sketch or foretaste of the brilliant perfection of *Pride and Prejudice*, which had behind it sixteen maturing years in the mind of an unequalled artist, and came forth at last not only with the solid excellence it had acquired in the process, but with as much shining in it of the morn and liquid dew of youth as if it had been the author's earliest work.

But at the moment of receiving a disappointment one cannot comfort oneself with feeling that sixteen years hence it may turn out to have been all for the best. It is impossible that she should not have been disappointed, though it is characteristic of her and of her family that there is no record of her saying so. What is most striking in the affair is the influence she allowed it to have over her. After all, her novel had not been condemned; it had never been looked at. The only person who had read it and was competent to criticize it was the Rev.

44

George Austen, and he had thought it good. No one whose first object in life was to attract the public notice would have been satisfied with such a rebuff as that; even a timid author might have persevered at least until he found a publisher who would go so far as to tell him that his work was useless. Such was not Jane Austen's way; when, after her death, Henry tried to give some account of his famous sister's manner of work, he said that 'though in composition she was equally rapid and correct' she had 'an invincible distrust of her own judgement.' It is as if when she had the pen in her hand she reigned undisputed; but when daily life returned upon her she was no more bold and unerring, but modest, reflective, attentive to anything that might be said. But had she merely accepted in silence Cadell's refusal to read her novel, however unusual, it would not have been of particular significance; the latter, it is true, prevented her doing anything further with *First Impressions*, but to herself it made no difference at all. The novel had been refused in the November of 1797; before the year was out she was deeply engrossd in a second one. She called it *Sense and Sensibility*.

1797 had brought disappointment to both sisters, but had Jane's been severer than it was, she would have despised herself if it had caused her more than a passing pang, when Cassandra's was so heavy. In the preceding February, Thomas Fowle had caught the yellow fever in San Domingo, and was dead.

Eliza said: 'This is a very severe stroke to the whole family, and particularly to poor Cassandra, for whom I feel more than I can express. . . . Jane says that her sister behaves with a degree of resolution and propriety which no common mind could evince in so trying a situation.' This is not Jane's language, but one can recognize beneath it the warmth of sympathy and distress, and the loving admiration, increased tenfold, of the strength of mind that was controlled in grief and not morose but silent.

Thomas Fowle had left his betrothed a thousand pounds. Lord Craven was greatly distressed, and said had he known that Fowle was an engaged man, he would never have taken him abroad; a tragic consequence of discretion.

45

CHAPTER SIX

The method in which Jane Austen's first three novels were produced makes it a matter of uncertainty to decide the order in which they should be considered. The schoolgirl's sketch, *Elinor and Marianne*, was followed by the youthful but mature *First Impressions*; *First Impressions* by *Elinor and Marianne* rewritten as *Sense and Sensibility*; *Sense and Sensibility* by *Northanger Abbey*; then, after an interval of eight years, *Sense and Sensibility* was 'prepared for the press,' and immediately after that *First Impressions* was arranged for publication and renamed *Pride and Prejudice*.

Our ignorance as to how much rewriting was involved in this preparation for the press, must make any method of arranging the first three novels on a chronological plan a question of personal opinion. A good case could be made out for placing *Northanger Abbey* at the head of the list, as the earliest example of a completed work; for though, with *Persuasion*, it was actually published the last of all the finished works, we know that it had not been retouched to any extent because the preface apologizes to readers of 1817 for anything that may seem out of date in a story written in 1803. Of the other two, one cannot but feel that, whatever its origins, *Pride and Prejudice* is the product of the time at which the author published it; spontaneous, topical, inspired no less by present enthusiasm than by earnest craftsmanship, and that it is *Sense and Sensibility* that, even more than *Northanger Abbey*, represents the carly work. It was obviously prepared for the press when Jane Austen's powers were approaching their zenith, and there is one indication at least of later workmanship. In *La Belle Assemblée* for March 1810, on the page headed Remarkable Occurrences, Deaths and Marriages, the following announcements occur under "Hampshire": 'At Ringwood, William Dyke Esquire of Vernham to Miss Elizabeth Steele of Ashmondsworth. At Cheriton, the Rev. John Courtney to Miss Ferrers, only daughter of the Rev. Edmond Ferrers.' But in spite of this indication of the source of two of the names in it, it seems possible to suggest that not the book's failings only, but, more important, its background and its atmosphere, relate it to the earliest period of her novel-writing.

Henry said that his sister had been, from a very early age, familiar with *Gilpin on the Picturesque*. The term 'picturesque beauty' has been defined as beauty capable of being formed into pictures, and the

46

cult of the picturesque in England reached its most ardent phase in the latter part of the eighteenth century. It was natural that the Rule of Taste should extend itself to landscape no less than to architecture. Those artists whose works were deemed models of the picturesque belonged in fact to a previous era; they were, notably, Salvator Rosa, Poussin and Claude Lorraine, and the savage abruptness of effect in the first, and the beautifully arranged landscapes of the last, with their indigo distances and bold masses of foliage, so frequently touched with the gilded bronze of approaching autumn, provide an immediate illustration of the general conception of the term. When Thompson's poem, *The Seasons*, with its detailed descriptions of landscape in the varied changes of the year, became known to the public, he was hailed as the Claude of poets; the enthusiasm extended itself from admiring a picturesque rendering of landscape to looking at an actual scene and deciding on its capacity for being formed into a picture, and the connoisseur had to assist him a 'Claude glass,' a little appliance, something like the view-finder of a camera, which reflected the scenery in a manner that brought out the picturesque values.

> *Much will the mirror teach, or evening grey*
> *When o'er her ample span some twilight ray*
> *Obscurely gleams; here Art shall best perceive*
> *On distant parts what fainter lines to give.*

This appreciation of picturesque beauty, celebrated in poetry and paint, greatly influenced landscape gardening. The formal laying out of gardens on a grand scale, such as one may see at the Palace of Versailles, yielded, among the fashionable landowners of the mid-eighteenth century, to a series of systems, each practised by the improvers of the day, of which the common feature was an ordered wildness, and in each of which landscape was disposed with the aim of achieving an emotional effect in the spectator. Of one of the earliest improvers it was said: 'When the united plumage of an ancient wood extended wide its undulating canopy, and stood venerable in darkness, Kent thinned the foremost ranks, and left but so many detached and scattered trees as softened the approach of gloom and blended the chequered light with the thus lengthened shadows of the remaining columns.' The dramatic contrast of light and shade, chiaroscuro, was an inseparable adjunct to the picturesque.

The best known of the improvers of estates, 'Capability' Brown, so called because he was accustomed to say: 'I perceive that your estate has great capabilities,' was noted for his abhorrence of a straight line.

47

Avenues of chestnut, oak and beech, under whose branches their owners had ridden off to the Civil Wars, caused Capability to shake his head. He thinned them out, until they became clumps of trees, irregularly disposed, and he aimed at the illusion of a sweep of grass coming from the horizon up to the windows of the dining-room. For the paling, which had hitherto divided the garden from the park, he substituted a ditch, invisible till one was almost in it, and called a ha-ha! from the exclamations of surprise it so frequently provoked. The flower-beds beloved of the Elizabethans, their red and white rosebushes and beds of lavender, the tulips whose parti-coloured, glossy ranks the seventeenth century had delighted to rear, were banished from a tasteful scheme and relegated to a rosegarden hidden in yew hedges or a walled enclosure for cut flowers, vegetables and fruit. In the case of one client, Capability Brown was able to realize his highest conception of the improver's art; he was permitted to excavate a deep depression and to sink in it the stables and all the offices, so that no excrescence marred the outline of the house amidst its verdure. Brown and his successor Repton were of course principally called in to improve a seat already in existence, but when a new mansion was built, care was taken that where possible it should crown rising ground, so as to command the finest view available.

The enthusiasm for picturesque beauty, as it implied a rearranging of one's own landscape, was of course confined to landowners, but appreciation of picturesque scenery as a pleasure for the private person was both crystallized and further stimulated by the works of Thomas Gilpin, a clergyman whose taste and capacity made him a leader of one of the most fashionable passions of the day, and who spent everything he made by his writings on this select subject, on improving the conditions of the poor in his parish. Between 1792 and 1798 he published five works, *Observations* on five separate districts of the western part of England, including the coastal scenery of Hampshire, 'chiefly relative to Picturesque Beauty.' Within the same period he produced shorter works on similar topics, such as *Picturesque Beauty*, *Picturesque Landscape* and *Sketching Landscape*. When Henry Austen referred to *Gilpin on the Picturesque,* he may have meant a collection of extracts of which the sources only have survived, or it may have been his way of mentioning the subject of Gilpin's works as a whole, but one passage of Gilpin's at least seems ascribable as the origin of a remark in the *History of England*. Gilpin said: 'England exceeds most countries in the Variety of its picturesque beauty,' for the following reasons: the prevalence of hedgerows, the predominance of oaks, the frequency of parks, its vaporous atmosphere, and the large number of its Gothic

48

ruins; as the perpetrator of which, said the History, Henry VIII had been of great use to the English landscape.

Gilpin's observations on Forest Scenery are plainly glanced at in *Sense and Sensibility*. 'How many forests have we, wherein you shall have for one living tree, two evil-thriving rotten and dying trees. What rottenness! What hollowness! What dead arms! Withered tops! Curtailed trunks! What loads of moss! Dropping boughs and dying branches shall you see everywhere!' But in the student of the picturesque such a spectacle would arouse not feelings of chagrin at the sight of fine timber going to waste, but the romantic agitation of a mind attuned to sensibility. 'When the dreary heath is spread before the eye, and ideas of wildness and desolation are required, what more suitable accompaniment can be imagined than the blasted oak, ragged, scathed and leafless, shooting its peeled white branches athwart the gathering blackness of some rising storm?'

There was actually in the Austens' neighbourhood a feature which would have delighted a connoisseur of the picturesque, but it is mentioned, not by Gilpin, but by Gilbert White. He speaks of 'two rocky, hollow lanes, the one to Alton, the other to the forest. . . . These roads . . . are by the traffic of ages and the fretting of water, worn down through the first stratum of our freestone, and partly through the second; so that they look more like watercourses than roads; and are bedded with naked rag for furlongs together. In many places they are reduced sixteen or eighteen feet below the level of the fields : and after floods and in frosts exhibit very grotesque and wild appearances, from the tangled roots that are twisted among the strata and from the torrents rushing down their broken sides; and especially when those cascades are frozen into icicles, hanging in all the fanciful shapes of frostwork. These rugged, gloomy scenes affright the ladies when they peep down into them from the paths above and make timid horsemen shudder while they ride along them.'

The fervent enthusiasm for picturesque beauty might no doubt be ascribed to the reaction against the unyielding canons of aesthetic propriety, and common sense which governed the century as a whole, and this reaction showed itself again in the cultivation of Sensibility. The maintenance of feeling at a high pitch as a matter of duty to oneself often outran the genuine emotion, but the genuine emotion was often there. When 'Perdita' Robinson wrote an account of her seduction and subsequent desertion by the Prince Regent, she appealed to that Being 'Who formed my sensitive and perpetually aching heart.' One does not doubt that her heart ached sorely, but, then, nothing was more fashionable than a heartache.

49

So widespread among the cultivated portion of society was this mania for Sensibility, that when Hannah More wrote her *Strictures on the Modern System of Female Education with a view of the principles and conduct among women of rank and fortune*, she devoted a long chapter to this quality and its dangerous abuse. Speaking of girls who were enthusiastic by nature, she said: 'Through this natural warmth which they have been justly told is so pleasing, but which perhaps they have not been told will be continually exposing them to peril and to suffering, their joys and sorrows are excessive. Of this extreme irritability . . . the uneducated learn to boast, as if it were a decided indication of superiority of soul, instead of labouring to restrain it. . . . It is misfortune enough to be born more liable to suffer and to sin, from this conformity of mind; it is too much to nourish the evil by unrestrained indulgence, it is still worse to be proud of so misleading a quality.' The *Strictures*, which had reached nine editions by 1801, did not come before they were needed. As early as 1775 the evil had been noticed, and it ran through every walk of feminine society from the impertinent Lydia Languish who had sent to the circulating library for *The Tears of Sensibility* to the girl whose epitaph in Dorchester Abbey says that: 'When nerves were too delicately spun to bear the Rude Shakes and Jostlings which we meet with in this transitory world, Nature gave way; she sank and died a martyr to Excessive Sensibility.'

In the brilliant lines of Sheridan no less than in the solemn harangues of Hannah More, we can only regard fashionable sensibility as something with the preserved appeal to our interests of an object in a museum. It is in *Sense and Sensibility* that we understand what it meant to a person in real life.

There is a peculiar loveliness in *Sense and Sensibility*. The book's shortcomings are obvious; the language is often stilted, and of the two heroines, the author's confessed favourite is not likely to be the favourite of anybody else. Even to-day it gives some surprise that Elinor Dashwood, who is meant to be not only admirable but charming, should be so constantly finding fault with her delightful mother and telling her what she ought to do; but these blemishes do not affect the romantic beauty of the work. With its too rational heroine and the immature stiffness of some of its expressions, it is like a blossoming landscape under a hoar frost. The heart of the book, the core of light by which the rest is illuminated, is the calamitous love affair of a selfish looseliver and a girl of seventeen, ardent, inexperienced, and trained to believe that caution or even common discretion are an offence against true feeling. The characters of Marianne Dashwood and Willoughby are in one sense among the most deeply interesting Jane Austen ever produced; they show a mingling of more serious evil with good than she afterwards attempted in any full-length character study. Marianne is more disastrously mistaken in her attitude to life than any of the other heroines, yet her essential, her passionate virtue, is one of the endearing things about her, and Willoughby, who for two-thirds of the book arouses the reader's detestation as a brutal scoundrel, is shown by a wonderful transition, whose suddenness is equalled only by its complete convincingness, to be actually an object of sympathy. It is, if one may adopt the language of the picturesque, a moral chiaroscuro, unique among her works and carried through with a ruthless logic, an unwavering pursuit of probability, even to the point of Marianne's ultimate happy marriage with Colonel Brandon, who had fallen in love with her at first sight, but whom she had declared to be, as a man of thirty-six, too far removed from youth, the period of acute feeling, to inspire any emotion but a respectful sympathy.

To turn for a moment to those parts of the book immediately recognizable as characteristic of Jane Austen, we find them, naturally enough, in the comic relief. The serious conversations in *Sense and Sensibility*, however excellent in matter, are frequently more suggestive of a particularly well written letter than actual speech, but the conversation of any character, comic, disagreeable or odd, is astounding. One aspect of her work is shown as truly in the comic portions of the early *Sense and Sensibility* as in whichever of the other novels may be the reader's favourite; it is the capacity to work up conversation to a pitch of comedy bordering nearly upon farce, and yet to sacrifice almost nothing— sometimes nothing at all—to photographic realism. We laugh at Mrs. Malaprop as at an excellent joke; we laugh at Mrs. Palmer and Robert Ferrars and Nancy Steele with the pleasure, and it is altogether different from the pleasure usually derived from humorous authors, that we get from something irresistibly funny in daily life. The perception that cuts out a self-portrait is conversation, as with a razor edge, was perhaps never better shown than in the celebrated second chapter of *Sense and Sensibility*, in which John Dashwood, the half-brother of Elinor and Marianne, and present owner of the family estate, has a discussion with his wife on the subject of how he is to carry out the promise made to his dying father, of taking care of the widowed Mrs. Dashwood and her daughters. To give an adequate idea of how the grasping and callous nature of the wife influences that of the superficially amiable husband who is at heart as selfish as she, but more anxious to view himself in a respectable light, it would be necessary to quote the greater part of the chapter in its entirety. By stages, exquisitely graduated yet rapid enough to maintain the stimulus of comedy, John Dashwood is brought to change his original idea of giving each of his half-sisters a thousand pounds, to that of helping them to move their things when they find a new house and sending them presents of fish and game when in season: and to think it a generous one.

The style, even in the serious passages, has a constant subdued sparkle, like that of a dark but quartz-shot stone; in the lighter narrative-portions, apart even from the achievements in character and episode, it scintillates with every turn.

The principal comic relief of the book is supplied by a figure who is not, for the purposes of comedy, seen from one angle only but whom we begin by ridiculing, despising and disliking, and end, as is so often the case in real life, by coming really to know and consequently to value with warmth and respect. Mrs. Jennings, the mother-in-law of the Dashwoods' Devonshire relation, Sir John Middleton, appears in the first volume of the book practically intolerable; her coarse good humour finds its most usual vent in joking about the supposed love affairs of everybody in her neighbourhood, and as both Elinor and Marianne are, from different causes, very susceptible to impertinent comment, the reader's view of Mrs. Jennings is naturally coloured by theirs. No less offensive is her blundering, unfeeling, remorseless curiosity with regard to some particularly painful private business of Colonel Brandon's; even her harmless conversation puts her in a contemptible light; as when she brings her second daughter, the pretty, stupid little Mrs. Palmer, to call on the Dashwoods. Mrs. Jennings said that she wished her daughter had not travelled so fast because it might have done her harm, as she was expecting a baby; she made this communication 'leaning towards Elinor, and speaking in a low voice as if she meant to be heard by no one else, though they were seated on different sides of the room. . . .'

It is in the second volume, when Marianne, knowing Willoughby to be in London, accepts Mrs. Jennings' invitation to spend some weeks at her town house, that Mrs. Jennings' character begins to develop itself. Elinor had at first declined the invitation, supposing that in doing so she was consulting Marianne's wishes even more than her own; but Marianne, thinking of nothing but Willoughby, said that if Elinor were frightened away by her dislike of Mrs. Jennings, at least *she* had no such scruples, adding: ' "I am sure I could put up with every unpleasantness of that sort with very little effort."

'Elinor could not help smiling at this display of indifference towards the manners of a person to whom she had often had difficulty in persuading Marianne to behave with tolerable politeness, and resolved

52

within herself that if her sister persisted in going, she would go like-wise, as she did not think it proper that Marianne should be left to the sole guidance of her own judgement or that Mrs. Jennings should be abandoned to the mercy of Marianne for all the comfort of her domestic hours.'

The visit thus embarked upon, with its immediate exploding of the mine which had been already laid for Marianne's happiness, brings out the essential qualities of Mrs. Jennings, of which—and herein lies the art of the portrayal—we were unconscious before, but which, when brought before us, we at once realize to have been latent in the charac-ter as previously described. Her extraordinary kindness to the girls, her good-tempered, humble recognition of herself as a silly old woman of 'odd ways,' her comically expressed but most genuine friendship for poor Colonel Brandon, and her instinctive condemnation of all the people whose falseness and cold hearts add so much to Elinor's un-happiness, make her by the end of the book appear as one of the pleasantest people in it.

But so much is merely what one would expect to find in the appren-tice work of Jane Austen. It is the romantic episode which affords the unique interest among her works, and though the course of it is an illustration of the title and the condemnation implied by its contrast: though Marianne is openly criticized on almost every page, her story is told with so much sympathy and so much conviction that in retro-spect we regard it, not as the tragic blunder it actually was, but as some-thing with the strange, essential beauty that attaches to profound human experience.

The outlines of the story are much more boldly drawn than in any of the other five novels, and the scenes, though they in no case over-step the limits of strict probability, are conceived on a larger scale. An instance of this difference is provided by a comparison of the first meet-ing of Marianne and her lover with the similar encounters in the other books. Catherine Morland has a casual introduction to Mr. Tilney at a crowded and fatiguing assembly; Elizabeth Bennet and Mr. Darcy have a very unpromising first encounter at a ball; Fanny Price, as a frightened child of ten, does not distinguish Edmund Bertram among the alarming cousins to whom she is introduced on the evening of her arrival at Mansfield Park; Emma Woodhouse would not have been able to remember that day in her childhood on which she became con-scious of Mr. Knightley's existence; we are not told how Anne Elliot and Captain Wentworth first saw each other, because they met eight years before the opening of *Persuasion*; but with Marianne we are in a different world at once. She and her younger sister had gone for a

53

walk on the downs which, varied with hanging woods, shut in Barton valley; it was autumn, and when the girls had reached the summit and were delighting in the excitement of a tearing wind, the clouds suddenly closed over their heads and a burst of rain made them run down the hillside to the shelter of the cottage once more. Marianne was ahead of her sister when she suddenly tripped, and on trying to get up, found herself helpless with a sprained ankle. 'A gentleman carrying a gun, with two pointers playing round him,' saw the accident and, putting down the gun, ran to her assistance, and finding that she could not walk, picked her up in his arms and carried her down the hillside, through the gate of the cottage, and the front door which Margaret on running in had left open, and straight into the parlour, where he deposited her in a chair under the astonished eyes of Mrs. Dashwood and Elinor.

The acquaintance thus begun opens as the bud in summer's ripening breath. Marianne, though so severely handled by her creator, is lovely and interesting to a degree. Her attractions are those of a breathing creature, wild and startling with life. 'Her skin was very brown, but from its transparency, her complexion was unusually brilliant; her features were all good; her smile was sweet and attractive; and in her eyes, which were very dark, there was a life, a spirit, an eagerness, which could hardly be seen without delight.' It is a type particularly well illustrated in portraits of the late eighteenth century of young women in their long-sleeved gowns with fichus, and hair turned loosely back from the face and arranged in so carefully careless a manner that it seems to be wandering at will. One of the indications that *Sense and Sensibility* was composed fourteen years at least before its publication may be found in the incident of Willoughby's cutting off a piece of Marianne's hair, as, although they were in the parlour, she was sitting with it 'all tumbled down her back.' The gentleman who had raped a lock from the Grecian coiffure of 1811, would have caused his victim to cry out with Belinda:

> *O hadst thou, cruel, been content to seize*
> *Hairs less in sight, or any hairs but these!*

Nowhere in the novel is the author's unerring touch upon character better shown than in the fact that Marianne, with all her exasperating faults, was of the type which was, quite irrespective of her personal beauty, strongly attractive to the opposite sex. 'Gaiety was never a part of *my* character,' says Edward Ferrars. Elinor replies: 'Nor do I think it a part of Marianne's. I should hardly call her a lively girl—she is

54

very earnest, very eager in all she does—sometimes talks a great deal, and always with animation—but she is not often really merry.' But Marianne's earnest animation was bewitching, and her 'eagerness of fancy and spirits' seized on the imagination more than any frivolity, however entertaining. Nor was her charm diminished by the fact that she was quite without a sense of humour. The present age has added so many decades to the period of youth that it is a little difficult to understand the impression Jane Austen meant to make in saying that Colonel Brandon was thirty-six; but a rough calculation is sufficient for one to realize the absurdity of Marianne's remarks when she debated the possibility of the Colonel, old as he was, finding some woman of seven and twenty or so who might be pleased to marry him. '"A woman of seven and twenty," said Marianne after pausing a moment, "can never hope to feel or inspire affection again, and if her home be un-comfortable or her fortune small, I can suppose that she might bring herself to submit to the offices of a nurse, for the sake of the provision and security of a wife. In his marrying such a woman, therefore, there would be nothing unsuitable. It would be a compact of convenience, and the world would be satisfied. In my eyes it would be no marriage at all, but that would be nothing"'; though the full effect of this pro-nouncement is perhaps not appreciated until it is discovered that Marianne herself, at the age of nineteen, became the Colonel's loving and devoted wife. The wrong-headedness of Marianne and Mrs. Dash-wood, in the one case leading her to hasty and altogether erroneous judgements, and in the other hurrying her favourite child to calamity, does not detract from the charm of its possessors any more than it would in real life; the opposite quality is the one dangerous to fas-cination; it is not that men positively admire a woman for defective powers of judgement, but that they feel instinctively ill at ease with one of calm and acute perception. Elinor was of the latter sort, and if the portrait of her lover Edward Ferrars seems colourless and flat, one can say at least this for it: that it represents the kind of man who might reasonably be expected to fall in love with Elinor.

Marianne's firm conviction that no one who understood the mean-ing of love could ever feel it twice was in harmony with all her other ideas and tastes. It seems strange to us that the sensitive, gentle, melan-choly Cowper should have afforded such ecstatic delight to a mind as ardent as Marianne's, but that does not mar our appreciation of the scene where she was obliged to listen to his verses read aloud by the well-meaning Edward. '"I could hardly keep my seat. To hear those beautiful lines which have frequently almost driven me wild, pro-nounced with such impenetrable calmness, such dreadful indifference!"

' "He would certainly have done more justice to simple and elegant prose. I thought so at the time; but you *would* give him Cowper."

' "Nay, mama, if he is not to be animated by Cowper!" '

Edward was equally deficient in a taste for the picturesque; he visited them at Barton, and when the sisters were showing him the views of the neighbourhood, he said the country was beautiful but that the bottoms must be dirty in winter; to which Marianne exclaimed: ' "How can you think of dirt with such objects before you?"

' "Because," he replied smiling, "amongst the rest of the objects before me, I see a very dirty lane."

' "How strange!" said Marianne to herself as she walked on.'

Edward gives an amusing comparison between the terminology of the student of the picturesque and that of the ordinary observer. When Marianne questions him eagerly as to the parts of the scenery he has most admired, he says: ' "You must not inquire too far, Marianne. . . . I shall offend you by my ignorance and want of taste if we come to particulars. I shall call hills steep, which ought to be bold; surfaces strange and uncouth, which ought to be irregular and rugged; and distant objects out of sight which ought only to be indistinct through the soft medium of a hazy atmosphere. . . . It exactly answers my idea of a fine country . . . and I daresay it is a picturesque one too, because you admire it; I can easily believe it to be full of rocks and promontories, grey moss and brushwood, but they are all lost on me." ' Marianne was not offended; she had too settled a conviction that she herself was right. Her sensibility was dangerous because it was so genuine; the impossibility of Elinor's task in trying to induce her to be more guarded in her attitude to Willoughby lay in the fact that Marianne thought that reserve or caution towards a man for whom she felt a mutual affection, though he had not as yet proposed to her, was not tiresome or prudish merely, but utterly ignoble. On every occasion where she might have been more comfortable by exercising self-control she regarded it as a moral obligation to herself to be as uncomfortable as possible. The day after Willoughby had left Devonshire, albeit his return was expected almost immediately, 'Marianne would have thought herself very inexcusable had she been able to sleep at all the first night after parting with Willoughby. She would have been ashamed to look her family in the face the next morning, had she not risen from her bed in more need of repose than when she lay down in it.' But at the climax of the affair, when Willoughby's desertion is made plain and announced in a manner of such startling brutality, the criticism of Marianne which is so perpetually implied is for once quite absent, and the scene is offered whole and entire in impartial conviction.

56

'Before the housemaid had lit their fire next day, or the sun gained any power over a cold, gloomy morning in January, Marianne, only half dressed, was kneeling against one of the window seats for the sake of all the little light she could command from it, and writing as fast as a continual flow of tears would permit her. In this situation, Elinor, roused from sleep by her agitation and sobs, first perceived her; and after observing her for a few moments with silent anxiety, said, in a tone of the most considerate gentleness, "Marianne, may I ask—" "No, Elinor," she replied, "ask nothing. You will soon know all." The sort of desperate calmness with which this was said lasted no longer than while she spoke, and was immediately followed by a return of the same excessive affliction. It was some minutes before she could go on with her letter; and the frequent bursts of grief, which still obliged her at intervals to withhold her pen, were proof enough of her feeling how more than probable it was that she was writing for the last time to Willoughby.'

She spent the time till breakfast wandering about the house, avoiding everybody, and after breakfast, during which Elinor had done her best to distract the attention of Mrs. Jennings, 'a letter was delivered to Marianne which she eagerly caught from the servant, and, turning of a death-like paleness, instantly ran out of the room. Elinor, who saw as plainly by this as if she had seen the direction, that it must come from Willoughby, felt immediately such a sickness at heart as made her hardly able to hold up her head, and sat in such a general tremor as made her fear it impossible to escape Mrs. Jennings' notice. That good lady, however, saw only that Marianne had received a letter from Willoughby, which appeared to her a very good joke, and which she treated accordingly by hoping with a laugh that she would find it to her liking.' She went on to talk of their forthcoming marriage, which had been the standing topic of conversation at Barton for the past several months; and Elinor tried in vain to make her believe that Marianne and Willoughby were not formally engaged; Mrs. Jennings put down all these denials to slyness, and assured her that was not to be taken in. Elinor at length gave up the unequal struggle; 'eager at all events to know what Willoughby had written, (she) hurried away to their room, where, on opening the door, she saw Marianne stretched on the bed, almost choked by grief, a letter in her hand, and two or three others lying by her. Elinor drew near, but without saying a word, and seating herself on the bed, took her hand and kissed her affectionately several times, and then gave way to a burst of tears which at first was scarcely less violent than Marianne's. The latter, though unable to speak, seemed to feel all the tenderness of this behaviour, and

57

after some time thus spent in joint affliction, she put all the letters into Elinor's hands, and then, covering her face with her handkerchief, almost screamed with agony.'

Allowing for the natural difficulty of one great creative artist properly to estimate another, it is not easy to understand what Charlotte Brontë meant by saying that Jane Austen's heroines have only so much acquaintance with the passions as their author would think lady-like.

After a period of distraught, oblivious misery, Marianne allowed Elinor to accept for them an invitation to go with Mrs. Jennings to the Palmers' house at Cleveland: because Marianne wanted to be at home and thought that this would be the quickest means of getting there. The Palmers were wealthy enough to have a house constructed on the rules of taste. It was 'situated on a sloping lawn. It had no park, but the pleasure grounds were tolerably extensive; and like every other place of the same importance, it had its open shrubbery and closed wood-walk; a road of smooth gravel winding round a plantation, led to the front; the lawn was dotted over with timber; the house itself was under the guardianship of the fir, the mountain ash and the acacia, and a thick screen of them altogether, interspersed with tall Lombardy poplars, shut out the offices.' Marianne, whose heart 'swelled with emotion' to think that Willoughby's seat, Combe Magna, was not thirty miles distant, determined that she would make her stay endurable with the relief of long walks alone in the twilight; and 'while the others were busily helping Charlotte show her child to the housekeeper, she quitted it again, and stealing away through the winding shrubberies, now just beginning to be in beauty, to gain a distant eminence; where, from its Grecian temple, her eye, wandering over a wide tract of country to the south-east, could fondly rest on the farthest ridge of hills in the horizon and fancy that from their summits Combe Magna could be seen.'

The long course of wretchedness in which Marianne had indulged made her so low in health that when she caught a chill it developed into something serious. 'Two delightful twilight walks on the third and fourth evenings of her being there, not merely on the dry gravel of the shrubbery, but all over the grounds, and especially in the most distant parts of them, where there was something more of wildness than in the rest, where the trees were the oldest, and the grass was the longest and wettest, had—assisted by the still greater imprudence of sitting in her wet shoes and stockings—given Marianne a cold so violent, as, though for a day or two trifled with and denied, would force itself by increasing ailments on the concern of everybody.'

The cold and sore throat having developed into what the apothecary

58

diagnosed as a putrid fever, Mrs. Palmer, nervous for her baby, left the house for a relation's and took Mr. Palmer with her. Mrs. Jennings and Colonel Brandon remained to help and comfort Elinor, and when at last Marianne became desperately ill the Colonel went off in his own carriage to fetch Mrs. Dashwood from Barton. While he was actually gone, Marianne took an unexpected turn for the better, and Elinor, who at first scarcely dared to believe her eyes, longed with passionate impatience for her mother to arrive and receive the good news herself.

'The night was cold and stormy. The wind roared round the house, and the rain beat against the windows; but Elinor, all happiness within, regarded it not. Marianne slept through every blast, and the travellers —they had a rich reward in store, for every present inconvenience.

'The clock struck eight. Had it been ten, Elinor would have been convinced that at that moment she heard a carriage driving up to the house; and so strong was the persuasion that she *did*, in spite of the *almost* impossibility of their being already come, that she moved into the adjoining dressing-closet and opened a window-shutter, to be satisfied of the truth. She instantly saw that her ears had not deceived her. The flaring lamps of a carriage were immediately in view. By their uncertain light she thought she could discern it to be drawn by four horses; and this, while it told the excess of her poor mother's alarm, gave some explanation to such unexpected rapidity.

'Never in her life had Elinor found it so difficult to be calm, as at that moment. The knowledge of what her mother must be feeling as the carriage stopped at the door,—or her doubt—her dread—perhaps her despair?—and of what *she* had to *tell*?—with such knowledge it was impossible to be calm. . . . The bustle in the vestibule as she passed along an inner lobby, assured her that they were already in the house. She rushed forwards towards the drawing-room—she entered it,—and saw only Willoughby.'

The dramatic surprise of this entry is sustained by the unexpected but convincing fashion in which Willoughby explains his conduct, though he cannot explain it away. His account of what led him to appear a scoundrel is not one of the arresting psychological studies, such as are furnished by the comic or satirical episodes; but it is perhaps, with the conversation of the second chapter, the soundest, most searching analysis of motive in the book. There are portions of the novel which one imagines may be the fruit of revision; when, for instance, Elinor disclosed to Marianne that Edward had for two years been entangled in an engagement with Lucy Steele, Marianne considered Lucy 'so totally unamiable, so absolutely incapable of attaching a sensible man, that she could not be persuaded at first to believe, and

59

afterwards to pardon, any former affection of Edward for her. She would not even admit it to have been natural; and Elinor left her to be convinced that it was so, by that which only could convince her, a better knowledge of mankind.' One does not know whether that last sentence was written by Jane Austen at twenty-two or Jane Austen at thirty-six; but the conduct of Willoughby is so integral a part of the story that it must have been conceived, with all its understanding of a weak, vicious yet fascinating character, at the time of the story's origin. The episode of Marianne and Willoughby is indeed condemned from its outset; it brings out the worst characteristics in each, and Marianne at least recovers from it as if from some painful disease; yet it is a thing of beauty, and it sounds a note Jane Austen never repeated, when Willoughby says to Elinor in asking her to tell Marianne of his confession: 'You tell me she has forgiven me already. Let me be able to fancy that a better knowledge of my heart, and of my present feelings, will draw from her a more spontaneous, more natural, more gentle, less dignified forgiveness.'

Even in this early work, Jane Austen's achievement suffers great injustice from an attempt to discuss it in parts, to illustrate it by detached quotations; for her very first novel shows a capacity for construction, and for making all her characters act upon each other amazing in a writer who was so young that one would have expected the book to be a series of passages, brilliant in themselves but not making each one an indispensable contribution to the whole. Art lies in concealing art, and it is true that the framework of *Sense and Sensibility* is obvious; that, in a sense, is why it is so remarkable; beneath the enthusiastic delight in creating character, the conscious preoccupation with some favourite ideas about conduct and common sense, the light and shade of romantic passion, and the itch that besets us all, to make a personal comment upon the trends and fashions of the day, is the instinctive, faultless sense of balance, the intellectual attack upon form, which matured into that unique quality of hers, the power to impose a shape upon her material without sacrificing anything to probability.

CHAPTER SEVEN

Jane Austen's existence was apparently without incident; the answer to such a comment lies in six works of art, and one cannot avoid the question of how much actual experience of character and scene she incorporated into her novels in recognizable form. Of trivial details there are not many, but there are some; perhaps it would be more accurate to say that some knowledge of her daily life enables one to guess, here and there, with some degree of confidence, that she is at least modelling her creation on experience, especially, one believes, with reference to visual description: the view from Mr. Darcy's drawing-room windows, the vast kitchen premises of Northanger Abbey, Donwell Abbey 'with all the old neglect of prospect.' A few, a very few minor characters seemed to her family ascribable to people they knew or had known. We ourselves are occasionally tempted to think that in the relationship, at least, of one character to another, if not in the characters themselves, as in Jane Bennet's influence on her brilliant sister, Emma Woodhouse's grateful affection for her older friend Mrs. Weston, Emma Watson's for an invalided father, there is a reflection of something to be seen in Jane Austen's own life. But to go farther than such speculations, to try to deduce from her novels a personal history of Jane Austen, is completely to misunderstand the type of mind she represents.

The creative mind of the first order is infinitely difficult to understand; Dryden understood it when he said of Shakespeare: 'After God, he has created most'; but there are numberless people who say 'Anne Elliot *must* be Jane Austen' because Jane Austen could never otherwise have understood how Anne Elliot would have felt; and the only thing that deters them from believing that Shakespeare smothered his wife in a fit of jealousy, was deeply distressed by a second marriage of his mother's, murdered a distinguished guest in the hope of succeeding him in his office, and was finally turned out of doors by his ungrateful children, is that the stories of Othello, Hamlet, Macbeth and Lear were published and widely known before he undertook them.

The highest type of creative genius owes to daily life at once everything and nothing; its implements, its medium, are supplied by observation of the topical existence, but its inspiration lies in the fact that owing to some extraordinary *lusus naturae* it is in touch with something that encompasses us but that the rest of us do not see; racial memory or basic consciousness, one knows not how to name this vantage ground, and dark as it is to us, there is no doubt that it was equally so to the conscious mind of its possessors. But when they postulated to themselves a human being in a particular situation, something nameless whispered to them all the rest. How else could Shakespeare, three hundred years before anyone had investigated the working of the subconscious mind, have understood that though Lady Macbeth had urged her husband not to be appalled by blood, which a little water could wash away, yet when her conscious mind was asleep, she was haunted by the nightmare that she would never get the bloodstains off her hands? When Macaulay mentioned Shakespeare and Jane Austen in the same breath, he did not suppose it necessary to state the obvious differences of their art and scope; admirers of Jane Austen understood what he meant in making the comparison, and feel that however far apart they stand, the two share the quality, in however differing degrees, of creating character.

It is this most unusual calibre of mind that she possessed which is the inmost secret of her skill and explains, in so far as words can explain, the miracle of her achievement; and an attempt to understand it, however faintly, provides a strong warning against the folly and the uselessness of attempting to establish definite connections between the world she lived in and the world of her imagination. Her creation is as much like the world of her experience as one human being is like another, in that they are both recognizable as belonging to the same species; but two human beings are not, in any other sense, the same.

One may, however, trace the sort of experience which, germinating in her mind, told her what hope was, and despair, and comfort and joy and every emotion, not as it shows itself in some superhuman form, but as it affects the so-called ordinary man and woman.

In December 1797, a month after the refusal of Messrs. Cadell to read *First Impressions*, Eliza de Feuillide was brought, not without some latent misgiving that she might be throwing herself away, to marry Henry Austen. Their courtship had been most characteristic of Eliza, and perhaps of the kind exactly calculated to increase the ardour and determination of a man so volatile and light-hearted. The handsome, brilliant, amusing Henry had to be serious, perhaps even distraught, for once in his life, before he could be 'immeasurably enlarged into a husband' and Madame de Feuillide permitted herself to dwindle into a wife. To woo Eliza was like attempting to hold the wind in a net. Eliza wrote to Phila Walter on the subject: 'I do not believe the parties will ever come together; not, however, that they have quarrelled, but one of them cannot bring her mind to give up dear Liberty and yet dearer Flirtation. After a few months' stay in the country she some-

62

times thinks it possible to undertake sober matrimony, but a few weeks' stay in London convinces her how little the state suits her taste.' But in the December of 1797 the marriage took place; Eliza announced it in a letter to Warren Hastings, in which she mentioned that Henry was fond of little Hastings de Feuillide, and, she was sure, would make him a good father. She said that the courtship in which she had at last acquiesced had been going on for two years.

Henry at the time of the wedding was a Captain in the Oxfordshire Militia, but he presently turned his attention to a more lucrative profession, and five years afterwards he was established as the partner of a brother officer named Maunde, as a banker and army agent with offices in Albany Street; he and Eliza lived in Upper Berkeley Street, and Mrs. Henry Austen continued, if on a slightly smaller scale, the social existence of the Comtesse de Feuillide. In the month of their marriage she was still writing a reference to Henry as 'my *cousin*,' adding, 'I have an aversion to the word husband, and never make use of it.' But in fact she and Henry were very happy. James had once wanted to marry Eliza, and she had refused him on the ground that he was a clergyman; such was her ostensible reason, but a profound instinct lay behind it. James, deeply emotional though of a quiet disposition, and of an earnest turn to his whole nature, that sometimes made him awkward and ungracious in his behaviour, would never have endured Eliza's manner of life when the first enchantment of her presence had worn off; nor would Eliza, quick and cool, have felt equal to the demands of James's grave, romantic nature; but to Henry, who liked society and shone in it, who was naturally cheerful and whose feelings were acute rather than deep, she was ideally suited. There was nothing in him that she could torment him upon, and for being perverse and cross with no reason at all, she herself was too rational, too elegant, with too much *savoir vivre*.

The only cloud upon the happiness of her second married life was that in 1801 poor little Hastings de Feuillide died of epilepsy. Warren Hastings had been acquitted at the close of his seven years' trial, six years before, but he was still a figure of public interest, and the death of his small namesake was recorded in *The Gentleman's Magazine*.

In the next year Jane began a story of a young girl who, having been brought up in a remote country parsonage, was taken for a season to Bath. This city was well known to Jane, because Mrs. Austen's brother, James Leigh Perrot, and his wife, Jane, had a house, No. 1 Paragon, near the upper end of the town, and the family from Steventon frequently stayed with them. Visits to Bath in these circumstances were not the unmixed delight they would otherwise have been to Cassandra and Jane. Jane Leigh Perrot and her husband were devoted to each

63

other, and she was attached to her sister-in-law Austen and her family and meant to be kind to them all; but her manner was not prepossessing, and her temper was rather gloomy and uncertain. Her nieces, accustomed to the affectionate, gracious, unconstrained atmosphere of home, could not be happy with their aunt, though their natural sense of justice gave her credit for meaning to do well by them. Jane Austen suffered fools gladly, but she did find it hard to bear a harsh, uncompromising behaviour, however it was supposed to conceal a heart of gold. Nevertheless she knew she owed a good deal to Mrs. Leigh Perrot's kindness. As an unmarried girl she could not go to stay at places by herself; she could not get to Bath except as somebody's guest, unless one of her relations wanted to take the waters and brought her with them, and Bath, for anyone to whom it did not spell rheumatism, gout or gravel, was a terrestrial paradise of gaiety, with plays, concerts and balls far superior to anything a country town could produce; with crescents and a circus of houses more beautiful than anything in London, and without London's bewildering vastness, noise and dirt; and, above all, ample arrangements for loitering and lounging in public, for the convenience of invalids and the dissipation of everybody else—the Pump Room, the Abbey yard, the colonnaded shop fronts, the public libraries, some displaying jewellery and toys among the latest novels, and others where people went to skim over the newspapers. That exciting contrast of town and country, lost now when towns straggle out in miles of suburbs which eat up the intervening greenery, was particularly marked in Bath, where Lansdowne Hill rises behind the highest crescent, and on the opposite rim of the cup Beechen Cliff rears its bold masses of foliage, shivering and whispering when one stands beneath them, but sculptured by distance to immobility.

Jane chose a heroine for this novel with a healthy love of pleasure, an enthusiasm for dancing and novels and dearest friends and the society of young men, and with just that degree of *naïveté* that enhanced the bustle and elegance of Bath into something absolutely glamorous. The exquisite naturalness of this story of a girl's holiday owes some of its convincingness at least to the manner in which, by touches so small and yet so sure, Jane Austen calls up around her walks and streets and buildings in so solid a form that when one visits those parts of Bath mentioned in *Northanger Abbey* after one has read the book, the experience strikes one as a confirmation.

Jane had been staying at No. 1 Paragon in the early part of 1798; in the early autumn she paid a visit of greater interest. Edward Austen's adopted father was dead, and Mrs. Knight now made over to Edward the great houses of Godmersham and Chawton. She wished the property

64

to be administered as well as it had been in her husband's time, and thought it better for the tenants and the neighbourhood that God-mersham should be inhabited by Edward and his growing family rather than by the small establishment of a widow. In October Mr. and Mrs. Austen with Cassandra and Jane paid their first visit to Edward as the master of Godmersham. The house, some eight miles from Canter-bury, stands in a beautifully timbered park. The most striking feature of the wide-stretched, white, classical building is the central hall, paved with marble, into which open four great rooms, through lofty arched doorways, flanked by white, fluted columns supporting a pediment over each lintel. The drawing-room has windows down to the floor, which command a view of rising ground, well wooded.

Edward and Elizabeth had four children at present: Fanny, aged five; Edward, four; George, three; and the baby William. Jane was fond of all the children, though she did not yet know how fond she was to be of Fanny; at the moment her special pet was Georgie, called Dordy by himself and her. So much of Elizabeth's time was taken up in lying-in, and in caring for the children, that Cassandra's presence in the household was most welcome as a companion to Edward and a help to her mild and beautiful sister-in-law. On the occasion of this visit the party had to leave Cassandra behind them, and when they stopped at Dartford on the journey home Jane wrote her a note from the parlour of the 'Bull and George.' The weather had been pleasant, and she used a happy word to describe it. 'We had one heavy shower on leaving Sittingbourne, but afterwards the clouds cleared away and we had a very bright *chrystal* afternoon.' As she wrote, her mother was sitting by the fire, and the Rev. George Austen was reading *The Midnight Bell*. She said that she should have begun to write the letter before, but she had been detained by discovering that her writing and dressing boxes had been put by mistake into a chaise which was just packing up when their own arrived at the inn, 'and were driven away towards Gravesend on their road to the West Indies.' But a man on horseback was sent out after them, and 'they were got about two or three miles off.' She added in a postscript: 'I flatter myself that *itty Dordy* will not forget me at least under a week. Kiss him for me.'

The following Saturday she wrote in answer to a long letter from Cassandra. Mrs. Austen had not borne the journey well and had been obliged to send for Mr. Lyford, the apothecary, when they got home. He prescribed laudanum as a composer, and Jane, in Cassandra's absence, had the dignity of dropping it out. She had bought some flan-nel—a stuff which, with her mania for elegance, she could not take

65

much interest in. She said: 'I fancy it is not very good, but it is so disgraceful and contemptible an article in itself that its being comparatively good or bad is of little importance.' Cassandra's letter had mentioned George, and she said: 'My dear itty Dordy's remembrance of me is very pleasing to me—foolishly pleasing because I know it will be over so soon. My attachment to him will be more durable. I shall think with tenderness and delight on his beautiful and smiling countenance and interesting manners till a few years have turned him into an ungovernable, ungracious fellow.'

And then she made a remark which to those who do not like Jane Austen is better known than anything in *Pride and Prejudice*. 'Mrs. Hall of Sherborne was brought to bed yesterday of a dead child, some weeks before she expected, owing to a fright. I suppose she happened unawares to look at her husband.' She was thinking, not of the dead baby, but of the father's ugliness. The very thoughtlessness of the thing is its excuse, but the sentence is an unfortunate one, and those who, at twenty-three, have never been guilty of an unfeeling remark about a stranger, do quite right to be very severe upon it.

Meantime, James and Mary were expecting a baby. In November Cassandra was still at Godmersham, and Jane wrote to say that she and her father had been over to see Mary, 'who is still plagued with the rheumatism, which she would be very glad to get rid of, and still more glad to get rid of the child, of whom she is heartily tired.' The high maternal mortality of the time made the birth of the first child a matter of grave anxiety. Jane went on: 'I believe I never told you that Mrs. Coulthard and Ann, late of Manydown, are both dead, and both died in child-bed. We have not regaled Mary with this news.' Happily, before the letter was sent off she was able to add a few lines saying that James had just sent a note to say that Mary had had a fine little boy at eleven the night before, and both were going on very well. Mrs. Austen had sensibly declared that she wished to know nothing about it till it was over, and Jane had managed to keep the news from getting to her although it was known in the house that Mary had been taken ill. Cassandra wrote to Deane at once, and Jane's next letter to her began: 'I expected to have heard from you this morning, but no letter is come. I shall not take the trouble of announcing to you any more of Mary's children, if instead of thanking me for the intelligence, you always sit down and write to James.' She had been over to Deane, and had a glimpse of the baby; he was asleep, but the nurse told her that 'his eyes were large, dark and handsome.' Mary was getting on wonderfully well, but Jane said she 'does not manage matters in such a way as to make me want to lie in myself.' Mary was not tidy or elegant, very

66

different from Elizabeth in the luxurious surroundings of Godmersham, who had looked so pretty in her draperies of immaculate white.

Jane had made some drawings for Georgie, which had been sent under cover to his Aunt Cassandra. She thought that really they would have answered George's purpose as well if they had been less carefully finished, but, she said, 'an artist cannot do anything slovenly.'

The letters are filled with domestic news. The Rev. George Austen and Edward used the correspondence of the girls to exchange news about their live-stock. Jane said: 'You must tell Edward that my father gives 25s. a piece to Seward for his last lot of sheep: and in return for this news, my father wishes to receive some of Edward's pigs.' The reply was satisfactory. 'My father is glad to hear so good an account of Edward's pigs and desires he may be told, as encouragement to his taste for them, that Lord Bolton is particularly curious in *his* pigs, has had pig-stys of a most elegant construction built for them, and visits them every morning as soon as he rises.'

As the daughters of the Rectory, they visited the cottagers in Steventon, and with Cassandra away, the whole of this duty devolved on Jane. 'I called yesterday on Betty Londe, who enquired particularly after you, and said she seemed to miss you very much, because you used to call in upon her so very often. This was an oblique reproach at me, from which I will profit. I will send George another picture when I write next.' She and Cassandra had each a stock of clothes, which they were continually making or collecting to give away; she asked Cassandra on one occasion whether she should give one of the village women something from Cassandra's store. On Christmas Eve she wrote: 'I have given a pair of worsted stockings to Mary Hutchins, Dame Kew, Mary Stevens, and Dame Staples; a shift to Hannah Staples, and a shawl to Betty Dawkins.'

Mrs. Austen's health was still unsettled, and earlier in the month Mr. Lyford had been with her again; he did not seem quite to know what to make of Mrs. Austen's symptoms. Jane said: 'He wants my mother to look yellow and to throw out a rash, but she will do neither.'

Mrs. Lefroy had been to see them, and Jane had managed to secure her to herself for some part of the visit. Mrs. Lefroy did not mention Tom, and Jane was too proud to ask after him, but presently Mr. Austen enquired for him, and then she heard that he had gone back to Ireland, where he had been called to the Bar and meant to practise. But Mrs. Lefroy did mention someone whom she thought Jane would hear of without even a momentary agitation; she had with her a letter from a young Mr. Blackall, a Fellow of Emmanuel, who had been staying with her husband, and who had shown a good deal of pleasure in

67

Jane's society. Jane had quite liked Mr. Blackall, but he was, albeit, good-natured, noisy and self-assertive, and a little too fond of instructing the ladies. That her simple, gay and friendly manner gave him no suspicion of her opinion is seen by the fact that Mr. Blackall would have liked, if his circumstances had allowed it, to have prosecuted his acquaintance with the Austen family, as he said in the letter, 'with a hope of creating to myself a nearer interest.' But, he said, he could at present see no prospect of being able to do so. Mrs. Lefroy said nothing about Mr. Blackall's admiration, only handed Jane the letter to read. Jane continued her account to Cassandra: 'There is less love and more sense in it than has sometimes appeared before, and I am very well satisfied. It will all go on exceedingly well, and decline away in a very reasonable manner.'

She had the healthy person's delight in any kind of good weather, but, as she loved to walk, she naturally preferred cold weather to hot. In the previous September she had exclaimed at the heat: 'It keeps one in a state of perpetual inelegance'; but now she said: 'I enjoyed the hard black Frosts of last week very much, and one day while they lasted walked to Deane by myself.—I do not know that I ever did such a thing in my life before.' The unusualness of a girl's taking a solitary walk is an indication of the roughness of the time; no one nowadays would be afraid to pass a gipsy encampment; but in *Emma*, when Harriet Smith, helpless and foolish, met gipsies on her way to Hartfield, she was harried by them as a matter of course; but Jane, fond of walking and knowing the neighbourhood like the palm of her hand, no doubt walked by herself to the extreme limit of what was thought possible, and in saying that she did not remember having walked alone to Deane before, she may very well have meant that the natural way of getting there was to be driven over by her father or by James.

She took considerable interest in her own dress and in Cassandra's; more in Cassandra's than the latter was disposed to take herself. Cassandra had thought that she ought to have a new dress at Godmersham but had apparently said something doubtful about the expense. Jane said she must certainly have it, and that she could perfectly well afford it, but if she supposed that she could not, Jane herself would give her the lining for it. They each had a stuff gown; when Jane said, writing in December: 'I find great comfort in my stuff gown,' one can appreciate her feelings only in remembering that the wear for elegant young women, though it had not yet reached the period of misty impalpability that was to usher in the nineteenth century, was already sufficiently fine and light to need some resolution in its wearers. Mus-

68

lin, spotted muslin, sarcenet, cambric, poplin and the softest possible cashmere, were already the usual materials of ladies' dress; and Jane, snug in her own woollen gown at the Rectory, yet felt obliged to say to Cassandra, moving in the superior elegance of Godmersham, 'I hope you do not wear yours too often.' She was going to a ball at the Ashford Assembly Rooms, and in preparing her dress, she said: 'I took the liberty of asking your black velvet bonnet to lend me its cawl which it very readily did, and by which I have been enabled to give a considerable improvement to the dignity of my cap.' The head-dresses drawn with evening gowns of the time are of very shallow, small crowns, worn far back on the head and fitting closely to it, with a frill, narrow over the brow and deepening to the back of the neck, and a small feather worn in the middle of the forehead, whose angle added to the wearer's height. Jane's cap, which owing to her raid on Cassandra's bonnet now appeared to be of black lace, had a narrow silver ribbon twisted twice round it, and instead of the black feather, which Cassandra had advised, she put in a poppy-coloured one, because it was smarter, and, she said: 'Coquelicot is to be all the fashion this winter.' She was so strongly impressed with this fact that when in her current story two girls met in the Pump Room, one was full of an extremely smart hat she had just seen in a shop window in Milsom Street— trimmed with coquelicot ribbon. She had also made herself a few caps to wear at home in the evening; they saved her 'a world of torment as to hairdressing, which,' she said, 'at present gives me no trouble beyond washing and brushing, for my long hair is always plaited up out of sight and my short hair curls well enough to want no papering.'

The ball, for which she spent the night with Catherine Bigg at Manydown, was a great success. Jane danced every one of the twenty dances and felt that she could have gone on dancing for a week together. 'My black cap,' she said, 'was openly admired by Mrs. Lefroy, and secretly I imagine by everybody else in the room.'

'How do you spend your evenings?' she asked. '—I guess that Elizabeth works, that you read to her, and that Edward goes to sleep.' The simple hours of the Rectory were different from the fashionable ones of Godmersham; the Rector's dinner was at half-past three, and was over before the Godmersham cloth was laid: 'We drank tea at half-after six.—I am afraid you will despise us.' After tea Mr. Austen read Cowper aloud and Jane listened when she had the time.

Books were as ever the principal amusement at Steventon. A Mrs. Martin was opening a circulating library in the neighbourhood and wrote to Jane, requesting her to be one of the subscribers. Mrs. Austen

69

paid the subscription and Jane took it out in Cassandra's name. She was surprised and pleased to find that Mary was to be a subscriber also; she went on: 'As an inducement to subscribe, Mrs. Martin tells us that her Collection is not to consist only of Novels, but of every kind of Literature, etc. etc.—She might have spared this pretension to *our* family, who are great Novel-readers and not ashamed of being so.' A suggestion of what true novel-readers the Austens were, and how whole-heartedly they read, however much they criticized, is afforded by the delightful glimpse of the Rev. George Austen, reading *The Midnight Bell* in the parlour of the 'Bull and George' on his way home from Godmersham. *The Midnight Bell* was one of a class of novels which no one could have been surprised at Mr. Austen's gravely disdaining look at, if he had not been just the man to find great entertainment in them.

The reaction against the uncompromising, classical elegance of the eighteenth century, which culminated in the Romantic Revival, had already produced the interesting cult of picturesque beauty; but it had a smaller, more artificial, sensational offshoot in the Gothic Revival. The Augustans had looked back upon all pre-Reformation English history as something violent, savage and uncouth, now happily lost in the dark backward and abysm of time. Their strongest term of reproach was to say that a person or a sentiment was 'positively Gothic.' With the impulse natural to the human mind, the period that marked the highest reach of rational elegance in society saw at the same time the reaction towards the fascination of the mysterious past; and people who liked to live in white-panelled rooms lighted with crystal lustres, who admired china in the delicious apple-green and rose colour of Sèvres, who had their carriages painted primrose colour or vermilion, and their waistcoats sprigged with rosebuds, derived an agreeable titillation from reading about ruins infested with bats and screech owls, the nodding horror of forest boughs at nightfall, and the discomforts and perils of life in a haunted Gothic fortress. When Thomson wrote to congratulate his friend Mallet on the latter's poem, *The Excursion*, he quoted some of the passages which seemed to him especially deserving of praise.

'You paint ruin with a masterly hand.

> *Ghastly he sits, and views with steadfast glare*
> *The falling bust, the columns gray with moss.*

This is such an attitude as I can never enough admire and even be astonished at.

70

Save what the wind sighs and the wailing Owl
Screams solitary—

Charmingly dreary!'

The charm of that emotion which Thomson enjoyed so avidly is far better explained by Horace Walpole, who, though not the earliest, was undoubtedly the most important and the most interesting of the pioneers of the Gothic Revival. He said: 'One must have taste to be sensible of the beauties of Grecian architecture; one only wants passions to feel Gothic. . . . It is difficult for the noblest Grecian temple to convey half so many impressions to the mind as a cathedral does of the best Gothic taste . . . the priests . . . exhausted their knowledge of the passions in composing edifices whose pomp, mechanism, vaults, tombs, painted windows, gloom and perspective infused such sensations of romantic devotion.'

Walpole, in his half-serious, wholly fashionable Gothic enthusiasm, had his house at Strawberry Hill furnished and adapted to suggest as many medieval features as possible without interfering with the comforts, or even the modern elegance, of a man of taste; his roof showed Gothic battlements, and his conservatory was so like an oratory that the French Ambassador took off his hat on coming into it. At the same time there was a vast china basin with goldfish swimming in it, and in the hall suits of plate armour stood side by side with cabinets of exquisite blue porcelain. The mania spread fast; where small Grecian temples and neo-classical statues had once been disposed in telling positions about the grounds, the best people now erected Gothic summer-houses with small leaded panes and Gothic ruins carefully constructed of cobbles and cement. The heyday of the revival in which whole country houses were built in sham Gothic did not, of course, mature until towards the middle of the next century; its opening years showed only the rather charming and amusing touches which were added to without seriously injuring the excellent simplicity of eighteenth-century taste.

Walpole's Gothic fervour showed itself in another manner, by which he had an infinitely wider influence on the taste and amusement of the general public, than by anything he did among his fashionable friends in the privacy of Strawberry Hill. He wrote the first historical novelette exploiting the mystery and terror of the Middle Ages. *The Castle of Otranto*, in which the eeriness the civilized mind feels in the presence of dark spiral staircases, secret passages, dungeons and imperfect lighting is combined with a supernatural element, was at once the perfect expression of the fashion and its pioneer. Gothic romances, such as

Emmeline, the Orphan of the Castle, and *Ethelinde, or the Recluse of the Lake,* were purveyed in their now-forgotten scores to the novel-reading public, who began to derive from their pages something of the pleasure that minds of a different stamp were finding in Percy's *Reliques of English Poetry* and a study of medieval architecture. In 1794, when Jane Austen was nineteen, there appeared the most famous of them all, Mrs. Ann Radcliffe's *Mysteries of Udolpho.*

This book enjoyed a widespread popularity which, compounding for the necessary differences between our time and its own, it is easy to understand. Compared with *The Old English Baron,* or indeed with *Otranto,* it is a novel of serious merit; it is thrilling, mysterious, subtly terrifying, and, at its climaxes, absolutely ghastly. Its weaknesses to the modern mind are almost all attributable to its unwieldy length. The tendency in the development of our own 'thriller' has been, since the days of Poe, to cut down by degrees all unnecessary flourishes until nothing interferes with the rapid movement of the narrative; and it would take far more skill than Mrs. Radcliffe possessed to sustain our interest over so much space. With her original readers, it was an object to have their pleasure and suspense prolonged to the last limit of possibility; with us, who have neither time, patience, nor credulity, and who know as much (or as little) about the Middle Ages as we do of any other period of history, and on whom, therefore, her incantations will not work, her methods are fatal to her success. Nevertheless when the book is read from curiosity rather than spontaneous desire for a story, it is most rewarding. One cannot believe in any of the characters, who are indeed little more than names; nor does Mrs. Radcliffe give one that inexpressible sensation of interest and awe that one feels in roaming over a ruined abbey by oneself. Her medievalism is precisely that of the illustrations which show a heroine in modish, nymph-like garb with laced sandals and hair unbound, wandering along some Gothic battlements, with a cross and beads hanging round her neck to suggest the historical atmosphere. But she can create and maintain the genuine note of terror, and the episodes of the figure who was seen walking up the avenue, chequered with moonlight and the wavering shadows of the trees, the hand that suddenly raised the counterpane in the great four-poster bed in the long-shut-up apartment where the lady of the castle had died, and the celebrated incident of discovering the worm-eaten corpse behind the Black Veil, are, in their contexts, most effective.

Another element in Mrs. Radcliffe's popularity with the general reader of the time was that she drew excellent word pictures of the scenery of the South of France and the Italian Alps, and thus gave something for readers like Henry and Eleanor Tilney to enjoy, even if these passages were skipped by Isabella Thorpe.

When we remember that *Udolpho* was to the seventeen-nineties what the railway bookstall thriller is to us, a short example of its style provides a comment beyond the power of whole volumes of social history to express.

'Towards the close of day the road wound into a deep valley. Mountains, whose shaggy steeps appeared to be inaccessible, almost surrounded it. To the east, a vista opened, and exhibited the Apennines in their darkest horrors; and the long perspective of retiring summits rising over each other, their ridges clothed with pines, exhibited a stronger image of grandeur than any that Emily had yet seen. The sun had just sunk below the tops of the mountains she was descending, whose long shadow stretched athwart the valley; but his sloping rays, shooting through an opening of the cliffs, touched with a yellow gleam the summits of the forest that hung upon the opposite steeps, and streamed in full splendour upon the towers and battlements of a castle that spread its extensive ramparts along the brow of a precipice above. The splendour of these illumined objects was heightened by the contrasted shade which involved the valley below.

' "There," said Montoni, speaking for the first time in several hours, "is Udolpho." '

The wild success of this novel gave a new impetus to the Gothic romance, or tale of terror, and by 1798 Isabella Thorpe, having started off her friend with *Udolpho*, could supply her with a list of others when she should be ready for them:

' "*Castle of Wolfenbach, Clermont, Mysterious Warnings, Necromancer of the Black Forest, Midnight Bell, Orphan of the Rhine* and *Horrid Mysteries*. These," said Isabella, "will last us some time."

' "Yes; pretty well; but are they all horrid? Are you sure they are all horrid?"

' "Yes, quite sure; for a particular friend of mine, a Miss Andrews, a sweet girl, one of the sweetest creatures in the world, has read every one of them." '

Among the crowd of Gothic novels was the unusual contribution of 'Monk' Lewis. *The Monk* differed from its fellows in being not only lurid but lewd, and it was one of the few titles John Thorpe could remember with any certainty.

It is simpler to refer to the story Jane Austen was now writing as *Northanger Abbey*, and to its heroine as Catherine Morland, but Jane originally called her Susan, and meant her name to be the title of the book. As Jane changed the name shortly before her death, Henry was

73

obliged, in posthumously publishing it, to choose another title, and decided upon *Northanger Abbey*. Though the novel was not completed till 1803, the importance it gives to the effect of sensational literature on those who don't know any better relates it closely to the couple of years before Jane Austen left Steventon. One may believe that many tales of terror found their way from Mrs. Martin's library to the Rectory, and were enjoyed by everyone from the Rev. George Austen downward.

CHAPTER EIGHT

In January of the New Year Cassandra was still at Godmersham, and on the morning of the 8th Jane was telling her what she meant to wear that evening at the ball given by Lord Dorchester at Kempshott House. This was one of the biggest private balls in the neighbourhood, and by a stroke of good luck, Jane was to make a most fashionable appearance at it. The battle of the Nile in the previous year had inaugurated a craze for things Egyptian among that portion of society called by *La Belle Assemblée* 'the first-rates'; and the first-rates were now exhibiting patriotism and *ton* by wearing such tokens as the Nelson rose feather, green morocco slippers laced with crocodile-coloured ribbon, Mameluke capes of red cloth, and Mameluke caps, modelled on the shape of the Egyptian fez. One of the Fowles had sent Mary a Mameluke cap, and Mary lent it to Jane for this occasion; the cap added distinction to her toilet of a white frock and green shoes, and the sister of Commander Francis Austen and Lieutenant Charles Austen put it on with particular delight. Unfortunately by the time Jane wrote her next letter she had caught a cold in one eye, so she said she should leave her mother to describe the ball, as Mrs. Austen was also writing. She did say, however, that she had taken her white fan, and referring to an escapade of little George's, she added: 'I am very glad he never threw it into the river.' A charming picture of George is gained, standing by Cassandra and choosing out the wafer with which she was to seal the letter to Aunt Jane. 'My sweet little George! I am delighted to hear that he has such an inventive genius as to face making. I admired his yellow wafer very much, and hope he will choose the wafer for your next letter.'

Mary had recovered from the birth of her baby, Edward, and she and James meant now to enter more into the society of the neighbourhood. On January 17th she went in Jane's party to the public ball at Basingstoke. Poor Mary had not the health and buoyancy of her young sister-in-law; still, Jane was pleased with her; she said Mary behaved very well and was not fidgety, and added the further praise that she had now become 'rather more reasonable' about her child's beauty; she did not now think him *really* handsome. The ball was not a particularly brilliant one, but Jane enjoyed it, because, she said: 'I do not think it worth while to wait for enjoyment until there is some real opportunity for it.'

Charles, 'our own little brother,' was now on shore leave. The mar-

75

riage of Jane Cooper with Captain Williams had been of great use to her young cousin, for he had thus been on board Captain Williams's frigate *Unicorn* when she captured *La Tribune* after a chase of two hundred and ten miles. Captain Williams was knighted for the exploit, and many of the crew received promotion. Charles was now second lieutenant in the *Scorpion*. His home-comings were always occasions of happy pride and loving delight. He took Jane about, and was much admired in the neighbourhood; some people thought him even handsomer than Henry. He had gone away with his hair tied at the nape of the neck and powdered, but he had come back with it in the newly fashionable crop. It seemed an eminently sensible fashion for a young man who spent most of his time on board, but Edward, in the stately retirement of Godmersham, was inclined not to think well of it. Edward had not been well for some time; in December, Jane had written: 'Poor Edward! It is very hard that he, who has everything else in the world that he can wish for, should not have good health too.' Now she said: 'I thought Edward would not approve of Charles' being a crop, and rather wished you to conceal it from him, lest it might fall on his spirits and retard his recovery.' Charles had brought with him a large piece of Irish linen which someone had told him he ought to buy, and Jane warned Cassandra that as soon as she came back her help would be demanded in making it up into shirts for him.

In spite of all her distractions, she was growing very weary of her sister's absence. She had, in letter-writing, a favourite device of understatement, and she used it here. 'What time in March may we expect your return in? I begin to be very tired of answering people's questions on that subject, and independent of *that* I shall be very glad to see you at home again.' She hoped that they would be able to secure Martha for a visit on Cassandra's return, and then she said: 'Who will be so happy as we?'

But the happy, busy, domestic life enjoyed, but never enjoyed in perfection unless Cassandra were there, did not remain uninterrupted for long. Edward's health grew worse, and a visit to Bath was decided upon, and this time it was Jane who left home to accompany him. The party was a large one; in May, Jane and Mrs. Austen, with Edward, Elizabeth and their two eldest children, Fanny aged six and Edward, five, set off from Steventon in two carriages, and arriving in Bath, took lodgings at No. 13 Queen's Square. The day after their arrival Jane gave Cassandra an account of their proceedings. They had spent the night at Devizes, where they had had good accommodation, and where the children had made 'so delightful a supper' off lobster, asparagus and cheese-cakes, 'as to endear the town of Devizes to them for a long

76

time.' It was raining when they entered Bath. Their road to Queen's Square in the lower part of the city led them past Paragon, and here they stopped to enquire after Mr. Leigh Perrot; it was so wet and dirty they did not get out, but were merely told at the carriage door that he was 'very indifferent' though he had had a rather better night than usual.

The house in Queen's Square proved most agreeable. The rooms were large and good; there was a stout landlady in mourning and a little black kitten playing about the stairs. They arranged the rooms so as to let Mrs. Austen and Jane have a bedroom each at the top of the house. Elizabeth had wanted Mrs. Austen to have a room on the first floor opening out of the drawing-room, but it would have meant moving a bed into it, and as Mrs. Austen felt strong enough not to mind the stairs, she said she would prefer to be above with Jane.

They had all stood the journey quite well; since their arrival, Elizabeth had had a letter from her nurse Sackree giving 'a very good account of the three little boys' left at Godmersham: George aged four, Henry, two, and the baby William; so she was quite at ease, and though Edward had seemed 'rather fagged' on his arrival, and was not very brisk this morning, Jane hoped that his spirits would be improved by his going out personally to order the tea, coffee and sugar, and to taste a cheese for himself. The weather was clearing; when they had come, umbrellas were up everywhere, but now, she said, 'the pavements are getting very white again.'

It was delightful to be in Bath—and not in Paragon. The north side of Queen's Square had been built in the middle of the century by the great Wood, at the time of his laying out the Royal Crescent, the Circus and the Assembly Rooms. It has a massive stone front, adorned with columns and pediments on a grand scale; Wood had meant the other sides of the square to correspond, but he had never completed his design, and the west wing and the south wing, of which No. 13 forms the corner, had been built some years later in a graceful domestic style, with ample sash windows and good doorways suggestive of space and comfort within. The green plot in the middle of the square is dignified by an immense monolith and made pleasant by some trees and shrubs. Jane said: 'I like our situation very much; it is far more cheerful than Paragon, and the prospect from which I write is rather picturesque as it commands a perspective view of the left side of Brock Street, broken by three Lombardy poplars in the garden of the last house in Queen's Parade.'

Brock Street leads from the Circus to the Royal Crescent, and thus connects Wood's two greatest achievements. The outside of a Georgian house, whether native or classical, is lovely, stimulating, satisfying;

77

but Wood took the ordinary classical house-front of the time, repeating and repeating it in perfect uniformity until he closed the whole in a giant circle, pierced by the roads leading out of it; thus imposing the majestic beauty of the circular formation on the small perfection of the component parts. The delicate Bath stone in which he embodied his inspiration is extremely susceptible to atmosphere, and dampness blackens it almost to the extent of smoke; the pillars and classical friezes, the doors and window-frames of many of these houses are painted black, and their façades appear to have suffered unusually from the darkening influence of the weather, with the result that the whole circle has a Plutonian* air, hardly relieved by the freshness of its trees and grass. Wonderful as it is, it is not until one passes through Brock Street and gains the paved walk before the Royal Crescent that one realizes the full splendour of Wood's genius. The first view of the Royal Crescent affects the mind like a great burst of music. The crescent contains as much of a semi-circle as is described by the crescent of a new moon. The vast curve of the façade is striped with pairs of stone columns, between which the windows, enormous as they are on a nearer view, appear in a very reasonable proportion. The material of this structure has escaped the darkening of the circle behind it; the porous stone seems filled with light as a honeycomb with honey; massive yet airy, gracious in line and hue but dazzling in its rigid uniformity, it is a unique example of classical domestic architecture, a visible manifestation of that spirit of the age from which people in the next century recoiled, ran into holes and corners and covered themselves up with ornaments and plush.

The Royal Crescent occupies a site a little less than half-way between the lowest point of the city where the Avon lies like a strip of looking-glass, and the highest line of buildings near the hill-top. On the higher levels Wood's successors erected further crescents: Camden Crescent of rich, wheat-coloured stone, whose promenade is supported on a row of arches jutting out of the hillside, and commands an unrivalled prospect of the opposite side of the valley and the city at its feet; and higher still, Lansdowne Crescent, less majestic but perhaps the loveliest of all, a tall and gentle sweep of pearl-grey stone, the gracious curve of its parapet supporting urns that stand up boldly against the sky. Its retired elegance and lofty grace are as different in character from the warm-toned, open Camden Crescent as from the powerful triumph of the Royal Crescent; but they bear to each other something of the relation of the movements of a concerto by Mozart.

* The houses in the circle have recently been restored to their original pale colour by cleaning (1973).

78

The more mundane quarters of the city do not suggest themselves in terms of poetry or music; they contain rows and groups of plain and elegant houses adorned with a wide variety of fairy-like porticoes and fanlights, and shop-fronts ennobled with fluted pillars and rich cornices: sometimes in spacious, excellent thoroughfares, sometimes hedging in streets so narrow that modern traffic finds difficulty in getting through them. The most famous thoroughfare is Milsom Street, with shop windows on its ground level and apartments of great spaciousness and dignity above. The most expensive shops were to be found in Milsom Street and in Stall Street, where there is a beautiful cream-coloured colonnade of shops, in the form of a semi-circle.

One could not come from a village to so noted a shopping centre without being charged with commissions by those who remained behind, and Jane had many to execute. Mary had asked her to get some stockings for little Anna, now six years old, and Jane said she should hope to get some such as Anna would approve of. Martha wanted some shoes, but Jane did not promise to get these; she said: 'I am not fond of ordering shoes.' She had had a cloak made for herself edged with lace, and was to procure one for Cassandra just like it; she made a little drawing of the lace, and said if Cassandra would like hers to be wider, she could buy some at an extra threepence a yard and yet not go beyond two guineas for the whole cloak. She was also to buy Cassandra an ornamental sprig for her hair, and she and Elizabeth were both interested to see what could be bought in that line. They discovered that though flowers were worn a great deal, artificial fruit was even more fashionable. Elizabeth bought herself a bunch of strawberries, but they were so expensive that Jane hesitated. Mrs. Leigh Perrot told her that she could probably get something cheaper in a shop near Walcot Church, beyond Paragon, but when they went to the shop, it had no fruit after all, only flowers. Jane began to think that Cassandra might be better pleased with flowers; for one thing, she could buy four or five very pretty sprigs for the cost of one Orleans plum; 'besides,' she said, 'I cannot help thinking that it is more natural to have flowers grow out of the head than fruit. What do you think on that subject?' Meanwhile, she bought a black lace veil for Mary as a joint present from Cassandra and herself. It cost sixteen shillings, and she said: 'I hope the half of that sum will not greatly exceed what you had intended to offer upon the altar of sister-in-law affection.'

The children made her put messages from them into her letters to Cassandra, sending love to Grandpapa, Uncle James, Aunt James, and little Edward, and hoping that the turkeys and ducks and chickens and guinea-fowl were all well, and asking for a printed letter each. Cassandra complied with this request; to save Jane the postage on the letters she enclosed them in one to her, and Jane sealed them up before delivering them, to make them look as if they had come through the post in their own right. 'The children were delighted with your letters,' she said, 'as I fancy they will tell you themselves before this is concluded. Fanny expressed some surprise at the wetness of the wafers, but it did not lead to any suspicion of the truth.' Sure enough, at the end of the letter came the notes dictated by Fanny and Edward. The latter said: 'My dear Aunt Cassandra, I hope you are very well. Grandmama hopes the white Turkey lays and that you have eat up the black one. We like Gooseberry Pye and Gooseberry pudding very much. Is that the same Chaffinch's nest we saw before we went away? And pray will you send me another printed letter when you write to Aunt Jane again, if you like it.'

In the meantime, the object for which they had come to Bath was not achieved. Edward remained very unwell, and they could only hope that he would begin to feel the benefit of the cure after he had got home. He became infected with the family's shopping fervour and bought a pair of black carriage horses for sixty guineas.

Jane had enjoyed Bath immensely, but as the time drew near which had been fixed for their all going back to Steventon, she became anxious to get home again. They had been to a firework display in Sydney Gardens, and it had been most effective and delightful, and they were going to the play on Saturday, but *that* she hoped would be the last of their engagements, as she did not want their return to be postponed. She said: 'It is rather impertinent to suggest any household care to a house-keeper, but I just venture to say that the coffee-mill will be wanted every day while Edward is at Steventon, as he always drinks coffee for breakfast.'

And so on June 27th the party set out for Steventon once more. They had said good-bye to the Leigh Perrots, and as the carriages drew past Paragon, that sombre and sunless dwelling, the spot least dear to Jane from situation and association of any that she knew in Bath, she had not an idea in her head of how she was next to hear of its inmates.

Mr. and Mrs. Leigh Perrot were not strikingly agreeable to the world in general, and perhaps the pleasantest part of their character was their great devotion to each other. So great was it that, reserved as they were, it was very generally known. The other circumstance affecting them that was public property was that Mr. Leigh Perrot was a man of considerable wealth.

In the beautiful colonnade at the junction of Bath Street and Stall

80

1. Drawing of the rear façade of Steventon Rectory, made by Jane Austen's niece, Anna Lefroy, in 1814.

2. Map of the grounds of Steventon Rectory.

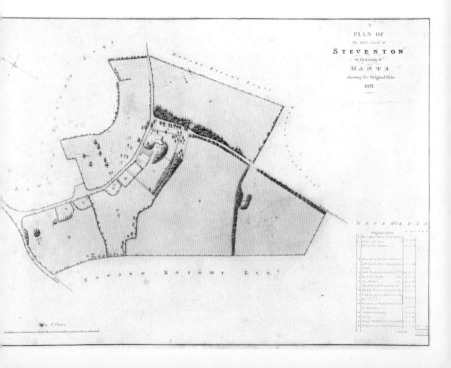

3. Jane Austen's father, the Rev. George Austen, from a miniature of 1801.

4. Silhouette of Jane Austen's mother.

5. The Reverend George Austen presenting his son Edward to Mr and Mrs Thomas Knight: silhouette, *c.* 1778.

6. Edward Austen, Jane's third brother, painted when he was twenty-one and on the Grand Tour.

7. The Reverend James Austen, Jane's eldest brother.

8. In 1792, James Austen married Ann Matthew: this portrait of the Matthew family shows Lady Jane Matthew, Mrs Austen (James's wife), Mrs Dewar and Mrs Maitland.

9, 10 and 11. Miniatures of three of Jane Austen's brothers. *Above:* Henry Thomas, born in 1771. *Below left:* Francis William, later Admiral Sir Francis Austen, born in 1774. *Below right:* Charles, later Rear Admiral Charles Austen, born in 1779.

12. Mrs Philadelphia Hancock, the Reverend George Austen's sister: after a miniature by J. Smart.

13. Eliza Hancock, Madame la Comtesse de Feuillide, Jane Austen's first cousin and later her sister-in-law.

14. Warren Hastings, Governor-General of India: portrait by T. Kettle. His son, George, was put in the care of the Reverend George Austen, and he stood godfather to Eliza Hancock.

PRISE DE LA BASTILLE le 14 Juillet 1789.
Par les Citoyens et les Ci devant Gardes Françaises

15. Detail from an engraving of the siege of the Bastille, 14 July, 1789.

16. Fanny Burney, Madame D'Arblay, whose novels were of such delight to Jane Austen. In 1796 Jane was included in the subscription list for her third novel, *Camilla*. Portrait by her cousin E. F. Burney.

17. Hall's circulating library in a seaside town, 1789.

Street was a milliner's shop which had once been the property of William and Mary Smith, and which, on their becoming bankrupt, was now in the hands of Mrs. Smith's sister, Miss Elizabeth Gregory. Part of the profits were drawn by Miss Gregory, and part were paid over to the trustees of the creditors, one of whom, William Gye, was ostensibly a printer, but who was suspected to have less reputable means of adding to his income.

Mrs. Leigh Perrot on the early afternoon of August 8th bought some black lace at the shop, and was walking past the shop a little later, accompanied by her husband and with the parcel still under her arm, when one of the assistants ran out and charged her with having a card of stolen lace in the parcel as well as what she had paid for. Mrs. Leigh Perrot replied that if she had another card, the shopman had wrapped it up by mistake. The parcel was undone there and then, and sure enough disclosed a second card of lace. The shopman now appeared, and he and his assistant loudly charged Mrs. Leigh Perrot with theft. Mr. Leigh Perrot took his wife away, saying that if anyone wished to speak to him, it was known where he was to be found; two days later it appeared that the shopman had lodged a formal accusation with the magistrates, and the magistrates, who knew the Leigh Perrots personally, had no course open to them but to commit Mrs. Leigh Perrot for trial at the next Assizes. These would be held at Taunton in March, and in the meantime she was lodged in Ilchester Gaol.

The situation to-day would be sufficiently startling, but in 1799 it was a hundred times worse. None of her friends remotely supposed her to be guilty; but were she judged so, the value of the alleged theft being about five shillings, she might legally be condemned to death. Sir F. D. Mackinnon* says: 'I do not think there was any serious danger of her being hanged; for I do not believe that Sir Soulden Lawrence would have "left her for execution." But there was a very real danger that, after being reprieved by him, she might have been transported to Botany Bay for fourteen years.' That Mr. Leigh Perrot understood this is shown by his making tentative negotiations for the realizing of his property, so that if his wife were transported, he could go with her. In the meantime, to await one's trial in the eighteenth century, unless one were a state prisoner in the Tower of London, was frequently an ordeal considerably worse than penal servitude to-day. John Howard's *State Prisons in England and Wales*, published in 1777, disclosed a condition among gaols which at its best was deplorable, and at its worst unspeakably dreadful. The state of the prisoners naturally varied very much from town to town, according to whether the gaol

* *Grand Larceny.*

were a modern building, or an antique one with waterlogged cells below the ground, or with its walls overlooking an open sewer; even more difference was made by the conduct of the gaolers, whether they were honest and humane, or of the type represented in Hogarth's picture where the naked prisoner is appealing on his knees to the committee of enquiry.

Judged by the standard of what might have happened to her, Mrs. Leigh Perrot was, on the whole, very fortunate, though she could scarcely be expected to think so. By 1800 Howard's exposition had begun to take some little effect; and had Mrs. Leigh Perrot been actually lodged in the prison, her plight would not have been, in the eighteenth-century view, desperate; there were no offensive sewers near Ilchester Gaol and the cells were whitewashed twice a year. As it was, however, her husband's money procured her special treatment, and they were both lodged in the house of the prison-keeper, Mr. Scadding.

Scadding had the reputation of a humane man, and he and his wife were sorry for the Leigh Perrots and certainly did their best to oblige them and make them comfortable; but for a person of Mrs. Leigh Perrot's nurture to be confined for eight months in a small and sordid lodging, with no privacy and only one smoky fire to which, although it was supposed to be for her use, the rest of the household naturally resorted, and waited upon by Mrs. Scadding, who licked her knife to clean it from fried onions, before she helped Mrs. Leigh Perrot to butter, entailed considerable suffering. Her plight was made much worse by compassion for her husband; Mr. Leigh Perrot was personally fastidious almost to a fault, but he bore with Scadding's children putting pieces of greasy toast on his knee, and upsetting table beer down his coat, with perfect fortitude; until presently he had an attack of gout so severe that he could not move without agony, and his wife, distracted as she was, dared not call in the only doctor in Ilchester, because, apothecary, surgeon, coal-dealer, brick and tile maker in one, he would, she felt, be likely to do more harm than good.

She had perhaps never showed herself in so good a light as now. Her situation made her family passionately anxious to do everything they could for her, but she absolutely refused to let others undergo what she endured herself. She wrote to a friend: 'My dear, affectionate sister Austen, though in a state of health not equal to trials of any kind, has been with the greatest difficulty kept from me.' James had been exceedingly anxious to come to her; he had been throughout, she said, 'a perfect Son' to her in affection; but unfortunately he had had a fall from his horse and was laid up with a broken leg, which meant that

82

neither he nor Mary could be with her at the Assizes, as they had meant to be. Mrs. Austen therefore suggested that Cassandra and Jane should come to stay with her in the Scaddings' house and sit by her through the trial, if their presence would give her any comfort and relief. When one considers what an exquisite consolation it would have been to have Cassandra's company and Jane's in the Scadding household; how they would have waited on Mrs. Leigh Perrot, talked to her and soothed her; how they would have nursed Mr. Leigh Perrot, and gently diverted the children's toast and beer, one cannot but very much admire the austere unselfishness of Mrs. Leigh Perrot in refusing to accept the offer. But she said she could not allow 'those Elegant young Women' to come to such a scene as she was undergoing; and as for having them beside her at the trial—'to have two young creatures gazed at in a public court, would,' she said, 'cut me to the very heart.'

The trial, which opened on the 29th of March, began at 8.30 in the morning and the court was densely crowded with spectators. The jury found no difficulty in coming to the conclusion that the prisoner was not guilty, and they returned a verdict to that effect after a consultation of less than fifteen minutes.

The scenes on Mrs. Leigh Perrot's release and her return to Bath were of uninterrupted joy and congratulations; she wrote to one of her friends apologizing for not having done so before, but her time had been almost entirely taken up with crying and kissing! The business had cost Mr. Leigh Perrot something nearer two thousand pounds than one; Mrs. Leigh Perrot said that from the point of view of their expenses it was a good thing they had no children, and as for themselves, she added, 'Lace is not necessary to my happiness!'

A residence in the Scaddings' house would have been a severe tax on Jane Austen's nerves and health, and though her virtue and common sense would have borne her up, she would not, in all probability, have come out of the eight months' confinement as well as her aunt. She was lively, and she was healthy, but she was not robust, and in the light of what happened some sixteen years later when she nursed her brother Henry, there is much to be thankful for in the self-denying decency of Mrs. Leigh Perrot.

83

CHAPTER NINE

In October, Cassandra was at Godmersham again. Edward and the younger Edward had been spending a little time at Steventon, and the latter had picked up some very fine chestnuts which he meant to take home and plant, and had also made a drawing for young George; unfortunately, he had left them both behind him, and his Aunt Jane said: 'The former will therefore be deposited in the soil of Hampshire instead of Kent; the latter I have already consigned to another element.'

The letter of the last week in October merely contained news of country visiting, and an account of some improvements that were being made in the garden—the bank under the Elm Walk was going to be planted with thorn and lilac-bushes—but the next letter was full of an important piece of news; a letter had come for Cassandra from Frank Austen, who was in his ship *Peterel* off the coast of Alexandria. The previous year, Frank had come into touch with his hero. When, in 1799, Admiral Brieux escaped through the blockade of Brest harbour and set sail for the Mediterranean, Lord St. Vincent sent word of the calamity to Nelson, who was then at Palermo. This urgent despatch was given to the captain of the *Hyena*, but when the *Hyena* came alongside the *Peterel*, the latter being the faster sailing-ship of the two, the *Hyena's* captain made over the despatch to Captain Austen. The log of the *Peterel* contains the entries in Frank Austen's handwriting, which mark his putting on shore the first lieutenant with despatches for Lord Nelson.

In March of 1800, the month of Mrs. Leigh Perrot's ordeal, Frank, cruising off the coast of Marseilles, fell in with *La Ligurienne*, and captured her without a single man of his own being killed or wounded and with the loss of only two killed and two wounded to the French. This capture was considered of such importance by the Admiralty that Frank was elevated to the rank of postcaptain; but as he was still cruising in the Mediterranean, his family heard the news of his promotion long before he did, and he was still unaware of it when he wrote to Cassandra in October.

Cassandra had been to London from Godmersham and had had her turn of shopping for the family: pink shoes, a comb and a cloak for Jane; a locket and a mangle for Mary; a looking-glass and some wine-glasses for the Rectory. She appeared to feel that some of the things might not be quite what was wanted, but Jane said: '*We* find no

84

fault with your manner to performing any of our commissions, but if you like to think yourself remiss in any of them, pray do.' There had been another ball at Basingstoke: 'Did you think of our ball on Thursday evening, and did you suppose me at it? You might very safely, for there I was.' She had had three offers of hospitality for the night, one from Mary, one from Mrs. Bramston of Oakley Hall and one from Mrs. Lefroy; 'and therefore with three methods of going, I must have been more at the ball than anybody else.' She said: 'I wore your favourite gown, a bit of muslin of the same round my head and one little comb.'

'The Debaries,' she said, 'persist in being afflicted at the death of their uncle, of whom they *now* say they saw a great deal in London.'

The next letter acknowledged the arrival of another of Cassandra's commissions. 'The Tables are come and give general contentment; . . . The two ends put together form our constant table for everything and the centre piece stands exceedingly well under the glass. . . . They are both covered with green baize and send their best love.'

One of the great houses in the vicinity of Steventon, Ashe Park, was rented by a Mr. Holder who had made his fortune in the East Indies; Jane had been over there with Mary for dinner and a quiet evening. 'I believe Mary found it dull,' said Jane, 'but I thought it very pleasant. To sit in idleness over a good fire in a well proportioned room is a luxurious sensation. I said two or three amusing things and Mr. Holder made a few infamous puns.'

The winter storms were blowing up, and on Sunday evening, Jane, sitting in the dining-room, heard an odd kind of crash. 'In a moment afterwards it was repeated. I then went to the window, which I reached just in time to see the last of our two highly valued elms descend into the Sweep ! ! ! ! ! The other, which had fallen I suppose in the first crash and which was the nearest to the pond, taking a more easterly direction, sunk among our screen of chestnuts and firs, knocking down one spruce fir, beating off the head of another, and stripping the two corner chestnuts of several branches in its fall.' The storm that wrought this sensational ruin was so high, blowing down some trees in the meadows besides those in the Rector's plantation, that they all felt considerable alarm. However, no damage was caused in the neighbourhood except to trees. 'We grieve therefore in some comfort.'

In the middle of November, with Cassandra still away, Jane was going to visit Martha at Ibthrop. Martha had suggested that if she had anything to read, she had better bring it. Jane said: 'You distress me cruelly by your request about books, I cannot think of any to bring with me, nor have I any idea of our wanting them. I come to you to be talked to, not to read or hear reading. I can do *that* at home.'

Before she went, there had been a visit from Charles. 'About two o'clock he walked in on a Gosport hack.' He seemed much better in health than they had expected to find him; he walked over with Jane to James and Mary's, where they had dinner, and went to a dance afterwards. 'He danced the whole evening and to-day is no more tired than a gentleman ought to be.' It says something for Charles's state of health that he felt nothing more than gentlemanly lassitude after a journey, a long ride, and a night spent in dancing from which they did not get back to Deane till nearly five in the morning. Cassandra and Jane had had gowns made out of the same length of stuff, and Jane wearing hers, Charles said he did not like it. James, however, liked it so much that he said it was the best dress of the kind he had ever seen, so the devoted Mary asked Jane to find out whether she might buy Cassandra's from her.

The Rectory received a parting visit from Mr. James Digweed, the son of the tenant of Steventon Manor. Mr. James Digweed was leaving Hampshire for Kent, and Jane said to Cassandra: 'I think he must be in love with you, from his anxiety to have you go to the Faversham Balls, and likewise from his supposing that the two Elms fell from their grief at your absence. Was not it a gallant idea? It never occurred to me before, but I daresay it was so.' Charles sent his best love to Cassandra and promised to write to her when he got back to his ship. The postscript added: 'Charles likes my gown now.'

The visit to Martha Lloyd was memorable for what happened imme-diately afterwards. Jane brought Martha back with her, and when they walked into the house, Mrs. Austen abruptly greeted them: 'Well, girls! it is all settled. We have decided to leave Steventon and go to Bath.' Mrs. Austen was not one to beat about the bush, but she may have regretted being quite so precipitate on this occasion, because Jane fainted. When she was a little girl she had made the heroine of *Love and Friendship* say: 'Run mad as often as you choose but do not faint,' and nothing but a very severe shock could have been responsible for making her faint herself. The circumstance indicates how extremely rapid her perceptions were. The ordinary girl, on being told that she is to leave the home where she has spent the first twenty-five years of her life, cannot understand, immediately, the full force of the statement: the realization comes by degrees; it is at first resisted by the mind and makes its way only with difficulty. When Jane received the news, in one instant she understood the whole of its implication, and the shock was too much for her. That she was extremely agitated by the idea of

86

leaving Steventon is suggested, as the family record points out, by the fact that though Cassandra was still at Godmersham, there are no letters from Jane to her preserved from November 30th, when Jane was still at Ibthrop, till January 3rd, 1801. This gap in a correspondence which sometimes extended to three or four letters a week would be significant, even if her descendants had not known that Cassandra Austen destroyed of set purpose the parts of Jane's correspondence which she thought showed too much intimate feeling to be made public. But by January of the new year Jane was quite herself again and looking forward to the move and all its attendant arrangements with interest.

James was to succeed his father as the Rector of Steventon, and it became necessary to find another curate for Deane. The curacy was offered to Mr. Peter Debary, but he declined it because he said he wanted to be nearer London. 'A foolish reason!' said Jane. 'As if Deane were not near London in comparison of Exeter or York!— Take the whole world through, and he will find many more places at a greater distance from London than Deane, than he will at a less.'

Mr. Austen then thought of offering it to James Digweed, but Jane did not think it would suit him, unless Cassandra were to remain there too. 'Were *you* indeed to be considered as one of the fixtures of the house! but you were never actually erected in it, either by Mr. Egerton Brydges or Mrs. Lloyd.' The arrangements connected with the church were Mr. Austen's province, but there was plenty to do indoors for Mrs. Austen and Jane. Cassandra's being away just now was very inconvenient, and Jane wanted her opinion on all kinds of things. In the middle of a long letter full of household concerns, she suddenly broke off to say: 'I have now attained the true art of letter-writing, which we are always told, is to express on paper exactly what one would say to the same person by word of mouth; I have been talking to you almost as fast as I could the whole of this letter.' Cassandra's advice, and also Mrs. Austen's, as to leaving things behind did not always meet with Jane's approval. They both thought a cabinet of Jane's might be very well left in the house for Anna. Jane said: 'You are very kind in planning presents for me to make, and my Mother has shown me exactly the same attention,—but as I do not choose to have generosity dictated to me, I shall not resolve on giving my cabinet to Anna till the first thought of it has been my own.' In the meantime, Mary wanted to know if Cassandra could let her have the pattern of 'the Jacket and Trowsers, or whatever it is, that Elizabeth's boys wear when they are first put into breeches.' As for their own clothes, Jane said she should want two new coloured gowns for the summer, as her pink one would not do more than 'clear her' from Steventon; but if Cassandra would buy her a length of brown cambric muslin in Kent, she should buy a yellow muslin when she got to Bath.

How long Cassandra stayed away once they had got her at Godmersham! Jane said: 'Neither my affection for you nor for letter-writing can stand out against a Kentish visit. For a three months' absence I can be a very loving relation and a very excellent correspondent, but beyond that I degenerate into negligence and indifference.' The move was to be made in May, and Cassandra would be at home for the previous two months; in May they would all go to the Lloyds at Ibthrop for a short visit, and then Mrs. Austen and Jane would go to Bath and leave Cassandra to follow them. Jane had become quite resigned to their departure now that she had had time to get used to it. She said: 'I get more and more reconciled to the idea of our removal. We have lived long enough in this neighbourhood . . . there is something interesting in the bustle of going away and the prospect of spending future summers by the sea or in Wales is very delightful.' A house had not yet been fixed upon; Mrs. Leigh Perrot had wanted to establish them in Paragon, or in Axford buildings opposite: but as, in Jane's words, they all united in a particular dislike of that end of the town, they hoped to escape. Jane and Cassandra had previously agreed that it would be very agreeable to be near Sydney Gardens, as they could then walk in the gardens every day; and the house finally chosen was to be No. 4 Sydney Place, overlooking the classical pavilion and the trees behind it.

While house-hunting was still in progress, Jane and her mother were to stay for a while at No. 1 Paragon, and when Cassandra joined them, they were to go to Sidmouth. Jane looked forward to this trip intensely, and was extremely glad that an invitation from some of the Coopers that would have interfered with it was refused. Another year, she said; *this* year the sea was more to them than their relations.

The journey to Bath with their personal possessions was accomplished without any accident except to Cassandra's drawing-ruler, which was found, on being unpacked, to have broken in two. Jane wrote to Ibthrop to tell her so, and to describe their doings in Paragon. This time they entered the city in fine weather, but she said: 'I think I see more distinctly through rain. The sun was got behind everything and the appearance of the place from the top of Kingsdown was all vapour, shadow, smoke and confusion.' The search for a suitable house went on, and Jane went with Mr. Leigh Perrot to look at one, having first been with him to the Pump Room for him to take his second glass of water. Her uncle and aunt took her to a ball at the Assembly Rooms,

88

for which, she said, 'I dressed myself as well as I could, and had all my finery much admired at home.' At this ball, she was on the look-out for a certain Miss Twistleton, whom she did not know by sight, but of whom she had heard a good deal. In describing how she picked her out, Jane said: 'I am proud to say that I have a very good eye at an adulteress, for tho' repeatedly assured that another in the same party was *she*, I fixed upon the right one from the first.'

The next evening Mr. and Mrs. Leigh Perrot had a staid party at home. Their niece said it was very stupid; three ladies—Lady Fust, Mrs. Busby and Mrs. Owen—were among the guests, and they had sat down to whist with Mr. Leigh Perrot 'within five minutes after the three old *Toughs* came in'; nor did the card-table break up until the Toughs' chairmen were announced.

A gentleman called Mr. Evelyn, whose name had been connected with Miss Twistleton's, was known to Mrs. Leigh Perrot, and though the latter seems to have been doubtful as to whether he ought to be encouraged in the circumstances, he was quite accepted by the neighbourhood, even to the extent of being given groundsel out of their gardens. Jane said: 'I really believe he is very harmless; people do not seem afraid of him here, and he gets groundsel for his birds and all that.' He asked to be allowed to drive Jane out in his phaeton: 'which,' she said, 'to confess my frailty, I have a great desire to go out in.' The next day she did go out in it; 'a bewitching phaeton and four,' it was. They drove over the top of Kingsdown and had a delightful airing; the home-coming was delightful too, for when Jane got back she found on the table a letter from Cassandra, and a letter from Charles, who had got thirty pounds as his share of prize money for the capture of a French privateer, and had bought for each of his sisters a topaz cross on a gold chain. Jane said: 'Of what avail is it to take prizes if he lays out the produce in presents to his sisters? . . . I shall write again by this post to thank and reproach him.—We shall be unbearably fine.'

The crosses were each formed of five stones; but in one the jewels were of an oval shape and all of the same size, while in the other they were rectangular, and the topaz forming the stem of the cross was twice as long as the other four. Topazes, with amethysts and garnets, were very fashionable, especially to wear with the white frocks that were the height of elegance; how nobly extravagant the presents were may be understood from the beautiful episode in *Mansfield Park*. Charles, flushed with prize money, had bought gold chains to go with the crosses; when the midshipman William Price bought an amber cross for his sister Fanny, he had wanted to buy a chain as well, but

89

he had not the money to do it. Such was Jane's last letter before Cassandra joined them for Sidmouth.

Eliza Austen writing to Phila Walter on the 29th of October in that year says: 'I conclude that you know of our uncle and aunt Austen and their daughters having spent the summer in Devonshire. They are now returned to Bath where they are superintending the fitting up of their new house.'

This letter covers the time of what was, to herself, one of the most important periods of Jane Austen's existence. It was certainly the year which has given rise to the most discussion and conjecture of any in her life.

The information we possess about this matter is derived solely from Cassandra Austen, and was given by her, many years after her sister's death, to her sister-in-law, Mrs. James Austen, and the daughter of James and Mary, Anna's half-sister, Caroline.

Caroline Austen's account of what her aunt Cassandra had said, and the manner in which Cassandra, usually so much reserved, had been led to give it, was this: that when they had all three been staying together at Newtown, the party had become acquainted with a young and very good-looking man in the Engineers, whom Caroline Austen refers to as Mr. H. E. Cassandra admired and liked the young man, and this struck her niece at the time as something unusual, because Cassandra 'so rarely admired strangers.' Shortly after they had left Newtown, they heard that Mr. H. E. had died of a sudden illness. The news shocked Cassandra out of her reserve, and moved by the coincidence which brought back to her what must have been, after the death of her own lover, one of the darkest periods of her life, she told her niece that when she and Jane had been staying in Devonshire, they had met a young man, of whom Mr. H. E. had strongly reminded her. He appeared to be greatly attracted by Jane; Cassandra's impression was that he had fallen in love with her and was 'quite in earnest.' He was very anxious to know where they would be the next summer, implying that wherever it was, he should be there too. Cassandra's opinion of him may be inferred from the fact that she thought him worthy of Jane, and she was certain also 'that he would have been a successful suitor.' They parted in the full expectation of meeting again but more happily. Shortly afterwards they heard that he was dead.

Such is the only existing mention of the story, and for the next three years none of Jane's letters has survived. The blank is complete, the darkness impenetrable. She was not the woman to be prostrated by a love affair, however tragic; she would not rudely have repulsed all attempts at sympathy and shut herself up in grief till the beauty of

90

the world became a torment instead of a consolation. She thought a person stood disgraced who abandoned him or herself to a private grief and disregarded the claims of others to decency and consideration. One may feel assured, without undue tendency to imagination, that she went about every daily occupation with more scrupulous attention rather than less, and that she recovered a certain peace of mind the more quickly because she meant to recover it. On the other hand, one cannot doubt that she suffered very much. She was not one of those women of whom men say that they are 'made for love'; but she had, with all the awe-inspiring qualities of her mind, a bright and loving nature, a sweetness and tenderness of affection, and though she could not feel passion without its spiritual accompaniments, when she fell in love at twenty-six, one feels that she did it with mind and body, with heart as well as soul. It is that which makes the tragedy complete. She was predisposed to love; no one knew better than she the support that woman's nature gains from man's; she thought a happy marriage the best fate for everybody; but her fastidiousness was such that, though she was prone to flirting and made herself agreeable by instinct, she found the utmost difficulty in finding a man—not a worthy or intelligent man, or even an attractive man, but one whom she could love, and when she had found him it was only to know him before she lost him.

The importance of what happened to her as it affected the development of her sensibilities and powers is great, but it lies in the fact that it acted as a pointer towards realms of undiscovered country; and the exquisite speech on woman's constancy written fifteen years afterwards is not uttered by Jane Austen in her own person, but by Anne Elliot, whom Jane Austen's experience enabled her to understand. Had Jane met another man as sympathetic with herself as the nameless companion of that summer of 1801, there is no reason to suppose that she would not have loved again and married him; she was difficult to please, but not incapable of being pleased. That she never met another man to equal, in her estimation, the one she had known, was a thing very likely to happen, and which did actually happen, but it was not an inevitable consequence of what had gone before. To say that people can get over their unhappiness is not to make light of it, or to underestimate its influence on their lives long after the pain has ceased to be felt; but to say of someone who, from duty, common sense and inclination, made as determined an effort as possible to overcome distress, who had such a relish for existence as transformed it, without the aid of external circumstances, into an adventure of entertainment, hope and joy: that such a person never recovered from a love affair that ended

91

disastrously in early life, or that she would never have been so unfaithful to the image of the past as to fall in love again, is surely to show an extraordinary lack of comprehension of the essentials of her character.

It is impossible not to long to know what he was like; 'young and handsome,' 'worthy' of Jane: on such a foundation one could erect a structure satisfying enough to one's own fancy, but as Henry Tilney said: 'If it is to be guesswork, let us all guess for ourselves.' At all events one feels justified in saying that his name was not Edmund Bertram or George Knightley or Captain Frederick Wentworth. It is enough that she knew him.

'Nameless here for evermore.'

92

CHAPTER TEN

The three years' residence in 4 Sydney Place which began with the return from Devonshire in 1801 is the period marked by the gap in Jane's correspondence. It is probable that Cassandra may have wished to be with her sister as much as she could: her constant presence must have been Jane's best, if not her only comfort for some time; but that there should have been no occasion for letters during three years would have marked so complete a change in the sisters' way of living as is not likely to have been the case. Henry and Eliza's house was now added to the round of establishments to be visited by both, and Edward is not likely to have forgone his claims on Cassandra; his seventh child, Marianna, was born in 1801, and Charles, his eighth, in 1803, and even had there been no visits in between, he would scarcely have done without Cassandra's usual services while Elizabeth was upstairs.

The move to Bath had been undertaken because of Mr. Austen, now over seventy, and in uncertain health, but it was his wife who was actually ill when they got there. Cassandra and Jane nursed their mother; Cassandra was especially capable in a sick room, as she was in housekeeping; they had besides a doctor whom they thought a great deal of, a Mr. Bowen; and the whole incident of Mrs. Austen's illness is commemorated in a few verses composed by the spirited old lady herself, entitled: *A Dialogue between Death and Mrs. A.*

> *Says Death: 'I've been trying these three weeks and more*
> *To seize on old Madam here at Number Four,*
> *Yet I still try in vain, tho' she's turned of three score;*
> *To what is my ill success owing?'*
> *'I'll tell you, old Fellow, if you cannot guess,*
> *To what you're indebted for your ill success—*
> *To the prayers of my husband, whose love I possess,*
> *To the care of my daughters, whom Heaven will bless,*
> *To the skill and attention of Bowen.'*

Another marriage in the family was imminent. Cassandra and Jane had been very fortunate in their first two sisters-in-law, Elizabeth and Mary, and if, as the family record suggests, some of the Austens thought that Eliza was too 'pleasure-loving' to be a suitable wife for the mercurial Henry, Jane at least was not likely to have been among them,

93

constant as she was to her early loves, of whom the wonderful grown-up cousin had been among the first. She was to be equally fortunate in the choice of her fourth brother. Frank was at present reduced to half pay and was employed in organizing 'the sea fencibles' whose duty it was to keep a look-out and give the alarm should Napoleon's fleet attempt a landing on an unsuspected part of the coast. While so employed he met Miss Mary Gibson at Ramsgate; and though his prospects were not yet sufficiently settled for him to be able to offer an immediate marriage, they became engaged. Cassandra and Jane both liked Mary extremely, and Jane's visiting her at Ramsgate is one of the few incidents of which we have any mention during this time. Mary Gibson can have had no notion when she first met her future sister-in-law of what her achievements were to be, and must therefore have had an unusually complete impression, in the most favourable circumstances, of Jane's personality as a simple member of society. To be prepared to like Frank's choice, and then to find that she truly did like her, would have brought out the most fascinating and endearing aspect of Jane's behaviour; and to be received by Jane Austen with open arms as a member of the family must have been, in its way, almost as delightful as becoming engaged to Captain Francis Austen. Only one thing marred the coming of Mary Gibson into the family circle; Cassandra and Jane had hoped that Frank might marry Martha.

Whatever might have been Jane's sensations during these three years, this was the period that finished and revised *Northanger Abbey*, and when one considers that exquisitely hilarious work, the most unrestrainedly witty of all the completed novels, it is strangely touching to see how noticeably graver the second part is than the first: it displays, for one thing, the cure of Catherine Morland's *entêtement*; it contains also the story of Eleanor Tilney's feelings for her dead mother; but even so, the prevailing character of the work is not affected. *Northanger Abbey* is not one of the great novels, but its style is the most consistently stimulating of any; it bubbles and sings with a cool and brilliant exhilaration, and one is never more conscious of the spirit of an age as inspiring different forms of art than when walking among the streets of Bath with a copy of *Northanger Abbey* in one's hand.

The characterization of *Northanger Abbey* is in its way as perfect as that of the later books, but it deals with simpler, more emphatic types than are found in *Pride and Prejudice, Mansfield Park, Emma* and *Persuasion*. One is fascinated by the vivid presentation of John Thorpe and Mrs. Allen—till one comes to consider Mr. Collins and Mrs. Bennet. Nevertheless the ring of characters in *Northanger Abbey* is realized with characteristic perfection, and they have that other excellence

94

peculiar to their author, that they all, even those in the most distinctly separate parts, react upon, and are seen in relation to each other. John Thorpe reflects upon General Tilney, General Tilney upon Mrs. Allen, Isabella Thorpe upon Henry and Eleanor, and thus the solidity and conviction of the whole are powerfully but imperceptibly strengthened with every succeeding turn of the action. In one respect the characterization is superior to that of *Sense and Sensibility*; there are no weak spots in it. One does not say of anybody in *Northanger Abbey,* as one says of Elinor Dashwood and Edward Ferrars: 'I understand what this character is meant to be, but I do not feel about him or her as I am meant to feel.' At the same time, none of the *dramatis personæ* is seen in situations of such depth and emotional significance as Elinor, when she discovers the secret engagement of Edward and Lucy, or Colonel Brandon in recognizing in Marianne a likeness to the sister-in-law he had loved and who had become a prostitute.

The book bears a likeness to *Sense and Sensibility* in one respect: it satirizes a prevalent fashion instead of merely viewing individuals from a satirical aspect. An exaggerated enthusiasm for sensibility and the picturesque has given place in this book to a ridiculing of the absurd conventions of the popular novel, and a mania for Gothic romance. The story opens by describing Catherine as going through the normal stages of childhood and gawky adolescence, 'noisy and wild,' developing gradually into the bloom of seventeen, when her interests began to turn in the direction of finery and balls, and when she had the pleasure of sometimes hearing her parents say: 'Catherine grows quite a good-looking girl; she is almost pretty to-day.' And having thus delineated a girl completely normal in character and circumstances, Jane Austen says that being what she was, Catherine Morland was of course quite unsuitable to be the heroine of a novel. The original achievement of Charlotte Brontë in creating the heroine of a powerful love story from a girl of unusual character but of appearance avowedly plain and insignificant has often been commented upon; the earlier feat of Jane Austen in demonstrating that a little ordinary girl was an interesting subject for a novel was quite as remarkable and new.

The two parts of the story, laid respectively in Bath and at Northanger Abbey in Gloucestershire, are connected by the mistake into which General Tilney was led, of thinking that Catherine, under the guardianship of the wealthy Allens, was herself the heiress to a large fortune, and his consequent invitation to her to spend some months at Northanger, with a view to marrying her to Henry, between whom and Catherine he had seen that there was already an interesting degree of friendship. His grossly brutal behaviour in turning the innocent guest out of doors when he had discovered his own mistake comes like a thunderclap; and well-nigh incredible as such behaviour at first appears in someone who, like the General, was not merely of gentle birth but piqued himself considerably upon being so, its genuine probability is established by the developing of the astutest character study in the book. General Tilney's affability and courtesy, so overwhelming as positively to alarm the simple Catherine, have something frightening about them from the start. 'The bustle of going was not pleasant. The clock struck ten while the trunks were carrying down, and the General had fixed to be out of Milsom Street by that hour. His great coat, instead of being brought for him to put on directly, was spread out in the curricle in which he was to accompany his son. The middle seat of the chaise was not drawn out, though there were three people to go in it, and his daughter's maid had so crowded it with parcels that Miss Morland would not have room to sit; and so much was he influenced by this apprehension that she had some difficulty in saving her own new writing desk from being thrown out into the street.' The entirely hollow nature of the General's good-heartedness, of which he himself was of course unconscious, is illustrated by almost everything he says. The *chef d'œuvre* of his speeches has been generally allowed to be that in which he condemned patched-on bow windows. Poor Catherine was so much embarrassed by his asking her opinion of every room in Woodstone as if she were to be its future mistress that she could not say anything in praise of what she saw; and though the General deprecated his possessions with ludicrous mock-modesty when anybody was impressed by their splendour, the least hint of any imagined criticism put him on his mettle at once. ' "We are not calling it a good house." said he. "We are not comparing it with Fullerton and Northanger. We are considering it as a mere parsonage, small and confined, we allow, but decent perhaps and habitable; and altogether not inferior to the generality; or, in other words, I believe there are few country parsonages in England half so good. It may admit of improvement, however. Far be it from me to say otherwise; and anything in reason—a bow thrown out, perhaps; though, between ourselves, if there is one thing more than another my aversion, it is a patched-on bow." '

General Tilney's thrusting Catherine out of doors when she was found not to be an heiress after all is exactly of a piece with utterances showing such a lack of integrity, such vanity and blind egotism, such childish lack of self-control; it is an audacious climax which few authors would have ventured upon; but on a careful study of General Tilney's character it rings faultlessly true: Catherine had been discovered to be poor, and therefore need be spared no unkindness or indignity.

96

Richardson revealed the barbarity that can underlie a polished behaviour, in deeds of violence and rape; Jane Austen does it, without going one step beyond the confines of everyday existence.

The part played in *Northanger Abbey* by the satire on Gothic romance is secondary to the attraction of the characters themselves, but is exceedingly entertaining in itself, and the more so to a modern reader because its chief value is not its intrinsic interest, but the effect it has on the minds of the different people who read it. The parody of Mrs. Radcliffe which Henry Tilney makes for Catherine's amusement when they are driving to Northanger is indeed not so much a parody, as another romance on the lines of *Udolpho*, and gives those who shirk reading that romance all that they need to know.

'He smiled and said: "You have formed a very favourable idea of the Abbey."

' "To be sure I have. Is it not a very fine old place, just like what one reads about?"

' "And are you prepared to encounter all the horrors that a building such as one reads about may produce? Have you a stout heart? Nerve fit for sliding panels and tapestry?"

' "Oh! yes, I do not think I should be easily frightened, because there would be so many people in the house; and besides, it has never been uninhabited and left deserted for years, and then the family come back to it unawares, without giving any notice as generally happens."

' "No, certainly we shall not have to explore our way into a hall dimly lighted by the expiring embers of a wood fire, nor be obliged to spread our beds on the floor of a room without windows, doors or furniture. But you must be aware that when a young lady is (by whatever means) introduced into a dwelling of this kind, she is always lodged apart from the rest of the family. While they snugly repair to their own end of the house, she is formally conducted by Dorothy, the ancient housekeeper, up a different staircase and along many gloomy passages, into an apartment never used since some cousin of kin died in it about twenty years before. Can you stand such a ceremony as this! Will not your mind misgive you, when you find yourself in this gloomy chamber, too lofty and extensive for you, with only the feeble rays of a single lamp to take in its size, its walls hung with tapestry exhibiting figures as large as life, and the bed of dark green stuff or purple velvet, presenting even a funereal appearance? Will not your heart sink within you?"

' "Oh! but this will not happen to me, I am sure." '

The state of mind into which Henry's narrative had thrown her made Catherine more than naturally predisposed to find enchantment

J.A.—6   97

in a house calling itself an Abbey; her first view of it was something in the nature of a disappointment because its rooms had been rendered so modern, elegant and comfortable. It was not until she went to bed that things began to take a different turn, and her sensations are described in a short passage which shows that when Jane Austen wished to create the atmosphere of eeriness as experienced by a real girl on going to bed in a strange country house, she had very little to learn from Mrs. Radcliffe's ebony and silver nocturnes and the harrowing whisper of their breezes.

'The night was stormy; the wind had been rising at intervals the whole afternoon; and by the time the party broke up, it blew and rained violently. Catherine, as she crossed the hall, listened to the tempest with sensations of awe; and when she heard it rage round a corner of the ancient building, and close with sudden fury a distant door, felt for the first time that she was really in an abbey. Yes, these were characteristic sounds; but *she* had nothing to dread from midnight assassins and drunken gallants. Henry had certainly been only in jest in what he had told her that morning. In a house so furnished, so guarded, she could have nothing to explore or to suffer, and might go to her bedroom as securely as if it had been her own chamber at Fullerton. Thus wisely fortifying her mind, as she proceeded upstairs, she was enabled, especially on perceiving that Miss Tilney slept only two doors from her, to enter her room with a tolerably stout heart; and her spirits were immediately assisted by the cheerful blaze of a wood fire. "How much better is this," said she, as she walked to the fender; "how much better to find a fire ready lit, than have to wait shivering in the cold till all the family are in bed, as so many poor girls have been obliged to do, and then to have a faithful old servant frightening one by coming in with a faggot! How glad I am that Northanger is what it is! If it had been like some other places, I do not know that, in such a night as this, I could have answered for my courage; but now, to be sure, there is nothing to alarm one."

'She looked round the room. The window curtains seemed in motion. It could be nothing but the violence of the wind penetrating through the division of the shutters; and she stept boldly forward, carelessly humming a tune, to assure herself of its being so, peeped courageously behind each curtain, saw nothing on either low window seat to scare her, and, on placing a hand against the shutter, felt the strongest conviction of the wind's force.' She decided 'not to make up her fire: *that* would seem cowardly, as if she wished for the protection of light after she were in bed. The fire therefore died away; and Catherine, having spent the best part of an hour in her arrangements, was beginning to think of stepping into bed, when, on giving a parting glance round the room, she was struck by the appearance of a high, old-fashioned black cabinet, which, though in a situation conspicuous enough, had never caught her notice before.'

The light and shade of the book is considerably varied; as between Catherine's friendships with the 'resolutely stylish' Isabella Thorpe, on the one hand, and the shy, elegant, well-bred Eleanor Tilney on the other; the Gothic terrors of romance and the very real horror and distress occasioned by the behaviour of General Tilney; Henry's sparkling good humour, and the gentleness, patience and forbearance of his sister; at the same time the impression the work leaves on the reader's mind is one of consistent liveliness and wit. Much of the humour is conveyed by the characters exposing themselves in conversation; but there are some instances of good things being said by the author that are dazzling but more summary, less exquisitely related to the matter in hand than is true of similar features in the later work. There is the instantaneous flash in which Mrs. Allen is printed on the reader's consciousness: 'Mrs. Allen was one of that numerous class of females whose society can raise no other emotion than surprise at there being any men in the world who could like them well enough to marry them,' and the brilliant contribution to that never-failing topic of whether intelligence in women is a handicap to their social success: 'Where people wish to attach, they should always be ignorant. To come with a well-informed mind, is to come with an inability of administering to the vanity of others, which a sensible person would always wish to avoid. A woman, especially if she have the misfortune of knowing anything, should conceal it as well as she can. I will only add, in justice to men, that though to the larger and more trifling part of the sex, imbecility in females is a great enhancement of their personal charms, there is a portion of them too reasonable, and too well-informed themselves, to desire anything more in woman than ignorance.' When one remembers the conversations of Emma and Mr. Knightley on the very subject of woman's beauty and woman's brains, one feels that after this, the last completed work of her early period, she relinquished this habit of stringent witticism without sacrificing any of her wit: that indeed in becoming less harsh, it became at the same time more penetrating and more luminous.

The book contains one picture of family affection, worthy to be put among those of the later works. It is the arrival of Catherine after her miserable journey from Northanger. 'The chaise of a traveller being a rare sight at Fullerton, the whole family were immediately at the window; and to have it stop at the sweep gate was a pleasure to brighten

99

every eye, and occupy every fancy; a pleasure quite unlooked for by all but the two youngest children, a boy and a girl of six and four years old, who expected a brother or sister in every carriage. Happy the glance that first distinguished Catherine! Happy the voice that proclaimed the discovery! But whether such happiness were the lawful property of George or Harriet, could never be exactly understood.

'Her father, mother, Sarah, George and Harriet, all assembled at the door, to welcome her with affectionate eagerness, was a sight to awaken the best feelings of Catherine's heart; and in the embrace of each, as she stepped from the carriage, she found herself soothed beyond anything that she had believed possible. So surrounded, so caressed, she was even happy!'

The conclusion of the book gives the reader an unusual degree of æsthetic satisfaction; not only in pleasure at the happiness of the people concerned, but because the behaviour of every one of the parties is so perfectly judged. All Jane Austen's novels have the property attributed to the pool of ink in the saucer of an Egyptian conjuror: the more each one is studied, the deeper into its interior the gazer's eye can strike; and when we read of Henry's being allowed to bring Mr. Morland the General's consent to the marriage in a page full of empty professions, we feel that we know exactly the manner in which the General treated his son and daughter-in-law and the degree to which it was likely to affect their happiness at Woodstone.

CHAPTER ELEVEN

The calamity that ended the friendship of the Devonshire summer holiday was not the only event that marked their stay in Sydney Place, letters treating of which may have been destroyed by Cassandra Austen.

In the November of 1802 Cassandra and Jane paid a visit to James and Mary, now occupying Steventon Rectory. The new Rector's family consisted of his own Anna and Mary's Edward, and there was ample room for them in the house which had sheltered the family of the Rev. George Austen.

Cassandra and Jane, who had arranged to give part of the visit to Catherine and Alethea Bigg, were, it was supposed, at Manydown when, on the morning of Friday, December 3rd, Mary was startled by their unexpected reappearance in the Biggs' carriage, accompanied by the sisters. She was still more surprised at the agitation with which the party, on alighting, took farewell of each other; the tears and convulsive embraces were so unlike anything she had been accustomed to in the Austen family. When the carriage had driven off, her surprise increased, for Jane, seconded by Cassandra announced that they must return to Bath immediately. As James would not wish them to go so far without an escort, and his going with them on a Friday would mean his having to find someone to preach for him on Sunday, Mary besought them not to think of going off so soon. A hint of causing inconvenience to one of her brothers would normally have been enough to deter Jane from almost any course of action; but, to Mary's increasing bewilderment, on this occasion both Jane and Cassandra brushed away all remonstrance on James's behalf, and insisted that he must take them home immediately.

The cause of this mysterious behaviour could not long be kept a secret, and when it came to light it showed how much more highly strung Jane was than anyone but Cassandra might have suspected. During the visit at Manydown, Jane had received a proposal from Harrison Bigg-Wither. Whether he had had it in mind to make it for some time, and had engineered the Austen's visit to give him an opportunity of doing so; or whether, having always regarded Jane with the affection of an invalidish man for a girl who was at once lively and gentle, he had been swept off his feet at the sight of her, reunited with old friends, at her gayest and most endearing, can be

101

now only conjectured; but on Thursday, December 2nd, he proposed to her, and she accepted him.

The match from her point of view was a good one. Her own provision in life was small and would be smaller, her father's income from the livings of Steventon and Deane would die with him, and though all her brothers were doing well in the world, none of them except Edward was rich enough to do very much beyond their own immediate families. A match with the heir of Manydown Park was one quite at the top of her reasonable expectation, and it had further inducements; not only had Harrison no serious drawbacks in himself, he was neither stupid nor unpleasing, but his sisters were her dear friends already; the marriage would place her in a very agreeable situation, near to James and Mary, and in the neighbourhood of Martha, and would enable her, when both her parents should be dead, to offer the security of a home to the person she loved best on earth. It was a marriage that would confer happiness on many, and it was reasonable to suppose that it would bring a large measure of it to herself.

She accepted; but in the night the struggle began, between every worldly advantage, common sense and even kindness on the one hand, and, on the other, an absolute rectitude of soul, the inescapable tyranny of a mind formed by nature and by training to put first things first. It was not that she did not want to marry, or that she undervalued the comfort, the importance, the security of being a married woman; she might have urged another woman, situated as she was, to accept Mr. Bigg-Wither, if she could; but when it came to doing it herself, to marrying for an establishment, to marrying without love, she could not do it. Whether she sat up in bed and waited for the morning when she could tell Harrison Bigg-Wither that she must take back her word; whether she could see him as soon as she was dressed, or had to sit through the torment of a leisurely pleasant breakfast, at which the family treated her with redoubled kindness as their sister-in-law to be; at all events, her nerves were so unstrung that by the time the Biggs had brought her back to the Rectory and had left her there in tears, not Steventon, not Hampshire, could conceal her sufficiently from the neighbourhood where she had been through such painful turmoil, and Cassandra could only second her entreaties and commands to be taken to Bath as quickly as possible.

Caroline Austen said of her aunt long afterwards: 'To be sure she should not have said "Yes" overnight, but I have always respected her for cancelling that "yes" the next morning.'

The following year, *Northanger Abbey* being now finished and entitled *Susan*, Jane took the manuscript with her on a visit to Henry

102

and Eliza at Brompton. She had decided upon a second attempt at publication. Her father, old and infirm, was naturally superseded in the matter by Henry, and Henry, from his living in London, his experience of the world and his eager interest in Jane's work, was the very one to assist her. He gave the manuscript to his man of business, Mr. Seymour, and Mr. Seymour took it to Messrs. Crosby and Sons, of London, who, in accepting it, promised to publish it at an early date and gave him £10 on behalf of the author, but having paid £10 for it, they did not, upon consideration, think it worth while to risk more in publishing it, and after the first pleasure, excitement and expectation, the image of it in published form faded from the mind of its modest and uncomplaining author, and she turned her imagination to a new enterprise.

It has often been said that Jane Austen's career as a novelist shows two periods of great fertility—in the first of which she produced *First Impressions, Sense and Sensibility* and *Northanger Abbey,* and in the second re-wrote *Sense and Sensibility, Pride and Prejudice* and composed *Mansfield Park, Emma* and *Persuasion*—and that the two periods are divided by a mysterious gap of eight years, namely from 1803 to 1811, in which she produced nothing. There are writers who have not scrupled to erect upon this lacuna the hopefullest of mare's nests. They are stimulated to an unparalleled degree by the discovery that Jane Austen had 'an eight years' silence' in her life, and that eight years was the time that elapsed between the parting of Anne Elliot and Captain Wentworth and their reconciliation. Surely, they say, this is of deep significance?

The fact that there was actually no eight years' mysterious silence at all will not, however plainly demonstrated, affect these theorists. Abraham in the parable said that there are people who would not hear, though one rose from the dead, and those who must have what the newspapers call the 'human story' are, one feels, among them. But to the more temperately minded very great interest attaches not only to the publication of the two fragments, *The Watsons* and *Lady Susan,* but to the detecting of the watermarks upon the paper of the manuscripts. *The Watsons* is written on quires bearing the watermark '1803' and '1804,' and *Lady Susan* on those bearing that of '1805.' The manuscript of the former contains so many erasures and alterations that the dates of the watermarks can hardly be taken as anything but the dates, roughly speaking, of the story's composition. That of *Lady Susan* is fair copy, beautifully written out with scarcely a correction; and of this work it might therefore be urged that the date of its being copied out is no indication of the date of its composition. Arguments for its being composed not before 1805 are, first that as the fragment is ended off, in however summary a fashion, it was clear to the authoress that she was not going to make it part of a long novel, and therefore there could scarcely have been a reason for copying it out a long while after its composition; and secondly it is in itself a piece of character-drawing maturer and more subtle than anything to be found in *Northanger Abbey*.

We have therefore, as many people would agree, evidence of Jane Austen's literary activity in 1804 and 1805, and we have also the evidence of something which, by causing her a painful shock and disturbance of mind, obliged her either to relinquish them when carried out to a certain length, or made her realize that her mind was too shaken and disturbed to do more than sketch out the plan that had suggested itself. In December 1804 Mrs. Lefroy was killed by a fall from her horse; in January 1805 the Rev. George Austen died at Bath.

To anticipate for a moment the remaining six years of the famous and controversial eight; in 1806 the family, Mrs. Austen, Cassandra and Jane, moved to Southampton, in 1809 they returned to Hampshire; when, the family record says, Jane Austen's authorship, the revising of *Sense and Sensibility* and what one may perhaps be allowed to call the re-creation of *Pride and Prejudice* were resumed; thus we account for the last two years before the publication of *Sense and Sensibility* in 1811. How much, apart from the losses of 1804 and 1805, she was affected by the business of removing from one home to another we may gauge from something she said to Cassandra apropos of the simple business of keeping house in her sister's absence: 'I find composition impossible with my head full of joints of mutton and doses of rhubarb.'* An upheaval that began with her father's death and ended in their leaving Bath seems ample reason for her to have abandoned further work on *Lady Susan* or any other project for the year 1806. If we adopt this mode of reckoning, the eight years' mysterious silence resolve themselves into three, from 1806 to 1809; and those who admire the exquisite solidity of Jane Austen's work of art will not feel that three years in which she apparently did nothing require a dramatic explanation.

In the late summer of 1804 Mr. and Mrs. Austen with Cassandra and Jane went to Lyme Regis. Henry and Eliza joined them, and the four younger people took long walks in the environs of Lyme. When the Henry Austens left the party they took Cassandra with them and went on to Weymouth. Jane delighted in Lyme, and when she wrote *Persuasion* at the end of her life the place was fresh and lovely in her re-

* Letter 133.

104

collection. She speaks in it of the principal street almost hurrying into the water; the view on either side of the bay of Lyme—Pinney, with 'its green chasms between romantic rocks,' and Charmouth, with 'its sweet, retired bay, backed by dark cliffs, where fragments of low rock among the sands make it the happiest spot for watching the flow of the tide, for sitting in unwearied contemplation'—and describes a before-breakfast walk, in which Anne Elliot and Henrietta Musgrove 'went to the sands to watch the flowing of the tide, which a fine south-easterly breeze was bringing in with all the grandeur which so flat a shore admitted.'

On Cassandra's leaving them they had moved into lodgings in a small brown-painted house on the Cobb's side of the bay, almost on the level of the shore. Jane told Cassandra: 'The servants behave very well and make no difficulties, tho' certainly nothing can exceed the inconvenience of the offices, except the general dirtiness of the house and furniture and all its inhabitants. . . . I endeavour as far as I can to supply your place and be useful, and keep things in order. I detect dirt in the water decanters as fast as I can.' They had a servant called James, who blacked Mrs. Austen's shoes as they had never been blacked before, waited excellently at table, was attentive, quick and quiet, and, to add to his perfections, wanted to return to Bath with them. Jane promoted his taking an afternoon walk to Charmouth with their maid Jenny. She said: 'I am glad to have such an amusement for him as I am very anxious for his being at once quiet and happy.' As he could read, she was anxious also to find some books for him; unfortunately he had read the first volume of *Robinson Crusoe*, but the Austens shared a newspaper with another family, and that, she said, she should take care to lend him. Although it was the 14th of September, it was still warm enough to bathe. 'The bathing was so delightful this morning . . . that I believe I staid in rather too long, as since the middle of the day I have felt unreasonably tired. I shall be more careful another time, and shall not bathe to-morrow as I had intended.' Perhaps one of the reasons for her fatigue was that she had been to a dance at the Assembly Rooms the night before. The era and those preceding it could show innumerable fascinating contrasts of sophisticated elegance deposited in surroundings altogether rural and remote—a theatre in a park, a marble boat-house with Latin inscriptions among the reeds and flags of a wasteland mere—and none of them perhaps more strangely charming than the Assembly Rooms of Lyme Regis, built on a projection of the sea-front at the left-hand side of the bay, with its glass chandelier and painted panels, and its windows from which the dancers could see nothing but sky and sea. Jane said the ball had been pleasant, though not

105

full for Thursday. Mr. Austen had left at half-past nine and 'walked home with James and a lanthorn,' though the lantern was not necessary, as the moon was up. Mrs. Austen had sat till Jane came away. The latter did not dance the first two dances, but she danced the next two, and might have danced more if she had allowed a friend to introduce to her a Mr. Granville, which offer she declined, and if she had encouraged the advances of 'a new, odd-looking man' who had been eyeing her for some time and at last, without any introduction, asked her if she meant to dance again. Jane thought from his free behaviour that he must be Irish; she thought he belonged to some Honourable Barnwells, who were, she said, 'the son and son's wife of an Irish viscount, bold, queer-looking people, just fit to be quality at Lyme.'

The girl who had asked to introduce Mr. Granville to Jane was a Miss Armstrong, whose acquaintance they had made at Lyme. Jane told Cassandra that Miss Armstrong, like many young ladies, was considerably genteeler than her parents. She had called on the family and been introduced to them, and Mrs. Armstrong had sat darning a pair of stockings the whole of Jane's visit. With a recollection of her own mother's practical habits, Jane added: 'But do not mention this at home lest a warning should act as an example.' Miss Armstrong had taken her for a walk on the Cobb afterwards; Jane said she was really very pleasant, but—'she seems to like people rather too easily.'

Cassandra had gone to Ibthrop on leaving Henry and Eliza, but they were all back in Bath for the winter, and Jane had written the opening chapters of the story to which she had given no name, and which was to be published long after her death with the title of *The Watsons*. With her first novel declined before it had been read, and her second languishing in Mr. Crosby's office, whatever just confidence she may have felt in her powers, she would have been surprised to know that the fragment she herself was soon to lay aside would one day be eagerly sought out, published with an *apparatus criticus*, studied with passionate earnestness and deplored only on account of being far too short. She talked to Cassandra about the story while she was still at work on it, and told her what were to be the ultimate fortunes of the characters, so that she had the completed scheme of the story in her mind and was at work on the first stages of filling it out. On December 16th she had her twenty-ninth birthday, and on that day, although unknown to her at the time, she suffered the second serious loss of her existence. The carnage of the modern roads is so shocking that on looking back to an age less congested and without the menace of motor traffic, we are apt to overlook the fact that a vicious or frightened horse could sometimes prove as fatal as a weighty mass of machinery

106

that has escaped control. There had already been one tragedy in the Austen family circle from such a cause: six years before, in 1798, Jane Williams, less than two years after her husband's triumphant capture of the *Tribune*, had been driving herself in a one-horse chaise, when a startled dray-horse rushed violently into the road and collided with her carriage; she was thrown out, and picked up dead. On December 16th, 1804, Mrs. Lefroy was out riding when her horse threw and killed her. There is no letter to show how deeply Jane felt the sudden horror of her loss; but four years later, on the anniversary of her birth and Mrs. Lefroy's death, she wrote some verses which showed that when she overcame grief she did not do it by oblivion. For the last three years of her life she had gone through much sorrow and distress, and her writing had taken the form of revising and finishing a work whose spring of inspiration had started in an earlier and happier time. The new novel she began did not carry itself far; she gave it up now. But she did not destroy the manuscript of *The Watsons*, and though one is conscious of acute disappointment as one becomes more and more interested in the characters and aware at the same time of the dwindling number of pages ahead, yet since we cannot have the story as a novel, we make a virtue of necessity and admit that as one of Jane Austen's fragments its value is great.

In *The Watsons* the characters are so completely realized that the expansion of the story through volumes could not add to our knowledge of them; yet the necessary information as to their circumstances and their past is conveyed in a manner more summary than was usual even with Jane Austen's economy. To say that we have an outline would be incorrect; we have, on the contrary, the solid figures of Emma Watson, her sisters Elizabeth, Penelope and Margaret, her brother Robert and her sister-in-law Jane, her invalid father; and we have not only the characters themselves, of whom we are conscious almost as if they were living beings, but we have that truest interest and delight among those a novel can furnish, the relation of these characters to each other and the variety of discord and harmony produced by the note which is struck by each mingling with those given off by the rest.

At the same time one may incline to believe that the relation of Emma's past life with the aunt who had adopted and meant to provide for her, and had then returned her penniless to the family, from whom she had been brought up as a stranger, would, in a finished version, have been conducted with slightly more detail, supplying more information as to how that event occurred, of whose complete probability we have already been convinced. In the same way we feel that here and there, there would have been a statement, a remark, two sentences of dialogue, which would have amplified our pleasure, in the sense that though one strawberry is all that is necessary to show how strawberries taste, it is pleasanter to have a dishful.

The actual structure of the sentences is characteristically perfect, but they seem sometimes to follow each other more abruptly than is usual in Jane Austen's style; and though she used dashes very frequently in the revised and complete form of her work, the number of dashes between sentences in *The Watsons* is higher than it is in the completed novels: they appear, in fact, as frequently as they do in the letters.

In examining the fragment from the point of view of learning what we can about Jane Austen's method of composition, we may come to different conclusions, but one fact is inescapable: that from the very foundation, her conception of her characters was as firm and faultless as it appears at the conclusion of one of her masterpieces. They grow into life before our gaze as she makes her magic passes, too rapid for the eye to follow; but to her they were distinct, separated from herself, fully born, in other words, before she had written the first chapter.

Mr. Edward Austen Leigh suggests that Jane Austen laid aside *The Watsons* because she had 'become aware of the evil of having placed her heroine too low, in a position of poverty and obscurity, which, though not necessarily connected with vulgarity, has a sad tendency to degenerate into it; and therefore, like a singer who has begun on too low a note, she discontinued the strain.' One cannot feel that this reason is a convincing one, if only because Emma Watson is shown to such triumphant advantage in the poverty and obscurity of her home, as on the occasion when the pernicious Tom Musgrave brought Lord Osborne to call just as he knew that the table would be laid for the Watsons' unfashionably early dinner.

Nevertheless, there *is* something painful in *The Watsons*. It is a study, of uncompromising realism, of three women desperately anxious to get themselves married. Of the four sisters, Emma is outside this circle, and Penelope, though we feel we know almost all there is to know about her, we do not actually see; Elizabeth, the eldest of all, and Margaret, the youngest except Emma, show this desire through the medium of their widely differing characters. Elizabeth, sane and good-natured, disposed to be fond of all her sisters, and welcoming Emma with a delight that is almost incredulous after her experiences of Penelope and Margaret, feels to the full how necessary a marriage is, both from the practical and the emotional aspect of happiness, and has also been badly treated both by Penelope and by a flirtatious young man some years before; yet she has not become soured; her disappointment does not interfere with a hearty cheerfulness and an innocent

108

delight in Emma's interest and happiness. Her attitude to marriage is contrasted with Emma's in a conversation between the two. 'You know, we must marry. I could do very well single for my own part—a little company and a pleasant ball now and then would be enough for me, if one could be young for ever, but my father cannot provide for us, and it is very bad to grow old and be poor and laughed at.' She goes on to narrate the adventures of Penelope, who is staying with her friends the Shaws, to be near 'a rich old Dr. Harding.' 'I suspect the Doctor to have had an attack of the Asthma—and that she was hurried away on that account—the Shaws are quite on her side.—At least I believe so—but she tells me nothing. She professes to keep her own counsel: she says, and truly enough, that "too many cooks spoil the broth."

' "I am sorry for her anxieties," said Emma—"but I do not like her opinions. I shall be afraid of her.—She must have too masculine and bold a temper.—To be so bent on marriage—to pursue a man merely for the sake of situation—is a sort of thing that shocks me; I cannot understand it. Poverty is a great evil, but to a woman of education and feeling it ought not, it cannot be the greatest. I would rather be Teacher at a school (and I can think of nothing worse) than marry a man I did not like."

' "I would rather do anything than be Teacher at a school——" said her sister, "*I* have been at school, Emma, and know what a life they lead; *you* never have.—I should not like marrying a disagreeable man any more than yourself,—but I do not think there *are* many very disagreeable men;—I think I could like any good-humoured man with a comfortable income, I suppose my aunt brought you up to be rather refined." '

Elizabeth inspires pity and liking; the element of horror is supplied by Margaret, with her features pretty but too sharp and restless, and her voice drawlingly soft and sweet in company and snappishly ill-tempered behind the scenes. Her character is exceedingly disagreeable, but the eagerness and frustration are depicted with such oppressive vividness that what would be contemptuous dislike gives way to a feeling of shocked sympathy.

It has sometimes been asserted that Jane Austen's novels are preoccupied to a sordid extent with the business of marrying. There is, in each of her novels, much anxiety expressed by the elder generation that the younger members should not throw away the chance of a good establishment for a mere whim of personal reluctance; but this is treated by Jane Austen either as material for comedy, as in the case of Mrs. Ferrars or General Tilney or Mrs. Bennet, or with severe criticism as in that of Sir Thomas Bertram and Lady Russell. She did, however, arrange for her heroines, as a matter of course, more financial security than the modern author would feel obliged to stipulate for; and there are some who will regard the existence of Mr. Darcy's park as sufficient to dispel the claims of Jane Austen to be considered a great novelist.

More interesting perhaps than the contention that she is preoccupied with the incomes of the suitors, is a discussion of the simple fact that Jane Austen depicts every heroine as marrying at the end of the book. To say that even nowadays the vast proportion of novels deal with the love affairs, if not the marriage, of the protagonist, is of course, in sober earnest, neither here nor there. From a writer of Jane Austen's eminence we have a right to expect that we shall be given a picture of life viewed from a rational rather than a popular angle, and it was clearly her considered opinion not only that a happy marriage was the best thing for everybody—in which, after all, many people would concur to-day—but that the great majority of women were concerned in getting themselves married as the most important accomplishment in their career. The people whom she approved of: women like Emma Watson and Elizabeth Bennet, did not regard an eligible marriage as the first object of existence, though a very desirable one; but quite pleasant, respectable girls of a less disinterested and exacting nature were prepared to command their affections to a very considerable extent. The overbearing desire for romance, or sexual satisfaction, or marriage, or all these, as such, irrespective of a genuine attraction, is shown constantly in her less important female characters: in the Steele sisters, in Isabella Thorpe, in Lydia Bennet and Charlotte Lucas, in Maria Rushworth and Harriet Smith, and Louisa Musgrove and Penelope and Margaret Watson; in fact, with all of them it really appears their most important consideration. The point at issue is whether Jane Austen gave undue importance to a state of affairs which existed only at a time when women of the upper middle class who were single and unprovided for had no refuge open to them but a post as governess or companion, or lingering out an existence in genteel distress.

In one instance, but in one only, we feel that modern conditions of wage-earning employment for women would have altered Jane Austen's treatment of a character had she been writing to-day. To-day, so sensible and respectable a woman as Charlotte Lucas, the intimate friend of Elizabeth Bennet, wouuld not have felt herself obliged to marry Mr. Collins.

But of the other characters, it is true that so realistic a writer as Jane Austen would to-day have described some—or perhaps all of them —as engaged in some wage-earning pursuit; they might be typists or assistants in a friend's hat-shop, or kennel maids or apprenticed to teachers of ballroom dancing and elocution, or students at an art school or an academy of music; but would their natures have been radically altered by these conditions? Would they have been less excited by the presence of men, less prone to think that pleasure means the admiration and society of the opposite sex, less anxious and hopeful in looking forward to a marriage that would put an end to the necessity of their earning a living?

Should we be justified in saying that the majority of women to-day are less interested in their actual or possible relations with men and their practical future as seen in terms of a successful marriage, than they were a hundred years ago?

We say that to-day the lot of spinsters is less hard to bear because of the innumerable opportunities now open to them; that, in fact, the lot of the spinster has ceased to be a hard one; so it has—if she thinks so. Multitudes of single women who would have suffered keenly from the restraints and tedium and emptiness of their lives had they lived a century ago are now happy and busy, interested and sane; but they are not all; one wonders even if they constitute the greater number. There must always have been unmarried women, even those with the normal attitude to marriage, who, like Jane Austen, could lead a full and happy life, loving and beloved, but just as the successful single women of to-day had their counterparts in the nineteenth century, so, too, the Margaret Watsons of 1804 have their pitiable and terrifying counterparts to-day.

In *The Watsons* Jane Austen was beginning a study, perfectly balanced in variety and of a stereoscopic distinctness, of a problem which she never touched again in so unrelieved a manner. That she was essentially capable of a realism as sordid as Flaubert's, is testified in those few startling pages, but the power of a great artist is sometimes something separate from his conscious personality; Mrs. Siddons never undertook the part of Cleopatra, because, she said, she would hate herself if she were to play it as she knew it should be played, and Jane Austen was no artless disciple of her own genius, following delightedly wherever it led her; her conscious likes and dislikes were pronounced. 'Let other pens dwell on guilt and misery; I quit such odious subjects as soon as I can,' runs the famous sentence in *Mansfield Park*; and it is not impossible to suppose that when she began to write again, and left *The Watsons* in obscurity, it was not because the heroine dined at three, but because something had been started in the story too near to morbidness to please the mind that had composed it.

CHAPTER TWELVE

In 1804 the Austens left Sydney Place for a house in Green Park Buildings, whose situation, although in a less elegant neighbourhood than that of Great Pulteney Street, was not unlike that of No. 4 Sydney Place, in that it stood in one of two quiet rows of houses overlooking a shady green; Green Park Buildings were much nearer the Pump Room, an advantage to the Rev. George Austen, who had become very feeble and who could not now walk without a stick. None the less, he seemed to enjoy a very reasonable state of health, and though he was now seventy-four, his daughters had no immediate idea of losing him.

But on January 19th he was unwell; on the following morning he was so much recovered that he got up and breakfasted with the family; soon after breakfast, however, he showed signs of a feverish attack, and these increased so rapidly that he presently sank into a stupor from which he never recovered, and in which he died at twenty minutes past ten the following morning.

Among the many concerns of the day, Jane wrote to Frank, aboard H.M.S. *Leopard*, lying, as she supposed, off Dungeness. She did her best not to break the news too suddenly, but as Frank's first intimation of the illness was the letter announcing his father's death, the task was no light one. 'I wish I could better prepare you for it. But having said so much, your mind will already forestall the sort of event which I have to communicate—our dear Father has closed his virtuous and happy life in a death almost as free from suffering as his children could have wished.' She told him that their mother was bearing the shock as well as could be expected. Mr. and Mrs. Leigh Perrot had been with them, and showed them 'every imaginable kindness,' and, said Jane, 'to-morrow we shall, I daresay, have the comfort of James's presence, as an express has been sent to him.' But when the letter had been posted, Jane discovered that the *Leopard* was not at Dungeness after all, but at Portsmouth, and so she was obliged to write again, repeating the substance of what she had said before: by the time this letter was written she was able to say that James had arrived; he begged his mother to go back to Steventon with him, but Mrs. Austen said she had rather stay where she was.

The funeral was conducted at Walcot Church, that building whose porch is entered on a level with a lane that leads from Belmont, and whose further end overhangs the street above a sheer precipitous drop.

1 Jane Austen: pencil and watercolour portrait executed by her sister, Cassandra.

II Cassandra Austen: portrait painted on plaster and bronzed by John Miers, *c.* 1809.

III Rowlandson's cartoon of Oxford undergraduates, 'Bucks of the First Head'.

IV and V Humphrey Repton's improvements to Harleston Park, Northamptonshire, from *Fragments of Theory and Practice of Landscape Gardening*, 1816. *Above:* before landscaping. *Below:* after improvements.

VI and VII   Watercolour sketches made by Cassandra Austen for *The History of England, from the reign of Henry the 4th to the death of Charles the 1st, by a partial, prejudiced and ignorant historian* written by Jane in 1790.   *Left to right, top row:* Henry IV, Henry V, Henry VI, Edward IV, Richard III, Henry VII, *middle row:* Henry VIII, Edward VI, Mary Tudor, Elizabeth I, Mary Queen of Scots, James I, *bottom row:* Charles I.

VIII and IX Aquatints by J. C. Nattes of Bath in 1805.
Above: Axford and Paragon Buildings.
Below: Sydney Gardens.

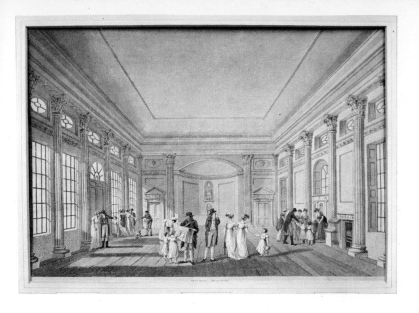

x and xi   Aquatints by J. C. Nattes of Bath in 1805.
Above: The Pump Room.
Below: Milsom Street.

XII 'Two young ladies, in calico gowns, taking an airing in a phaeton', from *Gallery of Fashion*, by N. Heideloff, 1794.

The church, a fashionable, neo-Grecian building, stands over a crypt of such antiquity that one of its walls contains a Roman window. One side of the crypt is open to the churchyard with its tombs and grass, and a few paces within, lies the grave of the Rev. George Austen, with a simple epitaph stating that he had been the Rector of Steventon and Deane in Hampshire. His true epitaph had been written by Jane, when she said: 'His tenderness as a father, who can do justice to?'

On the death of her husband, Mrs. Austen and her daughters, with one maid, removed to lodgings at 25, Gay Street; Gay Street runs steeply down hill out of the Circus, and is therefore in a much more fashionable and frequented quarter of the town than Sydney Place or Green Park Buildings. The houses are small but elegant. Cassandra and Jane might have rejoiced to find themselves in Gay Street, if they had not been growing tired of Bath.

Very shortly after they had moved in, Cassandra went to Ibthrop; her visit was especially welcome to Martha, for old Mrs. Lloyd was very ill and not expected to recover. Jane wrote to her, as usual, an account of every day. She said they had been to see a Miss Chamberlayne 'look hot on horseback,' and she recalled that seven years ago they had been to the same riding school to watch Mrs. Lefroy's daughter Lucy. 'What a different set are we now moving in! But seven years I suppose are enough to change every pore of one's skin and every feeling of one's mind.' She was now thirty; and to her mind the girl of twenty-three had quite disappeared; although to other people the alteration might seem less complete, for the grace and liveliness were still there, the eager interest in people and their doings, the open, delighted gaze upon the world, but her charm had suffered a sea-change; it was not now the over-lively fascination that had once alarmed Cassandra, but a simple elegance, a quiet but ready agreeableness, a friendliness that considered a little. Though she had not now the attraction of a brilliant girl, she was, to acquaintances in general, a centre of interest and appreciation; on the whole, people were rather more anxious for her company than she was for theirs, though they had not the remotest notion of what she was. She was glad of society but she did not want too much of it; and in Bath they had almost more friends than she could cope with. She 'endeavoured' to keep her intimacies in their proper place without their clashing with each other; after one particularly strenuous bout of entertaining, she hoped she might in future be preserved from so many dear friends all at once; but she had no trace of self-consciousness even in her private attitude towards them. Miss Armstrong, her friend of Lyme, was now in Bath, and, as Miss Armstrongs will, taxed Jane with showing 'a change' in her manner towards her. 'Unlucky me,' said Jane, 'that my notice should be of such consequence and my manners so bad!' but she took Miss Armstrong for a walk; she said she really was a pleasant girl, and added: 'Her great want of a companion at home, which may well make any tolerable acquaintance important to her, gives her another claim on my attention.'

Before she could send the letter, news arrived from Ibthrop that Mrs. Lloyd was dying. Jane wrote: 'The nonsense I have been writing in this my last letter seems out of place at such a time; but I will not mind it; it will do you no harm and nobody else will be attacked by it.'

The death of Mrs. Lloyd opened the way for a new arrangement; the Austens asked Martha to come and live with them. It says much for the reasonable nature of Jane and Cassandra's attachment to each other that, singularly profound as it was, they welcomed the idea of such a friend as Martha being included in their household. The plan was advantageous to everybody; now that Martha was alone, nothing could have been more welcome to her, and besides the pleasure of her society, her presence afforded Cassandra and Jane more freedom in going away without feeling that they were neglecting their mother.

Martha was with them by August, and in that month they both visited Godmersham. Edward's family had now increased to nine, his daughter Louisa having been born in 1804. Elizabeth was still the mild and lovely creature he had married; her husband's wealth relieved as far as possible the strain of bearing so many children in such rapid succession; and besides being the devoted mother of all her sons and daughters she was still the elegant mistress of a large country house, and a charming hostess to her younger sister-in-law. When the hairdresser came to Godmersham to arange a new coiffure for the lady of the house, he undertook Jane's hair as well. He charged Jane half a crown for cutting and dressing hers, which she agreed was a moderate charge, but she was shocked at his rapacity towards the wealthy Mrs. Austen; he charged five shillings for each time he dressed Elizabeth's hair in the new manner and five shillings for every lesson he gave her maid Sace in how to do it.

But the round of domestic interests, visits, pleasures, duties, was suddenly impinged upon; in the autumn of 1805 occurred an event which roused the nation at large, and through the medium of Frank Austen was brought peculiarly close to the Austen family. The war with France had continued intermittently for so long that though people living on the coast were almost always in a state of restlessness, and the girls in boarding schools near the sea kept under their beds blankets with tapes attached, known as Napoleon blankets, to be put on in case of a midnight alarm, the English people as a whole, excepting those with relations or friends in the Navy, tended to regard the war as something in the background of their lives; but despite this general lack of concern for the imminence of danger, and ignorance of the magnitude of its possible consequences, one man connected with the conduct of the war was a national idol. The procession of Nelson through the streets of London, in an open carriage with Lady Hamilton beside him, had caused scenes of frantic enthusiasm, and his person, his features, his characteristics, had impressed themselves on the public consciousness, as his extraordinary personality influenced those who served with him and under him.

In the October of 1805 Frank Austen wrote to Mary Gibson from off Tetuan, expressing a fear that, in spite of the nearness of a big engagement of the fleets, owing to the enemy's having escaped the blockade of Cadiz, he and his companions might be prevented by contrary winds from reaching it in time to join it. It was not, he said, that he liked fighting for itself, but 'after having been so many months in a state of constant and unremitting fag, to be at last cut out by a parcel of folk just come from their homes, where some of them were sitting at their ease the greater part of last war and the whole of this, till just now, is particularly hard and annoying.' When he wrote a week later his worst fears had been realized. 'Alas, my dearest Mary . . . The fleets have met, and, after a very severe contest, a most decisive victory has been gained by the English.' For a naval captain to have missed the battle of Trafalgar was the disappointment of a life-time, but the death of Nelson was to Frank Austen a grief that over-rode even that. He had seen the Admiral at close quarters, and felt the magic exerted by the puny, fragile, half-blind little man with the empty sleeve. 'I never heard of his equal, nor do I expect again to see such a man,' he wrote. 'He possessed in a superior degree the happy talent of making every class of persons pleased with their situation and eager to exert themselves in forwarding the public service.' Frank Austen's tribute is borne out by every other account of Nelson's achievement; but one cannot properly appreciate it without some knowledge, however slight, of what the situation was of those seamen whom Nelson managed, not merely to command as their Admiral, but to inspire as fellow-workers in the service of their country.

The question of Nelson's private life, than which few private lives have been more the public property, is especially interesting in connection with what Jane Austen said about the Navy; nor was it so much a variance with her view of the typical sailor's as might appear.

She was always struck by that aspect of the sailor which combined great courage, hardihood and an enthusiasm for his perilous profession, with a love of domestic happiness and a constant fidelity to it; and though Nelson's mistress, that overblown rose, glorious in Romney's portraits and in caricature obscenely gross, was something altogether alien to the taste and habits of the Austens themselves, yet the celebrated liaison did embody, though under so different a guise, something of what Jane Austen described as the characteristic relationship between sailors and the women they loved. She depicted them as husband and wife or betrothed lovers. But Nelson's constancy to Lady Hamilton was so entire that in the eyes of many it ranked as the devotion of a husband to his wife; and what Lady Hamilton's was to him he proved when he said: 'If there were more Emmas, there would be more Nelsons.' 'Be careful of my guardian angel,' he said, when the ship's carpenters, clearing the *Victory's* decks for action, took down Lady Hamilton's portrait from the mast; and the concluding paragraph of *Persuasion* is one side of the story, of which Lady Hamilton wrote the other when she scrawled across the letter Captain Hardy brought her after the Trafalgar action: 'O miserable, wretched Emma! O glorious and happy Nelson!'

In the following June Captain Frank Austen was married, and he and Mary settled at Southampton. Ultimately a house was taken large enough for him and Mary, Mrs. Austen, Cassandra, Jane and Martha to live in together; and 1806 saw the removal of the Austens from Gay Street 'with what happy feelings of release!' said Jane; but before the new year and the round of visits which preluded their arrival at Southampton she had finished her little sketch, afterwards to be known as *Lady Susan.*

The story is intrinsically interesting, but in a consideration of Jane Austen's work it is invaluable; it establishes once for all the dangers one may fall into in saying that this one or that of her characters 'is' some person in real life. The death of Mrs. Lloyd in April 1805 had perhaps recalled to Jane the story of the old lady's early years, or possibly it made her feel that there was now no harm in using a story which some scruple might have prevented her from treating while one of the actors in it was still living. The story of Lady Susan is of course based on that of 'the cruel Mrs. Craven'; the lovely, fascinating mother, so caressing and soft in her manners in public and so brutal to her daughter in private, and the condition of the daughter, brought on a visit by her mother, but kept as much as possible locked up in her mother's dressing-room and rendered stupid by misery and fear, make it unmistakable; and, this being the case, when one is confronted with a portrait

116

of Lady Susan, sketched lightly but with Jane Austen's skill, and having thus all the appearances of an actual woman, the temptation is to say that 'of course' Lady Susan 'is' Mrs. Craven. It is only when we remember that Jane Austen never saw Mrs. Craven, and that her study shows Lady Susan in relation to a variety of people, of whom her daughter is only one, that we see the essential falseness of such a conclusion, though it may at first sight appear irresistible.

The more the story is considered, the more widely it is seen to differ from its origin. From the scanty accounts of Mrs. Craven which have transpired, it is tolerably plain that the original was on a larger and darker scale altogether than the offspring. Lady Susan is cold-blooded and completely heartless, hypocritical, unscrupulous and mean; her callousness, indeed, makes her a formidable character; but what she does is done from a quite understandable, though entirely selfish standpoint. She is cruel because she wants to get her own way and does not intend to be influenced by a consideration of anybody's feelings, but she is not morbid or perverse; she is an extremely bad character, but she is not a nightmare; on the contrary, she is so completely convinced that her course of action is merely what she owes it to herself to do that she becomes, at times, almost disarming; and she is so far from physically ill-treating her daughter or wishing to degrade her, that she establishes her at a highly exclusive finishing school, of which, as she says, 'the price is immense, and much beyond what I can ever attempt to pay,' and is very angry at the girl's stupidity in refusing an eligible suitor.

The slightness of the tale is not a matter for regret such as we feel at the unfinished condition of *The Watsons*; it contains no one character of such charm and worth that we long to read the remainder of his history; but as it stands it is a remarkable structure, comprising, within a very little space, a great deal of light and shade, and that most satisfying kind of excitement which is produced in the reader by turns of action at once dramatic and inevitable. The threads of interest which converge upon Churchill, the country house of the Vernons, are a characteristic example of Jane Austen's instinctive brilliance in the handling of plot. Lady Susan, the widow of Mr. Vernon's brother, is invited by him to pay Churchill a long visit. Lady Susan is far from wishing to do anything so much in the nature of a dead bore, but she is obliged to leave the house of the Mainwarings where she has been staying, because, as she has made Mr. Mainwaring deeply in love with her, and drawn off his sister's suitor, Sir James Martin, Mrs. Mainwaring and Miss Mainwaring have combined to make the house impossible to her. Being extravagant and poor, she therefore avails herself

117

of the invitation to Churchill, to the annoyance of Mrs. Vernon, who, far shrewder than her good-natured, unsuspecting husband, has heard too much about Lady Susan's goings-on, and mistrusts her from the start. Nevertheless she is obliged to admire her beauty, so exquisitely fair, her grey eyes with their dark lashes and her youthful appearance which makes her appear twenty-five, though she is actually ten years older. Mrs. Vernon is also surprised at Lady Susan's manner, so simple, frank and unassuming, though her penetration allows her to see that it is only a pose to gain their confidence.

Mrs. Vernon's brother, Reginald de Courcy, hearing that the notorious Lady Susan is at Churchill, invites himself for a visit out of curiosity to see so finished a specimen of an adventuress. It is on the arrival of Reginald de Courcy, gay, self-confident and twenty-three, that the emotional interest of the story begins; he is rapidly and completely vanquished by Lady Susan, denounces all that he has heard against her as baseless calumny, and finally, notwithstanding the difference of their years, implores her to marry him. Though full of glee at her success, Lady Susan is always secretly annoyed at the sincerity of the young man who, even in the toils, will try to prove to himself that she is worthy of his devotion. She says in a letter to her friend Alicia Johnson: 'There is a sort of ridiculous delicacy about him which requires the fullest explanation of whatever he may have heard to my disadvantage, and is never satisfied till he thinks he has ascertained the beginning and end of everything. This is *one* sort of love, but I confess it does not particularly recommend itself to me. I infinitely prefer the tender and liberal spirit of Mainwaring, which, impressed with the deepest conviction of my merit, is satisfied that whatever I do must be right.'

The letters in which the story is carried on are written chiefly between Mrs. Vernon and her mother, Lady de Courcy, expressing their helpless fury at Reginald's gullibility, and between Lady Susan and Mrs. Johnson, who lives in London with an elderly husband who has become soured by his disillusionment about his wife. The correspondence of Lady Susan and Mrs. Johnson is Jane Austen's only contribution to the description of Regency society, beyond what can be gathered in *Mansfield Park* of the past life of Mary Crawford when she was living in the set of Lady Stornaway and Mrs. Fraser. 1805, the year of the story, was that of Lady Caroline Ponsonby's marriage to William Lamb, when the Prince Regent was living at Carlton House, known on that account as 'Nero's Hotel.' The first decade of the nineteenth century showed that renaissance of classical forms in architecture, decoration and dress which gives to the Regency its distinctive charm; classical porches on English house-fronts had long been familiar to the eye, and Grecian temples closing vistas of English trees, but in 1805 interior decoration showed the Grecian influence. Urns and mirrors framed between fluted columns adorned the walls, while furniture was designed to imitate the lines, exquisitely spare, of an altar or a tripod, and a procession of pallid nymphs and shepherds, heroes and deities, wound its way across marble mantelpieces, cameo necklaces, and the blue and black china services of Wedgwood. Female dress became violently Greek, with a waist beneath the breasts, heelless slippers and such headdresses as the Psyche knot with several fillets across the head, and the Minerva bonnet, modelled on a helmet with its plumes. It was not in shape alone that the first-rates imitated Grecian dress; the transparency of their robes was also ascribed to a classical origin. In 1806, a gentleman, calling himself Modestus, wrote from Bath on the topic,* recalling the fact that Grecian ladies had worn a drapery, transparent as glass, and with something of its texture, invented by the courtesan Pamphilia, of whom Pliny said: 'This woman ought not to be deprived of the glory which is due to her, that of having invented a dress which exhibits women perfectly naked.'* The gauzes and muslins of 1806, worn over a pair of blush-coloured silk stockings in the form of tights and a single, sleeveless petticoat, damped so as to cling revealingly to the figure, seemed to Modestus to answer very much the same purpose as Pamphilia's drapery of glass. The number of women who could dress in such a manner was of course exceedingly small, but a much larger number approached the ethereal ideal as nearly as they could.

The revealing nature of Regency dress had in it something peculiarly expressive of the spirit of the age; whether lewd or innocent it was characteristic of a boldness, a classical simplicity, a shamelessness which was either bad or good according to its possessor.

Lady Susan would not have worn transparent robes when staying at Churchill, nor discussed, like Byron's Lady Oxford, the more *risqué* portions of Greek literature, even supposing her to have known any Greek, and indeed she had something else to do; but the unvarnished character of her letters to Alicia Johnson is typical of the background against which we see her; had she lived thirty years later, her character would have been the same, but it would have expressed itself with a less refreshing openness.

The crisis occurs when Lady Susan, having given her sixteen-year-old daughter Frederica 'a hint' of her intention that Frederica shall marry Sir James Martin, is faced with the news that Frederica has run away from school and that though the mistress has recovered

* *Le Belle Assemblée, 1806.*

119

her, she will not take her back. Lady Susan's comment on the escape of her miserable daughter makes one feel for the moment that there was little to choose between her and Mrs. Craven: 'Such was the first distinguished exploit of Miss Frederica Susanna Vernon, and if we consider that it was achieved at the tender age of sixteen, we shall have room for the most flattering prognostics of her future renown.' The good-natured Mr. Vernon goes to town to bring her down to Churchill and in the meantime even Mrs. Vernon sympathizes with Lady Susan in having so rude and obstreperous a daughter. It is only when Frederica arrives, pale and distraught, speechless, her great, dark eyes filled with unhappiness and fright, that something of her mother's treatment begins to be understood.

Lady Susan's previous letter to Alicia Johnson has already made the reader understand it.

'You are very good in taking notice of Frederica, and I am grateful for it as a mark of your friendship . . . but I am far from exacting so heavy a sacrifice. She is a stupid girl and has nothing to recommend her. I would not therefore on any account have you encumber one moment of your precious time by sending for her to Edward St., especially as every visit is so many hours deducted from the grand affair of education, which I really wish to be attended to while she remains with Miss Summers.' Not, added Lady Susan, that she wanted Frederica to learn the arts and sciences; it was 'throwing time away.' French, Italian, German, music, singing and drawing might gain a woman some applause, but were nothing to the purpose in attaching a lover. 'Grace and manner,' said Lady Susan, 'are, after all, of the greatest importance. I do not mean therefore that Frederica's acquirements should be more than superficial, and I flatter myself that she will not remain long enough at school to understand anything thoroughly. I hope to see her the wife of Sir James within a twelve-month. You know on what I ground my hope, and it is certainly a good foundation, for school must be very humiliating to a girl of Frederica's age; and by the by, you had better not invite her any more on that account, as I wish her to find her situation as unpleasant as possible.'

Frederica is so desperately unhappy at the idea of being married to Sir James Martin that, gauche and timid as she is, she writes a letter to Reginald de Courcy, whom she supposes to be the person in the Churchill household having the most influence with her mother, imploring him to intercede on her behalf. Reginald, touched, immediately comes to Lady Susan and earnestly points out to her the cruelty of what she is doing; and it is at this point that Jane Austen shows her instinctive grasp of what one might call, without unjustifiable exaggeration, the criminal mentality, which believes that a course of action, however wrong in the abstract, is right when adopted by its possessor. Lady Susan ultimately turned the occasion into a further triumph for herself in Reginald's good opinion, but to Alicia Johnson she poured out the real state of her mind. 'He can have no regard for me, or he would not have listened to her; and she with her little rebellious heart and indelicate feelings, to throw herself into the protection of a young man with whom she had scarcely ever exchanged two words before. I am equally confounded at *her* impudence and *his* credulity. How dared he believe what she told him in my disfavour! Ought he not to have felt assured that I had unanswerable motives for all that I have done! Where was his reliance on my sense or goodness then?'

When Jane Austen began to write again it was not on such subjects as Margaret and Penelope Watson, or Lady Susan; she returned, in the prime of her powers, to that infinite variety comprehended in the normal; but her experiments show that her material was selected from choice, not natural limitation.

CHAPTER THIRTEEN

In the August of 1806 Mrs. Austen took her daughters to visit a branch of her own family, the Leighs of Adlestrop. The Reverend Thomas Leigh, Rector of Adlestrop, had recently and in a very unexpected manner come into an immense property, that of Stoneleigh Abbey in Warwickshire. The late owner, Lord Leigh, had left a curiously worded will, from which it was assumed that the Rev. Thomas Leigh occupied the position of his heir. There were other members of the family with a possible claim upon the estate, among them Mr. Leigh Perrot, who relinquished his for a sum of twenty-four thousand pounds down and an additional two thousand a year. As other claimants still might be found to come forward, the Rev. Thomas Leigh's solicitors advised his taking possession of the Abbey immediately and the decision being arrived at during this identical August, the party at the Rectory, including Mrs. Austen and her daughters, was swept off to Stoneleigh Abbey with its master.

The Austens were familiar with Godmersham, but Stoneleigh was on a scale quite new to them. Mrs. Austen wrote to Frank's wife, describing some of their experience in the vast house. The wings and corridors were so devious and extensive that the party were perpetually losing themselves, and Mrs. Austen thought that sign-posts should be erected. The day began with prayers in the chapel, still draped in black for the late Lord Leigh, and next followed breakfast, with 'chocolate, coffee, tea, plum cake, pound cake, hot rolls, cold rolls, bread and butter, and,' added Mrs. Austen, 'dry toast for me.' They spent a large part of the day walking in the grounds, for the woods were 'impenetrable to the sun, even in the middle of an August day.' Mrs. Austen's practical mind delighted in the kitchen garden, where, she said, 'the quantity of small fruit exceeds anything you can form an idea of.' The house party were very agreeable and considerate of each other's feelings; the only fly in Mrs. Austen's ointment being the presence of Lady Saye and Sele. This lady had figured already in the diary of Fanny Burney, and what she said to Fanny Burney explains exactly what Mrs. Austen meant by her subsequent comment. 'I am very happy to see you; I have longed to see you a great while; I have read your performance and I am quite delighted with it! I think it's the most elegant novel I ever read in my life . . . I must introduce you to my sister: she'll be quite delighted to see you. She has written a novel herself, so you are sister authoresses. A most elegant thing it is, I assure you. It's called *The Mausoleum of Julia* . . . Lord Hawke himself says it's all poetry . . . my sister intends to print her *Mausoleum* just for her own friends and acquaintances.'

Mrs. Austen said: 'Poor Lady Saye and Sele, to be sure, is rather tormenting, though sometimes amusing, and affords Jane many a good laugh, but she fatigues me sadly on the whole.'

The round of family visits was a long one, but in the new year of 1807 they were in Southampton, superintending the progress of their house. To this house, No. 2 Castle Square, a singular interest attaches; when, as an old man, in 1870, Mr. Edward Austen Leigh* wrote the memoir of his aunt, he drew together the facts of her previous life and the family history as he had been told it by other people; so much of his work might have been written by anybody; but when he dealt with the period of her living in Castle Square, he came to the point where his own recollections began, and as we read his description of the house, with its garden bounded by the old city wall, we realize with an indescribable sensation that we are listening to James's son Edward, that child whom Jane had first seen when he was asleep and of whom she had been assured by the nurse that his eyes were large, dark and beautiful.

The house was the property of the 'wicked' Lord Lansdowne. The outlook over the city wall to the sea was fine and open, but the windows on the square were curiously obstructed. In the middle of the square Lord Lansdowne had built a miniature castle. Mr. Edward Austen Leigh said it was 'a fantastic edifice, too large for the space in which it stood, though too small to accord well with its castellated style'; but what fascinated him in the castle was that in its courtyard he could see putting-to a little carriage for the Marchioness, drawn by pairs of cream-coloured ponies of diminishing size. He would watch the harnessing and unharnessing of this 'fairy-like equipage' with the greatest delight.

Southampton had been decided upon largely for the convenience of Frank Austen when on shore, and his presence among the family brought upon them a burst of society. 'Our acquaintance increase too fast,' Jane said. 'He was recognized lately by Admiral Bertie, and a few days since arrived the Admiral and his daughter Catherine to wait on us. There was nothing to like or dislike in either. To the Berties are to be added the Lances, with whose cards we have been endowed, and whose visit Frank and I returned yesterday. . . . We found only

* The Leigh was added to his name when he inherited the fortune of Mrs. Leigh Perrot.

123

Mrs. Lance at home, and whether she boasts any offspring beside a grand pianoforte did not appear. She was civil and chatty enough, and offered to introduce us to some acquaintance in Southampton which we gratefully declined.'

They had all hoped that Cassandra would be rejoining them very soon, but, as usual, her visit at Godmersham was extending itself. Frank and Mary wanted her advice on some of their final household purchases and told Jane to say that if she were not home in time to help them they would buy everything to spite her, 'knives that will not cut, glasses that will not hold, a sofa without a seat and a bookcase without shelves.' Frank was waiting to hear whether he was to have the command of a frigate; in the meantime, he had a very bad cold, 'for an Austen,' and was employing himself indoors with making fringe for the drawing-room curtains.

They had had a visit from James, and it had given rise to one of those very few criticisms of a brother that Jane Austen ever felt called upon to make. James had not fewer good qualities than the others; none of them was kinder to his mother, and Mrs. Leigh Perrot said he had been a perfect son to her in affection; but he had perhaps the least happy temperament. His face, with its sensitive mouth and brooding dark eyes, suggests it; he had not the brilliant insouciance of Henry, the untroubled good-humour of Edward, or the strong-nerved, cheerful dispositions of Frank and Charles. He was a scholar, and deeply interested in poetry, particularly poetry of the new school of sensibility, and in his contacts with daily life his inner self was sometimes concealed behind a mask of gaucheries and irritations, quite foreign to the social graces of his family. This time he drove even his devoted sister into saying: 'I am sorry and angry that his visits should not give one more pleasure, the company of so good and so clever a man ought to be gratifying in itself; but his chat seems all forced, his opinions on many points, too much copied from his wife's, and his time here I think is spent in walking about the house, banging the doors, and ringing the bell for a glass of water.'

Indoors they were still occupied with the finishing touches to curtains and beds, carpets and sofa-covers. They read aloud when they had time; and Mrs. Frank, who had not read so many books as her sister-in-law, was introduced to some that delighted her. They made one false start, however. 'Alphonsine,' said Jane, 'did not do. We were disgusted in twenty pages; as, independent of a bad translation, it has indelicacies which disgrace a pen hitherto so pure.' The first twenty pages of Madame de Genlis' Alphonsine, ou la tendresse maternelle, comprehend the flight of a lady who leaves a note for her husband,

124

excusing her conduct on the ground that their marriage had never been consummated, and her subsequent discovery, asleep in the arms of a page. As a girl, Jane had piqued herself on having a good eye at an adulteress in a ballroom, but she drew the line at reading this sort of thing aloud by the fire.

A little later she discovered Southey's *Espriella*, a collection of letters supposed to be written by a Spaniard and abusing English people and customs quite in the modern manner. Jane read the book aloud to the others by candlelight. Her comment on the stylish intellectualism of Mr. Southey was: 'He deserves to be the foreigner he assumes.'

In the meantime, they were laying out the garden. The gravel walk was bordered with roses and sweetbriar; the gardener said these shrubs were sickly, so they bought some stronger ones to plant among them. As Jane's 'own particular desire,' he bought them some syringas. She said, 'I could not do without a syringa, for the sake of Cowper's line.' She was thinking of the poet's *Winter Walk*, where he looked at the bare earth and longed for the beauty a few months would bring:

> '...*laburnum, rich*
> *In streaming gold, syringa, ivory pure.*'

She said they were thinking of a laburnum tree as well. Her sense of natural beauty was unusually fresh and strong. Her novels show it, and always in such a way that her brief descriptions heighten the emotional significance of the scene; but the descriptions are usually landscapes, and the only place where she mentions a flower which can compare with her syringa bush is the interesting little conservation between Catherine Morland and Henry Tilney, where she says to him: 'I have just learnt to love a hyacinth.'

Her love of children, like her love of Nature, has sometimes been ignored, and her description of the disagreeable children of Lady Middleton is made to symbolize her attitude to children as a whole. Even if she had not mentioned children in any novel but *Sense and Sensibility*, her portrayal of the young Middletons would not, one feels, constitute grounds for saying she disliked children. It is, as Dr. Johnson would say, 'no very cynical asperity' to think that noisy, insolent, greedy and deceitful children are disagreeable; most people think so, unless the children happen to be their own; but apart from such sympathetic studies of children as those of the little Gardiners and Fanny Price, Jane Austen displays what was, for the time, an unusually lenient attitude to spoilt children, in the passage where Emma says that little Anna Weston is certain to be spoiled, and what will become of her? To which Mr. Knightley replies: 'Nothing very bad. The fate of thousands. She will be disagreeable in infancy, and correct as she grows older.' Not the novels only, but her letters make one understand how very much surprised a child who had known Jane Austen would be to hear, from what eminent authority soever, that she was unsympathetic with children and disliked them in the true spirit of an old maid.

Frank Austen brought the little daughter of one of his friends to spend the day with them. He brought her home after church, and as Jane was writing to Cassandra, she said: 'She is now talking away at my side, and examining the treasures of my writing-desk and drawers, very happy I believe;—not at all shy of course.' Jane thought the modern child a great improvement on what she had been herself, but she was surprised at its ease. 'What is become of all the shyness in the world? Moral as well as natural diseases disappear and new ones take their places—shyness and the sweating sickness have given way to confidence and paralytic complaints.' She admired the child's manner —'all the ready civility one sees in the best children of the present day; so unlike anything that I was myself at her age, that I am often all astonishment and shame.' She was extremely grateful on this wet Sunday that they had a set of spillikins in the house; she thought the toy not the least important benefaction from the family of Knight to that of Austen.

In June of 1808 there was a large family gathering at Godmersham. The Castle Square household was represented by Jane this time; there came, beside, James and Mary with little Edward and his sister Caroline, aged three; Anna, on the other hand, was to stay in Castle Square with her aunt Cassandra. Anna was now fifteen; she adored her aunts, especially her Aunt Jane. In some ways she recalled what the latter had once been; she was lively and uncertain, what country people describe as 'easy cast up, easy cast down'; she had much of that sweetness which won upon the eye and ear of anyone who talked to her aunt; in Anna, it was a something at once wild and gentle. She had also a desire to write. She had shown it when, as a child of five, she had dictated stories to Jane in the dressing-room at Steventon; and when, at seven, she had written down for herself a drama based on that favourite of her aunt's, Sir Charles Grandison. At the same time, she was a fashionable young lady; she dismayed Jane by arriving with her hair in the mode of the moment, cut short behind like a boy's. Jane said she was reconciled to it only by the thought that two or three years would repair the damage.

At Godmersham, Jane was going to another niece who loved her as dearly as Anna loved her, and who, from her more equable temperament, could be a genuine companion to her. Fanny Austen was the same age as Anna, but while Anna was a much-beloved object of anxiety, Fanny was 'almost another sister.' Jane told Cassandra on this visit: 'I did not think a niece would ever have been so much to me.'

The welcome at Godmersham was more than satisfying. James, who had gone ahead to leave room for Jane in his carriage, was walking with Edward in front of the house when they drove up. Jane said it was not necessary to mention that she had a most kind welcome from Edward, 'but I do, you see, because it is a pleasure.' She had been given the Yellow Room, and was writing her letter in it at that moment. Fanny saw her Aunt James to her room first, because Aunt James was the married lady; then she flew to Aunt Jane; she stayed while Jane was dressing, and was 'as energetic as usual' in her wishes that her Aunt Cassandra could have come as well.

Elizabeth had been dressing when the party arrived, but she came to Jane's room now, bringing with her Marianne, Charles and Louisa, seven, five and four, and there was a rapturous welcome from everybody. Elizabeth was breeding again, but she seemed quite well; indeed, unusually active for her size. Jane tried to find out from Fanny if her mother tired herself in looking after the younger children; Fanny did not think so but Jane determined to take them off her sister-in-law's hands whenever she could, and took over at once the business of hearing Louisa read in the mornings.

The days passed delightfully; they breakfasted at ten, then Jane heard Louisa read, after which she usually spent an hour or two in the Yellow Room. She rejoiced particularly in the luxury of the space, for she had recently been staying at Brompton with Henry and Eliza, who had been obliged to give her very cramped quarters. The park with its river and the steep wooded hills of Godmersham afforded beautiful walks. They roamed about a good deal, and Edward drove James further afield. Jane was glad of it; she thought it would do James good to see a new country with its fine views. 'Edward certainly excels in doing the honours to his visitors and providing for their amusement.' Even the summer evenings were short, for they had not finished supper till ten, but when they had, in the coolness and the dusk James read *Marmion* to them. Jane could not but be interested in the poem, but she did not know whether she altogether liked it, as yet.

Mary was enjoying the visit very much; she found her sister-in-law's tribe of children 'less troublesome than she expected'; and indepen-

127

dently of them, as Jane observed, 'there is certainly not much to try the patience or hurt the spirits at Godmersham.' But Mary always had something about which to be a little nervous or unhappy. She had written to Anna, and because when Anna wrote to Jane she did not include any message to her stepmother, Mary supposed that she was not going to answer the letter. This was the sort of thing that Jane found most exhausting. The folly of Lady Saye and Sele's conversation had gone off her like water from a duck's back. There is poetry in such foolishness; but petty, useless, eating cares, which no sensible encouragement and advice can do away, because they grow like Hydra's heads, produce an effect on the vicitimized listener which is almost disintegrating. Jane was fond of Mary, and her personal kindness and her beautiful manners must have made her a most acceptable receiver of Mary's woes; but by the time Mary had finished, the burden probably sat as heavily on Jane's shoulders as on her own.

Of the children, Edward was having a fine time; he had play-fellows of about his own age in his cousins Charles and William, and his Uncle Edward 'talked nonsense to him most delightfully.' But his little sister, Jane thought, would be glad to get home; her cousins were too much for her.

In the meantime, she wanted to know everything that went on in Castle Square; she besought Cassandra to be minute. 'You know how interesting the purchase of a sponge cake is to me.' Would they send word of Anna's exact height? Godmersham wanted to know whether she or Fanny were the taller. Anna must not be surprised to hear that the idea of her hair's having been cut off was not at all popular. She was interested to hear that Cassandra had taken Anna over to the Isle of Wight; but as they had had to embark at four in the morning, she was afraid Cassandra must have had an almost sleepless night. A plan had been set on foot to bring little Edward home with them to Castle Square for a visit; she hoped they could manage to find the beds.

There was one incident which the letters discussed with unusual seriousness; its background has been elucidated by Dr. Chapman in his note to Letter No. 52. The *Morning Post* of June 18th records: 'Another elopement has taken place in high life. A Noble Viscount, Lord S, has gone off with a Mrs. P, the wife of a relative of a noble marquis'; and the issue of June 21st adds: 'Mrs. P's *faux pas* with Lord S——e took place at an inn near Winchester.' Jane said: 'This is a sad story about Mrs. Powlett. I should not have suspected her of such a thing. She stayed the Sacrament, I remember, the last time that you and I did.'

Jane Austen often referred, in letters, to this or that gentleman in

128

the neighbourhood as having taken a mistress; her attitude in regard to such doings among people she did not know was satirical and light. Elopements without benefit of clergy play an important part in the stories of *Pride and Prejudice* and *Mansfield Park*; and on both these occasions the differing attitudes of the surrounding characters are so vividly expressed that one is not exclusively conscious of a superimposed attitude, that of the author's own opinion. The better people in each novel regarded the episode as a guilty one, and an event to shock and mortify the family in which it occurred, but in each case there is a solid contribution of worldly common sense or even, in the case of Mary Crawford, fashionable cynicism, which prevents the reader's feeling that the dice have been loaded against the couple.

But just as Jane Austen, though she tossed off a flippant remark about an adulteress in a ballroom, would not read Madame de Genlis' account of such an affair, so, though she understood perfectly the varying attitude of society to sexual immorality, and reflected the tolerant as truly as the hostile, in her own heart she hated it. The idea of such a thing's happening in her own family would have caused her an unspeakable horror and distress; directly it approached her own particular orbit, it took on another colour altogether; and the fact that she and Mrs. Powlett had communicated at the same service was sufficient to make her regard the matter as a serious one. An airy reference to it in those circumstances, would have been impossible to her taste. It is the tradition of her family that though she was very devout, she so much distrusted the exploiting of religious feeling that she was almost exaggerated in her reserve about her own. The very few references she ever makes to it belong to a later period of her life, with the exception of this; but the passage on Mrs. Powlett is of great interest when one remembers the sensations of Fanny Price on hearing of the liaison of Maria Bertram and Henry Crawford: 'There was no possibility of rest. The evening passed without a pause of misery, the night was totally sleepless. She passed only from feelings of sickness to shudderings of horror; and from hot fits of fever to cold.' This is a picture, not of Jane Austen, who had been acquainted with the nature of elopements ever since she was old enough to read the novels in her father's eighteenth-century library, but of Fanny Price, seventeen years old, who had been brought up in the austere elegance of Mansfield Park, by a fashionable governess who worked under the eye of Sir Thomas Bertram; a girl protected by 'a youth of mind as lovely as that of person,' who was in a state of agitation in any case, being in love with Maria Bertram's brother, and having been proposed to with the utmost perseverance by Henry Crawford himself. Her situation fully justified her sleepness night; but had such a thing occurred in Jane Austen's own family, one believes that her feelings would have been more those of Fanny Price than of Mary Crawford.

By the end of June the house party was breaking up. 'In another week,' said Jane, 'I shall be at home—and then my having been at Godmersham will seem like a dream, as my visit to Brompton seems already.' Little Edward was to come with her. She supposed that when they got home it would be time to think about making the orange wine, but for the moment all was 'elegance, ease and luxury. The Hattons and the Millers dine here to-day—and I shall eat ice and drink French wine, and be above vulgar economy.' But even in resigning the comforts and elegance of Godmersham, there was something to go home for. 'Luckily the pleasure of friendship, of unreserved conversation, of similarity of taste and opinions, will make good amends for orange wine.'

For July, August and September these pleasures were enjoyed, but in October it was Cassandra's turn to be at Godmersham again. The baby, John, was born just before his aunt's arrival; Jane was glad of that, and said: "His mama has our best wishes, and he our second best for health and comfort—though I suppose unless he has our best too, we do nothing for her.' But the wishes this time were of no avail. Elizabeth had had eleven children in fifteen years, and the eleventh killed her. The anguish of her loss was felt for at Southampton as much as if they had all been at Godmersham. 'We have felt, we do feel for you all—as you will not need to be told—for you, for Fanny ... for dearest Edward, whose loss and whose sufferings seem to make those of every other person nothing. God be praised! that you can say what you do of him—that he has a religious mind to bear him up, and a disposition that will gradually lead him to comfort.' Her heart was with Fanny. 'My dear, dear Fanny!—I am so thankful that she has you with her!—you will do everything to her, you will give her all the consolation human aid can give.' To Cassandra's next letter, she said: 'Your accounts make us as comfortable as we can expect to be at such a time. Edward's loss is terrible, and must be felt as such, and these are too early days indeed to think of moderation in grief ... but soon we may hope that our dear Fanny's sense of duty to that beloved father will rouse her to exertion. For his sake, and as the most acceptable proof of love to the spirit of her departed mother, she will try to be tranquil and resigned.' She said she had sent the news to their cousin Edward Cooper, but she did hope he would not send 'one of his letters of cruel comfort to my poor brother.' Cassandra had sent news of all the children then at home, and mentioned particularly the eight-year-old Lizzie. Jane thought that such an event ought to make a solemn impression on a child's understanding, and yet, she said, 'one's heart aches for a dejected mind of eight years old.'

Soon she had an opportunity, gratefully accepted, of doing something for the children. George and his brother Edward, thirteen and fourteen years old, were at Winchester, but their father had removed them for the time being until the shock of their mother's death should be something passed; they had been first with their uncle James at Steventon, and now they came for a few days to Southampton. They came down perished with cold, having chosen to ride outside, and without their greatcoats; the coachman, Mr. Wise, had kindly spared them as much of his as possible, but they arrived in such a state that Jane thought they must be going to be laid up with chills. They were not, however; they had never been better. They cried next day over a letter from their father, whom they spoke of with great affection, but after that they cheered up and Jane devoted herself to amusing them. They played bilbocatch, spillikins, paper ships, riddles, conundrums and cards; one evening Jane introduced speculation, and 'it was so much approved that we hardly knew how to leave off.' Out of doors there was endless amusement by the tidal river; they walked to the quayside after church, 'when George was very happy as long as we could stay, flying about from one side to the other and skipping on board a collier immediately.' Her eagerness in promoting their enjoyment and taking their minds off their grief was the more remarkable because, to a certain point, she believed that the grief ought to be felt. She was glad to see that Edward had been much affected by the sermon, of which the text happened to be taken from the Litany, on the subject of 'All that are in danger, necessity or tribulation.' In the evening they read the Psalms and Lessons and a sermon, to which the boys were very attentive, but, said Jane, 'you will not expect to hear that they did not return to conundrums the moment it was over.' The next day they all went from Itchen Ferry up to Northam, where they landed, 'looked into the 74,' and walked home. 'The boys rowed a great part of the way, and their questions and answers, as well as their enjoyment, were very amusing.' George, often, by his eagerness in everything, reminded Jane of his Uncle Henry.

Their aunt at Steventon had written pleasantly of them, which was more than Jane had hoped for; but Mary had only been able to get them one suit of mourning in Basingstoke, so it devolved on Jane to see to the rest in Southampton. She herself was already in mourning, in a black crape gown and bonnet and a black velvet pelisse; she had supposed that black coats only would be needed for the boys, but she

131

found that they considered black pantaloons equally indispensable. Jane was doubtful, but she said: 'Of course one would not have them made uncomfortable by the want of what is usual on such occasions.' She gave a picture of the two boys as she wrote: 'George is most industriously making and naming paper ships, at which he afterwards shoots with horse chestnuts, brought from Steventon on purpose and Edward equally intent over the "Lake of Killarney," twisting himself about in one of our great chairs.'

The death of Elizabeth Austen had far-reaching consequences in her own family. It meant, for one thing, the end of Fanny's childhood, and that before she was sixteen she was the mistress of Godmersham, responsible for her father's comfort, and for that of her brothers and sisters, of whom the youngest was a few weeks old. It also affected Edward with a desire to have his sisters, the aunts of his children, somewhat nearer to him. They had been thinking of a remove from Southampton. The Frank Austens now had a baby, Mary Jane, born in 1808; in 1809 they were to have another, Francis. Charles also was married. In 1807 he had married Frances Palmer, the daughter of the Attorney-General of Bermuda, and their daughter, Cassy, was born in 1808; Cassandra and Jane were the only unattached members of the family. An independent establishment for them with their mother and Martha Lloyd was desirable, and Edward wanted it to be near him. He offered his mother a choice of two small houses, one near the grounds of Godmersham, the other at Chawton, opposite the park of the Great House.

There were many reasons for their preferring the latter. Jane called their branch of the family 'the Hampshire-born Austens,' and it was an attractive proposal that they should be once more settled near to Steventon and Deane. Godmersham was lovely in itself, but to Jane at least the neighbourhood outside it was not so pleasing as that of Alton and Basingstoke. She did not like Canterbury. And there was another consideration; so large a family as the Austens and their connections made up provided in itself a society, and a most agreeable one, outside which its members scarcely needed to go for variety and amusement. They all felt that it was so, but family tradition says that Jane was the most keenly alive to it, and thought the tendency should be strenuously withstood. However deep one's private attachments might be, however much one felt that the truest pleasure could only be found at home, any feelings which caused one to appear abstracted, or inattentive to the claims of society as a whole, seemed wrong to her. There was a moral reason for the view—that of doing one's duty by one's neighbour; there was also a social reason—no normal person could

132

lead a full and happy life confined to one circle, however pleasing and attractive its members might be; but there was yet another reason, though perhaps unconsciously felt—such a preoccupation with the affairs of one's own family was against the interests of vitality, and counter to the artist's instinct for self-preservation. Had she and Cassandra been established at the gates of Godmersham, they would have been out of their own house much oftener than they were in it; their whole lives would have been absorbed, a willing, eager sacrifice to the interests, cares and pleasures of somebody else. Whereas at Chawton, not removed and yet detached, they stood upon their own feet, the centre of their individual sphere, and radiated their influence instead of being drawn into another orbit. When one considers that *Pride and Prejudice* was rewritten, and *Mansfield Park*, *Emma* and *Persuasion* actually composed in that cottage built upon the side of the village street, one realizes something of its significance as a home, and may believe that, however unknown to herself, Jane Austen's mind was actively working in its own best interests when she gave her voice in the family discussions as to which of Edward's offers they should accept.

She longed to go to Chawton, as soon as it was decided that they should. Cassandra was at Godmersham in December 1808, and Jane's letters were frequently interspersed with talk of what they should do in their new home. They would certainly have a piano, as good a one as could be got for thirty guineas, and Jane promised herself to practise country dances, to be able to provide amusement for the nephews and nieces. Their change of home was already being discussed by their connections. The present Rector of Chawton, Mr. Papillon, was a bachelor, and old Mrs. Knight thought it would be a good thing for Jane to marry him. Jane said: 'I am very much obliged to Mrs. Knight for such a proof of the interest she takes in me, and she may depend upon it that I *will* marry Mr. Papillon, whatever may be his reluctance or my own.'

At Godmersham, the ten-year-old William, who had been kept indoors with a cold, had found great comfort in his cross-stitch; he was now working a footstool for Chawton. Jane said: 'We shall never have the heart to put our feet on it. I believe I must work a muslin cover in satin stitch to keep it from the dirt. I long to know what his colours are—I guess greens and purples.' She hoped they would be in the cottage 'in time for Henry to come to us for some shooting in October at least;—but a little earlier, and Edward may visit us after taking his boys back to Winchester.' Meantime they were having a last fling at the gaieties of Southampton. She meant to make up a party for a play; she thought Martha ought to see the inside of the theatre before she left, and Jane imagined that one visit would be enough. She and Martha went to some of the assemblies. One of them she said: 'It was the same room in which we danced fifteen years ago!—I thought it all over,—and in spite of the shame of being so much older, felt with thankfulness that I was quite as happy now as then.' She went on: 'You will not expect to hear that *I* was asked to dance, but I was—by the gentleman whom we met *that Sunday* with Captain D'Auvergne.' At another one she was so well entertained she would have liked to stay longer 'but for the arrival of my list shoes to convey me home, and I did not like to keep them waiting in the cold. The room was tolerably full, and the ball was opened by Miss Glyn;—the Miss Lances had partners, Captain D'Auvergne's friend appeared in regimentals. Caroline Maitland had an officer to flirt with, and Mr. John Harrison was deputed by Captain Smith, being himself absent, to ask me to dance. Everything went well, you see, especially after we had tucked Mrs. Lance's neckerchief in behind, and fastened it with a pin.' She regarded a ball now as more in the nature of a party, when people of her age were occasionally asked to dance but expected more of their entertainment in the tea and card room or among the spectators' benches; but she delighted to hear of Anna, whose dancing season had just begun. Anna had been to a ball at Manydown, which turned out to be a very small affair. Jane was glad Anna had enjoyed it, but she said: 'At *her* age it would not have done for *me*.' Anna had been to a much bigger one afterwards, and sent Jane a 'very full and agreeable account of it.' 'The grandeur of the meeting,' said Jane, 'was beyond my hopes. I should like to have seen Anna's looks and performance— but that sad cropped head must have injured the former.'

In January, Henry was at Godmersham, and when Jane had a letter from Charles, she said she should say as little about it as possible, as 'that excruciating Henry' was sure to have had one too, and would make her information valueless. The letter was from Bermuda, and all were well. She reproached Cassandra with not returning her a due amount of news. Something had been in the air about Edward Cooper's sermons being published, but had Cassandra told her anything of it? 'I tell you everything, and it is unknown the mysteries you conceal from me.'

Jane's passion for news was insatiable, not only for receiving but for giving it; but fond as she was of writing letters she sometimes felt she had had enough. 'As for Martha, she has not the least chance in the world of hearing from me again, and I wonder at her impudence in proposing it.—I assure you I am as tired of writing long letters as you can be. What a pity that one should still be so fond of receiving them?'

Another time she concluded a letter with saying: 'Distribute the affectionate love of a heart not so tired as the right hand belonging to it.'

The letters of Jane Austen will always be a source of controversy, for a sound judgement of them is rendered impossible from the start. Most collections of letters are edited for publication, but hers is the only one which has been given to the public on the understanding that everything of an interesting nature has been first cut out. What remains is, to some readers, trivial and flat, its insipidity relieved only by touches of startling frankness and that remorseless clarity of perception and expression that will always make some people uncomfortable. The intrinsic merits of the letters can be decided only by the reader's personal taste. No one would read them for a picture of the age, for they are the letters that are written in every age and have been since letter-writing began. Nor do they convey, as Byron's letters convey, a complete and instantaneous portrait of the writer. At best they give a side-light only on Jane Austen's character. Here and there, as when she writes to the Prince Regent's librarian or to a schoolboy nephew, an objective impression of the writer's personality emerges for a moment; but the vast majority of the letters were written to someone with whom her intimacy was so complete that, as regards normal daily life, everything but trivial detail was too well known to need or to be capable of expression.

The mass of small and disintegrated detail, of persons, places, episodes and anecdotes, appears, on a casual reading, unintelligible; but the notes supplied by Dr. Chapman cause such a blossoming of comprehension in the reader's mind that it is possible under its influence to see, however obliquely, something of the letters' value to their original recipient. That Jane Austen herself regarded them as of no importance and was even dismayed at the idea of anyone else's doing otherwise was shown when she heard how much Fanny Austen cherished her letters. She wrote to Cassandra: 'I am gratified by her having pleasure in what I write—but I wish the knowledge of my being exposed to her discerning criticism may not hurt my style.' She would have been considerably embarrassed if she had known that in 1930 one of her letters was to be sold for a thousand pounds.

To those who are fond of Jane Austen the letters need no apology, for even without the elucidation of Dr. Chapman's notes they provide a treasury of interest and delight, shot through as they are with sentences that cast a ray of light on something that she saw or felt, a country walk in a hard frost or on roads disagreeable with wet and dirt, a hamper of apples to be unpacked, a leaky store closet, a gown or a pair of shoes, the comings and goings of her family, the occasional

135

outbreak into words of her love for Cassandra: 'Adieu, sweet You!' But they have an importance for even the indifferent reader: they reveal how much conscious art went to the formation of the novels.

The letters are an impression, as it were, of the raw material, unsifted and unrefined, out of which the novels were composed. They are exquisitely written, with a racy, careless perfection the novels themselves do not surpass; but there is an earthiness about some of them which the novels, despite their directness of attack, do not smack of; yet such is the intense vitality of the latter, it implies in their author a full apprehension of life, an outspoken plainness in her own consciousness, at least. One of the erasures made by Cassandra Austen* suggests that the sisters spoke plainly to each other of their bodily functions. Of a lady whose family increased too fast Jane said: 'Good Mrs. D! I hope she will get the better of this Marianne, and then I would recommend to her and Mr. D the simple regimen of separate rooms.' Visiting a young Craven at a fashionable boarding school, she said: 'The appearance of the room, so totally unschool-like, amused me very much . . . if it had not been for some naked Cupids over the mantelpiece, which must be a fine study for the girls, one would never have smelt instruction.' Elizabeth Bennet or Anne Elliot would not have made these remarks, but Jane Austen was not either of these women; she was the person who created them both, and that was a different matter.

But the most striking aspect of the letters so far as their relation to the novels is concerned is their very lack of objective impressiveness. In a letter written daily to Cassandra everything was merely noted down. Cassandra knew the people and the scenes of which Jane wrote as well as Jane knew them herself, and the simple mention of them was enough to bring the living image before Cassandra's mind. In a novel, where the reader knew nothing but from the author's information, every detail must be charged with significance, every word must tell. A comparison of one of the letters with the opening chapters of *Pride and Prejudice* conveys some idea, however inadequate, of the concentration of energy which has gone to form the work of art.

The making of verses was a social pastime in an age without mechanical amusement. Jane Austen had no talent for poetry though she wrote excellent charades, spirited and neat. To congratulate Captain Frank Austen on the birth of his son she wrote an entire letter in doggerel, quite as bad as anyone's sister might have written; but though she could not carry her extraordinary felicity into rhyme, one set of verses remains which shows that what she felt passionately she could express with simplicity. On her thirty-third birthday, the third anniversary of

* Letter 69.

136

Mrs. Lefroy's death, she wrote a short poem expressing the hope that when she was dead she might see Mrs. Lefroy again.

From her writing it is easier to see how much the world about her cared for poetry rather than the extent to which she cared for it herself; but one may judge how well the revivers of Shakespeare had done their work when in 1813 Henry Crawford was made to say: 'Shakespeare one gets acquainted with without knowing how. He is part of an Englishman's constitution. His thoughts and beauties are so spread abroad that one touches them everywhere; one is intimate with him by instinct.' Jane Austen herself had had an education in poetry in common with the circle in which she moved. She thought that one of Edward's visitors must be a man of taste because she saw him in the Godmersham library reading Milton. One might have expected that she herself would have been a whole-hearted admirer of Pope. It is true that by the end of the eighteenth century Pope's great fame had suffered an overthrow correspondingly complete; but in spite of the lack of sentiment, the indifference to natural beauty, and the use of clichés derived from classifical literature which obliged Marianne Dashwood to make sure, before capitulating altogether to the charm of Willoughby, that he admired Pope 'no more than was proper,' one might have supposed that some of his qualities would have kindled a responsive admiration in Jane Austen; his delineation of character, conveyed, as in a streak of lightning, his devastating satire and the diamond-like lucidity of his expression. Some of his couplets are what, had she been a poet, she might have written herself, such as

> *Men must be taught as if you taught them not,*
> *And things unknown proposed as things forgot.*

But the only sign of familiarity with them that she gives is one misquotation, in a letter, from the *Essay on Man*, and a quotation from the *Elegy of an Unfortunate Lady* which she cites as one of the tags that formed Catherine Morland's education. Her indifference speaks much for the truth of the tradition that James Austen helped to form her taste, and perhaps it is a rebuke to our tendency to fit a character to the Procrustean bed of a previous conception; perhaps we can learn something of importance about Jane Austen from the conclusion that she admired Pope 'no more than was proper.'

The same passage in *Northanger Abbey* makes perfunctory mention of Thomson, and though much of Thomson's work would have become ponderous to a circle attuned to the simplicity of Gray and Cowper, many passages of the Claude of Poets, his descriptions of meadows in the spring evening and the autumn woods, 'a crowded umbrage, dusk and dun,' could not but give pleasure to one who thought that beauty of landscape must make one of the joys of Heaven.

Her genuine criticism is, in an interesting manner enough, reserved for the poets contemporary with herself. Burns, if one may accept the opinion of *Sanditon*'s heroine as her own, she admired but thought too rough and profligate to be considered as of the first rank. The conversation of Anne Elliot and Captain Benwick was upon 'the richness of the present age' in poetry, but they confined themselves to Scott and Byron. Jane Austen said on first hearing *Marmion* that she did not know whether she liked the poem or not, but afterwards her favourable opinion of it increased, and she demanded praise for having sent her copy of it abroad to Charles. Anne Elliot's gentle hint to the love-lorn Captain Benwick, apropos of Lord Byron's 'impassioned descriptions of hopeless agony' that she thought it the 'misfortune of poetry to be seldom safely enjoyed by those who enjoyed it completely; and that the strong feelings which alone could estimate it truly were the very feelings which ought to taste it but sparingly,' is beautifully in harmony with the characters, their previous history and the scene; it was what Anne Elliot would have thought, and it was advice sorely needed by Captain Benwick; but that Jane Austen herself could be credited with such extreme sensibility to Byron's poetry seems doubtful. Her one reference to him in the published correspondence is as follows: 'I have read *The Corsair* and mended my petticoat and have nothing else to do.'

It is difficult to-day to associate the mass of Cowper's neat and thoughtful verse with ardent, youthful enthusiasm, yet Marianne Dashwood said she had been 'driven nearly wild' by his lines—perhaps it was *The Castaway* she was thinking of rather than *The Sofa*. But strange as it seems to us that lovers of poetry were once ravished with enthusiasm for Cowper's work, it is partly explained by the fact that the readers of 1800, though in full revolt against the conventions of the Augustan age, had had as yet no opportunity of reading Keats or Shelley, or even Scott and Byron. *Lyrical Ballads* had been published in 1798, but the newness of Wordsworth's style made it at first a sealed book to the common readers. Cowper gave them the ideas and feelings of sensibility, clothed in a language which, though to them it appeared the perfection of simplicity after the tarnished splendours of poetic diction, was more comfortably close to what they were used to, than the disconcerting nakedness of Wordsworth.

Jane Austen herself was not one of those people who cannot exist without poetry. She would scarcely have supported Wordsworth when

138

he said: 'To be incapable of a feeling for poetry, in my sense of the word, is to be without love of human nature and without reverence of God.' But she had the sensitiveness of an educated taste; it is not a reflection on the latter that she had not, by 1806, discovered the *Lyrical Ballads* for herself, and that when she roamed about the February earth, delightedly planning a garden, it was *The Task* she thought of, rather than the *Lines written in Early Spring*.

Cowper remains alive, even to our unsympathetic age, by virtue of a few poems, but one versifier, though he was far more in accordance with modern thought, has perished altogether. Yet a study of Crabbe's verse tells us something of unique value and interest about Jane Austen. Her fondness for his work was well known to her family. She had been known to say that had she ever married, she would have liked to be Mrs. Crabbe; and when we remember some of the assertions made about her, we can hardly smile at Mr. Austen Leigh for begging us to understand that this was meant as a joke. She only knew that Crabbe was married when she heard of his wife's death. 'Poor woman!' she wrote, 'I will comfort *him* as well as I can, but I do not undertake to be good to her children. She had better not leave any.' It has been suggested that what attracted her in Crabbe's verses was his minute and highly finished detail. The Tales are indeed amply furnished with detail, but it is detail of a most grinding and prosaic kind. *Tales of the Hall* are anecdotes of middle-class life, but *Tales of the Borough* and *Tales of the Village* are pictures of poverty and hardship whose realism was evolved for a very definite purpose. Crabbe objected to *The Deserted Village* as giving a false impression of the happiness of village life; the reader had only to look about him, he said, to be convinced of Goldsmith's disingenuous romanticism, and describing a peasant's existence as he himself saw it, Crabbe exclaimed:

> *By such examples taught, I paint the cot*
> *As Truth will paint it and as Bards will not.*

It is no doubt most unfair that Goldsmith's poem should read as freshly as when it was written, and the eminently respectable works of Crabbe be found to have withered beyond hope. But though he had not that touch that would have brought him as near to us as he was to his contemporaries, the content of his work is perfectly understandable, and those who assert that Jane Austen was narrow in her sympathies and lacking in humanity towards any but the comfortable portion of mankind, might be interested to glance at a characteristic extract from the works of her favourite poet, such as his description of the Dying

Pauper. No one would read this poem, or any of Crabbe's pictures of the Workhouse, or the Pauper Lunatic Asylum, or the fearful stories of Ellen Orford or Peter Grimes, for the charm of their highly finished detail, or indeed for anything except the interest of their subject-matter. Stark realism of treatment, a ruthless exposing of every fictitious compliment paid to the romance of a humble life, which was an insult to those who knew its privations, were to Crabbe a matter of urgent moral duty. 'Will you,' he asks.

> *'praise the healthy, homely fare*
> *Plenteous and plain, that happy peasants share?*
> *O trifle not with wants you can not feel,*
> *Nor mock the misery of a stinted meal,*
> *Homely, not wholesome, plain, not plenteous, such*
> *As you who praise would never deign to touch.'*

It is not difficult to see why Jane Austen liked to read Crabbe's work; such sound common sense and such an excellent heart, and a method which went out of its way to avoid false sentiment, never more mischievous than when indulged in by the well-to-do at the expense of the poor, appealed to her with particular force. We remember her biting allusion to Lady Catherine de Burgh's method of visiting her poor tenants 'to scold them into peace and plenty' and that Emma Woodhouse, deficient as she was in self-knowledge and modesty, was yet tentative and respectful in her efforts to help the poor of Highbury, and that Anne Elliot, the only one of the Elliots really to suffer in leaving Kellynch, made a call at every one of the cottages in the neighbourhood because she had heard that the villagers wanted a farewell visit. When old Betty Londe said that she missed Cassandra Austen because the latter had seemed to call in on her so often, Jane took it as a rebuke to herself and determined to visit the old woman more regularly; she told Cassandra joyfully of Edward's having given them ten pounds to spend among the Chawton cottagers. Her fondness for Crabbe is an indication of more than her literary taste.

CHAPTER FOURTEEN

Before leaving Southampton Jane had made an effort to secure the publication of *Northanger Abbey*. In a letter, calling herself Mrs. Ashton Denis, she recalled the transaction of six years ago and expressed her surprise that no attempt had been made to publish the novel; she could only suppose, she said, that the publishers might have mislaid the script; if that were the case, she could provide them with a copy, though she would not be able to let them have it before August. She added: 'Should no notice be taken of this address, I shall feel myself at liberty to secure the publication of my work by applying elsewhere.' Messrs. Crosby, in reply, denied that when they bought the manuscript they had undertaken to publish it at any particular time, and added that if the author or anyone else attempted to publish the work they should take proceedings to stop the sale; they offered in conclusion to return the script on receipt of the £10 which had been paid for it.

To pay £10, which would be more nearly the value of £100 to-day, out of a very slender income, and for a work which it was always possible might be published if she left it where it was, was not at present worth while, perhaps it was not even possible, to Jane Austen; she left *Susan* to linger in Messrs. Crosby's cupboards for another four years; and in the meantime, when the visits had been gone through, her energies and interests were concentrated upon the new house at Chawton.

The cottage, whose last tenant had been Edward Austen's steward, had received many alterations to make it a pleasant dwelling-house. It stands at the end of the village street, very near to what was once a large pond, opposite the cross-roads which lead to Gosport and Winchester. It opens directly on to the street itself. This being so, it was thought more comfortable to have the big window to the left of the front door bricked up, and the left-hand parlour made to look out into the garden. The window of the right-hand parlour remained overlooking the street as before, and very shortly after the family's settling in Mrs. Knight received an account of them 'looking very comfortable at breakfast, from a gentleman who was travelling by their door in a post chaise.'

The nearness to the Winchester road meant that the cottage was perpetually alive to the stimulating noise of wheels and hoofs, and James's daughter Caroline remembered how comforting it was, when

141

she stayed as a small child with her grandmother, 'to have the awful stillness of night frequently broken by the sound of passing carriages, which seemed sometimes even to shake the bed.' Her grandmother, too, Caroline thought, enjoyed the cheerful bustle of frequent traffic. Mrs. Austen, from the time of her arrival at Chawton, had completely given over the affairs of the household to Cassandra and Jane; the latter made breakfast every day at nine, and looked after the stores of tea, sugar and wine; Cassandra saw to everything else. Mrs. Austen herself was very energetic in the garden, however; and not merely in delicately clipping and pruning; she put on 'a round green smock like a labourer's' and dug the potatoes. Within doors, she employed herself in devising and making a splendid patchwork quilt; she had also taken to knitting gloves, and found the work quite absorbing.

The left-hand parlour was the larger of the two, and Jane's piano stood there; but in the right-hand one, which was the common sitting-room, was kept her mahogany writing-desk. She had, says her nephew, no separate study to retire to; there was no dressing-room here as there had been at Steventon in which she worked with no one near her but her 'other self.' She wrote now in a living-room overlooking the road, in which any caller immediately perceived her to be at home, where the children from Steventon were constantly walking in. Her sole protections against the world were, a door which creaked, whose hinges she asked might remain unattended to because they gave her warning that somebody was coming, and the blotting-paper under which she slipped her small sheets of exquisitely written manuscript when a visitor was shown in. The many long spells of quiet when the others had walked out, her mother was in the garden and she had the room to herself; or when the domestic party was assembled, sewing and reading, with nothing but the soft stir of utterly familiar sounds and no tones but the low, infrequent ones of beloved, familiar voices—these were the conditions in which she created *Mansfield Park, Emma* and *Persuasion*. They seem inadequate, it is true; the important novelists of to-day, who have their agents and their secretaries, whose establishments are run entirely for their own convenience and who give out that they must never in any circumstances be disturbed while they are at work—these have, in every respect, a superior régime to that of Jane Austen's unprofessional existence—but their books are not so good.

Hers were not conditions in which any but a mind of exceptional strength could have exerted itself to full advantage; but the shaping spirit of imagination that created human beings, whole and entire, was a force too powerful to be thrown out of gear by having to break off in a conversation or a paragraph because a child wanted to talk to her.

142

When James's Edward, in his Winchester holidays, or the young lady Anna, or the four-year-old Caroline, or one of the tribe of Godmersham cousins, on a visit to the great house opposite, came into the right-hand parlour of the cottage, they remembered afterwards that their Aunt Jane had frequently been writing at her desk before, at their entrance, she turned to greet them with her gay, affectionate manner. Their remorse, afterwards, for the mischief they might have done was intense; it could not be otherwise, when they considered that they had interrupted her in *Mansfield Park*, or *Emma* or *Persuasion*; but they did no injury; she put the sheet under the blotting-paper with a smile.

It is of this period that the children's recollections of her were the strongest. For a couple of years Fanny and Anna had known and loved her, though their closest intercourse with her was yet to come; but now the little Caroline began to know her, too. Caroline had of course seen Aunt Jane the previous year when she had come with them in the carriage to Godmersham. The Godmersham visit had not been a very happy one for Caroline, who, as her Aunt Jane saw, had been over-powered by her blooming, noisy cousins; but at Steventon and Chawton, where everything was quieter, she began to learn how delightful her Aunt Jane was. She said in later years: 'As a very little girl, I was always creeping up to Aunt Jane, and following her whenever I could, in the house and out of it.' Mary was afraid that Caroline might be a nuisance, and told her privately that 'she must not be troublesome to her aunt'; but the attraction was irresistible. Caroline explained it in the words: 'She seemed to love you, and you loved her in return.' That was the earliest charm; then when Caroline was old enough to understand them, came 'delightful stories, chiefly of Fairyland.' One is not sur-prised to hear that Aunt Jane's fairies 'had all characters of their own.' The same entertainment had been produced for Anna long ago in the dressing-room at Steventon, and she spoke for herself, for Caroline and the younger Godmersham Austens, when she said that the 'long, circumstantial stories' were 'begged for on all possible and impossible occasions.' Another pastime at which Aunt Jane excelled was dressing up and pretending. When the children in the cottage played at this, Aunt Jane provided clothes out of her own wardrobe, and she was the visitor in the make-believe house. An occasion that stuck in Caroline's memory was when Aunt Jane, pretending that Caroline and her cousins, Frank's Mary Jane and Charles's Cassy, were grown up, invented a conversation between the three ladies on the day after a ball.

Edward Austen Leigh wrote down a description of her appearance at the time of which he first became conscious of it, in the years be-ginning with the family's removal from Southampton. He thought

143

her 'very attractive.' She was tall and slender; her face was rounded, with a clear brunette complexion and bright hazel eyes. Caroline said that her Aunt Jane's was the first face she remembered thinking of as pretty. She was not so handsome as Cassandra, but her face had 'a peculiar charm of its own to the eye of most beholders.' Her curly brown hair escaped all round her forehead, but from the time of her coming to live at Chawton she always wore a cap, except when her nieces had her in London and forbade it, obliging her to have her hair all 'curled out' and bound with a ribbon, which was something against her better judgement, but to which she was partially reconciled by their saying how charming it looked. Edward said that in the Chawton period, which began when she was thirty-four, though she was always dressed with beautiful care, she had given up being fashionable and he thought he remembered that people in general said she was too young and attractive to be so regardless of making the most of herself.

One characteristic that impressed them all was the wonderful regularity of any of her handiwork. Her handwriting, controlled and flawless as the cutting on a gem, remains for us to see; but the family remembered how deftly her letters were always folded. 'In those days there was an art in folding and sealing. No adhesive envelopes made all easy. Some people's letters always looked loose and untidy; but her paper was sure to take the right folds, and her sealing wax to drop into the right place.' She sewed exquisitely, with such regular stitches 'as might almost have put a sewing machine to shame.' A great deal of her sewing was done on garments for the poor, but she usually had a piece of embroidery at hand that she might take up if visitors were there; satin-stitch was her especial forte; on one occasion she sent Fanny an embroidered strip; and there still exists a large muslin scarf bordered with her handiwork. She was the deftest of any at games requiring dexterity of hand, such as spillikins or cup and ball. She amazed Edward by what she could do with the latter; sometimes she caught the ivory ball upon its point over a hundred times in succession.

She seems to have had, besides a dislike for much expression of religious enthusiasm, a dislike for anything bordering on an affectation of enthusiasm for music. To-day such an affectation is almost unknown; the majority of people who do not care for music do not imagine that they make themselves more interesting by pretending that they do; but when diversions were relatively few, and, while general information was scanty, the standard of accomplishments was high, there was a temptation to pretend to musical fervour which is quite outside

144

18. Tom Lefroy, whose name was linked with Jane Austen. In 1796, Jane wrote to her sister 'He is so excessively laughed at about me at Ashe that he is ashamed of coming to Steventon.' Tom became eventually Lord Chief Justice of Ireland and declared that 'he had once been in love with the great Jane Austen . . . but it was a boy's love.'

30   Diary Supplement, 1794.

III. QUERY, *by Mr. Tho. Hornby, Wombleton.*
What is the reason that a piece of burnt limestone, when water is poured upon it, falls to powder?

IV. QUERY, *by Mr. Tho. Ridout, Canterbury.*
By what operation of nature are flints produced?

Of the SOLAR *and* LUNAR ECLIPSES, *&c. this year.*

There will happen this year six eclipses of the two great luminaries, viz. Four of the Sun and two of the Moon, and one of each will be visible in these parts. They happen in the following order:

I. The SUN is visibly eclipsed on Friday January the 31st, in the forenoon. This will be but a small eclipse, but will be visible here as well as in the more northern parts, viz. Denmark, Sweden, Norway, &c. where the defect will be much larger than with us. The times and appearances, and type at the middle, for Greenwich or London, &c. will be as below, where b is the place of the beginning of the eclipse, about $40\frac{1}{2}$ degrees below the vertex on the right hand, and e the end of it a little below the vertex on the left hand.

Jan. 31, morning.
Beginning   - $10^h 56^m$
Middle   -   11 45
End of ecl.   -   0 $33\frac{1}{4}$ aftern.   Digits eclipsed   -   2° 40´.

II. *February* the 14th, in the afternoon, is a total and visible eclipse of the Moon, and almost central, as the centre of the moon passes nearly through the centre of the earth's shadow; consequently the eclipse will be very large, and of long duration. At the middle of the eclipse the moon is vertical to the southern parts of Nubia in Africa, near the side of the Red Sea, opposite its middle part, in about $12\frac{1}{2}$ degrees of north latitude, and 28 degrees of longitude east from London; but at the beginning of it she is vertical near the island of Socotora, at the mouth of the Red Sea, in latitude 13 degrees north, and long. 57 degrees east

19. Supplement to the Ladies Diary for 1794, giving details of the eclipses of the moon, vital information when planning balls and evening parties.

20. Miniature by R. Cosway of Elizabeth Austen, Edward's wife.

21. Portrait of Edward Knight.

22. In 1798, Thomas Knight died and Mrs Knight made over to Edward Austen the great houses of Godmersham and Chawton. This engraving shows the great house at Godmersham Park. In October of that year Jane visited Godmersham to see Edward newly installed as master of the house.

23. Horace Walpole's house at Strawberry Hill, one of the earliest and most influential houses to be built in the Gothic revival style.

MIRROR.

OLD ENGLISH BARON.

24. Illustration from the 'Gothic' novel, *The Old English Baron* by Clara Reeve, written in 1780.

25. General view of Bath in 1805, showing the newly-built crescents and squares stretching up Lansdowne Hill: engraving by J. C. Nattes.

By May 1800, Edward Knight's health had deteriorated so much that he decided to take the waters at Bath. Jane accompanied her brother, and stayed in Queen's Square.

26 and 28. Engravings of the Royal Crescent (*below*) and the Circus (*right*) at Bath built by John Wood in the mid-eighteenth century.

27. Sydney Hotel, Bath: In 1801, Jane Austen moved, with her parents and Cassandra, to No. 4, Sydney Place, close to the hotel.   Aquatint by J. C. Nattes.

29.   Exterior of the Pump Room at Bath: aquatint by J. C. Nattes.

30.   Rowlandson's cartoon of a subscription concert held at the Assembly Rooms in Bath in 1798.

." But talks of the *Op'ras* and his *Signora*,
Cries *Bravo, benissimo, bravo, encora*,   Yet *I* think, though she's at it from morning till noon,
                                                    The dear little thingumbob's never in tune."

31 and 32. 'Comforts of Bath', Rowlandson's satirical view of the waters of the Pump Room and the King's Bath in 1798.

33 and 34.   Silhouettes of James and Jane Leigh Perrot. Mrs Leigh Perrot was Mrs Austen's sister.   In 1800 Mrs Leigh Perrot was accused of stealing lace from a milliner's shop in Bath, and was lodged in Ilchester Gaol to await her trial. Here she and her husband lived in comparative comfort, but the experience was a tremendous shock to them both.

35.   This engraving from Rowlandson's and Pugin's *Microcosm of London* shows the Yard of the King's Bench Prison.

our experience. A vivid illustration of this is supplied by Mrs. Elton. Jane frequently, in private life, displayed a determination not to show more pleasure in music than she actually felt. In Bath she had said of a public concert in Sydney Gardens that happily the gardens were large enough for her to get out of earshot of the strains; and though we might take that as a not unjust reflection on the orchestra, she said of a singer in town, 'that she gave *me* no pleasure is no reflection upon her, nor I hope upon myself, being what nature made me on that article.' She did not think a defective appreciation of music was an unsympathetic trait in a heroine; at a party, Elinor Dashwood who 'was neither musical nor affecting to be so,' 'made no scruple of turning away her eye from the grand pianoforte when it suited her, and unrestrained by the presence even of a harp and a violoncello, would fix them at pleasure on any other object in the room.' Yet her own genuine fondness for music was considerable. The piano at Steventon had been hers, and the instrument bought for thirty guineas that stood in the left-hand parlour at Chawton was hers also. On this, she used to practise every day before breakfast, because, as her nephew thought, she disturbed the household least at that hour. The children thought her singing voice very sweet; Caroline remembered standing by her at the piano while she played and sang. The greater part of the airs and pieces she played were from manuscript copies she had made herself.

It was the opinion of her descendants that she had no sooner settled down after the move to Chawton—and such upheavals were very disturbing to the workings of her mind—than she began to write once more; and her writing took the form of a reconsideration of *Sense and Sensibility*. *Northanger Abbey* was lost to her, *Pride and Prejudice* had not yet been tried in the refiner's fire, but *Sense and Sensibility*, which in its original state had been nearer to what she deemed the standard of publication than the previously composed *First Impressions*, was the natural choice. Eleven years had passed since the completion of the story, and those eleven years—her life since the age of twenty-three—comprised everything that could be accounted her development as a human being and as an artist. What she had learned from this apparently eventless existence is shown by the amazing rapidity with which she composed those three later novels, whose worlds of experience are so solid in their detachment, so infinite in the associations they bring about in the reader's mind with depths upon depths of human nature, that one would imagine they had been the slow growth of half a life-time, instead of, as they are, that of little more than a twelve month each.

Another writer might have altogether outgrown the work of eleven such years ago; but it was characteristic of Jane Austen's singular integrity of mind that she seems never to have put down anything of which she could afterwards be ashamed. *Sense and Sensibility* is certainly the least regarded of her works, and she applied to it hardly any of those expressions of interest and personal love which, in the strict privacy of her family circle, she made use of in connection with every other novel; but she thought, with ample justice, that it contained material, which made over, was worthy to represent her in her mature appearance before the world.

Henry, naturally, was the man to come forward with assistance at this point. He and Eliza had moved to a house in Sloane Street, next door to Mr. and Mrs. Tilson; and Henry not only put his experience and encouragement at his sister's service, but his hospitality, while she wished to be in touch with the printers, correcting the proofs.

The publisher who undertook the work was Mr. Thomas Egerton, but he would not do it at his own risk. Jane Austen did not hand over a sum of money to him to defray expenses of publication, but she undertook to reimburse him in case of loss, and set aside a sum for the purpose.

She arrived in Sloane Street in the middle of April, and plunged immediately into the round of sightseeing and diversion that a visit to Henry and Eliza invariably spelled. One of the first expeditions she made was to a couple of art exhibitions, one at the Liverpool Museum and the other at the British Gallery. She said: 'I had some entertainment at each, though my preference for men and women always inclines me to attend more to the company than to the sights.' She had the usual shopping commissions to fulfil; at the great draper's, Grafton House, the crowd was so thick she had to wait half an hour at one counter before getting attention; but when she had secured it, she bought some bugle trimming and some silk stockings very satisfactorily.

Jane was accompanied to Grafton House by one of Eliza's servants, because Eliza meanwhile was out on her own account ordering in things for a grand evening party. Eighty people had been invited for the next Thursday evening. The next day, however, they planned, if it were fine, 'to walk into London' together. Jane said: '*She* is in want of chimney lights for Tuesday: and *I* of an ounce of darning cotton.'

She was much taken up with the idea of going to the theatre. Mrs. Siddons had returned to the stage in 1809, and though her astonishing beauty was no more, and the lovely, fragile, large-eyed creature had become an unwieldy bulk, so that when Isabella knelt to Angelo attendants had to help her to her feet, her power had no whit dim-

146

inished, rather it had increased. It is impossible to say with any authority what her affect would be on an audience to-day; one can only recall, by fits and starts, the almost petrifying influence of her acting upon audiences who saw it. A play-goer who went to see her in *Hermione* has recorded the impression made upon him by the difference between the silence of an ordinarily well-bred audience, full of small rustlings and sounds, and the deathly hush that settled over the theatre as Mrs. Siddons opened her mouth.

The party from Sloane Street meant to go to Drury Lane on the night of Thursday, April 18th, to see Mrs. Siddons as Constance in *King John*. Constance was a role in which she had made her name some years before; the young Miss Kelly who was her Arthur said when Mrs. Siddons wept over her her collar was always wet with Mrs. Siddons' tears; and Mrs. Siddons herself said that it was her practice to leave her dressing-room door open throughout the play, because she wanted to hear, as she said, 'going on upon the stage . . . those distressing events . . . the terrible effects of which . . . were to be represented by me.' Jane in particular was most eager to see this celebrated performance, but when they got to the box office they found that *King John* was to be replaced that evening by *Hamlet*, in which Mrs. Siddons did not appear. They therefore drove to No. 10 Henrietta Street, to ask Henry what should be done. Henry said they had better put off the theatre altogether until Monday, and then see Mrs. Siddons as Lady Macbeth. But Mrs. Siddons was in an uncertain state of health or spirits. When Henry went to secure seats on Monday, the box-office keeper told him that she was not going to appear that evening either; Henry walked away much discomfited at the thought of disappointing his family, and his feelings were not relieved when they all heard, a little later, that Mrs. Siddons was to appear that night after all, but that to get tickets now was, of course, out of the question. Jane told Cassandra she could have sworn quite easily.

On Tuesday night all was forgotten in the party, which was a resplendent success. The first floor of the Sloane Street house was composed of a rectangular drawing-room, an octagonal back drawing-room, and a passage between the two, so broad that is was almost like an ante-room. At half-past seven, the musicians arrived in two hackney coaches. At eight the company proper began to arrive, and the rooms filled so rapidly and became so hot that Jane was glad to seek the comparative coolness of the broad passage, where, besides being more comfortable, she had a very good view of everybody who passed out and in. She was 'surrounded by gentlemen' most of the evening. One of them, Captain Simpson, told her: 'On the authority of some other Captain, just arrived

147

from Halifax, that Charles was bringing the *Cleopatra* home, and that she was probably by this time in the Channel.' But Jane said the news could not be altogether depended on, because Captain Simpson was obviously something the worse for drink; however, there was enough in it to make her feel it was not worth while to write to Charles again until they heard something definite.

The last guests had not left till after midnight, and the party was commented on in the *Morning Post* two days afterwards.

Cassandra enquired how the proof-correcting of *Sense and Sensibility* was going on; she thought perhaps in the middle of these distractions Jane might scarcely have leisure to think about it; but Jane said: 'No, indeed, I am never too busy to think of S. and S. I can no more forget it than a mother can forget her sucking child; and I am much obliged to you for your enquiries.' The sheets she had received so far carried the story to Willoughby's appearance. She had received some suggestion, albeit rather late in the day, that the incomes mentioned in the opening of the story were not exactly in accordance with probability, but the second chapter, in which Mrs. Dashwood's financial position is discussed, was already in type. She said to Cassandra: 'The *Incomes* remain as they were, but I will get them altered if I can.'

Mrs. Knight said how much she was looking forward to the book's appearance, and Jane, though much gratified by her interest, could not feel altogether sure that the old lady would be pleased with it when she read it. She said: 'I think she will like my Elinor, but cannot build on anything else.'

The letters from Sloane Street were sent to Cassandra at Godmersham. In Cassandra's absence Anna had been staying at Chawton with Mrs. Austen and Martha and both the latter were very much pleased with her. Jane said of her: 'She is quite an Anna with variations—but she cannot have reached her last, for that is always the most flourishing and shewy—she is at about her third or fourth which are generally simple and pretty.'

When Jane returned to Chawton in May, Cassandra was still at Godmersham, and she had much to tell her about Anna's various amusements. There was a party on Selborne Common with 'Volunteers and felicities of all kinds' and another one, an evening party, with 'syllabub, tea, coffee, singing, dancing, a hot supper at eleven o'clock, everything that can be imagined agreeable.' Anna sent her best love to her cousin Fanny, and promised to write her an account of the day on Selborne Common before she left Chawton.

The flowers in the rambling garden were doing well. Cassandra's mignonette, said Jane, made a wretched appearance; but 'our young

148

peony at the foot of the fir tree has just blown and looks very handsome; and the whole of the shrubbery border will soon be gay with pinks and sweet-williams, in addition to the columbine already in bloom. The syringas, too, are coming out.' The Orleans plums were likely to do well, but not the mulberries. The peas, however, would soon be ready. 'You cannot imagine,' she wrote, on May 31st, 'it is not in human nature to imagine what a nice walk we have round the orchard. The row of beech look very well indeed, and so does the young quickset hedge in the garden. I hear to-day that an apricot has been detected on one of the trees.'

The pleasantness of the month had been spoiled by frequent thunderstorms. She hated them. When they visited the Digweeds, 'we sat upstairs and had thunder and lightning as usual. I never knew such a spring for thunder storms as it has been. Thank God! we have had no bad ones here. I thought myself in luck to have my uncomfortable feelings shared by the mistress of the mansion, as that procured blinds and candles.' 'We have had a thunder storm again this morning. Your letter came to comfort me for it.'

In June the fruit was ripening. 'Yesterday I had the agreeable surprise of finding several scarlet strawberries quite ripe. . . . There are more gooseberries and fewer currants than I thought at first—we must buy currants for our wine.' Martha was in town and had chosen a breakfast set at Wedgwood's for Mrs. Austen. Jane said: 'I hope it will come by waggon to-morrow. I long to know what it is like.'

The death of King George III was thought to be imminent this month, and people were buying mourning to be in readiness for it. Anna was back at Steventon, but she meant to go over to Alton to buy mourning, and, accompanied by her friend, Harriet, she called in at Chawton to ask her Aunt Jane to go with them. The latter put aside her letter to do so; when she returned she wrote in it: 'I am not sorry to be back again, for the young ladies had a great deal to do—and without much method in doing it.'

July brought Cassandra home; summer passed into autumn and in October, *Sense and Sensibility* was published. It was announced in a list, containing Maria Edgeworth's *Tale of Fashionable Life*, and *Traits of Nature*, by the half-sister of Fanny Burney. The only item on the list which is now of any value had the least pretentious title and was published anonymously. '*Sense and Sensibility*, by a Lady': It was in three volumes and offered for sale at fifteen shillings.

Maria Edgeworth not only earned a great contemporary reputation for herself; *Castle Rackrent*, the only one of her works which has perfectly withstood the test of time, had the honour of inspiring a Russian novelist. Turgenev said that he might never have written of the Russian peasants as he did, had he not first seen what Maria Edgeworth had done for their Irish counterpart. Yet it is one of the curiosities of literature that Henry Austen should have said, after his sister's death, that *some* had thought her works not unworthy to stand on the same shelf with a D'Arblay or an Edgeworth.

None the less, Jane Austen never, after her work was published, suffered the sensation of failure, or of not receiving what she felt was her due of public estimation. On the contrary, she was delighted by the admiration she called forth, and she took a most healthy delight in the fortunes of her work; but she had no intention whatever that her own neighbourhood should know her to be an authoress. At the end of September, a month before *Sense and Sensibility* made its appearance, Cassandra wrote to Fanny at Godmersham, and Fanny recorded in her diary of September 28th: 'Letter from Aunt Cass. to beg we would not mention that Aunt Jane wrote *Sense and Sensibility*.' And so well was the secret kept that even Anna knew nothing of it. Anna one day accompanied her Aunt Jane to Alton, and they turned into the circulating library, on whose counter, among other novels, was *Sense and Sensibility*. Anna, her aunt standing beside her, picked up the first volume, looked at it, and threw it scornfully down upon the counter again. That one, she said, *must* be rubbish. She could tell it from the title.

The success of the book was not sensational, but the sales not only covered the expenses of printing, the first edition was sold out in twenty months, and brought the authoress one hundred and forty pounds; and it made its mark at once among novel-readers of a serious nature. In the correspondence of Lady Bessborough with Lord Granville Leveson-Gower occurs the following notice of it: 'God bless you, dearest G. Have you read *Sense and Sensibility*? It is a clever novel. They were full of it at Althorpe, and though it ends stupidly, I was much amused by it.'

Jane Austen would have gone on writing had nothing of her work ever seen the light, but the delightful stimulus of success was now added to her absorbing private pleasure; and her next project was to take up the second of her early works, the *First Impressions* that Messrs. Cadell had not thought it worth while to look at.

What she did to it we can never know; considering the difference between the greenish, unripe promise of *Sense and Sensibility* and the brilliant perfection of *Pride and Prejudice*, it seems probable that the revision was thoroughgoing; there are, for instance, no hints about this work as there are in the former, that its conception belonged to a

150

time before the present—the worldly, the interesting, the wide-awake year of 1812 to 1813. There are no ideas of abstract interest, such as an unwise indulgence in sensibility, or discussions on the picturesque. The book is topical—not only of that year but now; the conversations in it, the relationships of its men and women are essentially those of to-day.

The depth, the perspective of impression conveyed by *Pride and Prejudice* is so intense that when one re-reads the book one is astonished by its brevity. The people in the story are so distinctly present to one's mind that one searches in vain for the actual passage of description that made them so.

There is none; and in this lies the most characteristic aspect of Jane Austen's art, and the one most difficult to discuss and understand. What Macaulay said of Milton might with more aptness be said of her: 'There would seem at first sight to be no more in his words than in other words. But they are words of enchantment. No sooner are they pronounced, than the past is present, and the distant, near . . . Change the structure of the sentence . . . and the whole effect is destroyed. The spell loses its power, and he who should hope to conjure with it would find himself as much mistaken as Cassim in the Arabian tale, when he stood saying Open Wheat, Open Barley, to the door which obeyed no sound but Open Sesame.'

Jane Austen uses a perfectly simple sentence, stating a commonplace fact; none of the words in it is beyond the scope of daily conversation; but used by her they have an evocative power entirely unsuspected; as a ball, bounced on to a hard surface, soars into the air, as one stroke of a tuning fork produces a volume of echo, so a few ordinary words put together by Jane Austen produce a scene of absolute solidity and conviction. She uses none of the aids to creating an impression in the reader's mind that other writers use; her words are those we hear round the breakfast table; they are not, as indeed Milton's often are, haloed with association and musical in their concrete sound. She was, for instance, quite oblivious to the associations most of us connect with names. Not many people agree that 'That which we call a rose, by any other name would smell as sweet,' but Jane Austen seems to have thought so. She supplied her characters, every one of them, with a name which we feel to be exactly suitable—Fitzwilliam Darcy, William Larkins, Admiral Croft, Miss Bates, Lucy Steele—but it was a perfect arrangement of material, rather than one drawn from an extensive choice; in the collection of Letters written as a child she evolved names which she afterwards drew upon when she was grown up; Willoughby, Dashwood, Crawford, Annesley. Her use of Christian names

151

is remarkable; not only does she use the names of her brothers with complete unself-consciousness—James Morland, Edward Ferrars, Charles Bingley, Henry Crawford, Frank Churchill—but she gives her own to Jane Bennet and Jane Fairfax; even stranger, she uses a name which is consecrated by her readers to one character, for another: Elizabeth Bennet gives her name to the repulsive Elizabeth Elliot, and Jane Bennet to the even more obnoxious Mrs. Robert Watson.

There is no answer to the mystery as to why a plain statement made by her does the work of an architectural description of somebody else. She had the capacity to clear away the hackneyed, battered surface upon words and use them so that we perceive their pristine meaning; but that is the magical aspect of her genius. One cannot learn to do it for oneself by reading her work, any more than one can learn to play the piano by listening to Schnabel playing it. It is the secret which she could not have imparted even if she would; but there are a few things we can see as to the manner of her work, and they help us to understand a little how she managed to create an effect of startling realism, almost entirely without the use of descriptive detail.

The structure of *Pride and Prejudice* explains what she meant by saying to Anna Austen that two or three families in a small area was the very thing to work upon and just the situation she liked herself. She did not mean it to be inferred that a pleasant round of gossip and intrigue and an absence of anything of external interest were all that she herself felt fitted to cope with; but that, for her method of establishing conviction, it was essential to keep the threads of the story converging upon a single point and to show the various characters, not only as she saw them, or as two of them saw each other, but as each of them appeared to his or her acquaintance as a whole.

In *Pride and Prejudice* this interlacing of the characters forms, as it were, the steel structure upon which the work, with its amazing buoyancy, is sprung. Every important fact in the story is shown to be the inevitable consequence of something that has gone before. The fact that Bingley, pliable as he was, should be deterred by Darcy from his courtship of Jane Bennet is at first surprising; and Darcy's explanation is that Bingley was very modest, and really believed Darcy's representation of Jane's indifference; which, added Darcy, he genuinely believed himself. He saw that Jane liked Bingley, but he did not believe her to be in love, and therefore liable to be injured except in a worldly sense by Bingley's withdrawal. We then remember what Charlotte Lucas had said, very early in Jane and Bingley's acquaintance, when Elizabeth had remarked to her that though Jane was falling in love with

Bingley, her serenity and self-control were such that Elizabeth did not think anyone else would be able to notice it.

' "It may perhaps be pleasant," replied Charlotte, "to be able to impose on the public in such a case : but it is sometimes a disadvantage to be so guarded. If a woman conceals her affection with the same skill from the object of it, she may lose the opportunity of fixing him; and then it will be but poor consolation to believe the world equally in the dark. There is so much of gratitude or vanity in almost every attachment, that it is not safe to leave any to itself. We can all *begin* freely; —a slight preference is natural enough; but there are very few of us who have heart enough to be really in love without encouragement. In nine cases out of ten, a woman had better show *more* affection than she feels. Bingley likes your sister undoubtedly; but he may never do more than like her, if she does not help him on."

' "But she does help him on, as much as her nature will allow. If *I* can perceive her regard for him, he must be a simpleton indeed not to discover it too."

' "Remember, Eliza, he does not know Jane's disposition as you do." '

The suddenly brought about marriage of Charlotte and Mr. Collins, which is in its way one of the most interesting things in the book, is led up to before the reader has any suspicion of what is to happen. At the Netherfield Ball, before Mr. Collins has made his famous proposal to Elizabeth, he exacerbates her almost beyond endurance by his pertinacious attentions; as she has refused to dance with him, she is not able, in the etiquette of the day, to accept another partner; therefore she has to sit and endure Mr. Collins, who says he had rather sit by her than dance with anybody else. Her only moments of relief are when Charlotte Lucas comes to them and kindly diverts some of Mr. Collins' conversation to herself.

The difference between the meretricious, dishonest Wickham and his father, who had been the trusted steward and lifelong friend of old Mr. Darcy, is explained in a single statement. The elder Wickham had had an extravagant wife.

The celestial brightness of *Pride and Prejudice* is unequalled even in Jane Austen's other work; after a life of much disappointment and grief, in which some people would have seen nothing but tedium and emptiness, she stepped forth as an author, breathing gaiety and youth, robed in dazzling light. The penetration, the experience, the development of a mature mind, are latent in every line of the construction, in every act and thought; but the whole field of the novel glitters as with sunrise upon morning dew. The impression cannot be wholly analysed and accounted for, but it is worth while noting that in this book there

153

are no people who are thrown in upon themselves by an unsympathetic atmosphere, like Fanny Price; no one who is labouring under a painful secret like Jane Fairfax; no one whose natural frame of mind is one of stormy light and shade, like Marianne Dashwood; no one whose life has been radically altered by a killing past of unhappiness like Anne Elliot; there is disappointment in the book, and agitation, and acute distress, but the characters are all, even Wickham's, of an open kind, despite their individual variety.

Much of the novel's charm is created by the relationship of the two sisters; the idea that we have here something of the relationship of Jane and Cassandra is inescapable, particularly in such a passage as: 'I was uncomfortable enough—I was very uncomfortable—I may say, unhappy. And with no one to speak to of what I felt, no Jane to comfort me, and say that I had not been so very weak and vain and nonsensical as I knew I had! Oh, how I wanted you!' Cassandra Austen is to us something of a sybil; she is a veiled presence whose face we never see. Her sister is always talking to her; and we listen to her sister's voice and watch the changing expression of her face, but we never see the person to whom Jane is turned. Even the people who tried to give some account of her said very little. She was devoted to Jane, and thought nobody good enough for her, but one; she admired Jane's work with a full, intelligent participation. She was exceedingly reserved; she had very strict and delicate notions of honour. Her nephews and nieces remembered her as 'sensible and charming': Fanny was 'energetic' in her longings for her Aunt Cassandra when a party had come to Godmersham without her. Jane had fancy and invention and a delicious faculty for nonsense; but Caroline Austen remembered that she was sometimes 'very grave'; in their early middle age Cassandra seemed, to the younger generation, the more equably cheerful of the two. So much we piece together; but one quality of Cassandra's we recognize for ourselves: she had a striking sense of humour. In acknowledging one of her letters, Jane declared her to be 'one of the finest comic writers of the age.' Would Cassandra but read her own letters through five times, she might get some of the pleasure out of them that her sister did. Jane sent delighted thanks for the 'exquisite piece of workmanship' which had been brought into Henry's breakfast-room among the other letters.

Now a letter from Jane Bennet would never have ranked as an exquisite piece of workmanship. A partial sister could not have described her as one of the first comic writers of the age. If she had been, Mr. Bingley would not have fallen in love with her. Some characteristics of hers seem to suggest Cassandra Austen: she was perfect with Mrs.

154

Gardiner's children, and when Lydia inadvertently burst out with the information that Mr. Darcy had been at her wedding, and then exclaimed: 'But, gracious me! I quite forgot! I ought not to have said a word about it. I promised them so faithfully! What will Wickham say? It was to be such a secret!' Jane replied: 'If it was to be a secret, say not another word on the subject. You may depend upon my seeking no further.'

But Jane Bennet would not have been described as one who 'admired so few people'; on the contrary, she had the lovely, gentle, candid approach that both men and women find so charming; even Bingley's sisters were attracted to her; she 'looked to like.' Elizabeth said, when she found that her sister was pleased with Bingley: 'I give you leave to like him. You have liked many a stupider person.'

Jane delighted in Elizabeth's liveliness, but she never said a lively thing herself; but for the fact that the term conveys a sense of reproach, we should say she had no sense of humour. She was inclined to take Elizabeth's remarks *au pied de la lettre*; she said she could hardly be happy, even if Bingley did propose to her, knowing that his relations and friends were against the match; Elizabeth said: ' "You must decide for yourself, and if, upon mature deliberation, you find that the misery of disobliging his two sisters is more than equivalent to the happiness of being his wife, I advise you, by all means, to refuse him." "How can you talk so!" said Jane, faintly smiling. "You must know that though I should be exceedingly grieved at their disapprobation, I could not hesitate." '

'Mild' and 'steady' are words used in describing her; her very beauty was of the reposeful cast; she was not so light nor so used to running as Elizabeth; she was the sooner out of breath when they pursued Mr. Bennet across the paddock. In every respect she forms the ideal contrast to her mercurial sister, whose face, Miss Bingley said, was too thin, and whose eyes enchanted Mr. Darcy with 'their shape and colour, and the eye-lashes, so remarkably fine.'

Of the young men, Bingley and Wickham sustain the sense of gaiety and open good humour which is a part of the novel's atmosphere. Bingley is simple, modest, easily led; but with a disposition to be pleased. His impulsively affectionate behaviour to Jane when she and Elizabeth are at Netherfield; his sending his enquiries to Elizabeth by a housemaid very early in the morning, long before she received any from the two elegant ladies who waited on his sisters; his piling up the fire and his anxiety lest Jane should be sitting in a draught when she came down after dinner, are all a part of his character; so is his weakness, his dependence on Darcy's stronger mind; but even in that he laughs at himself. It is he who supplies that masterpiece among thumbnail sketches, of Darcy at Pemberley. 'I declare I do not know a more awful object than Darcy on particular occasions, and in particular places; at his own house especially, and of a Sunday evening, when he has nothing to do.'

The character of Wickham, though so base, is not of a kind to cloud the brilliant surface of the mirror. A curious degree of sexual attraction often goes with a lively, unreliable disposition, which may either be somewhat superficial but perfectly well-meaning, or, driven by circumstances which it has not the strength to withstand, become that of a scoundrel. Wickham was well on the way to being a scoundrel; but his sexual fascination was so great that Elizabeth Bennet, who was normally of a very critical turn of mind, saw at first absolutely nothing in him but what made him seem the most charming man she had ever met. Even Mrs. Gardiner thought him delightful and only warned Elizabeth against him because he was not in the position to support a wife. 'You have sense, and we all expect you to use it.' Even when the whole of his very discreditable story had been exposed, and Mr. Darcy had with difficulty brought him into marrying Lydia Bennet, Wickham's vanity made him still exert all his known powers of attraction on the family. The goaded Mr. Bennet said to Elizabeth: ' "He is as fine a fellow as ever I saw. He simpers and smirks and makes love to us all." ' Wickham's epitaph in the story is perhaps Mr. Bennet's finest flight. Speaking to Elizabeth: ' "I admire all my three sons-in-law highly," said he; "Wickham, perhaps, is my favourite; but I think I shall like *your* husband quite as well as Jane's." '

Elizabeth Bennet has perhaps received more admiration than any other heroine in English literature. Stevenson's saying, that when she opened her mouth he wanted to go down on his knees, is particularly interesting because it is the comment of a man on a woman's idea of a charming woman. Not less significant is Professor Bradley's: 'I am meant to fall in love with her, and I do.' She is unique. The only girl between whom and herself there is any hint of resemblance is Benedict's Beatrice. The wit, the prejudice against a lover, the warm and generous indignation against the ill usage of a cousin or a sister, remind us, something, one of the other. She attacks the mind in two ways:

> *... when she moves you see*
> *Like water from a crystal over-filled,*
> *Fresh beauty tremble out of her, and lave*
> *Her fair sides to the ground.*

She is also completely human. Glorious as she is, and beloved of her

156

creator, she is kept thoroughly in her place. She was captivated by Wickham, in which she showed herself no whit superior to the rest of female Meryton. She also toyed with the idea of a fancy for Colonel Fitzwilliam, who was much attracted by her. 'But Colonel Fitzwilliam had made it clear that he had no intentions at all, and, agreeable as he was, she did not mean to be unhappy about him.' Above all there is her prejudice against Darcy, and though their first encounter was markedly unfortunate, she built on it every dislike it could be made to bear; her eager condemnation of him and her no less eager remorse when she found that she had been mistaken, are equally lovable.

The serious side of her nature is perhaps nowhere better indicated than in the chapter where Charlotte Lucas secures and accepts Mr. Collins's proposal and then has to tell Elizabeth that she has done so.

'The possibility of Mr. Collins's fancying himself in love with her friend once occurred to Elizabeth within the last day or two; but that Charlotte could encourage him seemed almost as far from possibility as that she could encourage him herself; and her astonishment was consequently so great as to overcome at first the bounds of decorum, and she could not help crying out—

'"Engaged to Mr. Collins! my dear Charlotte, impossible!"

'The steady countenance which Miss Lucas had commanded in telling her story gave way to a momentary confusion here on receiving so direct a reproach; though, as it was no more than she expected, she soon regained her composure, and calmly replied—

'"Why should you be surprised, my dear Eliza? Do you think it incredible that Mr. Collins should be able to procure any woman's good opinion, because he was not so happy as to succeed with you?"

'But Elizabeth had now recollected herself; and making a strong effort for it, was able to assure her, with tolerable firmness, that the prospect of their relationship was highly grateful to her, and that she wished her all imaginable happiness.

'"I see what you are feeling," replied Charlotte. "You must be surprised, very much surprised, so lately as Mr. Collins was wishing to marry you. But when you have had time to think it all over, I hope you will be satisfied with what I have done. I am not romantic; you know. I never was. I ask only a comfortable home; and, considering Mr. Collins's character, connections and situation in life, I am convinced that my chance of happiness with him is as fair as most people can boast on entering the marriage state."

'Elizabeth quietly answered: "Undoubtedly," and after an awkward pause, they returned to the rest of the family.'

It is a scene between two young women, both of them normal,

pleasant and good; the conversation is of the briefest; in it the more remarkable of the two speaks only twice, and less than a dozen words in all; but what a world of thought and feeling, experience and philosophy it conjures up!

Mr. Darcy would not perhaps have acknowledged it, but of all her attractions it was Elizabeth's independence which charmed him most; by standing off from him, she gave him, unconsciously, an opportunity really to see her. His quiet reply to Miss Bingley that there was meanness in *any* of the deceptions women sometimes condescended to use for captivating men, suggests that though she was the worst offender, she had not been the only one. For the first time in his life he met an attractive woman who not only did not try to draw him in, but turned on him with anger and disgust when she found that, all unwittingly, she had done it. Her rejection of his proposal is of course the climax of his experience in finding that he had to be agreeable to a woman before she would be agreeable to him; but the reader perceives, long before Elizabeth perceives it herself, how much he was attracted by her unself-conscious behaviour; as, for instance, when she almost ran from Meryton to Netherfield before breakfast to see Jane, 'jumping over stiles and springing over puddles with impatient activity.' When she was shown into the breakfast-room, with the hem of her petticoat deep in mud, she had not the least idea that Mr. Darcy, while wondering whether the occasion justified her coming so far in such a manner, was admiring 'the brilliancy which exercise had given her complexion.'

The character of Fitzwilliam Darcy has been said to have no counterpart in modern society. The error is a strange one. Darcy's uniting gentle birth with such wealth is indeed an anachronism. To-day death duties would have felled the Pemberley woods and the estate passed into the hands of ales and stout. But Darcy's essential character is independent of circumstances. He had the awkwardness and stiffness of a man who mixes little with society and only on his own terms, but it was also the awkwardness and stiffness that is found with Darcy's physical type, immediately recognizable among the reserved and inarticulate English of to-day. That his behaviour in the early part of the book is owing to a series of external circumstances rather than to his essential character is very carefully shown, and we have a further proof of how easy it was to misunderstand him: when he and Elizabeth were becoming reconciled to each other at Lambton, and Elizabeth had suddenly to give him the news of Lydia's elopement, he was quite silent and took an abrupt departure. She thought his behaviour owing to his redoubled disgust at her family; it was really consterna-

158

tion at a state of affairs for which, as one who had failed to expose Wickham to society, he thought himself partially responsible.

That his character was actually quite different from what it appeared to be on the surface is of course revealed by his behaviour once the shock of Elizabeth's abuse has made him realize how it struck other people. It is a piece of extremely subtle characterization that when Elizabeth first met Lady Catherine, she thought that she and Mr. Darcy were alike, and after she had fallen in love with Darcy, she wondered how she could ever have imagined a resemblance. We do not, however, doubt that the resemblance was there. It was a family likeness, accentuated on the one hand by a harsh and arrogant nature and on the other by a shy and uncommunicative one. This view of Darcy is borne out by the drawing of his sister. Georgiana Darcy was a very well-meaning girl, but she was so extremely shy that society was an agony to her; and though for her brother's sake she was longing to please Elizabeth and Mrs. Gardiner, it was all that her gentle, pleasant governess could do to guide her through the occasion of their call as became the lady of Pemberley.

That some of his real nature had been, if unconsciously, perceived by Elizabeth before their reconciliation is proved by one of Jane Austen's rare and very beautiful touches of sensibility. It occurs when Elizabeth and her party are being taken round Pemberley by the house-keeper and arrive at the picture-gallery. 'In the gallery were many family portraits, but they could have little to fix the attention of a stranger. Elizabeth walked on in quest of the only face whose features would be known to her. At last it arrested her—and she beheld a strik-ing resemblance of Mr. Darcy, with such a smile over the face, as she remembered to have sometimes seen when he looked at her.'

It is true that in an attempt to see whether Darcy's character would stand the test of time, it is necessary to see how it would appear were he denuded of his wealth; but from the point of view of his position in the work of art that presents him to us, the background of Pember-ley, that Derbyshire landscape with its trees in the variegated beauty and the stillness of summer, is truly harmonious. 'The hill, crowned with wood, from which they had descended, receiving increased abruptness from the distance, was a beautiful object. Every disposition of the ground was good; and she looked on the whole scene, the river, the trees scattered on its banks, and the winding of the valley, as far as she could trace it, with delight. As they passed into other rooms, these objects were taking different positions; but from every window there were beauties to be seen.' When they were walking round the park, 'they had now entered a beautiful walk by the side of the water,

159

and every step was bringing forward a noble fall of ground, or a finer reach of the woods to which they were approaching.'

They took the usual path, 'which brought them again, after some time, in a descent amongst hanging woods, to the edge of the water and one of its narrowest parts . . . the valley, here contracted into a glen, allowed room only for the stream, and a narrow walk amid the rough coppice-wood which bordered it.'

Sir Walter Scott's statement that Elizabeth Bennet, on seeing the grounds of Pemberley, felt she had made a mistake in rejecting their owner, has been amply dealt with by distinguished admirers of Elizabeth; but it is worth while noticing another instance of the penetrating honesty of Elizabeth's portrayal. To walk through such a house and grounds and not feel a slight pang at the idea that they might have been one's own is not in normal human nature; but Darcy's letter had long since brought about a partial change in Elizabeth's feelings. Had it not, she might not even have thought of the park in possible relation to herself; for though, when she thought she was going to the Lakes, she exclaimed in ecstasy: 'What are men to rocks and mountains?' the personal consideration was actually so pre-eminent with her, that at the moment the idea that she might have been the mistress of Pemberley struck her, walking as she was with Mr. and Mrs. Gardiner, she remembered that, as Mr. Darcy's wife, she would not, so she thought, have been allowed to continue her intercourse with her aunt and uncle. 'This was a lucky recollection. It saved her from something like regret.'

There is such intense psychological interest in Jane Austen's work that it is possible, strange as it may seem, to forget for a moment that they are primarily creations of comedy; not only are they so in the broader sense, by which one implies that in the development of the plot a character which begins with a mistaken attitude to life is brought back to the angle of normality, and reformed in the process, but Jane Austen's own attitude to the various characters is largely satirical, in however mildly luminous a degree; there is none of her figures whom she treats in a consistently serious manner. Most important of all, she has comic portraits whose effect is that of 'straight' comedy, though their foundation is of the most brilliant and subtle excellence. Mr. Bennet is one of the most remarkable figures in the whole range of English comedy. Dean Swift is one of the few English masters of irony; it is not perhaps too much to say that Mr. Bennet is another. Of every other one of Jane Austen's male characters we may say that they are men as they appear to women; and that they are so is no reflection upon her powers. Man's aspect as he appears to women is after all as

160

important, neither more nor less, as his aspect as he appears to men. But Mr. Bennet is the unique exception; he might have been drawn by a man, except that it is difficult to think of a man who could have drawn him so well. It is relatively easy to be witty at somebody else's expense; but to create the character of a genuinely witty man is, one would say, for a woman, next door to impossible. Male characters of unconscious humour, women, with their capacity for acute observation, achieve very well. George Eliot was highly successful in this genre, so was Fanny Burney; even Emily Brontë relaxed her sternness over the delineation of old Joseph; Jane Austen herself is of course inimitable; but Mr. Bennet was something extraordinary even for her. To detach his remarks from their context is to deprive them of half their subtlety and force: as, for instance, his reply to the endless maunderings of Mrs. Bennet on the subject of the entail in Mr. Collins's favour. ' "How anyone could have the conscience to entail away an estate from one's own daughters, I cannot understand, and all for the sake of Mr. Collins, too! Why should *he* have it more than anybody else?"

' "I leave it to yourself to determine," said Mr. Bennet.'

One can appreciate the full aroma of that only after having read the twenty-three chapters that precede it.

Of Mrs Bennet and Mr. Collins, those two creations of unconscious humour, the only method of doing justice to them would be to repeat every word uttered by either; but it is one of the remarkable aspects of Jane Austen's comedy that though such characters are brilliantly funny, one can at the same time see them in relation to every aspect of ordinary life. We not only see Mr. Collins in the ballroom, 'awkward and solemn, apologizing instead of attending,' making such an exhibition of himself to Mr. Darcy as caused that gentleman to eye him 'with unrestrained wonder,' and making his celebrated proposal to Elizabeth; we see him also at Hunsford, being borne with by his wife. 'Poor Charlotte! It was melancholy to leave her to such society; but she had chosen it with her eyes open; and though evidently regretting that her visitors were to go, she did not seem to ask for compassion. Her home and her housekeeping, her parish and her poultry, and all their dependent concerns, had not yet lost their charms.'

The distinguishing of novelists as 'subjective' and 'objective' is essentially misleading, since a purely objective presentation of character is, to a human being, an impossibility; but the degree to which novelists appear to be either is sometimes very marked. In the last four of Jane Austen's works we are insensibly drawn in to believing that her rendering of the characters of Mrs. Bennet and Mrs. Norris and

Miss Bates and Mary Musgrave gives us the actual scientific truth about those characters. It is impossible, almost, to have any other opinion of them than that held by Jane Austen herself. She makes none of those violent assaults upon our prejudice and our imagination which the writer makes who is eminently subjective; she seems to leave us quite free to form our own judgement on the most mature of her master-pieces, but really the guiding is there, only it is so firm and skilful that we have not the opportunity to perceive it, excepting just now and again. *Pride and Prejudice* perhaps affords an example in Lydia Bennet. Lydia is very interesting because she shows that the type of girl known as 'modern' is perhaps one of the best and earliest known to society; bouncing, rowdy, indiscreet, with no attraction but 'youth and a toler-able person,' a success with the majority of young men by reason of health and noise, full of enthusiasm for her own concerns and pleasures, and not so much inattentive to advice and entreaty from anybody else, as actually deaf to it. Jane Austen disliked her very much; so do we when we read of her in relation to Jane and Elizabeth, and Mrs. Gar-diner, and even poor silly Mrs. Bennet, when the latter said: 'O my dear Lydia, when shall we meet again?' and Lydia replied: 'O Lord! I don't know. Not these two or three years, perhaps.' But though we do not question the truth of the portrayal, there are moments, when we have closed the book, when we wonder if we dislike her quite so much, after all. She interrupted Mr. Collins when he was reading aloud one of Fordyce's Sermons; she bought a bonnet, and when her sisters said it was very ugly, she said that there had been several in the shop much uglier, and had thought she might as well buy it as not; and she ran away at sixteen with Mr. Wickham without actually sup-posing she would be married to him, though at the same time she thought it would be very good fun if she were. She seems at times a sympathetic character; but then one remembers her overbearing wildness, her selfishness, how when she was invited to Brighton and the miserable Kitty was not, 'wholly inattentive to her sister's feelings, Lydia flew about the house in restless ecstasy, calling for everyone's congratulations and laughing and talking with more violence than ever'; and one feels that Jane Austen was right after all; she does indeed dislike Lydia Bennet, but there is nothing warped or desiccated in the portrayal of this robust, noisy, natural creature; as much sap went to her composition as to the divine reality of her elder sisters.

The dialogue of Jane Austen's men and women is so strikingly in character, what they say is at once so expressive of themselves and so material in forwarding the action, that although her stories are built on a structure which, solid as it is, contains very little incident, the

162

idea of the theatre naturally rises in the mind when one is considering some of it.

A dramatization of *Pride and Prejudice* compiled by Miss Helen Jerome has had a very successful run in London, and it is an interesting comment on the age that a work which purported to bring Jane Austen's novel on the English stage should have been tolerated in the language of Miss Jerome. Had Jane Austen been able to attend one of the performances herself and to hear some of the remarks put into the mouth of her Elizabeth, she would have echoed the words of Mr. Woodhouse: 'I live out of the world, and am often astonished at what I hear.'

CHAPTER FIFTEEN

In the autumn of 1812 Edward Austen brought his family to stay at the Great House, opposite Chawton Cottage. The visit was mutually delightful; Cassandra and Jane always enjoyed the Great House's being occupied, whether by the owners or Frank and Mary with their Mary Jane, Frank and Cassy, or Charles and Frances with their Cassy, Harriet and little Frances; but the visit of Edward's family meant that Jane had the favourite Godmersham children, and the especially favourite Fanny.

Fanny was by now taken into confidence over the writing; some of it was read aloud to her in manuscript. Her younger sister Marianne, aged eleven at the time of this visit to Chawton Great House, remembered when she was grown up that her Aunt Jane when in the library at Godmersham would sometimes burst out laughing, jump up and go over to a desk, at which she wrote something down, and then return to the company as if nothing had happened. Marianne remembered also of this Chawton visit, that she often stood outside a closed door, curious and disappointed, behind which her older sister and her aunts were uttering peals of laughter. The room in Chawton House where Jane usually sat with the children is one over the porch, lined with panelling and known as the Oak Room.

This occasion, during which *Pride and Prejudice* was being worked upon, was the last time of the Godmersham Austens appearing under that name; towards the close of 1812 old Mrs. Knight died, and upon her death Edward adopted the name of Knight, and Jane had to grow accustomed to addressing letters to Miss Knight at Godmersham Park.

In November 1812 Jane Austen submitted the manuscript of *Pride and Prejudice* to Mr. Egerton, and on this occasion there was no suggestion of the author's meeting the expenses of the printer. Egerton paid her £110, and the novel was to appear in January, in three volumes, at eighteen shillings the set. The title announced that it was by the author of *Sense and Sensibility*.

Jane was not so much elated by the prospect of this second publication that she could think of nothing but that; she had begun the first story of an entirely new nature that she had attempted since the sketch of *Lady Susan* in 1805. *Mansfield Park* was already forming in her mind, and she was careful that no slightest inaccuracy of detail should mar the reality of the whole. Very early in January Cassandra was

164

staying at Steventon, and Jane wrote to her: 'I learn . . . that there is no Government House at Gibraltar. I must alter it to the Commissioner's.' She was referring to William Price's remark that when the ladies of the Commissioner's House at Gibraltar came out in the new style of hairdressing, he had thought it outlandish, but when he saw it on his sister's head, he was reconciled to it. But her preoccupation with her own work did not make her any the less interested in the works of other people. The general interest in novels and literary work of all kinds is shown, not only by the flourishing of the circulating libraries, but by the establishment of Book Societies in various districts. Chawton possessed one, and now Jane heard that the Miss Sibleys wanted to begin one like it on the other side of the county. She was delighted. What could be stronger proof, she asked, of how much better theirs was than that at Manydown or Steventon? 'No emulation of the kind was ever inspired by *their* proceedings.'

On January 29th, however, nothing could be thought of but *Pride and Prejudice*. Jane had received a set from Mr. Egerton, and wrote to Cassandra: 'I want to tell you that I have got my own darling child from London.' Henry had been entrusted to despatch the others, and wrote to say he had given one to Charles and sent another by coach to Godmersham. 'Just the two sets which I was least eager for the disposal of,' she exclaimed. She wrote to beg Henry to send her the remaining two so that she could despatch them to James and Mary, and to Frank at Portsmouth; but Henry had left town for a day or two, so delay was unavoidable; but Jane consoled herself by saying to Cassandra: 'For *your* sake I am as well pleased that it should be so, as it might be unpleasant to you to be in the neighbourhood in the first burst of the business.' On the day of the volumes' arrival Miss Benn dined at the cottage, and Mrs. Austen, Martha and Jane told her they had got a new novel from town, of which they had heard before its publication, and had asked Henry to send them as soon as it came out. They suggested reading it aloud after dinner, and Miss Benn was all acquiescence. Mrs. Austen did the reading, and Jane thought Miss Benn was genuinely amused; 'she really does seem to admire Elizabeth.' Jane added with complete candour: 'I must confess that I think her as delightful a creature as ever appeared in print, and how I shall be able to tolerate those who do not like *her* at least, I do not know.'

She said: 'The second volume is shorter than I could wish, but the difference is not so much in reality as in look, there being a larger proportion of narrative in that part.' She then made a casual mention of something that showed what consummate care had gone into the achieving of that compact and buoyant masterpiece. 'I have lop't and crop't

165

so successfully, however, that I imagine it must be rather shorter than S. and S. altogether.'

The next morning Miss Benn came again to hear the reading, but this time Jane was not so much pleased as she had been before. She thought that perhaps the work did not make its proper impression owing to Mrs. Austen's reading too rapidly and without giving the conversations their proper emphasis. 'Though she perfectly understands the characters herself, she cannot speak as they ought.' 'Upon the whole, however,' Jane said, 'I am quite vain enough and well satisfied enough.' In the fullness of her glee, she added: '[It] is rather too light, and bright, and sparkling; it wants shade; it wants to be stretched out here and there with a long chapter of sense, if it could be had; if not, of solemn specious nonsense, about something unconnected with the story; an essay on writing, a critique on Walter Scott, or the history of Bonaparte, or anything that would form a contrast and bring the reader with increased delight to the playfulness and epigrammatism of the general style.'

But in spite of the exquisite delight of seeing *Pride and Prejudice* in its published form—far keener than that attending the appearance of *Sense and Sensibility*, for it contained the dearest of her inspirations, 'as delightful a creature as ever appeared in print'—she did not forget the new creation. She said to Cassandra, thinking James might have more knowledge on this subject than Chawton could afford: 'If you could discover whether Northampton is a county of hedge-rows, I should be glad.' What episode in *Mansfield Park* she had seen in a hedgerow, we can only imagine, since one must conclude that Cassandra's enquiries did not produce anything satisfactory; but the idea stayed in her mind, and three years later, Wiltshire having been, perhaps, discovered to be a county of hedgerows of the high and hollow kind, she placed in such a one the conversation Anne Elliot overheard between Louisa Musgrove and Captain Wentworth.

In April something happened that brought back to Jane many memories of childhood and youth. Eliza had been ill for a long while, and in this month she died. That vivid, anxious existence, connected as it was with great scenes and persons of the past, could not cease without reminding Jane of her early years at Steventon, when, as a child of fourteen, she had dedicated *Love and Friendship* to Madame la Comtesse de Feuillide. It was strangely suited to Eliza's character that she should be mourned for in anguish, but not long. Jane, in writing to Frank on board H.M.S. *Elephant* in the Baltic, telling him how their brother was, could say, three months after Eliza's death: 'Upon the whole, his spirits are very much recovered—If I may so express

166

myself, his mind is not a mind for affliction. He is too busy, too active, too sanguine.' Then, too, she said that the blow had been made easier to bear by the fact of Eliza's being ill so long. 'He very long knew that she must die, and it was indeed a release at last.'

In May, Jane went to stay with him in Sloane Street. Henry took her to town in his carriage, and the journey, in perfect weather, was delightful. The Chawton family had provided for their refreshment on the way; they ate three of the buns that had been put up, and when they arrived at Sloane Street, Mr. and Mrs. Tilson drank tea with them and were offered the remaining three.

Now, when Henry was out, Jane had the house to herself, except for two French servants, Madame Bigeon and her daughter, Madame Perigord. She said: 'I am very snug with the front drawing-room all to myself, and would not say thank you for any companion but you. The quietness of it does me good.'

But Henry was proposing now to leave Sloane Street and live over the bank at 10, Henrietta Street; preparations were being made already to fit up the upper floors for him. Jane went down there the following day, and told Cassandra: 'I . . . walked into No. 10, which is all dirt and confusion, but in a very promising way'; she was present 'at the opening of a new account, to my great amusement.' After that she and Henry went to an exhibition of water-colours in Spring Gardens. Jane amused herself by seeing if any of the portraits would do for Jane or Elizabeth Bennet. She said: 'I was very well pleased—particularly (pray tell Fanny) with a small portrait of Mrs. Bingley, excessively like her. I went in hopes of seeing one of her sister, but there was no Mrs. Darcy;—perhaps however I may find her in the Great Exhibition which we shall go to if we have time.' 'Mrs. Bingley's,' she said, 'is exactly herself, size, shaped face, features and sweetness; there never was a greater likeness. She is dressed in a white gown with green ornaments, which convinces me of what I had always supposed, that green was a favourite colour with her. I daresay Mrs. D. will be in yellow.'

But Jane went through the whole of the Great Exhibition, and an exhibition of Sir Joshua Reynolds', without finding a resemblance of Elizabeth in either; she said: 'I can only imagine that Mr. D. prizes any picture of her too much, to like it should be exposed to the public eye.—I can imagine he would have that sort of feeling—that mixture of love, pride and delicacy.' The more she would consent to go on with the characters in *Pride and Prejudice*, the more she was begged to do it. Fanny wanted a letter, as from Miss Georgiana Darcy; but her aunt said: 'I am much obliged to Fanny for her letter;—it made me laugh heartily; but I cannot pretend to answer it. Even had I more time, I

167

should not feel at all sure of the sort of letter that Miss D. would write.'

Jane said that Henry would not be settled in Henrietta Street till the autumn she thought. In the meantime, as he was occupied in the bank for most of the day, she drove about alone in the carriage. The weather was warm and an open carriage delightful. Much as she found pleasure and satisfaction in her own work, it seems never to have occurred to her that the author of *Pride and Prejudice* could advance any claims to consideration on behalf of Miss Jane Austen. She said of her thus driving about: 'I liked my solitary elegance very much, and was ready to laugh all the time at my being where I was—I could not but feel that I had naturally small right to be parading about London in a barouche.'

In July, Edward Knight brought his family to the Great House again. Fanny was now eighteen, and her intimacy with her Aunt Jane grew with the growth of what she had to tell. When she fell in love, her Aunt Jane had to hear all about it; for Fanny was of a serious and practical cast of mind, and on so important a topic she liked to test the reliability and degree of her emotions by laying them before the person whose judgement she admired so much, and with whom the most intimate confidence was easy. Anna was very different; Anna's love affairs were impulsive and could be managed by nobody but herself. When her brother Edward had gone back to Winchester after the holidays, she found herself so dull that she got herself engaged to Mr. Michael Terry. The match did not please James and Mary; they did not approve of the young man, and it was very awkward and disagreeable to a father incapable of taking things lightly, and a stepmother so prone to worry and distress herself, that Anna persisted in being engaged in spite of them. But worse followed. Anna discovered for herself that Mr. Terry would not do, and threw him over. Her action in doing so showed an unsteadiness that was even worse than her flying in her father's face and forming the engagement in the first place. Anna also was very intimate with her Aunt Jane, but, volatile as she was, she instinctively forbore to talk to her about this sort of affair. Fanny's artless, forthright mind did not engage in anything she could not lay before her aunt with a request for advice or encouragement. The summer at Chawton meant that she could see the latter every day, and in her diary she frequently recorded their meetings. 'Aunt Jane and I had a very interesting conversation'; 'Aunt Jane and I had a delicious morning together.' 'Spent the evening with Aunt Jane'; and, one August day: 'Had leeches on for a headache. Aunt Jane came and sat with me.'

Edward as well as his daughter was very happy in the visit; in writing to Frank, Jane said: 'Edward is very well and enjoys himself as thoroughly as any Hampshire-born Austen can desire.' Henry, too, was so much recovered that he had planned to make a tour in Scotland, and take his nephew, young Edward Knight, with him. The enterprise was a great success. Jane Austen's passion for scenery enabled her to take a vicarious delight in the views seen through her brother's eyes. 'I wish,' she said regretfully, 'that he had had more time and could have gone farther north, and deviated to the Lakes on his way back.' But what Henry had seen had given him very great pleasure, much of which he communicated to his sister. 'He met,' she said, 'with scenes of higher beauty in Roxburghshire than I had supposed the south of Scotland possessed.' On young Edward, however, these beauties of landscape had been, comparatively speaking, thrown away. He had enjoyed the tour because it was very agreeable to travel with Uncle Henry, but he really cared for the country only as he could hunt or shoot in it. But he was a dear boy, who behaved very well to his father, and was extremely kind to his young brothers and sisters, and his Aunt Jane said: 'We must forgive his thinking more of grouse and partridges than lakes and mountains.'

Besides news of the family, she had something to tell Frank of a mutual acquaintance, an old admirer of her own. The Mr. Blacknall, who had once told Mrs. Lefroy that if it had been possible he would have liked to improve his acquaintance with the Austen family because of Miss Jane Austen, had married at last, a lady called Miss Lewis. Jane remembered him as 'a piece of perfection, noisy perfection'; she had always rather liked him; from what she recalled of him, she drew a thumbnail sketch of what Miss Lewis should be like to suit him. She could wish her, she said, 'to be of a silent turn and rather ignorant, but naturally intelligent and willing to learn;—fond of cold veal pies, green tea in the afternoon and a green window blind at night.'

She concluded with the news that many people might have put first. Every copy of S. and S. was sold and had brought her £140. So that with the £110 for which she had sold the copywright of *Pride and Prejudice* she could say: 'I have now therefor written myself in to £250 —which,' she added, 'only makes me long for more.' Then she had a favour to ask. She had 'something in hand,' which she hoped would sell on the credit of P. and P., 'though not half so entertaining'; she said, would Frank mind if she mentioned in it the *Elephant*, and two or three other of his old ships? 'I *have* done it,' she confessed; 'but it shall not stay, to make you angry. They are only just mentioned.' Frank gave his permission for the names to be used, and so in *Mansfield Park* William Price, having escorted Fanny to their home in Portsmouth,

169

is greeted by his father with the news that Captain Walsh thinks William will certainly have a cruise westward in the *Elephant*, and that he himself had been on the platform two hours, looking at William's ship, where she lay, close to the *Endymion*, between her and the *Cleopatra*.

Mansfield Park had, in some form at least, reached what is now its thirty-eighth chapter. In September, Jane went to Henry again. He was now settled in Henrietta Street. At the same time Edward arrived with Fanny, Marianne and Lizzie, attended by Mrs. Sace; but the Godmersham party put up in an hotel near by, excepting Fanny, who was to be with her Aunt Jane. They arrived at quarter past four of a September afternoon, and were welcomed by Henry and by Madame Perigord. Madame Bigeon was below, dishing up, and a little after five they sat down to a dinner of soup, fish, bouillee, partridges and an apple tart. Fanny and her aunt had a room with a dressing-room leading out of it, and the large bed that had been Eliza's, and were very spacious and comfortable.

No. 10 had been made very presentable with cleaning and painting, and the Sloane Street furniture; Jane said: 'It seems like Sloane Street moved here.' There was a large front room which Henry used as a dining- and common sitting-room, and the back room opening out of it was quite large enough for any drawing-room accommodation he was likely to want. He did not mean to give parties now. Madame Bigeon and Madame Perigord lived near at hand, and came in as often as he wanted them. Madame Bigeon still did all his marketing for him, and with the visitors at No. 10, she was there almost the whole time to do the work.

On the evening of their arrival Henry took the party to *Don Juan* at the Lyceum. They had the stage box, and the little girls were enraptured, but Jane's delight was 'very tranquil.' She sat in the back of the box and talked to Henry. The latter had a piece of news and a letter for her to see which were of extreme and delightful interest. He had sent a copy of *Pride and Prejudice* to Warren Hastings, and Warren Hastings from his retreat at Daylesford had written to praise the novel warmly. Jane could not but be charmed by this approval; but she did wish that Henry had respected her desire of having the authorship kept a secret. Henry, however, was not the man to keep secrets, particularly agreeable ones. Frank, on the other hand, was silent as the grave, and Jane wrote to thank him for it: 'Henry heard P. and P. warmly praised in Scotland, by Lady Robert Kerr and another lady; and what does he do in the warmth of his brotherly vanity and love, but immediately tell them who wrote it! A thing once set going in that way—one knows how it spreads!—and he, dear creature, has set it

170

going so much more than once. I know it is all done from affection and partiality,—but at the same time, let me here express to you and Mary my sense of the *superior* kindness which you have shown on the occasion, in doing what I wished.'

But it was impossible to be really annoyed with Henry, when his actions proceeded from brotherly feeling and when staying with him in town was always so festive and amusing. London, as ever, meant shopping;—Edward gave Fanny and Jane £5 each. They set out to make the necessary rounds of the great shops, but they managed first to pay a call of ten minutes or so in Hans Place upon the Tilsons. Mrs. Tilson was in an advanced stage of pregnancy. 'Poor woman!' said Jane. Fanny, from much experience at home, prophesied that the child would come in three or four days. Free to devote themselves to the serious business of the day, from eleven to half-past three they were hard at it: silk stockings at twelve shillings a pair, cotton at four shillings, ribbons and lace, poplin for dresses, rose colour and dark slate; a beautiful square veil for Fanny, some net for a frock for Anna; a set of fingering exercises for beginners at the piano, and a visit to Wedgwood's, where Edward and Fanny chose a dinner service. The characteristic productions of the firm showed white classical figures on the black or azure ground; a tea service in the height of the Grecian mode had cups and saucers bordered with a key pattern in black, while the sides and centre of the vessels were ornamented with a medallion in sepia of a classical figure beside an altar or a tripod; but the firm also produced more ordinary patterns. The dinner service chosen for Godmersham was bordered with small purple lozenges between lines of narrow gold, and was to bear the family crest.

The expeditions were not all of them of a pleasant nature, as Lizzie and Marianne had to be taken to the dentist.—Jane said: 'Going to Mr. Spence's was a sad business and cost us many tears; unluckily we were obliged to go a second time before he could do more than just look.' Edward went with the children both times; the second visit took an hour, and in it Lizzie's teeth were filed, and pronounced to be of a very perishable nature, while poor Marianne had two taken out. When the extractions had been decided upon, Jane, with Fanny and Lizzie, went into the next room, where they heard 'each of the two sharp, hasty screams.' Fanny's teeth were examined also, and Jane said: 'Pretty as they are, he found something to do to them, putting in gold and talking gravely.' He wanted them all to be brought to him again in two months' time, but Edward would not promise. Jane was not at all pleased with Mr. Spence; she said she could understand that the little girls' teeth might be in a critical state, but that 'he must be a lover of teeth and money and mischief to parade about Fanny's.'

For their second visit to the theatre, to see Garrick's *Clandestine Marriage*, Jane was put into the hands of the hairdresser. She said: 'He curled me out at a great rate. I thought it looked hideous, but my companions silenced me by their admiration.' As she was accustomed to wearing a cap, she had thought that, with nothing but a bit of velvet round her head, she might catch cold, but she did not; 'the weather,' she said, 'is all in my favour.'

When the visit to Henrietta Street was over, Jane went back with the party to Godmersham. Henry's establishment, to say nothing of Edward's, had accustomed her for the moment to a state of luxury and elegance quite removed from the simplicities of Chawton, but it had not made her less mindful of the affairs of the cottage. She wanted to know if they had begun on the store of new tea, and on the new white wine. 'My present elegancies have not yet made me indifferent to such matters. I am still a cat if I see a mouse.'

The principal happening at Godmersham in September was the annual fair at Goodnestone. The development of shops and stores all over the country makes it difficult for us to understand the importance of fairs to those living out of range of the towns in the early nineteenth century. The booths supplied a bewitching variety of goods, from the severely practical to the altogether frivolous. Jane described the Goodnestone Fair as that famous one 'which makes its yearly distribution of gold paper and coloured persian through all the family connections.' To be on the spot, Fanny went for a day or two to her grandmother at Goodnestone Farm; Lizzy and Marianne accompanied her, and so did their father, who had been repenting very much of his promise to do so, and had hoped the day would turn out wet, but unfortunately for him the morning was perfectly clear. Jane was writing in the library, and had it therefore entirely to herself; she thought of Cowper's *Alexander Selkirk*; 'I am mistress of all I survey,' she said, and added that if she liked to repeat the whole poem there was nobody to stop her.

She constantly sent news to Chawton of the children. She disapproved rather of Edward and George, who were now at home: they seemed to think of nothing but field sports out of doors, and showed themselves idle and greedy in the house; but afterwards she wished she had not said this; she was touched by their both staying to the Communion Service on Sunday. As she said: 'After having much praised or much blamed anybody, one is generally sensible of something just the reverse soon afterwards.' In the evening, at least, their occupation was innocent

172

enough: they sat side by side making rabbit nets, 'as deedily . . . as any two Uncle Franks could do.'

But the boys were inclined to be something of a nuisance. At Chawton there was a Mary Doe; the little girls had left a hare behind and told her that if she would look after it till they came again they would give her something for her trouble. Mary had been gathering nuts, with some idea that the young Mr. Knights wanted them, and Cassandra wrote about this in her letter. Jane read that part of the letter to the old nurse Sackree, and Sackree did not approve at all. 'She saw some signs of going after her in George and Henry, and thinks if you could give the girl a check, by rather reproving her for taking anything seriously about nuts which they said to her, it might be of use.'

The thirteen-year-old Lizzie had had a letter from her Aunt Cassandra, and her Aunt Jane was much amused by her saying that she *would* answer it, but she had so much to do, it might be four or five days before she could. Jane said: 'This is quite her own message spoken in rather a desponding tone.' Louisa, who was nine, sent best love and 'a hundred thousand million kisses.'

Jane was glad to hear that Alethea Bigg and her sister Mrs. Heathcote, with their friend Miss Charlotte Williams, had been at Chawton and found much to approve of in the cottage. She was delighted by the warmth of Charlotte Williams's appreciation; besides, Miss Williams had the eyes Jane always admired. 'Those large dark eyes always judge well. I will compliment her by naming a heroine after her.'

On October 13th Charles arrived at Godmersham with his wife, little Cassy and the baby. They were so late that dinner had reached the stage of dessert, and their coming had been given up for that day by everyone but Jane. She and Fanny hurried out to the hall to meet them; little Cassy was so tired and bewildered that at first she did not seem to know anybody, but by the time they reached the library she had kissed her Aunt Jane very affectionately. 'It was quite an evening of confusion as you may suppose—at first we were all walking about from one part of the house to the other—then came a fresh dinner in the breakfast-room for Charles and his wife, which Fanny and I attended—then we moved into the library, were joined by the dining-room people, were introduced and so forth—and then we had tea and coffee which was not over till past ten.'

The next day the gentlemen went out to shoot. Jane said: 'I wish Charles may kill something, but this high wind is against their sport.' The coldness suited Edward very well; he was extremely cheerful, but Jane imagined that poor James at Steventon must be running his toes into the fire. Within doors Jane improved her acquaintance with her

173

sister-in-law and her little niece. Mrs. Charles, née Palmer, had handed on a good deal of her family's appearance to little Cassy. 'Poor little love,' said her Aunt Jane. 'I wish she were not so very Palmery, but it seems stronger than ever.' Charles was so extremely devoted to his wife and children that he kept them on board with him; but Cassy had lately suffered so much from seasickness that her Mama was beginning to think she ought to be left on shore. The difficulty was, Cassy could not bear to leave her parents, and her papa was most unwilling to part from her. He was so much engrossed with his family that it was quite difficult to get him out. Jane said to Cassandra on October 21st: 'I think I have just done a good deed—extracted Charles from his wife and children upstairs and made him get ready to go out shooting, and not keep Mr. Moore waiting any longer.'

'Southey's Life of Nelson!' she exclaimed. 'I am tired of Lives of Nelson, being that I never read any. I will read this, however, if Frank is mentioned in it.' To Frank himself she sent, while at Godmersham, an interesting piece of family news: the temperamental Anna had become engaged again, this time in sober earnestness, to Mr. Ben Lefroy. Ben, the son of Mrs. Lefroy and brother of the present Rector of Ashe, was in many respects a good match for Anna Austen; he was sensible, religious, well connected and possessed of a moderate income. Anna's aunt said: 'We are anxious to have it go on well, there being quite as much in his favour as the chances are likely to give her in any matrimonial connection.' The family had not actually foreseen this event, but Anna's behaviour had been such that they were kept in a constant preparation for something. The chief drawback to the match that Jane could see was that 'he hates company and she is very fond of it; this with some queerness of temper on his part and much unsteadiness on hers, is untoward.'

Mrs. Austen sent Jane a very 'comfortable' letter, 'one of her foolscap sheets quite full of little home news,' saying among other things that Anna had been on a short visit to Chawton. Ben was to come over and meet his prospective grandmother-in-law, and Jane said this would be an excellent time to pay his visit, 'now that we, the formidables, are absent.' For Cassandra was in Henrietta Street. Henry's servant had given notice because he wanted a place in the country. When Jane first heard of his going, she was afraid Henry had been obliged to turn him off. Now she said: 'I am glad William's going is voluntary and on no worse grounds. An inclination for the country is a venial fault. He has more of Cowper than of Johnson in him, fonder of tame hares and blank verse than of the full tide of existence at Charing Cross.'

Sense and Sensibility had gone into a second edition. Mary, who had

174

been staying at Cheltenham, had heard it well spoken of there, and said that one of their acquaintance meant to buy it. Jane said: 'I wish she may . . . I cannot help hoping that *many* will find themselves obliged to buy it. I shall not mind imagining it a disagreeable duty to them, so as they do it.'

The autumn was darkening into winter, and the party at Godmersham was cleared of the visiting family and the gentlemen who had been staying there to shoot. Fanny, as the mistress of the house, was necessarily occupied some part of the day about its concerns. There was a great deal of time and peace in which to work upon *Mansfield Park*.

At noon of a November day Jane broke off her writing with the words: 'I did not mean to eat, but Mr. Johncock has brought in the tray, so I must—I am all alone. Edward has gone into his woods. At the present time, I have five tables, eight and twenty chairs and two fires all to myself.'

She had said of *Pride and Prejudice* that it was too light and bright and sparkling, that it wanted shade. Such a charge could never be brought against *Mansfield Park*. *Pride and Prejudice* and *Mansfield Park* stand to each other in something of the relation of *L'Allegro* and *Il Penseroso*; the spirit of beauty which informs each book is in one case that of lively, and the other, pensive pleasure.

When Henry Austen entitled the story of Catherine Morland *Northanger Abbey*, he was adopting a method his sister had already used; but *Mansfield Park*, on which she bestowed the name herself, is named with far greater justice than *Northanger Abbey*. *Mansfield Park* has not the powerful structure of the novels that immediately precede and follow it, but there is a unity imposed on its story by the fact that it takes place almost exclusively in the house and its immediate neighbourhood. Mansfield Park itself is the matrix of the story to an extent that could not be claimed for Northanger, or Pemberley, or Hartfield, or Kellynch. We have, it is true, Fanny's excursion to Portsmouth; an eventful day is spent at Sotherton; there is a description of Edmund's Thornton Lacey; Fanny's brother comes ashore; Sir Thomas Bertram returns from a voyage to Antigua, in the course of which he was nearly nabbed by a French privateer; but for the greater part of the book we are conscious of no life, in village or town or distant county, except what is within Mansfield Park itself, and the Parsonage at one side of its park, and the White House at another. In the seclusion of this green retreat, where some of the characters are fixed, and from and to which the others go and come, the heroine is, for the greater part of the book, immovably settled; as the lowest and the least, the fagger of errands

175

for Mrs. Norris and the tacker on of Lady Bertram's patterns, she has no gaieties to take her out, dances in neighbouring great houses, or public balls at Northampton, or extended rides, since when the others took them, her horse was wanted for Mary Crawford. Edmund's determined efforts for her pleasure took her as far as joining the expedition to Sotherton and dining one evening at the Parsonage. All she sees and hears, all she thinks and feels and suffers for the important part of the book, is experienced in the radius of the house with its great and lofty rooms, the park, with its scattered trees and closer wood, the rose garden, the shrubbery and the lane. It is this characteristic that gives the book something of a spell, a legend; the sensation of faery is heightened by the fact that the heroine is, morally speaking, in a beleaguered castle, surrounded with fear and grief and loneliness and despair; placed at a disadvantage with the worldly by the insignificance of her position, and with almost everybody else by her own nervousness, and still further handicapped by a passion which she believes to be hopeless, she makes the appeal of the heroine in distress. Her story has the psychological attraction of Cinderella's.

To be able to say so much of a novel invested with all Jane Austen's powers of realism, which contains, moreover, her strongest portrait of a truly hateful woman and her one contribution to the painting of squalid interiors, is to give some idea of the story's complex and subtle strength. Fanny Price wanders through forests and enchantments drear; she is also nagged by Mrs. Norris, and banished to her father's home, where her mother is perpetually whining about a torn carpet and the doors are slammed till her temples ache.

The character of Fanny is not of a kind to be generally popular, and yet there is, as Professor Bradley has pointed out, a select band of those who prefer *Mansfield Park* to *Pride and Prejudice*. The dissatisfaction which many people feel with her has perhaps been best explained by the suggestion of Lord David Cecil that Jane Austen has not exactly caught the likeness she meant to convey; and the people who like and are attracted by Fanny are those who can visualize the original from the somewhat imperfect portrait.

The difference between *Pride and Prejudice* and *Mansfield Park* is epitomized in the difference between their heroines. Fanny possesses just those qualities which make a person an object of interest and sympathy rather than an object of desire. Her misfortunes are so keen that were not her fortitude quite equal to them, she would be a downright nuisance.

But though a character like Fanny's, in a situation such as hers does not constitute a spontaneous attraction to the opposite sex, it has a very

176

XIII Watercolour portrait by Cassandra Austen of Fanny Knight, Edward's eldest daughter.

XIV and XV   In 1809, Cassandra and Jane Austen moved to Chawton in Hampshire, to a small house opposite the park of the Great House.   *Above:* Early eighteenth-century gouache of the Great House and park at Chawton.
Below: Oil painting of Chawton House and church, in 1809.

XVI Detail of a patchwork quilt made by Mrs Austen with the assistance of Jane and Cassandra Austen. Jane makes mention of this in her letters after their move to Chawton.

XVII Needlecase made by Jane Austen for her niece, Louisa.

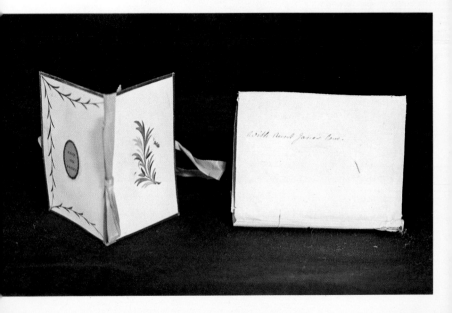

XVIII and XIX   Illustrations by Rowlandson and Pugin from Ackermann's *Microcosm of London*, published in 1809.   *Above:* Vauxhall Gardens.   *Above right:* The Queen's Palace in St James's Park.

xx *Below:* Wedgwood and Byerley's Warehouse in York Street, St James's Square, from *Repository of Arts*, 1800. In 1813, during a visit to Henry Austen at Henrietta Street, Jane Austen went to Wedgwoods with Edward Knight to choose a dinner service for Godmersham.

WEDGWOOD & BYERLEY,
York Street, St. James's Square.

MARIA

XXI Watercolour by Cassandra Austen of the heroine in Lawrence Sterne's novel, *Maria*.

XXII and XXIII Coloured engraving of Carlton House from W. H. Pyne's *The History of the Royal Residences*, 1819. *Above:* The Entrance Hall. *Below:* The Gothic Conservatory. In 1815, the Prince Regent, through his librarian, Rev. J. S. Clarke, invited Jane Austen to view the palace.

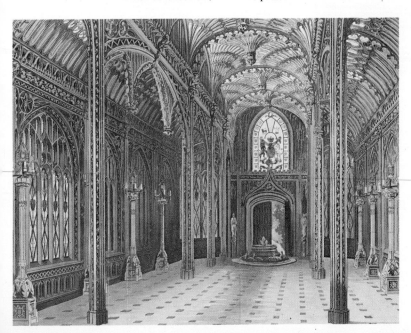

xxiv   The Old Wells and Pump Room at Cheltenham, which Jane Austen visited in May 1816 in the hope of improving her health. Engraving by H. Merke, 1813.

great charm, and one which may, given favourable circumstances, create that feeling of affection and confidence and comfort out of which sexual love can naturally develop. And there is no more exquisite example of perfect probability than the course of Edmund's love; his immediate infatuation for Mary Crawford, the manner in which he suffered from the abortive effects of two such disparate natures to join in a mutually acceptable scheme of life, the ready way in which he turned for sympathy to Fanny, with a confidence in her that had been built up in the past eight years of her life at Mansfield, and the inevitable effect upon his sore heart of her affection and sympathy and her unconsciously spoken admiration.

That he did very well for himself by falling in love with her, few people would deny. Her character had a sensibility and depth that is most attractive, though it is not of the kind that will necessarily, as Lady Susan put it, 'add a single lover to the list.' Much of her sensibility is shown in nervousness and alarm, but her love for Edmund is sometimes shown with the intensity of poetry.

Her passion for Edmund and the life-and-death importance of the struggle she made so that no one should suspect it are expressed at their highest pitch when she is leaving Mansfield for Portsmouth, and her feelings were in such a state that she 'could neither speak nor look nor think when the last moment came with *him*,' and she did not realize till it was over that he had kissed her good-bye.

The extreme sensitiveness and timidity of Fanny's nature are agreeably contrasted by the robustness, both physical and mental, of William Price. William's affection for Fanny, and his vigorous enjoyment of dancing, and the bold manner in which he addressed Sir Thomas despite his gratitude and respect, and the eagerness with which he accepted Henry's offer of a horse, without, as a sailor, understanding either the mettle of a highly-fed hunter or the value of the loan, the admirable manner in which he related his adventures at sea, his despair in thinking he would never be promoted, and the splendid figure he cut in his uniform when Admiral Crawford had procured him his commission—all these form a picture not only of great historical interest, and of great interest in the biography of Jane Austen, but one which, first and foremost, adds a most striking variety to the whole in which it is placed. The influence of William's presence is reflected by the various characters, and nowhere is the varying nature of such an influence better expressed than in the actual moment of his arrival at Mansfield. 'Fanny . . . found herself . . . watching in the hall, in the lobby, on the stairs, for the first sound of the carriage which was to bring her brother.

'It came happily while she was thus waiting; and there being neither ceremony nor fearfulness to delay the moment of meeting, she was with him as he entered the house, and the first minute of exquisite feeling had no interruption and no witnesses, unless the servants chiefly intent upon opening the proper doors could be called such. This was exactly what Sir Thomas and Edmund had been separately conniving at, as each proved to the other by the sympathetic alacrity with which they both advised Mrs. Norris's continuing where she was, instead of rushing out into the hall as soon as the noises of the arrival reached them.'

Another of those scenes, which most authors would treat from one aspect only, but which gain indescribably from being presented, as only Jane Austen does present them, with light converging upon them from a variety of angles, is the episode of Sir Thomas encountering the altogether unexpected resistance of Fanny to his desire that she should accept Henry Crawford's proposal. The scene occurs in the East Room, where Mrs. Norris long ago stipulated that Fanny should never have a fire. 'She was all attention . . . in placing a chair for him, and trying to appear honoured; and in her agitation had quite overlooked the deficiencies of her apartment, till he, stopping short as he entered, said, with much surprise : "Why have you no fire to-day?"

'There was snow on the ground and she was sitting in a shawl. She hesitated. "I am not cold, sir; I never sit here long at this time of year."

' "But you have a fire in general?"

' "No, sir." '

Sir Thomas is much annoyed at this evidence of Mrs. Norris's interference, whose existence he had never suspected; but the question is lost sight of in the interview that follows : in which Fanny reveals that unexpected strength concealed in a nature at once gentle and moral, and Sir Thomas, putting as well as it can be put, the case for considering the feelings of other people besides one's own on the question of a marriage, feels that she has behaved extremely badly and reads her a lecture that reduces her to hopeless crying. He leaves her in great displeasure, advising her to try to control herself by taking a walk in the shrubbery; 'she was struck, quite struck, when, on returning from her walk and going into the East Room again, the first thing which caught her eyes was a fire lighted and burning. A fire! it seemed too much; just at that time to be giving her such an indulgence was exciting even painful gratitude. She wondered that Sir Thomas could have leisure to think of such a trifle again; but she soon found, from the voluntary information of the housemaid, who came in to attend it, that so it was to be every day. Sir Thomas had given orders for it.'

178

In *Mansfield Park*, beauty and brilliance are not the adornments of virtue.

The two most fascinating characters of the book occupy what would be, in a novel less true to life, the positions of villain and villainess. The Crawfords are not villainous; but though each had 'the moral good taste' to appreciate the integrity of Edmund Bertram and Fanny Price, they were both by nature coarse-grained and unscrupulous. Fanny knew that it was so; when she suspected that Mr. Crawford had some share in the trick of the necklace, 'She could not be convinced that he had not, for Miss Crawford, complaisant as a sister, was careless as a woman and a friend.' Mary Crawford is amusing enough when she meets the Bertram brothers, and finding that she at first preferred Tom, she reflects: 'She had felt an early presentiment that she *should* like the eldest best. She knew it was her way.' But her letter to Fanny when she believes Tom on the point of death, and jokes about the possibility of Edmund's becoming Sir Edmund Bertram, is distasteful to a degree. So is her behaviour on her last interview with Edmund after the elopement of Maria and Henry. Her own attitude to adultery is much more that of the present day than Edmund's was; but that is beside the point. She knew—at least, she should have known —that Edmund was in very great distress, and she treated him without one impulse of sympathy, or even of common tact; and after their interview had become stormy and he had left her in disillusionment and grief, she put her head out of the door and called him back, with 'a saucy, playful smile.' The insensitiveness that could turn their delightful gaiety and humour into something horrible, like the grin of a mermaid over dead men's bones, is characteristic of both brother and sister. Henry shows his complete inability to understand Fanny Price until he set himself to do so, by the way in which he jokes about the desirability of adverse weather for Sir Thomas's homeward journey, and his suggestion that he and Fanny should come to the first service conducted by Edmund, that they might stare him out of countenance.

The best part of Mary's character is associated with her charm, her spontaneous good nature, her readiness in the interests of those she is fond of; and her liveliness and grace are particularly interesting to us, since we have the authority of the Austen family for believing that the character, in some respects, is modelled on that of Eliza de Feuillide. The idea is a delightful one, but even with such sanction, one must take care not to build too much upon it. In the first place, Henry Austen himself said that, contrary to what might have been supposed, his sister never copied from life, but only took suggestions from it. Eliza died in 1813, and the following year Jane performed the famous journey to

179

London with the widower, reading *Mansfield Park* aloud to him in the coach. When one considers that the judgement on Mary Crawford is on the whole markedly unfavourable, and that the best that even her lover can say for her is that she might have been very different had she not been ruined by bad training, one cannot imagine that Jane Austen would have read all this aloud to her favourite brother within a year of his wife's death, if he had supposed, or if she had conceived the possibility of his supposing, that Mary Crawford was intended for a picture of that wife. The point is perhaps worth elaborating, because it illustrates once more the sort of error those people are constantly falling into who attempt to find originals, rather than suggestions, for Jane Austen's characters among her family and friends.

The points of similarity between Eliza de Feuillide and Mary Crawford are that Eliza was said to have refused James Austen on the ground that he was a clergyman, and Mary expressed great dislike of Edmund's taking orders; that they were both very fond of private theatricals, and both 'somewhat small' but very lively and dashing; that Eliza was rather fonder of pleasure than some of the Austens liked, and Edmund very much regretted the frivolous tone of Mary's mind and manners.

The list of resemblances is a formidable one, and quite sufficient to justify the ordinary reader in thinking that Mary Crawford 'was' Eliza de Feuillide; yet if we examine the only one of the aspects common to both of which we have a knowledge in either—namely, their connection with theatricals—we see how very differently Mary and Eliza played their parts. Madame de Feuillide was, by common consent, the inspirer and organizer of the theatricals at Steventon. The plays chosen were those that she had seen; she took the principal female parts, and we may be convinced that real ability went to her direction of all the matters in hand. None of this was true of Mary Crawford. She is brought in by her brother as an 'under-strapper'; she accepts the post of the lively Amelia when it is found that Julia Bertram is not suited to it; she is alarmed at the nature of some of the speeches, and really uneasy until the part of Anhalt is cast and she may know to whom she is to say them. Lively and impudent as she is, her feelings for Edmund are such that she really shrinks from the awkwardness of proposing to him in the guise of Amelia and tries to harden herself by practising the scene on Fanny. One cannot imagine Eliza de Feuillide taking another girl aside and reading a scene with her until she could have the countenance to deliver it to a man. Private theatricals would never materialize if the people who got them up were affected with such interesting reluctance. Mary's embarrassment is of course chiefly caused by her extreme consciousness of Edmund; but

180

even before he had consented to take part, and she thought she was to be opposite to the unknown Mr. Madox, she was somewhat nervous, and said she should shorten a good many of his speeches and her own. There was something cooler, one fancies, in the original.

In spite of the gaiety of the character, we feel that it is a doomed one almost from the start; partly because we so often have to dislike the form taken by her wit, and because so often Mary is shown, in small ways, to be subtly in the wrong. The *coup de grâce* is administered to her, not at the end of the book, when her callousness has lost her the one man she truly cares about, but at a simple evening party in the course of which they sit down to cards. Mary secured William Price's knave 'at an exorbitant rate,' saying: ' "If I lose the game, it shall not be from not striving for it." The game was hers, and only did not pay her for what she had given to secure it.'

The poignant interest attaching to Mary Crawford arises from her capacity to appreciate, though she cannot imitate, a much better nature than her own; and it is precisely this touch of moral tragedy about her which makes one believe, independently of probability and of the evidence of Henry Austen himself, that Mary Crawford could never have been supposed to be an actual portrait of Eliza de Feuillide by people who were acquainted with the latter. What obviously suggested Eliza, beside the personal appearance, was the brilliant vivacity that seized upon the imagination of everybody whether they approved of it or not; the fact that when Mary Crawford was in the room, she was the central point of interest and animation, and that, in addition to her natural powers, she had the air of sophistication and fashion which made her seem as of another world in the eyes of her friends and relations in the country.

To say that it is the war of good and evil in Mary Crawford and her brother that invests them with their interest is to attempt a definition in black and white of what Jane Austen has accomplished in the infinitely subtle gradations of human character; but Henry Crawford, like his sister, is attracted by someone who, he feels, offers him a more solid chance of happiness than any woman of his own circle with whom he has previously been acquainted. It is another instance of Jane Austen's complete freedom from any romantic falsity that she explains the attraction Fanny Price has for Henry Crawford as she does. There have been many novels, of which *Jane Eyre* was perhaps the first, in which an insignificant heroine captivates a man against what are apparently great odds; but to Jane Austen's mind that was not the normal course of events, and she most carefully smoothes away the improbabilities inherent in the situation of a handsome, experienced and wealthy man's falling in love with a girl of very moderate attractions and who is almost always seen under a disadvantage before she allows that situation to arise.* The strongest weapon in the hand of the unconscious Fanny is her genuine indifference to Mr. Crawford's charms and her actual dislike of him as a man. Most men do not discover a charm in indifference and dislike, but the majority of men are not unusually attractive to women and accustomed to being run after by them from their earliest years. That such men do exist, however infrequently, and that they find a unique challenge in a woman's lack of response, had been amply demonstrated in those years immediately prior to the publication of *Mansfield Park*. Lord Byron's marriage proves once and for all that Jane Austen was correct in her view of the man, blasé with female attention, when he meets a woman who does not like him. The only intelligent action of Lady Caroline Lamb in her connection with him was her refusal, when they first met, to allow him to be introduced to her.

But the charm of Fanny's coldness is not allowed to operate on Henry Crawford until her beautiful cousins are out of the way, and he is left at Mansfield with no other female society beside his sister and Mrs. Grant. He had already been described as feeling the want of something to do, and he undertook to make Fanny fall in love with him merely as the diversion of an idle fortnight. It was her totally unexpected resistance which made him examine her with such attention, fancy that she was grown taller and see for the first time how beautiful her delicate complexion was. Once his attention was truly concentrated upon her, he was able to perceive the charm of her moral qualities, and 'that sweetness which makes so essential a part of every woman's worth in the judgement of man, that though he sometimes loves where it is not, he can never believe it absent.' When the time comes, we feel that it is perfectly natural that he should be able to see so much; but a less conscientious realist than Jane Austen would, to increase the heroine's triumph, have made him out as able to see it far too soon.

Another aspect of the honesty with which the emotional interest of *Mansfield Park* is handled lies in the author's candid admission that had Henry Crawford but refrained from entangling himself again

---

* See also Jane Austen's handling of Edmund's falling in love with Fanny: 'I purposely abstain from dates on this occasion, that every one may be at liberty to fix their own, aware that the cure of unconquerable passions, and the transfer of unchanging attachments, must vary very much as to time in different people.' Ch. 48.

with Mrs. Rushworth, he would certainly have overcome Fanny's resistance in the end. The marriage of Edmund and Mary, which was on the point of being brought about when Maria's elopement caused the general upheaval, would, Jane Austen says, have been of great assistance to Crawford, because it would have given Fanny the most urgent incentive to overcome her passion for her cousin; and with that obstacle removed, Crawford's assiduity and tact and his very great powers of pleasing would not have been permanently withstood by an inexperienced girl of eighteen. She had, in fact, begun to like him already.

Mrs. Norris is the most strongly disagreeable of all Jane Austen's creations, yet the character is a subtle one. She exhibited the very curious state of mind which made her go out of her way to get Fanny adopted by the Bertram family, and then watch with ferret-like eagerness to see that she was never treated as anything but an inferior dependant; the opportunity for her activities being provided by the passive, uncomplaining nature of Fanny, the sloth of Lady Bertram and the fact that Sir Thomas, dignified and aloof, knew very little of the domestic details of Mansfield. The reconciliation of two such different lines of conduct lies, of course, in Mrs. Norris's passion for gratifying her sense of power. She was moderately well off herself, but she could not bear to spend her own money, but only that of other people; 'nobody knew better how to dictate liberality to others.' ' "Well, and if they were *ten*," she cried, when Mr. Rushworth mentioned that Repton's terms were five guineas a day, "I am sure *you* need not regard it. The expense need not be any impediment. If I were you, I should not think of the expense. I would have everything done in the best style and made as nice as possible. For my own part, if I had anything within the fiftieth part of the size of Sotherton, I should be always planting and improving, for, naturally, I am excessively fond of it. It would be too ridiculous for me to attempt anything where I am now, with my little half-acre. It would be quite a burlesque." '

The avid anxiety to connect herself with the wealth and luxury of Mansfield Park and to behave almost as if she owned it, which is rendered possible by the torpor of Lady Bertram, is shown in small ways: she was in agony, on the evening of Sir Thomas's return, because 'It had left her nothing to do.' 'Would Sir Thomas have consented to eat, she might have gone to the housekeeper with troublesome directions, and insulted the footmen with injuctions of despatch; but Sir Thomas resolutely declined all dinner; he would take nothing, nothing till tea came—he would rather wait for tea. Still, Mrs. Norris was at intervals urging something different; and in the most interesting moment of his

183

passage to England, when the alarm of a French privateer was at the height she burst through his recital with the proposal of soup.'

Her anxiety that no one should infringe upon the prerogatives she has acquired for herself makes her resentful of Susan's arrival with Fanny when the latter returns from Portsmouth. 'She felt her as a spy, and an intruder, and an indigent niece, and everything most odious.' And her desire that no one but herself outside the immediate family of Mansfield should receive anything that might be going, as well as her eagerness to domineer, are shown with extraordinary imaginative power in the scene when she talks to Fanny when it has been decided that the latter shall accompany Edmund to the Grants' dinner-party.

Of the good side of her nature, which, however small, could not, in so convincing a portrait of a human being, be altogether absent, Jane Austen has indicated an aspect when she says that though Mrs. Price would have done as well in a situation of ease as Lady Bertram, Mrs. Norris would have made much better work of bringing up nine children on a small income. Another is her affection for the Bertram nephews and nieces. This is so inextricably mingled with her desire to associate herself with the family of Mansfield Park, and her base and selfish desire bears fruit in something so natural and good, the complexity gives the reader a sensation of uneasiness and pain. One does not despise her because, when catastrophe overwhelms the family, she is reduced to impotence; her appearance, stupefied by shock, is much more respectable than her practical and overbearing behaviour throughout the previous part of the book; and her blind championing of Maria, though it may be ascribed to a desire to vindicate herself, is something so nearly approaching what is lovable, that though everybody, including Jane Austen, is delighted to see the last of her, one feels as she makes her exit that here is something profounder than comedy, even in its deepest interpretation.

Mansfield Park contains more than any of the other novels of those fragments which we can recognize as of Jane Austen's own biography. There is the amber cross given by William to Fanny; the tradition that William Price's character, in its boldness, its love of dancing, and its brotherly affection, contained many elements of that of Charles Austen; the likeness of Mary Crawford to Madame de Feuillide which has already been touched upon; and the interest of a house-party in private theatricals.

Jane Austen's treatment of the episode of Lover's Vows is an illustration of how true her material is to the unvarying essence of human nature even where the medium in which it is presented has gone out of fashion. Edmund Bertram's principal objection to the Mansfield

184

theatricals—that there was something intrinsically improper in undertaking them at all—seems at first sight groundless not only by our standards, but by those of his own time.

The frankness of the present day and its lack of prejudice are much nearer to the spirit of the early nineteenth century than to that of the Victorian era. At the same time, the ideas regulating ordinary behaviour in country districts were altogether different from our own. It is true that in London, the Duchess of Devonshire, canvassing for Fox, beguiled votes from butchers and chimney-sweeps with kisses; that Lady Caroline Lamb visited Lord Byron's rooms at night dressed as a boy; that men emblazoned with stars and orders crammed into Harriet Wilson's modest opera box, while their duchesses bridled in haughty isolation on the opposite tiers. All this was a commonplace in the world of Mary Crawford. But when Mary came to Mansfield, she felt the difference with a vengeance. There, as in the remote country it still does, propriety ruled unchallenged; and interminable rehearsals with people, four of whom were very conscious though unacknowledged lovers, and two of whom were making love under the jealous and resentful eye of the man to whom the lady was engaged, provided something to which a well-bred man of conventional views such as Edmund Bertram might very reasonably object. Of more importance to the fundamental reality of the novel, the situation was one which, quite apart from any question of propriety, was bound to cause very strong feelings of excitement and unrest in the different characters.

With regard to the condemnation of the play, chiefly conveyed to us through Fanny's opinion of it, one is at first surprised at its being considered 'totally unfit' for home presentation. The language of Mrs. Inchbald's translation is so decorous that it is difficult at first sight to see why it should not have been pronounced by anybody; but such an opinion is the result of a failure in imagination. Mrs. Inchbald called her translation *Lover's Vows*, but Kotzebue had called the original *Das Liebes Kind*—in plain English, *The Bastard*. The sub-plot, which was to have been supported by Edmund and Mary, concerns the wooing by Baron Wildenheim's daughter of her tutor Anhalt, who loves her but feels it out of the question to say so; but the main theme concerns the rescue of Agatha by her illegitimate son, the latter's recognition by his father, Baron Wildenheim, and the Baron's belated reparation in marrying the waiting-maid he had seduced twenty years before. There is nothing in this of a startling character, and none of the Mansfield party, not Edmund, not even Fanny, would have objected to seeing *Lover's Vows* in the professional theatre. But Edmund put his finger on the genuine objection to the business when he drew the distinction between 'good, hardened acting' and the efforts of ladies and gentlemen. Anyone who has seen an amateur company attempt such a play as *Rain* before an audience of their fellow townsmen who punctuate the performance with loud guffaws in the wrong place, can realize at once the real force of Edmund Bertram's, or indeed Jane Austen's, objection to the party's choice of *Das Liebes Kind*. In the Mansfield production of the play Agatha and Frederick faded out of the picture: it was Maria Bertram who clasped Henry Crawford to her bosom and hailed him as her illegitimate son, and Mr. Yates who repented of having seduced her and offered to make the position good.

It is characteristic of Jane Aus.en that though she presents the theatricals in a wonderfully varied light, using the episode as a touchstone to bring out the essential attributes of every single person in any way connected with them, yet her final rounding-off of the situation is one of brilliant comedy. Sir Thomas, having arrived at Mansfield and exchanged greetings with his family, finds he cannot settle down to his first evening at home without having one look at his own dear room, and walks away to it before any one has time to warn him of the rehearsal his sudden appearance has broken off.

'Sir Thomas had been a good deal surprised to find candles burning in his room: and on casting his eye round it, to see other symptoms of recent habitation and a general air of confusion in the furniture. The removal of the bookcase from before the billiard-room door struck him especially, but he had scarcely more than time to feel astonished at all this before there were sounds from the billiard-room to astonish him still further. Someone was talking there in a very loud accent; he did not know the voice—*more* than talking—almost hallooing. He stepped to the door, rejoicing at the moment in having the means of immediate communication, and opening it, found himself on the stage of a theatre, and opposed to a ranting young man, who appeared likely to knock him down backwards. At the very moment of Yates perceiving Sir Thomas, and giving perhaps the very best start he had ever given in the whole course of his rehearsals, Tom Bertram entered at the other end of the room; and never had he found greater difficulty in keeping his countenance. His father's looks of solemnity and amazement on this, his first appearance on any stage, and the gradual metamorphosis of the impassioned Baron Wildenheim into the well-bred and easy Mr. Yates, making his bow and apology to Sir Thomas Bertram, was such an exhibition, such a piece of true acting as he would not have lost upon any account.'

The portion of the story which takes Fanny to her home in Portsmouth is Jane Austen's only excursion into the rough and sordid, but

186

is accomplished with such force as dispels the illusion that her range was restricted to the narrow circle of the well-to-do.

Mr. Price's squalid household is redeemed by the tang of sea air that sweeps through it, given to us with particular strength in the description of the Sunday walk the Prices, accompanied by Henry Crawford, take on the ramparts.

'The day was uncommonly lovely. It was really March; but it was April in its mild air, brisk soft wind, and bright sun, occasionally clouded for a minute; and everything looked so beautiful under the influence of such a sky; the effects of the shadows pursuing each other on the ships at Spithead and the island beyond, with the ever-varying hues of the sea, now at high water, dancing in its glee and dashing against the ramparts with so fine a sound, produced altogether such a combination of charms for Fanny, as made her gradually almost careless of the circumstances under which she felt them.'

But it is within the house that Jane Austen exhibits her capacity for a realism which reminds one of the French school.

'She was deep in other musing. The remembrance of her first evening in that room, of her father and his newspaper, came across her. No candle was *now* wanted. The sun was yet an hour and a half above the horizon. She felt that she had indeed been three months there; and the sun's rays falling strongly into the parlour, instead of cheering, made her still more melancholy, for sunshine appeared to her a totally different thing in a town and in the country. Here, its power was only a glare; a stifling, sickly glare, serving but to bring forward stains and dirt that might otherwise have slept. There was neither health nor gaiety in sunshine in a town. She sat in a blaze of oppressive heat, in a cloud of moving dust, and her eyes could only wander from the walls, marked by her father's head, to the table cut and notched by her brothers, where stood the tea-board never thoroughly cleaned, the cups and saucers wiped in streaks, the milk a mixture of motes floating in thin blue, and the bread and butter growing every minute more greasy than even Rebecca's hands had first produced it. Her father read his newspaper, and her mother lamented over the ragged carpet as usual, while the tea was in preparation, and wished Rebecca would mend it.'

The Price family was drawn with a vigour which is the more arresting when one compares it with the delicate and sensitive nature of Fanny and the calm elegance and good breeding of the Bertram party.

The children, with the exception of Fanny, are conceived on a robuster scale than any other in Jane Austen's work. There is William, 'with spirits, curiosity and courage up to anything,' at home equally in the elegance and comfort of Mansfield and the rough disorder of the house at Portsmouth; eagerly entering into his father's conversation about the ships and not forgetting an attempt to recommend Fanny to his indifferent kindness; 'imposing on her as fast as he could' at speculation, bringing her home an amber cross, and, when got ready by the united exertions of the household, coming down to show himself to her in his lieutenant's uniform, and looking so proud and touching in it that she burst into tears as she kissed him. More vigorous still are the midshipman Sam and the schoolboys Charles and Tom. 'The only interruption which thoughts like these received for nearly half an hour was from a sudden burst of her father's, not at all calculated to compose them. At a more than ordinary pitch of thumping and hallooing in the passage, he exclaimed: "Devil take those young dogs! How they are singing out! Aye, Sam's voice louder than all the rest! That boy is fit for a boatswain. Holloa, you there! Sam, stop your confounded pipe, or I shall be after you."

'This threat was so palpably disregarded, that though within five minutes afterwards the three boys all burst into the room together and sat down, Fanny could not consider it as a proof of anything more than their being for the time thoroughly fagged, which their hot faces and panting breaths seemed to prove, especially as they were still kicking each other's shins, and hallooing out at sudden starts immediately under their father's eye.'

Mansfield Park not only presents extreme opposites in character-drawing, and demonstrates a range of imaginative experience in Jane Austen which might otherwise have remained unsuspected; it also contains two statements which have a bearing of the first importance upon her art.

They constitute, in fact a paradox; when she rounds off the elopement of Maria and Henry Crawford with the sentence: 'Let other pens dwell on guilt and misery. I quit such odious subjects as soon as I can,' she gives the impression, or she would give it, were the sentence divorced from its context, that she had no interest in anything but tranquillity and joy; but she has actually given the whole emotional history of Maria's elopement; not, it is true, in the persons of the principal characters; she has shown it all in the demoralization of Mrs. Norris, the self-condemning wretchedness of Sir Thomas, the horror and anguish of Edmund and Fanny, and in the fact that the shock was such it had actually turned Lady Bertram from a slug into a human being. 'By one of the suffering party within, they were expected with such impatience as she had never known before. Fanny had scarcely passed the solemn-looking servants, when Lady Bertram came from the drawing-room to meet her; came with no indolent step; and falling on her neck, said: "Dear Fanny! Now I shall be comfortable!"' It is impossible to read *Mansfield Park* and feel that the episode of Maria Rushworth's adultery has been slighted; on the contrary, it constitutes so ugly a wound in the texture of the story one's only feeling is whether too much emotional significance has not, after all, been attached to it.

The other passage which has a great and as it were a technical interest, is her audacious sweeping aside of what might be supposed to be the novelist's duty—that of dealing at full length with the emotional climax of the novel.

When Edmund has confessed his love to Fanny and asked for hers in return, and been told that he has possessed it long since, the author says: 'It must have been a delightful happiness. But there was happiness elsewhere which no description can reach. Let no one presume to give the feelings of a young woman on receiving the assurance of that affection of which she has scarcely allowed herself to entertain a hope.'

Even Jane Austen's epigrams, torn from the strong and delicate weaving of their context, lose something of their lively sheen; but this passage, unless it be read exactly where it was intended to be read, is almost meaningless. But the reader who has enjoyed *Mansfield Park* knows when he has come to that paragraph that it says all that need be said, and all that, without anti-climax, *can* be said. The story which has grown in slow intensity from the moment at which Edmund, in his holidays from Eton, finds Fanny, a child of ten, crying on the attic stairs, unable to write to William because she has no paper, to the point at which he comes to fetch her from Portsmouth, looking so ill that to see him once more, and in such trouble, absolutely takes away her power of speech, and she feels almost ready to faint, has become so deeply charged with Fanny's emotion, that even if Jane Austen could have described her happiness, she could have told us nothing we did not know already; the cup is so full, it could hold no more.

189

CHAPTER SIXTEEN

In the January of 1814 Jane Austen began her new novel, with the heroine whom no one but herself was expected to like very much; but her absorption in the work did not diminish her interest in the one just completed. In March there was another visit to Henry; he and Jane journeyed together from Godmersham to Henrietta Street, and on the way Jane read *Mansfield Park* aloud to him. Henry was delighted; so far as they read in the carriage, Jane said 'His approbation is equal even to my wishes.' He said it was very different from *Sense and Sensibility* and *Pride and Prejudice*, but he thought it, in its own way, quite as good. When they got to town he took the manuscript into his own hands; he admired Henry Crawford very much; by the time he reached the third volume he was saying he liked it better and better; nor did his enthusiasm fall off; the last half of the third volume he found particularly interesting. His appreciation filled his sister with delight; now that her feelings on this very important point were set at rest, nothing remained but to enjoy the visit.

Fanny was with them; she slept with her aunt as before, and when Jane wrote to Cassandra before breakfast, she said: 'Fanny, I left asleep.—She was doing about last night when *I* went to sleep a little after one.' They went to the theatre, this time to see Kean as Shylock. Jane thought the *Merchant of Venice* a good play to take Fanny to, because there was nothing in it, over which she could get too much wrought up. Kean's performance Jane thought quite wonderful. 'It appeared to me as if there were no fault in him anywhere, and in his scene with Tubal there was exquisite acting.'

She had a lilac sarcenet gown—that colour most becoming to the dark-haired—and an ermine tippet in which they told her she looked extremely well. In the house she took a delicate and tactful interest in the housekeeping. She spoke to Madame Perigord about making Henry a boiled pudding, and then it came out that Henry had no raspberry jam. Madame Perigord had some herself, 'which,' said Jane, 'of course she is determined he shall have'; but could not Cassandra bring up a pot from Chawton on her forthcoming visit?

While Henry had been occupied with *Mansfield Park*, Jane had been reading *The Heroine*. This novel by Eaton Stannard Barret was a skit, written eleven years after the composition of *Northanger Abbey*, upon Radcliffian romance; the heroine, Cherry, who alters her name to

Cherubina, is positive that she cannot indeed be the daughter of Farmer Wilkinson, and that the latter must have abducted her in childhood and concealed her true parentage from her. ' "Were even my legitimacy suspected," she exclaims, "it would be a comfort, since in that case I should assuredly start forth . . . the daughter of a nobleman who lives retired and occasionally slaps his forehead." ' As it was, she felt that no explanation covered her circumstances except the theory of her abduction by Farmer Wilkinson.

The adventures of Cherubina, who set off with a band-box under her arm, containing a satin petticoat, a pair of satin slippers and her spangled muslin dress, form at almost every point a burlesque upon Mrs. Radcliffe's most popular characteristics; when she tries to discontent the rustic Mary with her way of life; and persuade her to become a heroine also, she says: ' "And then, Mary, though your own cottage is tolerable, is it, as in Italy, covered with vine leaves, fig trees, jessamine, and clusters of grapes? Is it tufted with myrtle, or shaded with a grove of lemon, orange or bergamot?"

' "But ma'am," said Mary, "it is shaded with some fine old elms."

' "True," cried I, "but are the flowers of the *agnus castus* there?" '

The Gothic portion of the tale is concerned with the heroine and her henchman, Jerry, taking possession of a ruined castle that stood in the grounds of somebody else's estate, and setting up an establishment among bats, cobwebs and dirt.

Jane Austen said it was 'a delightful burlesque, particularly on the Radcliffe style.' On the evening of her arrival in town she wrote to Cassandra: 'We have drank tea and I have torn through the third volume of the *Heroine*. I do not think it falls off.' It was an astonishing tribute to Mrs. Radcliffe that nearly twenty years after the publication of *Udolpho*, so clever a young man as Eaton Stannard Barret should choose to devote a full-length novel to the burlesque of her style, and that his work should be intelligible to the reading public of 1814 when he had done so. Crabbe also, in his *Tales of the Borough* of 1810, draws a contrast between the sordid hideousness of Ellen Orford's woes and the fantastic ones of the heroines in novels, and describes the latter in the vein of Mrs. Radcliffe's school. He said he had often marvelled at the vicissitudes of such ladies,

> *Who hemmed with bands of sturdiest rogues about*
> *Find some strange succours, and come, virgins, out.*

The topic had already been treated, but it was characteristic of Jane Austen that, even in writing to Cassandra, her praise of the *Heroine*

191

was not followed by any reference to the entombed *Northanger Abbey*.

In May, Egerton brought out *Mansfield Park*. Mrs. Austen's cousin, the Reverend Samuel Cooke, the Rector of Bookham, who was Jane's godfather, thought the novel the most sensible he had ever read. Cassandra preferred it to *Pride and Prejudice*; Mrs. Austen did not like it so well; a Mrs. B. was 'much pleased with it, particularly with the character of Fanny,' and 'thought Lady Bertram like herself'; but what is perhaps the most striking expression of opinion ever uttered on Jane Austen's works came from Mrs. B's daughter-in-law, Mrs. Augusta B, who 'owned that she thought S. and S. and P. and P. downright nonsense, but expected to like M.P. better, and having finished the first volume, flattered herself she had got through the worst.' Jane wrote it all down most carefully; there is no indication of what the public thought, except that the first edition of *Mansfield Park* was sold out by the autumn.

In June she paid a long-promised visit to the Cookes. The village of Bookham, in Surrey, is within easy distance of Leith Hill, and the fact that 1814 was the year of *Emma's* composition adds particular interest to the fact that there is a Randalls Road on the outskirts of Leatherhead, and in Leatherhead Church a memento that in 1761 a Mr. Knightley earned the thanks of the parish by remodelling the pulpit and reading-desk at his own expense. Jane gave Anna high credit for thinking of so good a name as Newton Priors,* and when she herself came upon two such plain, well-sounding words as Randalls and Knightley she caught them up at once. To attempt to identify Hartfield with a particular village in Surrey because it was near Leith Hill, and because the names of Randalls and Knightley are to be found in Leatherhead, seems as misguided and unprofitable as to try to establish an actual person as the original of one of her characters. She would have been at a loss what to say to someone who asked her to identify that particular village with its draper's shop and its baker's with the little bow window, its brick houses, sash windows below and casements above, with any one actual village in Surrey.

People who would like to deduce from Jane Austen's novels the story of her life are apt to be nonplussed when they consider those novels in their chronological order. There is of course ample reason for saying that in *Persuasion* she showed signs of a new method, and of a new sensibility; it forms, they feel, that fitting close towards which the trend of her development had set, and had she not been untimely lost, it might have been, not the close, but the new beginning. This idea that her attitude to life was undergoing a radical alteration, that

* Letters 100 and 106.

192

the pointed brilliancy of youth was maturing gradually into the profounder, more tranquil vision of middle age, would receive much greater stimulus were the order of her novels other than it is. Could we suppose that she declined from the unclouded radiance of *Pride and Prejudice* and *Emma*, through the shadowed loveliness of *Mansfield Park* to the autumnal beauty of *Persuasion*, we should have a line of development so clear and so suggestive that it might not be beyond the bounds of common sense to build some theory upon it. But Jane Austen's achievement was not one to be explained by reference to a biography. We cannot say of her that her brilliant work was conceived before the tragedy of 1802, and that what was created after that shows the unmistakable influence of grief; because actually the novels run in the very disconcerting order of: *Mansfield Park, Emma, Persuasion*, and that glittering fragment, *Sanditon*.

Emma has been described as Jane Austen's most finished comedy. One imagines that few of her admirers have the affection for it which they entertain for *Pride and Prejudice*; the author gave warning that she was about to choose a heroine whom nobody but herself would like very much, and if she thereby under-rated Emma's claims, scarcely anyone would maintain that Emma is as charming as Elizabeth Bennet. Nevertheless the books have more of an affinity with each other than either has with *Mansfield Park* or *Persuasion*. The strong gold light, as of early midsummer, that illumines every corner of that world composed of a Surrey village and a couple of country seats, within a morning's drive of Box Hill, is even more cordial and revealing than in *Pride and Prejudice*. Emma has not the heavenly air of Elizabeth Bennet, nor has Mr. Knightley hidden qualities like those of Mr. Darcy; he kept his affections to himself, it is true, but no one meeting him, in any circumstances, could have formed an idea of him as mistaken as those to which Mr. Darcy's behaviour gave rise. The one character who is invested with a secret is not a frail creature such as Fanny Price, 'indomitable in her feebleness,' but a sophisticated young woman, unfortunate, but quite capable of taking care of herself; and the mystery, when it is brought to light, is, though interesting, on a smaller and more homely scale than the real badness of Wickham. Considering that the whole of a highly complicated plot turns on mystification and misunderstanding, it is extraordinary that the atmosphere of the book should be so brilliant and serene; when Emma said she loved things to be 'decided and open' she seems, by a remarkable paradox, to have dictated the tenor of the book that bears her name.

The structure of Emma not only exemplifies Jane Austen's own peculiar method of showing each character in relation to all the rest;

193

it suggests that of a Chinese ivory ball, and has an intricacy no less complicated and distinct.

The heroine in her wrong-headed folly spins six separate interlacing, circles of delusion. On this highly formalized base the characters move to and fro with a naturalness that defies description. In no other of her books do we so luxuriate in our ability to listen and to look. The triumph of *Emma* in a general sense is perhaps that although the plot is intricate and formal in so striking a degree, yet every phase of it springs inevitably from the characters of those concerned. Emma's own misapplied quickness and her self-conferred right to interfere with other people's concerns are of course the mainspring of the story; but it could not proceed as it does without the foolish ductility of Harriet Smith, the coarseness and conceit of Mr. Elton, the calm good nature of Mr. Knightley, the mercurial character and undignified lack of scruple of Frank Churchill, the poise of Jane Fairfax that even wretchedness cannot defeat.

Newspaper-writers sometimes describe an idea of female weakness and timidity as reminiscent of 'one of Jane Austen's young ladies.' Could they be supposed to have read Jane Austen's works, they might conceivably be thought to have Fanny Price in mind. In none other of the five heroines can one discover an explanation of this strange abuse of language, and Emma Woodhouse, with her forwardness and over-bearing insensibility, is almost too strong for the modern stomach. She is the only one of Jane Austen's heroines who suffers from the limita-tions of her time; her troubles arose from her having a great deal of health and vigour and nothing at all to do.

With all her intelligence, Emma was not capable of finding enough occupation for herself to keep her rational; she had never taken the trouble to practise sufficiently, and though she could never have played as well as Jane Fairfax, she had the honesty to be ashamed, considering her talents, of not playing better than she did. With her drawing it was the same thing. She was always meaning to read a great deal, and often drew up lists of books, but the resolve never came to anything; as Mr. Knightley said: '"I have done with expecting any course of steady reading from Emma. She will never submit to anything requiring in-dustry and patience, and a subjection of the fancy to the understand-ing."' Her abounding energy, for which she had no proper outlet, made her throw herself with undue eagerness and interest into the amuse-ment of influencing other people's lives. The attitude is a tiresome one at best; but when it concerns the love affairs of others it is something worse. Mr. Knightley accused Emma of indelicacy; we should frame

194

the criticism in another manner, but in the substance of what he said we should agree exactly.

Indeed, Emma's conduct with regard to Harriet Smith was not only most severely condemned in the result, by which Harriet, having been talked into love with Mr. Elton, has perforce to be very wretched when the mistake is discovered, but is repellant to the normal mind from the beginning. To give a friend's affairs a helpful push in the right direction is one thing; but to decide upon a match and endeavour to bring it about as if the two people concerned were merely clay in the hands of a superior being, is highly distasteful, and not any the less so because Emma was in fact cleverer, richer and better born than any of her neighbours in Highbury. In that readiness to acknowledge her own faults which is one of her most sympathetic characteristics, she owned the wrongness of what she had been doing. 'It was assuming too much, making light of what ought to be serious,—a trick of what ought to be simple.' It is her capacity to recognize her faults and to try to cure them that is responsible for most of our warmth of feeling towards Emma. Elizabeth Bennet is mistaken and repents, but the process in her is a much more spontaneous one. Emma had committed herself to a course of arrogant meddling implying so much that is disagreeable in the nature that indulges in it, that it is the sign of a really honest and courageous character that she can shake off her weakness as she does, and that once she has seen her conduct in its true colours, she makes no attempt whatever at self-justification.

'When it came to such a pitch as this, she was not able to refrain from a start or a heavy sigh, or even from walking about the room for a few seconds: and the only source whence anything like consolation, or composure, could be drawn, was in the resolution of her own better conduct, and the hope that, however inferior in spirit and gaiety might be the following and every future winter of her life to the past, it would yet find her more rational, more acquainted with herself, and leave her less to regret when it were gone.'

The mood of the day that culminated in this misery is enhanced by one of Jane Austen's most emotional passages of natural description. 'The evening of this day was very long and melancholy at Hartfield. The weather added what it could of gloom. A cold stormy rain set in, and nothing of July appeared but in the trees and shrubs, which the wind was despoiling, and the length of the day, which only made such cruel sights the longer visible.' Even more emotional is the passage which immediately follows this one in the next chapter. Emma has come out into the garden, from which, though she is as far as possible from knowing it, she will return engaged to Mr. Knightley.

'The weather continued much the same all the following morning; and the same loneliness and the same melancholy seemed to reign at Hartfield, but in the afternoon it cleared; the wind changed into a softer quarter; the clouds were carried off; the sun appeared, it was summer again. With all the eagerness which such a transition gives, Emma resolved to be out of doors as soon as possible. Never had the exquisite sight, smell, sensation of nature, tranquil, warm and brilliant after a storm, been more attractive to her.'

The episode of Mr. Knightley's strawberry party contains a picture of landscape, full of that character which Jane Austen recognized and loved as truly English, though she had never been outside of England. Mrs. Elton's conversation has driven the usually serene Jane Fairfax to ask Mr. Knightley to show them the whole extent of the grounds, and the party accordingly begin to walk.

'It was hot . . . they insensibly followed one another to the delicious shade of a broad, short avenue of limes, which, stretching beyond the garden at an equal distance from the river, seemed the finish of the pleasure grounds. . . . It was a charming walk, and the view which closed it was extremely pretty. The considerable slopes, at nearly the foot of which the Abbey stood, gradually acquired a steeper form beyond its grounds; and at half a mile distant was a bank of considerable abruptness and grandeur, well-clothed with wood; and at the bottom of this bank, favourably placed and sheltered, rose the Abbey Mill Farm, with meadows in front, and the river making a close and handsome circle around it.

'It was a sweet view—sweet to the eye and the mind. English verdure, English culture, English comfort, seen under a sun bright without being oppressive.' Jane Austen herself seems to have been so much penetrated by the fairness she was describing, and her mind so full of all the lovely prospects she had ever seen, that she made in this passage what is perhaps her one and only mistake on a question of detail. She goes on to describe the surroundings of the farm as 'rich pastures, spreading flocks, orchards in blossom and light columns of smoke ascending.' When the master of Godmersham had come to this point in his sister's work, he said: 'I should like to know, Jane, where you get those apple trees of yours that blossom in July?'

Another passage of the novel which recalls the background of the Austen family is the pastime of Harriet Smith in making up an album of charades. A collection exists of charades made by Mr. Austen, Cassandra, James and Jane herself; one of her contributions was upon a bank note.

196

You may lie on my first by the side of a stream,
And my second compose to the nymph you adore,
But if, when you've none of my whole, her esteem
And affection diminish, think of her no more.

The episode of the charade submitted by Mr. Elton, which Emma applies to Harriet though it is really intended for herself, offers another instance of the complex yet clear and brilliant structure so characteristic of the book. It takes her barely a moment to resolve the word into 'courtship' 'while Harriet was puzzling over the paper in all the confusion of hope and dullness.'

Thy ready wit the word will soon supply,
May its approval beam in that soft eye!

and Emma admits that 'soft' is the justest epithet that could be given to Harriet's eye. The previous line is less strikingly apposite.
' "Harriet's ready wit! All the better. A man must be very much in love, indeed, to describe her so." ' And when Harriet is prevented by a sore throat from coming to the party at Randalls, and Mr. Elton has not availed himself of the opportunity of staying at home that Emma has held out to him, she reflects: ' "What a strange thing love is! He can see ready wit in Harriet, but he will not dine alone for her." ' When the fearful truth of the real nature of Mr. Elton's attachment has burst upon her on the drive home, and she is at last alone in her bedroom in the turmoil of mind the discovery has produced, she goes over all the incidents of Mr. Elton's behaviour which she had thought at the time to be a sign of his devotion to Harriet. ' "To be sure, the charade, with its 'ready wit'—but then, the 'soft eyes'—in fact it suited neither; it was a jumble without taste or truth. Who could have seen through such thick-headed nonsense?" '
The description of Mrs. Goddard's school, from whence Emma selected the lovely, stupid Harriet to be her chosen friend and companion, has frequently been compared with the Abbey School at Reading, as described by Mrs. Sherwood. The excellent, good-hearted, non-academic Mrs. Goddard does, in her attitude towards the business of female education, suggest that of Mrs. Latournelle. 'Mrs. Goddard was the mistress of a school—not of a seminary, or an establishment, or anything which professed in long sentences of refined nonsense, to combine liberal acquirements with elegant morality, upon new principles, and new systems—and where young ladies for enormous pay might be screwed out of health and into vanity,—but a real, honest,

old-fashioned boarding-school . . . where girls might be sent to be out of the way, and scramble themselves into a little education, without any danger of coming back prodigies . . . she had an ample house and garden, gave the children plenty of wholesome food, let them run about a great deal in the summer, and in winter dressed their chilblains with her own hands.' One recollects Mrs. Sherwood's account of the Abbey School's very elastic time-table; of the long summer evenings spent in wandering under the trees of the garden; and when Jane Austen speaks of Mrs. Goddard's 'leaving her neat parlour, hung round with fancy-work' to spend the evening by Mr. Woodhouse's fireside, one remembers that Mrs. Latournelle's parlour was decorated with weeping willows and tombstones embroidered in chenille. But the difference between the plain and sensible Mrs. Goddard, and old Mrs. Latournelle with her passion for anecdotes of theatrical life, is as fundamental as that between the Highbury boarding-school, whence its twenty young couples walked to church every Sunday, and that truly romantic establishment, formed partially of an abbey gate-house, in whose turrets the girls might sit gossiping and dreaming as long as they pleased. The Abbey School would not have done for Highbury, and old Mrs. Latournelle would have startled Mr. Woodhouse.

The aspect of *Emma* which is disagreeable to the modern reader is its dwelling upon distinctions of class in so bold and uncompromising a manner. This element has an importance in the historical aspect of Jane Austen's work. Her work as a whole is of so diamond-like a quality in the immutability of its value, that this is perhaps its only aspect of temporal importance—namely, the rise and self-conscious development of the middle class; to us it is painful. Most of this trouble is of course centred in Emma herself; a great deal of the book is quite untainted by it. Mr. Knightley, for example, is entirely free from it. Again, the character of Mrs. Elton, which occupies, with that of Mr. Woodhouse and Miss Bates, the most important position in the novel's comic relief, owes nothing to a scale of social values in the author's mind. Mrs. Elton is extremely funny in her conviction that Miss Augusta Hawkins had held such a place in society as Mrs. Elton only could surpass; her self-complacent assumption of social equality with Miss Woodhouse, and the patronizing good nature she showed Jane Fairfax because the latter, though infinitely more educated, elegant and better bred than Mrs. Elton, was, at the same time, in much narrower circumstances, do depend for a great deal of their comedy on the conditions of the then-existing social structure; but the character of Mrs. Elton, like that of Mr. Collins, is one fundamentally suited to the purposes of comedy. In any society, Mrs. Elton would have been delightfully intolerable. If self-consequence and meanness, a total lack of humility, perception and real goodness of heart, cannot show themselves in one sort of behaviour, they will in another. Such qualities are like the damp in a house's structure, that walks along the fabric until it finds a weakened spot, then shows itself upon the ceiling. A society in which there are no well-born heiresses to be insulted by the bumptious familiarity of a social climber, will still recognize the essential truth of Mrs. Elton's character.

Nevertheless, it is difficult not to be disgusted with Emma for the ruthless way in which she detached Harriet from her friends, Robert Martin's sisters, who had been at school with her: and disgust is the one impression that a heroine ought not to provoke. Nor is it possible to deny that this episode would have seemed less horrible in 1815 than it does to-day. At the same time, though one cannot think that Jane Austen would have been shocked, in the same manner that we are by Emma's handling of the Miss Martins, yet the drawing of these young women, in their simple, dignified reception of truly disgraceful treatment, and the extent to which poor Harriet suffered from being obliged through her blind admiration and affection for Emma, to throw them off, make it plain enough that Emma's conduct is condemned.

'A bad business,' indeed, but though Emma is proved to be, and comes to realize herself mistaken in her attitude, the book strikes an uncongenial note, because that sort of mistake, and that particular attitude, are, to our minds, absolutely repellent. Emma is the only heroine of whom we can say that her mistakes are those to which she was rendered liable by her time, rather than by the common failings of humanity.

At the same time, one of the charms of the book is that of her conversations with Mr. Knightley, not only of dramatic interest because they display so clearly the character of each, but because, though somewhat better expressed, they are those that we hear among intelligent men and women of to-day; in particular that to which the proposal of Robert Martin and Harriet's refusal of it under Emma's influence gave rise.

" '. . . She is a greater simpleton than I ever believed her. What is the foolish girl about?"

' "Oh, to be sure," cried Emma, "it is always incomprehensible to a man, that woman should ever refuse an offer of marriage. A man always imagines a woman to be ready for anybody who asks her."

' "Nonsense! A man does not imagine any such thing." '

Emma continues:

199

' "Supposing her to be, as you describe her, only pretty and good-natured, let me tell you, that in the degree she possesses them, they are not trivial recommendations to the world in general, for she is, in fact, a beautiful girl, and must be thought so by ninety-nine people out of an hundred; and till it appears that men are much more philosophic on the subject of beauty than they are generally supposed, till they do fall in love with well-informed minds instead of handsome faces, a girl, with such loveliness as Harriet, has a certainty of being admired and sought after, of having the power of choosing from among many, consequently a claim to be nice. Her good-nature, too, is not so very slight a claim, comprehending as it does, real thorough sweetness of temper and manner, a very humble opinion of herself, and a great readiness to be pleased with other people. I am very much mistaken if your sex in general would not think such beauty and such temper the highest claims a woman could possess."

' "Upon my word, Emma, to hear you abusing the reason you have, is enough to make me think so, too. Better be without sense, than misapply it as you do."

' "To be sure," cried she playfully. "I know *that* is the feeling of you all. I know that such a girl as Harriet is exactly what every man delights in—what at once bewitches his senses and satisfies his judgement." ...

' "I have always thought this a very foolish intimacy," said Mr. Knightley presently, "though I have kept my thoughts to myself; but I now perceive that it will be a very unfortunate one for Harriet." '

To-day there are numerous openings for women, and to many of these, marriage is even a hindrance; but this has not altered the desire of most women to be attractive to men; when the topic of what makes them so is under discussion, the substance of this argument comes home with a force that time has not diminished.

Mr. Knightley, although Lord Brabourne did not like him, is thought by some to be the most satisfactory of Jane Austen's heroes. For one thing: though he is presented to us through the eyes of women, he is drawn in a more detached manner than Darcy, Edmund Bertram or Captain Wentworth. We see the qualities of those men as they appear to women's resentment or gratitude or admiration, but it is difficult to imagine with what difference Mr. Knightley would appear to a man. He is calm, good-natured, honest, and has the dignity of a human being who has an essentially reasonable standard of values. His powers of judgement are as sound as Emma's are weak. He told her from the beginning that she was mistaken in thinking she would be able to influence Mr. Elton's destiny, in spite of Mr. Elton's excessive amiability and his anxiety to ingratiate himself at Hartfield. He pointed out, what no one else apparently was able to see, that there could be no satisfactory reason for Frank Churchill's delaying his visit to Randalls on his father's second marriage. ' "There is one thing, Emma, which a man can always do if he chooses, and that is, his duty." ' He also warned Emma that she might not quite understand the degree of intimacy between Jane Fairfax and Frank Churchill, and was laughed to scorn for his pains. He never relaxed his logical and forthright manner of speech, and yet even Mrs. Elton was not offended by it; his protective kindness to Miss Bates and Jane Fairfax was such that Emma supposed at one time he might be in love with the latter; but his behaviour was inspired by nothing more interesting than goodness of heart and the quickness of a practical man in putting his impulse of kindness into action. He is also excellent in his relations with other men. Mr. Elton liked him, and that, considering how Mr. Elton must have appeared to him, was much in his favour. Mr. Woodhouse liked and depended on him, although Mr. Knightley never pandered to Mr. Woodhouse's idiosyncrasies. Mr. Weston and Mr. Cole both liked and respected him; so did Robert Martin, while William Larkins had for him that irascible and proprietary fondness that is a tribute equally to servant and master.

The only person to whom, unsatisfactory as he is, Mr. Knightley appears to do less than justice, is Frank Churchill, and it is in connection with the latter that Mr. Knightley's very endearing weakness is made known. His otherwise concealed love for Emma is perhaps first genuinely apparent to the reader in the ball at the Crown, when Emma says she will dance with him, if he likes, adding: ' "You know, we are not really so much brother and sister as to make it at all improper" ', to which he replies: ' "Brother and sister!—no, indeed!" ' But the first manifestation of his jealousy of Frank Churchill comes at a time when it cannot be recognized for what it is.

' "I will say no more about him," cried Emma—"you turn everything to evil. We are both prejudiced! you against, I for him; and we have no chance of agreeing till he is really here."

' "Prejudiced! I am not prejudiced!"

' "But I am very much, and without being at all ashamed of it. My love for Mr. and Mrs. Weston gives me a decided prejudice in his favour."

' "He is a person I never think of from one month's end to another," said Mr. Knightley with a degree of vexation, which made Emma immediately talk of something else, though she could not comprehend why he should be angry.'

The mainspring of his attitude to Frank Churchill is described in the paragraph which concludes the chapter in which he proposes to Emma in the garden after the storm.

'He had found her agitated and low. Frank Churchill was a villain. He heard her declare that she had never loved him. Frank Churchill's character was not desperate. She was his own Emma, by hand and word, when they returned into the house; and if he could have thought of Frank Churchill then, he might have deemed him a very good sort of fellow.'

Frank Churchill's secret engagement to Jane Fairfax is another of those episodes on which opinion to-day would be essentially the same as that of 1815, though the criticism would be couched in different terms. No one now supposes that any blame attaches to a secret engagement or to corresponding with a person of the opposite sex to whom an engagement has not been publicly announced. On the other hand, Frank Churchill's conduct would strike a circle of acquaintances to-day very much as it impressed the people of Highbury. To be engaged to one girl and go about 'with manners so very disengaged,' almost making love to another; and for two people to have such an alliance with each other, unknown to the rest of society, and to mix with that society as if nothing of the kind existed, would certainly cause a feeling—not of moral indignation, but that an unfair advantage had been taken of unsuspecting people. A girl who had denied all particular knowledge of a young man, when she was in fact engaged to him, as Jane Fairfax denied any special knowledge of Frank to Emma; and a young man who had carried on with an unattached girl as Frank had carried on with her, would, to-day, be scarcely popular in a small town when their secret and long-standing engagement was finally announced.

Jane Fairfax herself is a most interesting creature. Her appearance is described in quite as lovely a passage as Emma's. 'It was not regular, but it was very pleasing beauty. Her eyes, a deep grey with dark eyelashes and eyebrows had never been denied their praise; but the skin which she had been used to cavil at, as wanting colour, had a clearness and delicacy which really needed no fuller bloom. It was a style of beauty of which elegance was the reigning character.' We know that Jane's hair was dark, because in the happy conclusion to her story Frank was having some of the family jewels reset for her in an ornament for the head, and said to Emma: '"Will not it be beautiful in her dark hair?"'

One of her keenest misfortunes, to rank with an uncongenial home and the misery of even the illusion of disappointed love, was the prospect, though that also proved illusory, of her having to go for a governess. The vivid presentation of the horrors of such a fate is the more interesting because it occurs in the same book as Mrs. Weston, who, as 'poor Miss Taylor that was,' had occupied a position of such confidence and affection at Hartfield, that when she married her one regret was that she was leaving 'friends who could ill bear to part with her.' Emma's love for Mrs. Weston is most beautifully displayed in the sentences that open the fateful party at Randalls. There was 'not anyone to whom she related, with such conviction of being listened to, and always understood, of being always interesting and always intelligible, the little affairs, arrangements, perplexities and pleasures of her father and herself; . . . the very sight of Mrs. Weston, her smile, her touch, her voice, was grateful to Emma.'

The character of Mrs. Weston is perhaps the most attractive in the book, with its common sense only overcome by her affection for Emma, 'My Emma,' her extraordinary kindness to Mr. Woodhouse, her devotion to her husband and her acute anxiety that for his sake everything about Frank Churchill's behaviour shall be satisfactory; nor was she, delightful as she was, undervalued by the family with whom she lived. But Jane Fairfax takes it for granted that when she becomes a governess she is to 'retire from all the pleasures of life, of rational intercourse, equal society, peace and hope.' And to Mrs. Elton's officious enquiries and offers of assistance in helping to find a situation, she says: ' "When I am quite determined as to the time, I am not at all afraid of being long unemployed. There are places in town, offices, where enquiry would soon produce something—offices for the sale, not quite of human flesh, but of human intellect."

' "Oh, my dear, human flesh! You quite shock me; if you mean a fling at the slave trade, I assure you, Mr. Suckling was always rather a friend of the abolition."

' "I did not mean—I was not thinking of the slave trade," replied Jane; "governess trade, I assure you, was all that I had in view; widely different, certainly as to the guilt of those who carry it on, but as to the greater misery of the victims. I do not know where it lies." '

In *Mansfield Park*, when the casting of 'Lovers' Vows' is under discussion, and it is proposed that Julia should take Cottager's Wife, the enamoured Mr. Yates exclaims: ' "Cottager's Wife! What are you talking of? The most trivial, paltry, insignificant part; the merest commonplace; not a tolerable speech in the whole. Your sister do that! It is an insult to propose it. At Ecclesford the governess was to have done it. We all agreed that it could not be offered to anybody else." '

On the whole it must be confessed that the position occupied by Lord Ravenshaw's governess was more typical of the governess in general than that of Miss Taylor at Hartfield. At the same time it is almost impossible, when one considers Miss Taylor at one end of the scale, and Agnes Gray at the other, to form a generalized estimate of the position of the governess in the first half of the nineteenth century. Mrs. Barnard's Miss Meadows, and Dickens's Ruth Pinch—we fully believe in the authenticity of each. It can only be supposed that a position which depended for its comfort almost entirely on the character of the employer, varied as much as human nature itself. Jane Fairfax was thinking of the misery of exile from friends, uncongenial occupation and society in which she held, on however easy a tenure, the position of an upper servant; but as regarded the physical conditions of employment, an elegant, well-bred girl, as highly accomplished as herself, going into a family who could afford to pay for her, might, according to Mrs. Elton, be fairly comfortable. ' "Your musical knowledge alone would entitle you to name your own terms, have as many rooms as you like, and mix in the family as much as you chose; that is —I do not know—if you knew the harp, you might do all that, I am very sure; but you sing as well as play; yes, I really believe you might, even without the harp, stipulate for what you chose,—and you must and shall be delightfully, honourably and comfortably settled, before the Campbells or I have any rest."

' "You may well class the delight, the honour and the comfort of such a situation together," said Jane, "they are pretty sure to be equal." '

The humour of *Emma* is implicit in every turn of the works and it has not only excellent comic characters such as the Eltons and Harriet Smith, but it is decorated, in the persons of Mr. Woodhouse and Miss Bates, with two of the masterpieces of English comedy. To this gallery Jane Austen had already contributed the portraits of Mr. Bennet, Mr. Collins and Mrs. Norris; but in their way the two latest achievements surpass even the earlier ones; at least they represent the apotheosis of that method that consisted in picking up garden pebbles with the hand of Midas. Mr. Bennet was a man of unusual intellect; Mr. Collins one of nature's strongest efforts in foolishness; Mrs. Norris was a singularly disagreeable woman; but there is, in the abstract, nothing outstanding about either of the supreme comic creations of *Emma*; one is a feeble and silly old man, the other a garrulous and boring old woman. But not when we see them as Jane Austen saw them; never has such commonplace human material been so filled with light. Mr. Woodhouse makes many appeals to our sympathies. He is touching, when he tries to remember a charade for the girls, and tells Emma regretfully that her mother had been so clever at that kind of thing; when he 'fondly notices' the beauty of Emma's dress before she goes to the Coles' dinner-party; when, as the company are playing Word-Making and Word-Taking, he occasionally picks up a letter to remark how well Emma had written it; in his apologetic courtesies to the guests at Hartfield, wishing his health allowed him to be a better neighbour; but none of these appeals is made directly; they steal upon us with unresisted power as we watch the presentation of Mr. Woodhouse, and that is made purely through the medium of comedy. Mr. Woodhouse is first and foremost a comic character; his valetudinarianism is a charming folly because it takes as much thought for other people's nerves, colds and indigestion as for his own; his great scenes are concerned with his proposing a boiled egg to Mrs. Bates, or his suggesting that the company, which includes Mr. Knightley and Mr. John Knightley, shall join him in a basin of gruel, or finding fault with the portrait of Harriet Smith because it makes her look as if she were sitting down outside: ' "But, my dear papa, it is supposed to be summer; a warm day in summer. Look at the tree."

' "But it is never safe to sit out of doors, my dear." '

It is the same thing with Miss Bates; Miss Bates is a more exemplary and sympathetic character than Mr. Woodhouse; when the latter was not the prey of his almost unceasing agitation on the score of his own and other people's health and safety, he was having a very pleasant time of it, living in a beautiful house and surrounded by an adoring daughter and friends, whose first concern it was that he should be made as little uneasy as possible on every occasion. But Miss Bates lived on the extremest verge of genteel poverty, with the care of an infirm old mother; yet she was none the less overflowing with cheerfulness, good-will, and gratitude for the innumerable blessings she felt that she enjoyed. At the same time, she also is presented to us, her comic aspect foremost. She has been described as a bore; indeed, Emma thought her so; but the flow of her garrulity has that balanced and dramatic quality which it is stimulating to listen to; the sentences frequently run into each other, but they have that emphatic vividness that shows a mind thoroughly alive to diverse interests; her tiresomeness consists in a tendency to what the psycho-analysts describe as 'total recall,' and it is precisely this quality which makes her superbly comic. Miss Bates' bravura passages are all of great length: as, for example, her conversation, partly delivered out of the window to Mr. Knightley, partly to the company who have come to hear Jane Fairfax's new piano, and the monologue which she keeps up as Frank Churchill conducts her and Jane from the ballroom to the supper-room at the Crown. It is not that what she says is ridiculous, but quite the contrary; her comments

205

and remarks are all, in themselves, evidence of a nature that is only too trusting and easily pleased; it is simply that they are poured forth in such unstinting abundance that the listener becomes hypnotized beneath their flow. But though Miss Bates is presented for the purpose of making us laugh, we are not allowed for a moment to lose sight of a proper scale of human values. Emma, at the Boxhill picnic, makes a pert remark to Miss Bates on the subject of her verbosity, and without any sentimentality, indeed with unadorned severity, Mr. Knightley afterwards takes her to task about it, and Emma drives home with the tears running down her cheeks.

Lord David Cecil has accounted for the extraordinary depth of the impression which Mr. Woodhouse and Miss Bates make upon us by the explanation that, highly individualized as each character is, they are not only characteristic of themselves, but of the whole world of the feeble and the foolish as well: that is perhaps why, when we read of Miss Bates and the baked apples, and Miss Bates and her niece's letters, and of her imperceptive, generous gratitude to Mrs. Elton, and her pure, unselfish bliss at the publication of Jane's engagement ('Miss Bates looked about her, so happily')—we are touched far more deeply than the mere occasion seems to warrant.

The figure of Miss Bates is the production of a genius, the touch that called her into life is something we believe in but can never understand; but that a hint, a spark that set imagination alight may have been caught by Jane Austen from one of her most prosaic rounds of visiting, is the suggestion of Mr. A. B. Walkley.

In the circle of acquaintances Godmersham visited in Canterbury were included a Mrs. Miles and her daughter. Jane Austen liked old Mrs. Miles 'because she is cheerful and grateful for what she is at the age of 90 and upwards.' In her Godmersham visit of October 1813 she described a call the party made on Mrs. Miles, in the course of which her daughter came in. Jane said of her: 'Miss Miles was as queer as usual and provided us with plenty to laugh at. She undertook *in three words* to give us the history of Mrs. Scudamore's reconciliation, and then talked on about it for half an hour, using such odd expressions, and so foolishly minute, that I could hardly keep my contenance. The death of Wyndham Knatchbull's son will rather supersede the Scudamores. I told her that he was to be buried at Hatch. She had heard, with military honour at Portsmouth. We may guess how that point will be discussed evening after evening.'

Jane Austen's novels all reflect her view that physical health was essential to female beauty. Marianne Dashwood and Catherine Morland with their fondness for the open air, and even more the lively,

206

agile Elizabeth Bennet, are in keeping with this kind of attraction. The effects of ill-health seemed to Jane Austen nothing but a disadvantage, the destruction of attractiveness. She was entirely at variance with the attitude, so popular with the nineteenth-century novelist, that ill-health could be interesting, that the symptoms of consumption were beautiful, or that a hot-house delicacy of figure or complexion conferred a charm. In none of the heroines, however, is the ideal of vital beauty realized so fully as in Emma. Mrs. Weston says of her: 'There is health not merely in her bloom but in her air, her head, her glance. One hears sometimes of a child being "the picture of health"; now Emma always gives me the idea of being the complete picture of grown-up health. She is loveliness itself.'

CHAPTER SEVENTEEN

Emma has been described as being, in some respects, the most polished example of that method of novel-writing which Jane Austen made particularly her own; and by a strangely apt coincidence, the year of its composition was also the year in which she wrote a series of letters containing advice on the method of novel-writing as practised by herself.

Anna Austen was not married till the November of 1814, and she amused herself during the summer of her engagement in writing a novel. First of all it was called *Enthusiasm* and then the title was changed to *Which is the Heroine?* She sent the chapters, as they were written, to her Aunt Jane, and though her aunt was writing *Emma* at the time, she had the leisure to read them and be amused by them and return them with her comments.

Which is the Heroine? must have been good, because Jane not only treated it with the generous enthusiasm she kept for the doings of her nephews and nieces, but she said over and over again that she had been amused with the manuscript and looked forward to reading the next instalment. Considering her own preoccupation at the time, her interest was a high tribute to Anna's powers of entertainment.

The bulk of the criticism is directed to the ends of naturalness and probability, and its importance lies much more in its relation to her work than to novel-writing as a whole. Many female writers, perhaps most, possess keen powers of observation; many are accurate and painstaking; there may be some who would never have made even that solitary blunder of causing strawberries and apple blossom to come together. There is nothing very remarkable in these qualities, even when they are possessed in an eminent degree; but they become inexpressibly important when they are the medium by which the spirit of genius is made visible to us. The novels of Jane Austen are not what they are because she almost never makes a mistake over detail, or because the tenor of life in them is outwardly tranquil and unadventurous; the medium itself becomes transfigured, and all its details take on a new significance, because of the power which burns behind it. Reviewers seldom say a more foolish thing than when they describe some ambling tale of domestic relationships as 'quite in the Jane Austen manner.'

But some hints on the practice of this manner was all of her method that she could impart. She could not say: you must be exquisitely witty; you must have one fixed viewpoint in your mind from which

208

37. Nelson's victory at the Battle of the Nile in 1799 inaugurated a craze for things Egyptian. When Jane Austen went to the ball of Lord Dorchester in January 1800, she wore a Mameluke cap rather like the cap shown in this illustration from a Ladies Fashion Magazine of 1804.

36. Horatio Nelson, drawn in 1797 in Naples by Charles Grignon. When Nelson was killed at the Battle of Trafalgar in 1805, Frank Austen wrote 'I never heard of his equal, nor do I expect again to see such a man.'

38. A composite engraving of all Nelson's ships. Behind the *Victory* lies HMS *Elephant* which Nelson commanded at the Battle of Copenhagen. It became the ship of Jane's brother, Frank Austen, and she mentions it in her novel *Mansfield Park*.

39 and 40. Watercolour views of Lyme Regis. Jane Austen visited Lyme with her parents and sister in the late summer of 1804, and took lodgings in a cottage on the Cobb side of the Bay. In *Persuasion*, Jane recalled her visit to Lyme, and caused Louisa Musgrove to fall off the Cobb, at the climax of the novel.

41. Handkerchief worked by Jane Austen.

42. Title page to one of Jane Austen's music books.

SENSE

AND

SENSIBILITY:

A NOVEL.

IN THREE VOLUMES.

BY A LADY.

VOL. I.

London:

PRINTED FOR THE AUTHOR,

By C. Roworth, Bell-yard, Temple-bar,

AND PUBLISHED BY T. EGERTON, WHITEHALL.

1811.

43. Titlepage to the first edition of *Sense and Sensibility*, published in 1811 by Thomas Egerton, under anonymous authorship.

44. Playbill of *Lovers' Vows*, a translation by Mrs Inchbald of Kotzebue's *Das Liebes Kind*. This was the play produced by the family in *Mansfield Park*.

THEATRE ROYAL, COVENT-GARDEN,

This present FRIDAY, Dec. 27, 1799,

Will be presented (47th Time) the New Play of

LOVER's VOWS.

Frederick by Mr POPE,

Verdun by Mr SIMMONS,

Being His FIRST appearance in that Character,

Anhalt by Mr. H. JOHNSTON,

Count Cassel by Mr KNIGHT,

Baron Wildenhaim by Mr. MURRAY,

Cottager, Mr DAVENPORT, Landlord. Mr THOMPSON,

Agatha Friburg by Mrs JOHNSON,

Cottager's Wife Mrs DAVENPORT, Country Girl Miss Leserve

And Amelia Wildenhaim by Mrs. H. JOHNSTON.

After which will be performed (3d Time) a New Grand Serio-Comic PANTOMIME, called THE

VOLCANO:

Or the RIVAL HARLEQUINS.

With entire New Music, Scenery, Machinery, Dresses and Decorations.

The OVERTURE and MUSIC composed by Mr. MOORHEAD.

The Pantomime invented by Mr T. DIBDIN — and produced under the direction of Mr. FARLEY.

The Dances by Mr. BOLOGNA, Jun.

Harlequin Whitesword, Mr. BOLOGNA, Jun.

Harlequin Blacksword, Mr. KING,

Clown, Mr. BOLOGNA,

Infernal Spirit, Mr. DELPINI, Columbine's Father, Mr. WHITMORE, Jun.

Old Beau, Mr HARTLIN, Hermit, Mr LEWISS,

And Colombine, Mrs. PARKER.

The Other Pantomime Characters by

Mess. Wilde, Blurton, Platt, Abbot, Lee, T. Cranfield, Sweeny, Viah, Howell, L. Bologna, Klanert, Atkins, Mills, Wilkins, Webb, Lettency, Griffith,

Mrs Watts, Mrs Follett, Mrs Bologna, Mrs Iageville, Mrs Cox, Miss Coombs, &c.

Vocal Characters,

Crateen (Demon of the Mountain) Mr. DENMAN,

Ballad-singers, Mr. EMERY and Mr. SIMMONS,

Principal Demon, Mr. LINTON, Second Demon, Mr. STREET,

Chorus of Infernal Spirits, Mess. Gardner, Thomas, Oddwell, Smith, J. Linton, Kendrick, Sawyer, Tett,

Florizel (Spirit of the Air,) Miss WHEATLY,

Attendants on Florizel—Mesdames Sims, Iliff, Gilbert, Lesserve, Norton, Masters, Sydney, Blurton,

Castelle, Burnet, &c. &c.

The Pantomime to conclude with an Allegorical Procession of the Seasons, Months and Hours, to the

TEMPLE of DOMESTIC HAPPINESS.

The SCENERY by Mess. PHILLIPS, LUPINO, HOLLOGAN, WILKINS, BROMLEY, the two

WHITMORE, & Mr. POWELL.

The Machinery by Mess. CRESSWELL, SLOPER, GOODTREE, C. DIBDIN, Jun. &c.

The Dresses by Mr. WEBB & Mrs EGAN.

The Second representation of the New Pantomime was honoured by an overflowing Theatre with

as loud and universal applause as on the first night—Those Ladies & Gentlemen who could not

procure Places, are respectfully acquainted it will be performed Tomorrow, after the new Co-

medy of the *Wise Man of the East*; and on Monday after the Historical Play (not acted these

two years) of KING HENRY the FOURTH — and repeated Every Night next Week.

Mr. KEAN as Shylock.

45. In March, 1814, Jane Austen visited her brother Henry at Henrietta Street, and went to the theatre to see Edmund Kean as Shylock in *Merchant of Venice*. Jane wrote 'it appeared to me as if there was no fault in him anywhere'.

46. In the November of the same year, Jane Austen returned to London and this time went to see Eliza O'Neal in *The Fatal Marriage*. Her comments on this were less complimentary: 'I do not think she was quite equal to my expectation. She is an elegant creature, however, and hugs Mr Young delightfully.'

PRIDE

AND

PREJUDICE:

A NOVEL.

IN THREE VOLUMES.

BY THE
AUTHOR OF " SENSE AND SENSIBILITY."

VOL. I.

London:
PRINTED FOR T. EGERTON,
MILITARY LIBRARY, WHITEHALL.
1813.

TO

HIS ROYAL HIGHNESS

THE PRINCE REGENT,

THIS WORK IS,

BY HIS ROYAL HIGHNESS'S PERMISSION,

MOST RESPECTFULLY

DEDICATED,

BY HIS ROYAL HIGHNESS'S

DUTIFUL

AND OBEDIENT

HUMBLE SERVANT,

THE AUTHOR.

47. In January 1813 Jane Austen's second novel, *Pride and Prejudice*, was published by Thomas Egerton. This time, Jane was described as 'the author of *Sense and Sensibility*', and she still retained her secret, even within the family circle. This copy belonged to Lady Caroline Lamb.

48. At the invitation of the Prince Regent, Jane Austen dedicated her novel, *Emma*, to the Prince. Her publisher for *Emma* was John Murray.

49. John Murray, publisher of many illustrious writers, including Jane Austen, Lord Byron and Walter Scott.

50. Jane Austen died on 18 July, 1817, and was buried in Winchester Cathedral. This engraving of the nave and aisle of the Cathedral was executed for a *History of Winchester Cathedral*, 1817.

you survey all your scenes and characters, and though that viewpoint is essentially comic, its comedy must cover a range, both wide and deep, of sympathy as well as laughter. Above all, I recommend you so to form your characters that when you have introduced them and let them speak for half a page, the reader feels that he is in the room with them.

The first instalment of Anna's manuscript was received in March. Jane read it aloud to Mrs. Austen and Cassandra, and they were all much amused by it. Jane commended the drawing of Devereux Forester, whom she liked 'a great deal better than if he had been very good or very bad.' 'A few verbal corrections' were all she felt moved to make. She pointed out, for one thing, that 'as Lady H. is Cecilia's superior, it would not be correct to talk of *her* being introduced; Cecilia must be the person introduced.' Then she demurred at the lovers' speaking in the third person, which, she said, sounded too much like Lord Orville (who, it will be remembered, on seeing Evelina unexpectedly at the opera, exclaimed, 'Good God! Is it possible that I see Miss Anville?'). Jane thought the habit unnatural; but she added: 'If *you* think differently, however, you need not mind me.'

Of the next instalment she said, 'My corrections have not been more important than before.' Here and there she and Cassandra thought the sense might have been expressed in fewer words, and Jane had scratched out Sir Thomas from walking out to the stables the very day after breaking his arm; because, she said, 'though I find your papa *did* walk out immediately after *his* arm was set, I think it can be so little usual as to appear unnatural in a book.' Then a question of geography presented itself. 'Lyme will not do. Lyme is towards forty miles distance from Dawlish and would not be talked of there. I have put Starcross instead. If you prefer Exeter, that must be always safe.' This instalment also contained a mistake over introductions. 'I have also scratched out the introduction between Lord P. and his brother, and Mr. Giffen. A country surgeon (don't tell Mr. C. Lyford) would not be introduced to men of their rank.'

Then came a very important piece of advice. 'We think you had better not leave England. Let the Portmans go to Ireland, but as you know nothing of the manners there, you had better not go with them.' And another: 'You describe a sweet place, but your descriptions are often more minute than will be liked. You give too many particulars of right and left.'

'Your Aunt C.,' said another paragraph, 'does not like desultory novels, and is rather fearful yours will be too much so.' But Aunt C. had read in manuscript at least one of the most remarkable novels in the English language, and her standards were necessarily high; Aunt Jane, who had merely written it, was more lenient. 'I allow much more latitude than she does, and think nature and spirit cover many sins of a wandering story.'

But over what she did think important, she was ruthlessly exacting. 'A woman, going with two girls just growing up, into a neighbourhood where she knows nobody but one man, of not very good character, is an awkwardness which so prudent a woman as Mrs. F. would not be likely to fall into. Remember, she is very prudent;—you must not let her act inconsistently.' Henry Mellish, she was afraid, would be 'too much in the common novel style,—a handsome, amiable, unexceptionable young man (such as do not abound in real life) desperately in love, and in vain.' Miss Egerton did not satisfy her either; Jane said that she was 'too formal and solemn in her advice to her brother not to fall in love, and it is hardly like a sensible woman; it is putting it into his head. We should like a few hints from her better.' The question of language was commented upon. Sir Thomas was not allowed to say— Bless my heart! It was too familiar and inelegant for him; and— 'Devereux Forester's being ruined by his vanity is extremely good; but I wish you would not let him plunge into a "vortex of dissipation." I do not object to the thing, but I cannot bear the expression; it is such thorough novel slang,—and so old, that I dare say Adam met with it in the first novel he opened.'

But the letters contained as much praise as criticism; from the aesthetic point of view, the latter is perhaps less interesting, except that Jane Austen said the work was so good that, 'I hope when you have written a great deal more, you will feel equal to scratching out some of the past.' She felt a responsive sympathy with the scene of some of the chapters. 'You are now collecting your people delightfully, getting them exactly into such a spot as is the delight of my life; three of four families in a country village is the very thing to work on, and I hope you will write a great deal more and make full use of them while they are so very favourably arranged.' She commented with interest upon Anna's choice of names; beside Newton Priors, she praised the name of Lesley, though Rachel, she said, was as much as she could bear. She was especially delighted with Progillian; it came home to her with such force that she and Anna rejoiced in it as in a sort of talisman which could not be expected to operate outside the family. Anna had shown Ben Lefroy the novel; quite rightly, Jane said; she was very glad to hear how much Ben liked it; but, she added, 'We have no great right to wonder at his not valuing the name of Progillian. *That* is a source of delight which he hardly ever can be quite competent to.'

Mrs. Austen, who was exceedingly fond of Anna, loved to hear the novel read aloud, and followed it minutely. 'Your grandmother,' said Jane, 'is more disturbed by Mrs. F.'s not returning the Egertons' visit sooner than by anything else. They ought to have called at the Parsonage before Sunday.' Mrs. Austen was making a pair of shoes for Anna, a process which the fashion for silk and satin shoes sewn on to a soft kid sole allowed to be followed out at home; when these were finished, the old lady thought they would look very well. But the public readings of *Which is the Heroine?* were interrupted; in the middle of September news arrived of a family tragedy: Mrs. Charles Austen had died of her fourth baby, while her husband was stationed off the Nore. She died leaving him three little girls, of whom the eldest was six; the baby died with her.

Mrs. Austen was now seventy-five, and such news was the worse because she was not young enough to be resilient. Jane could only tell Anna when she wrote next that 'Your Grandmother does not seem the worse *now* for the shock.' Jane did not send back the manuscript; she was keeping it to read to Mrs. Austen a little later; meanwhile she read it to Cassandra in their bedroom while they undressed—'and with a great deal of pleasure.' She said: 'I have made up my mind to like no novels really, but Miss Edgeworth's, yours and my own.'

In November, Anna was married quietly from Steventon Rectory. There was no wedding party except of the immediate family: Anna's father and stepmother, Edward, who had the morning off from Winchester, the Rector of Ashe and his wife, and Ben's brother Edward Lefroy. Caroline and Ben's niece, little Anne Lefroy, were the two bridesmaids, and wore white frocks and bonnets trimmed with white; the bride wore a white muslin robe and a silk shawl of palest yellow, embossed with white satin flowers, and a small cap trimmed with lace.

The bride, with Mrs. James Austen and the two little bridesmaids, went in the carriage to church between nine and ten. Caroline remembered the cold grey light of the November morning coming through the narrow windows of the church, as her father gave the bride away and Mr. Lefroy married them. Afterwards they all drove back to Steventon Rectory for a simple wedding breakfast, which was made into a feast by the wedding cake and chocolate being added to the usual hot rolls, buttered toast, tongue, ham and eggs.

Ben and Anna were to begin their married life by sharing a house with Edward Lefroy at Hendon, and they made haste away from their wedding breakfast because they did not want to be crossing Hampstead Heath after dark; there were still highwaymen upon it.

Anna's marriage did not put a stop to her novel-writing, of which she continued to send fresh instalments to her Aunt Jane. The latest one said that Sir Julian had previously been in love with Cecilia's aunt before he was attracted by Cecilia. Jane said: 'I rather like the idea:— a very proper compliment to an aunt—I rather imagine indeed that nieces are seldom chosen but in compliment to some aunt or other. I daresay Ben was in love with me once, and would never have thought of *you* if he had not supposed me dead of a scarlet fever.'

Anna also wrote describing her surroundings. Her aunt said: 'I think I understand the country about Hendon from your description. It must be very pretty in summer.' She used the irate Cobbet's term for London: 'Should you guess you were within a dozen miles of the Wen from the atmosphere?' 'Make everybody at Hendon admire *Mansfield Park*,' she said.

At the end of November she paid a brief visit to Henry, who had moved house once more and was now back again two doors off his old quarters in Hans Place. She went over to see Anna, and Anna begged her to come again, but the visit was to be so short and Henry had made so many plans that Jane had to say it was impossible. In the letter to Anna which said how sorry she was not to be able to manage it, she said they had been to the theatre the night before to see Miss O'Neal in *The Fatal Marriage*. Eliza O'Neal, who was twenty-three at the time, with features of a Grecian cast and jet-black ringlets, was making a name for herself as a tragic actress. Jane said: 'I do not think she was quite equal to my expectation. I fancy I want something more than can be. Acting seldom satisfies me. I took two pocket-handkerchiefs but had very little occasion for either. She is an elegant creature, however, and hugs Mr. Younge delightfully.'

Poor Charles Austen's three little girls were being looked after in a house in Keppel Street off Russel Square. Jane told Anna that she was going to see them. 'Cassy was excessively interested about your marrying, when she heard of it, which was not till she was to drink your health; and asked innumerable questions in her usual way—what he said to you? and what you said to him?' Jane was glad that Anna had heard, on her marriage, from her cousin Charlotte Dewar. 'I am glad she has written to you. I like first cousins to be first cousins, and interested about each other.'

In the meantime, despite the claims of Anna's wedding and Anna's novel, Jane Austen's favourite niece of all had been much on her mind. Fanny Knight had for some time thought herself in love with a Mr. Plumtree, of Fredville in the same county. But when Mr. Plumtree had fallen in love with her, she began seriously to doubt whether she did love him after all, and wrote to tell her Aunt Jane all about it. Jane was quite taken by surprise; she had had no idea of any change in Fanny's feelings, and she felt it was very difficult to know what to say. One thing, however, was clear to her: 'I have no scruple in saying you cannot be in love. My dear Fanny, I am ready to laugh at the idea; and yet it is no laughing matter to have had you so mistaken as to your own feelings, and with all my heart I wish I had cautioned you on that point when you first spoke to me, but though I did not think you *then* so much in love as you thought yourself, I did consider you as being attached in a degree—quite sufficiently for happiness, as I had no doubt it would increase with opportunity. And from the time of our being in London together, I thought you really very much in love.— But you certainly are not at all—there is no concealing it.' She thought Fanny's own explanation was the true one, that feeling sure of Mr. Plumtree's affections had caused her own to cool. Jane was so full of curiosity and concern that her first letter on hearing the news would, she was sure, contain nothing of any help to Fanny's judgement. She thought perhaps Fanny had fallen in love originally because Mr. Plumtree had been the first man to fall in love with her. 'That was the charm, and most powerful it is.' But, whatever the reason, she said Fanny had no cause to despise herself, because Mr. Plumtree was not only very eligible (and to be thought a respectable suitor for Mr. Knight's daughter, he must have been eligible indeed), but he was very pleasant, and his character was excellent; he had from that point of view everything, said Jane, 'that *you* know so well how to value. *All* that really is of the first importance,—everything of this nature pleads his cause most strongly.' The more she thought about him, the more strongly she was inclined to feel the desirability of Fanny's falling in love with him again if possible. Fanny, once she had admitted the spirit of criticism, began to view Mr. Plumtree as somewhat too silent and retiring. Jane said: 'If he were less modest, he would be more agreeable, speak louder and look impudenter;—and is it not a fine character of which modesty is the only defect?' Besides, she said: 'I have no doubt that he will get more lively and more like yourselves as he is more with you.' Fanny had also become rather frightened of her lover's being so good. Her own nature was serious, and she wondered very earnestly if she would be able to live up to such a husband. In this year she had written in her diary: 'Plagued myself about Methodists all day.' The evangelical movement of the early nineteenth century occupied very much the position in the minds of the seriously thinking public that revolutionary political doctrines occupy to-day; it might be unwelcome, but its claims to attention were insistent, and if its tenets were

213

not wholly adopted, at least they formed a touchstone by which to test values taken hitherto for granted. Jane said: 'As to there being any objection from his *goodness*, from the danger of his becoming an Evangelical, I cannot admit *that*. I am by no means convinced that we ought not all to be Evangelicals, and am at least persuaded that they who are so from reason and feeling must be happiest and safest.' Then Fanny was rendered nervous by the fact that her brothers were so much wittier than Mr. Plumtree. Jane told her not to think of it: 'Wisdom is better than wit, and in the long run will certainly have the laugh upon her side; and don't be frightened by the idea of his acting more strictly up to the precepts of the New Testament than others.' She thought Fanny might be in danger of exacting too high a standard from a man whom, if she were more reasonable, she would find it easy to love. She reminded her niece that though 'there *are* such beings in the world perhaps, one in a thousand, as the creature you and I should think perfection, where grace and spirit are united to worth, where manners are equal to the heart and understanding, such a person may not come your way, or if he does, he may not be the eldest son of a man of fortune, the brother of your particular friend, and belonging to your own country.'

But having said so much, her feelings began to veer; she thought it right to remind Fanny of the advantages of the match and to caution her not to do anything silly; but the idea of hastening the child towards a marriage, to which in her innermost heart she had really become unwilling, filled her aunt with dismay. '. . . Now . . . I shall turn round and entreat you not to commit yourself farther, and not to think of accepting him unless you really do like him. Anything is to be preferred or endured rather than marrying without affection.' If Fanny's feelings could allow of her dwelling on his drawbacks in manner, Jane's advice was that Fanny should give him up immediately. As she said: 'Things are now in such a state that you must resolve upon one or the other, either to allow him to go on as he has done, or whenever you are together, behave with a coldness which may convince him that he has been deceiving himself.'

Fanny wrote back to the effect that she was prepared to do whatever her aunt thought right, but Jane would not have this. She answered the letter from Hans Place, saying: 'Your affection gives me the highest pleasure, but indeed you must not let anything depend on my opinion. Your own feelings, and none but your own should determine such an important point.' None the less, she could not but lay it before Fanny as her opinion that Fanny's feelings were at least not such as to stand the strain of a long engagement. The marriage could not take place

214

for an indefinite period, and as Jane said: 'You like him well enough to marry, but not well enough to wait.' And she pointed out the great and very probable danger of Fanny's meeting someone else in the next six or seven years whom she would truly love. The situation of obliging Mr. Plumtree to understand that, if he had not been exactly deceiving himself, somebody else had come rather near to deceiving him, was of course going to be very awkward; but if Fanny made up her mind against the match, it had to be gone through. Jane sympathized, but was firm. 'The unpleasantness of appearing fickle is certainly great— but if you think you want punishment for past illusions, there it is— and nothing can be compared to the misery of being bound *without* love, bound to one and preferring another. *That* is a punishment which you do *not* deserve.'

She said she was sure that Mr. Plumtree would suffer a great deal when he found he must give Fanny up, but she added something which might be of interest to those who attach such overwhelming importance to the story of her early life; 'it is no creed of mine, as you must be well aware, that such sort of disappointments kill anybody.'

The carrying on of this correspondence, so important and so private, brings to light one extraordinary quality of Jane Austen's mind. A sister on terms of quite ordinary intimacy with another might have told that other what had been going on in her niece's affairs; that Jane should withhold something from Cassandra seems at first sight incredible; but she did so. Cassandra had been dining with Frank Austen's family at the Great House on the evening that Fanny's first letter arrived, and Jane had said it was a good thing Aunt Cassandra was out of the way, because once she had begun it, she could not bear to put it down. Another one was brought by Mr. Edward Knight himself, who 'most conscientiously hunted about' till he found Jane 'alone in the dining parlour' before he gave it to her; but Cassandra had already seen that he had a packet of some sort to deliver, only happily Fanny had put the letter into a piece of music. 'Your sending the music was an admirable device; it made everything easy; and I do not know how I could have accounted for the parcel otherwise. . . . As it was, however, I do not think anything was suspected.' On another occasion when Fanny was in the thick of the matter and raining down letters whose arrival everyone must notice, Jane implored her: 'Write something that will do to be read or told!'

The fact that both Cassandra and Jane could be relied upon implicitly to keep the confidence of their nieces even from each other, was recorded in his memoir by Mr. Edward Austen Leigh. In Jane's case particularly, with her acute interest in the heroine of the story, it is

215

astonishing that she could have denied herself the pleasure of talking over the matter with Cassandra; but it was a matter of which Cassandra knew the essentials already; she would have had no wish to know the details which it seemed to Fanny just at present so important to keep quite private between herself and her Aunt Jane. There was every reason for Jane's refraining from discussing the matter with her sister, except that in such circumstances almost nobody would have refrained from so doing.

Before Jane left Hans Place she wrote to tell Fanny of the visit she had made to Anna. She said that as Fanny's father had also paid a visit from Hans Place, Fanny would be able to gather most of what she wanted to know from him. 'Your papa will be able to answer *almost* every question. I certainly could describe her bedroom and her drawers and her closet better than he can, but I do not feel that I can stop to do it.' Her letter showed that Anna, even though the married lady, was an interesting child, and Fanny almost another sister. Though Fanny was exactly Anna's age, for they were both twenty-one, Jane spoke to her of the bride as if Fanny herself were on quite a different level of intelligence and sense. She told Fanny she was sorry to hear that Anna *was* to have a piano after all: 'It seems throwing money away. They will wish the twenty-four guineas in the shape of sheets and towels six months hence, and as to her playing, it never can be anything.' When Anna's trousseau was being prepared, her aunts from Chawton had seen it, and knew very well the standard, in number of garments and their degree of elegance, which the Steventon family could afford, and Anna's new life make necessary or suitable. Jane was surprised on visiting Hendon to see Anna in a violet pelisse whose existence had been quite unsuspected by her. Not, as she said, that she blamed Anna for having bought it. 'It looked very well, and I daresay she wanted it. I suspect nothing worse than its being got in secret, and not owned to anybody. She is capable of that, you know.'

She told Fanny also of a visit to Keppel Street, when 'dear Uncle Charles' was at home with the little girls. The two-year-old Fanny was 'a fine, stout girl,' who talked all the time with a lisp and indistinctness that were very charming. Harriet, who was four, sat in her Aunt Jane's lap and was very affectionate. Cassy, however, who was old enough to remember having seen Aunt Jane before, did not rise to the occasion; the latter said: 'That puss Cassy did not show more pleasure in seeing us than her sisters, but I expected no better;—she does not shine in the tender feelings. She will never be a Miss O'Neal; —more in the Mrs. Siddons line.'

In the year of October 1814 to 1815, Anna and Ben left Hendon

216

and came back to Hampshire once again. They took possession of Wyards, near Alton, an old farm-house which had been converted into a private dwelling. Anna's baby, Anna Jemima, was born in October 1815, and the young mother had so much to do that *Which is the Heroine?* was put aside. After her Aunt Jane's death Anna burnt the manuscript, and one of her little daughters remembered sitting on the rug and watching it burn, 'amused with the flames and the sparks which kept breaking out in the blackened paper.' When the child was old enough, she said how sorry she was her mother should have burnt the story, but Anna told her that she could never have borne to finish it; it brought back the loss of her Aunt Jane too vividly.

Which is the Heroine? was laid by, but *Emma* was finished. Jane went, as usual, to Henry while arrangements were made for its publication. In the middle of October she was writing to Cassandra from Hans Place; the letter began with congratulations on the new cook at Chawton being able to make good apple pies; it went on to speak of the new publisher. Mr. Egerton was no longer acting for her, the fame of *Pride and Prejudice* and *Mansfield Park* was such that the second edition of the latter had been undertaken by the most fashionable and talked-of publisher in London—none other than the celebrated Mr. Murray. The fact that Murray had published for Lord Byron and enjoyed much of his confidence, and had been, consequently, involved in Byron's meteoric career: visited and consulted by Byron's agitated friends, and hoaxed out of a portrait of his lordship by a forged letter presented by Lady Caroline Lamb, made of Mr. Murray something more than a publisher. To be undertaken by him was not only a sign of successful authorship; it was an honour. It might have been expected that Jane Austen, writing to a sister in the country, would have devoted a good deal of space to talking of Mr. Murray. Actually, she summed him up in a sentence: 'He is a rogue, of course, but a civil one.' Mr. Murray offered £450 for *Emma*, but he said the contract must include the copyright of *Mansfield Park* and *Sense and Sensibility*; and therefore for *Emma* alone he was offering roughly one-third of this sum; and as Jane Austen had made £140 on the first edition of *Sense and Sensibility*, as an author quite unknown, something in the nature of £150 for *Emma*, which was to include the copyright of that novel, was not as much as she, or as Henry for her, would naturally accept. But Mr. Murray *was* very civil; he sent Jane a letter containing so much praise as quite surprised her.

The weather of the sixteenth of October was like summer still. It did not suit Henry, who came home from Henrietta Street feeling feverish and bilious, and went straight to bed, leaving Jane to dine

217

tête-à-tête with Mr. Seymour; Jane hoped he would be better by the morning.

But he was not; he stayed in bed all Tuesday, and on Wednesday Jane wrote to Chawton: 'It is a fever—something bilious but chiefly inflammatory. I am not alarmed but I have determined to send this letter to-day by the post that you may know how things are going on.' She called in the apothecary from the corner of Sloane Street, Mr. Haden, a very attentive and clever young man who seemed to understand the case, and reassured her somewhat. 'Henry,' she said, 'is an excellent patient, lies quietly in bed and is ready to swallow anything. He lives upon medicine, tea and barley-water.' He was in bed 'in the back room upstairs.' Jane added: 'I am generally there also working or writing.' In a day or two Henry seemed better and was able to dictate a letter to Mr. Murray in which he thanked him for his politeness and said that his favourable opinion of *Emma* was most gratifying; but that the sum Mr. Murray was offering for the three copyrights was not equal to the amount Jane Austen had actually made already by one edition of *Mansfield Park*, and a still smaller one of *Sense and Sensibility*.

But before the matter could be agreed upon, Henry had suffered a sharp relapse. On October 22nd Jane sent expresses to Godmersham, Steventon and Chawton, for Edward, James and Cassandra. Edward arrived immediately, and James, who had gone to Chawton to fetch Cassandra, arrived with her the day after. For a week they thought Henry was dying. Jane and Cassandra nursed him night and day, in an unrelieved horror of suspense; but Henry's mercurial temperament was capable of startling seizures and equally rapid recoveries. After a week the two brothers felt able to go back to their families, leaving Jane with Cassandra, and at the end of October Jane was able to write to another niece who was engaged in literary composition; the ten-year-old Caroline was writing a story, and had sent it to Aunt Jane to look at.

Jane said: 'I have not yet felt quite equal to taking up your manuscript, but I think I shall soon.' Caroline was staying at Chawton with her grandmother, and her Aunt Martha, and her Aunt Jane said: 'You will practise your music, of course, and I trust to you for taking care of my instrument and not letting it be ill-used in any respect.—Do not allow anything to be put on it, but what is very light.'

The birth of Anna Jemima had exalted Caroline to the dignity of an aunt, and Jane concluded the letter by saying: 'I am sorry you got wet in your ride; now that you are become an aunt, you are a person of some consequence and must excite great interest whatever you do. I

218

have always maintained the importance of aunts as much as possible, and I am sure of your doing the same now. Believe me, my dear Sister-Aunt, yours affectionately, Jane Austen.' A couple of months later she was writing to say—'My dear Caroline, I wish I could finish stories as fast as you can.—I am much obliged to you for the sight of Olivia, and think you have done for her very well; but the good-for-nothing father, who was the real author of all her faults and sufferings, should not escape unpunished. I hope *he* hung himself, or took the name of Bone or underwent some direful penance or other.'

In the meantime Henry's illness had been the cause of Jane Austen's making a very interesting acquaintance. Mr. Haden, the clever young apothecary, was a friend of the Rev. J. S. Clarke, who was librarian to the Prince Regent at Carlton House. A great deal of what we hear of George IV is unfavourable, but he was an artist. That monument to his taste, the Pavilion at Brighton, with its blending of Chinese and Hindu architecture, conveys something of the breadth of the Prince Regent's taste. Another aspect of it is indicated by the fact that by 1815 he had become a profound admirer of the novels of Jane Austen. He had a set of those already published in each of the houses he was accustomed to occupy; his admiration was so well known to his librarian, that when Mr. Haden told his friend that the lady who had written *Pride and Prejudice* was actually in London, and that he had met her at the bedside of one of his patients, Mr. Clarke knew that the news would be well worth while carrying to his employer. The Regent asked Mr. Clarke to invite Miss Jane Austen to see the library at Carlton House, and to show her every attention in his power. Jane had been distressed at Henry's habit of doing away with her anonymity wherever he went, but here was a result of his behaviour that could not but please her. Carlton House, built for the Regent by Holland, presented a classical exterior, with the pillars that now adorn the National Gallery, but behind this façade, the ruling tone was one of Gothic fantasy. The hall, it is true, with its black-and-white marble pavement, its walls of verd antique and pillars of brown sienna marble, was classical in design; but the rooms were decorated in such colours as recall Horace Walpole's descriptions of the emotional effects of Gothic art: there were the ante-rooms in crimson and gold, blue and rose-colour; the blue velvet closet in blue, gold and bronze, the great crimson drawing-room, decorated in green and crimson, rose colour and gilt; the dining-room was all Gothic, with pillars whose capitals were formed by the carved plumes of the Prince of Wales; the conservatory was also Gothic, with a fan-vaulted roof, a nave and two aisles; from scientific regard to the plants, the tracery of the roof was filled in with clear glass, but the windows to the north and south were of rich stained glass, showing armorial bearings.

Into this astonishing establishment walked Miss Jane Austen on the morning of November 13th. Mr. Clarke was exceptionally attentive, and kindness itself. He not only had had instructions from the Prince Regent to do everything in his power, but he was a personal admirer of Jane Austen's work, and his care of her dispelled the nervousness that attends the private person on first entering a royal residence; not that Jane Austen was likely to have been so much overcome as many; she was accustomed to large houses. Carlton House itself was not the size of Stoneleigh Abbey, but the scene was so extraordinary that whether from nervousness or interest and surprise, or from all three, when she had come away she realized that she was not absolutely certain of what Mr. Clarke had said; she *thought* he had said that the Prince Regent would take it kindly if her next novel were dedicated to him; and that if she would like so to dedicate it, he was empowered to tell her that she could do so without any further ceremony; but it was so dream-like in her recollection that she could not feel certain of it. She was obliged to send a note to Mr. Clarke, asking him to repeat what he had said; she apologized for troubling him, but it was really necessary to be quite sure, as she said: 'I should be equally concerned to appear presumptuous or ungrateful.'

Mr. Clarke replied the following day. He said: 'It is certainly not *incumbent* on you to dedicate your work now in the Press to His Royal Highness; but if you wish to do the Regent that honour, either now or at any future period, I am happy to send you that permission which need not require any more trouble or solicitation on your part.' He went on to praise the novels already published. 'Your late works, Madam, and in particular *Mansfield Park*, reflect the highest honour on your genius and your principles; in every new work your mind seems to increase its energy and powers of discrimination. The Regent has read and admired all your publications.' There was an idea very near to Mr. Clarke's heart, which was that he himself was a very interesting man, both from character and attainments and because he was one who, like Dogberry, had had losses, and was now in a very honourable worldly position. He thought that the story of such a man would take the reading world by storm if presented by the genius of this remarkable novelist. He said: 'I also, dear Madam, wish to be allowed to ask you, to delineate in some future work the habits of life, and character and enthusiasm of a clergyman—who should pass his time between the metropolis and the country—who should be like Beattie's Minstrel—

Silent when glad, affectionate tho' shy
And now his look was most demurely sad
And now he laughed aloud, yet none knew why.'

The clergyman was to be 'fond of, and entirely engaged in literature' and 'no man's enemy but his own.'

Mr. Clarke wrote from the metropolis—from Carlton House, in fact—but said in the postscript that he was just going into the country.

When Jane Austen wrote in December to tell Mr. Clarke that *Emma* was on the eve of publication, and that she had not forgotten his kind recommendation of 'an early copy for Carlton House,' she replied also to his letter of the previous month. She thanked him most sincerely for his high praise of her novels and said: 'I am too vain to wish to convince you that you have praised them beyond their merits.' Her greatest anxiety at present, she said, was that *Emma* should not disgrace what was good in the four others; but she was, she admitted, 'strongly haunted with the idea that to those readers who have preferred *Pride and Prejudice* it will appear inferior in wit, and to those who have preferred *Mansfield Park* inferior in good sense.' Then she dealt with perfect seriousness with Mr. Clarke's suggestion.

'I am quite honoured by your thinking me capable of drawing such a clergyman as you gave me the sketch of in your note of Nov. 16th. But I assure you I am *not*. The comic part of the character I might be equal to, but not the good, the enthusiastic, the literary. Such a man's conversation must at times be on subjects of science and philosophy, of which I know nothing; or at least be occasionally abundant in quotation and allusions which a woman who, like me, knows only her own mother tongue and has read little in that, would be totally without the power of giving. A classical education, or, at any rate, a very extensive acquaintance with English literature, ancient and modern, appears to me quite indispensable for the person who would do any justice to your clergyman; and I think I may boast myself to be, with all possible vanity, the most unlearned and uninformed female who ever dared to be an authoress.'

In her haste to prove herself quite unequal to the demands of Mr. Clarke, Jane Austen very naturally exaggerated her own limitations; she sank her knowledge of French and Italian altogether and belittled the extent of her reading in English literature; what she said about her own acquirements in this context is not of value; but her first-hand opinion of the influence which personal circumstances must exert upon the novelist's choice of material makes the letter as valuable as those she wrote to Anna Lefroy upon *Which is the Heroine?* The getting of

Emma through the press was now a matter of doubled urgency. Jane wanted to leave town in December, and she could not do so till she had corrected the proofs, and she also wanted personally to make sure that the Prince Regent's copy had been despatched. Her relations with Mr. Murray, despite their financial dealings, became very much more cordial. It was impossible to withstand the charm of Mr. Murray's courtesy. He lent Henry a copy of Scott's *Field of Waterloo* and Miss Williams's *Narrative of the events which have lately taken place in France*; and when he apologized to Jane for a delay in transmitting the proof sheets, which, he said, was the printer's fault, not his, Jane said: 'He is so very polite indeed that it is quite overcoming.' She made a mistake when she asked him to see that the title-page bore the dedication to H.R.H. the Prince Regent. Mr. Murray, in some surprise, wrote to ask if she really meant the title-page? Of course she did not; her having said so was owing to her ignorance only, and to her never having noticed the proper place for a dedication. She thanked him for putting her right; as she said: 'Any deviation from what is usually done in such cases is the last thing I should wish for. I feel happy in having a friend to save me from the ill-effect of my own blunder.' When she was about to leave town, she returned the books Mr. Murray had lent her, saying: 'I am very sensible, I assure you, of the attention you have paid to my convenience and amusement.'

In the meantime Mr. Clarke did not despair of persuading Jane Austen to write such a biographical romance as he wished to see. He became wider and wider of the mark. 'Make all your friends send sketches to help you—and *Memoirs pour servir*—as the French term it.' As for the clergyman: 'Do let us have an English clergyman after *your* fancy—much novelty may be introduced—show, dear Madam, what good would be done if tithes were taken away entirely, and describe him burying his own mother—as I did—because the High Priest of the parish in which she died did not pay her remains the respect he ought to do. . . . Carry your clergyman to sea as the friend of some distinguished character about a court.' He had asked Mr. Murray to send to Jane Austen two little works of his: 'Sermons I wrote and preached on the ocean.' It is difficult to see where Jane Austen's own fancy was to have come in.

Mr. Clarke's next letter was written in an official capacity, and from the Pavilion at Brighton.

'DEAR MISS AUSTEN,
    'I have to return you the thanks of his Royal Highness the Prince Regent for the handsome copy you sent him of your last excellent

222

novel. Pray, dear Madam, soon write again and again. Lord St. Helen and many of the nobility who have been staying here, paid you the just tribute of their praise.'

The marriage of the Princess Charlotte to Prince Leopold of Coburg was about to be celebrated, and the Regent had just appointed Mr. Clarke Private English Secretary to the bridegroom. Mr. Clarke was to remain at the Pavilion 'with His Serene Highness and a select party' until the marriage, and this turn in his fortunes had given him a new idea to suggest to Jane Austen. 'Perhaps when you again appear in print,' he said, 'you may choose to dedicate your volumes to Prince Leopold: any historical romance, illustrative of the history of the august house of Coburg, would just now be very interesting.'

Mr. Clarke was naïve in his foolishness, but he was very kind, and Jane Austen was sincerely grateful to him. Of his advancement, she said: 'You have my best wishes. Your recent appointments are I hope a step to something still better. In my opinion, the service of a court can hardly be too well paid, for immense must be the sacrifice of time and feeling required by it.' She showed her genuine appreciation of Mr. Clarke's kindness and admiration by the serious manner in which she dealt with his suggestion of an historical romance. 'I am fully sensible that an historical romance founded on the House of Saxe-Coburg, might be much more to the purpose of profit or popularity than such pictures of domestic life in country villages as I deal in.' But she went on to say: and here was the pearl produced by the foreign body of Mr. Clarke's preposterousness: 'I could no more write a romance than an epic poem. I could not sit seriously down to write a serious romance under any other motive than to save my life; and if it were indispensable for me to keep it up and never relax into laughing at myself or at other people, I am sure, I should be hung before I had finished the first chapter. No, I must keep to my own style and go on in my own way; and though I may never succeed again in that, I am convinced that I should totally fail in any other.' She signed herself: 'Your very much obliged and sincere friend, J. Austen.'

The pleasure of the Prince Regent's notice must have been very great; but such a tribute to success did not make her any more absorbed in herself, or one degree less interested in the daily life going on around her. Indeed, by the accounts she was now sending to Cassandra at Chawton, she gave evidence of that wonderful power to shut away concerns of self and participate with single-minded eager sympathy in the interests of other people, which is one of her most revealing attributes. For Cassandra had been replaced in Henry's house by

223

Fanny, the only person who could be regarded as Cassandra's substitute. Henry was much better and able to sit up to dinner, and Mr. Haden was not only in professional attendance but he came to dine as well. He was immediately attracted by the very pretty Miss Knight, and Miss Knight, who had now ceased to speak of Mr. Plumtree, was immediately attracted by the lively, intelligent, delightfully mannered Mr. Haden. 'To-morrow,' wrote Jane, 'Mr. Haden is to dine with us. There's happiness!—We really grow so fond of Mr. Haden that I do not know what to expect.' They had a very pleasant little evening circle; Fanny played and Mr. Haden sat and listened and suggested improvements; and he did not appear less attractive in the eyes of the company because when the footman came in to tell him that 'the Doctor was waiting for him at Captain Blake's,' he jumped up and rushed away with all imaginable speed. Jane said: 'He never does appear in the least above his profession or out of humour with it.' But though Mr. Haden left the piano at the call of professional duty, he was so extremely fond of music that he quite shocked Jane by what he said about it. After one of his visits to Henry, she wrote: 'I have been listening to dreadful insanity,—it is Mr. Haden's firm belief that a person *not* musical is fit for every sort of wickedness.' She said: 'I ventured to assert a little on the other side, but wished the cause in abler hands.' It was bad enough when people rhapsodized about music; it was too much to bear when those who could not take an ecstatic delight in it were supposed thereby to exhibit a criminal tendency.

But even this did not seriously detract from Mr. Haden's charms. He came to another evening party. Henry had invited two ladies, Mrs. Latouche and Miss East. After dinner Henry and Jane sat with the two ladies on the sofa, 'making the best of it,' while opposite to them sat Fanny and Mr. Haden in two chairs. ('I *believe* at least they had *two* chairs'), talking together uninterruptedly. 'Fancy the scene! And what is to be fancied next? Why, that Mr. H. dines here again to-morrow.' Mr. H. was reading *Mansfield Park* for the first time and 'preferred it to P. and P.' Henry continued to improve. Jane said: 'He is so well, I cannot think why he is not perfectly well.' 'Perhaps,' she added, 'when Fanny is gone, he will be allowed to recover faster.' Jane said that Fanny had heard everything she had written about her to Cassandra; the latter, said Jane, seemed to be under a mistake about Mr. Haden. 'You call him an apothecary; he is no apothecary . . . he is a Haden, nothing but a Haden, a sort of wonderful nondescript creature on two legs, something between a man and an angel.'

Henry was now able to get about; 'he sets off this morning by the Chelsea Coach to sign bonds and visit Henrietta Street.' Meantime

Jane and Fanny did not want visitors; they liked the house to themselves. Jane had caught a slight cold and they made that do yeoman service. Mr. Tilson called and so of course did Mr. Haden; but they saw nobody but Mr. Tilson and 'our Precious.'

By the end of December, Jane was at home again, and *Emma* was published. Jane had felt, owing to a connection with Lady Morley and some very warm appreciation of her previous novels expressed by her ladyship, that it would be suitable to send Lady Morley a copy of *Emma*. Lady Morley in acknowledgment said she had been anxiously waiting for an introduction to *Emma*, and was 'infinitely obliged' for Jane Austen's 'kind recollection' of her, 'which will procure me the pleasure of her acquaintance some days sooner than I should otherwise have had it.' Her ladyship had begun the book immediately. 'I am already become intimate in the Woodhouse family, and feel that they will not amuse and interest me less than the Bennets, Bertrams, Norrises, and all their admirable predecessors—I *can* give them no higher praise.'

Jane was pleased with Lady Morley's note. While the reception of the book was still uncertain she said such praise was the more accceptable; and by it, she said: 'I am encouraged to believe that I have not yet—as almost every writer of fancy does sooner or later, overwritten myself.'

Beside the presentation copy to Lady Morley, one more was sent out from Chawton.

'MY DEAR ANNA,
  'As I wish very much to see *your* Jemima, I am sure you will like to see *my* Emma, and have therefore great pleasure in sending it for your perusal. Keep it as long as you choose. It has been read by all here.'

The host of press-cuttings received by a modern author makes him so conscious of the impression, whether good, bad or indifferent, that his work has made upon the public, that it would occur to few writers of to-day to put down a list of the opinions of their acquaintance, but with Jane Austen the reverse was the case. The few professional reviews of her work which have transpired are of exceptional interest, but novels upon the whole attracted much less attention in literary publications than histories and essays and books of travel, or even poetry; the outside comments upon her work were so few and far between that they did nothing to take off the keen edge of interest and pleasure she received from hearing the views of private people.

225

After the publication of *Emma* she made out a list of the comments that had come round to her. Captain Frank Austen 'liked it extremely; observing that though there might be more wit in P. and P., and an higher morality in M.P., yet altogether, on account of its peculiar air of Nature throughout, he preferred it to either.' The air of nature Captain Frank Austen had admired struck other people also but in various manners. 'Mrs. Guiton thought it too natural to be interesting,' while Mrs. Cage wrote this to Fanny: . . . 'I like it better than any . . . I am at Highbury all day, and I can't help feeling I have just got into a new set of acquaintance. No one,' added Mrs. Cage, 'wrote such good sense; and so very comfortable.' Cassandra liked it—'Better than P. and P. but not so well as M.P.,' and we know so little from first-hand information of Cassandra, that it is very interesting to hear that she preferred the serious work to the brilliant one. Fanny Knight—'not so well as either P. and P. or M.P. could not bear Emma herself. Mr. Knightley delightful. Should like J.F. if she knew more of her.' Fanny's father thoroughly approved of the portrait of Mr. Knightley. 'Mr. K. liked by everybody.' Mrs. Austen herself 'thought it more entertaining than M.P. but not so interesting as P. and P. No characters equal to Lady Catherine or Mr. Collins.' The opinion ascribed to Mr. and Mrs. Leigh Perrot is one of the pleasantest things we know about them. They 'saw many beauties in it, but could not think it equal to P. and P. Darcy and Elizabeth had spoilt them for anything else.' 'Mr. Haden —*quite* delighted with it. Admired the character of Emma.' Miss Isabella Herries was one of a well-known order of novel readers: 'Convinced that I had meant Mrs. and Miss Bates for some acquaintance of theirs. People whom I had never heard of before.' So was Mrs. Dixon, who 'liked it the less for there being a Mr. and Mrs. Dixon in it.' Anna Lefroy 'thought that if there had been more incident, it would be equal to any of the others. . . . Did not like the heroine so well as any of the others. Miss Bates excellent, but rather too much of her. Mr. and Mrs. Elton admirable, and John Knightley a sensible man.' 'Mr. Jeffreys of the *Edinburgh Review* was kept up by it three nights.' While 'Mr. Fowle read only the first and last chapters, because he had heard it was not interesting.' Captain Charles Austen, who was on board and had had a set of the volumes sent to him, wrote: 'Emma arrived in time to a moment. I am delighted with her, more so, I think, than even with my favourite, *Pride and Prejudice*, and have read it three times in the passage.'

CHAPTER EIGHTEEN

In 1815 Jane Austen had begun her sixth novel, but it did not proceed very fast in that year; not only was the proof-correcting of *Emma* on her mind, and the distracting circumstances of its publication, but she had had the severe strain of Henry's illness to bear. It would scarcely be too much to say that he recovered from it, but she did not.

Jane was not robust, but she had always given the impression of being healthy; her clear complexion and brilliant eyes, her slender, graceful, light-moving figure, her cheerfulness and serenity all suggested vitality and health; but she had within her the seeds of a weakness which it required only a general degree of ill-health and prolonged nervous strain to develop into dangerous activity. The symptoms of which she gave her own account in letters, and the course the illness took, suggest a malignant affection of one of the internal organs.* The doctor, who was consulted at Winchester, knew that she was dying the moment he looked at her. The ravages of the disease might have been indefinitely delayed if nothing had happened to create the general weakness which it immediately attacked; but Jane Austen had not only suffered acutely from distress and fatigue in nursing Henry; for the past three years her mind had been continually on the stretch; to what extent is revealed if we consider the energy and conviction, as well as the meticulous care with which her work was performed, and remember that *Pride and Prejudice* had been revised, and *Mansfield Park* and *Emma* actually written, since the year 1812.

At the beginning of 1816 she was forty years of age; whatever strength she now had, physical or intellectual, she had not the resilience of youth; she took things to heart more than she had done, could throw them off less easily, and there were family troubles which all played their part in disquieting the atmosphere. Two years after he had received the legacy and adopted the name of Knight, Edward became involved in a law-suit. The estate of Godmersham carried an annual income of £5,000, but that of Chawton was nearly twice as valuable, and the Chawton property was now claimed by a member of the Knight family. There had been a technical error in the instrument that made over the property to Edward Knight, and it now looked as if he might

* See Sir Zachary Cope, "Jane Austen's Last Illness", reprinted from the *British Medical Journal*, 18 July 1964, in "Collected Reports of the Jane Austen Society 1949–65," p. 267.

be obliged to relinquish it altogether. If he were to do so, he would not, while he possessed the Godmersham estate, be reduced to beggary, but to a man with eleven children, seven of whom were sons to be put out into the world, the loss of two-thirds even of a large income was an alarming prospect. But there was worse than this. The beloved Henry, whose fortune was so much smaller and therefore more vulnerable, met with a sudden tide of ill-luck; the bank at Alton which had been backed by the house of Austen, Maunde and Tilson, failed, and involved the latter in its own destruction. In March 1816 Henry was declared a bankrupt.

He was not only professionally ruined; besides losing other people's money he had lost a good deal belonging to his own family. Mr. Leigh Perrot lost £10,000; Edward Knight lost a considerable sum, though Jane Austen herself came off comparatively lightly with the loss of £13 which had been some of the profits of *Mansfield Park*; but there is reason to believe that poor Madame Bigeon's savings had been swallowed up.

No personal blame attached to Henry Austen, nor was there the least coldness between him and the relations who had been the victims of his misfortune; at the same time, many men would have been crushed by such a reverse, and for a time at least, not known what to turn to. But the buoyancy of Henry's disposition stood him in good stead. With perfect cheerfulness, with perfect sincerity, with perfect conviction, he decided upon the Church, and set about getting himself ordained immediately; he began to revise his knowledge of the Greek Testament, and by the time he was ordained he surprised the bishop with his erudition.

But however he was able to surmount these vicissitudes, they did not do Jane any good; sometimes she felt languid and ill at ease, and sometimes positively ill; but her natural cheerfulness and her standard of what was due by the people she lived with, though it was in a cottage and they her nearest relations, disguised from most people the fact that she was not quite well. She wrote, though it was sometimes an effort, as it had never been before; yet her style, so far from showing signs of ill-health, was more silvery and soft, more harmoniously simple than it had ever been, her creation of character as magical as before, and the whole work a structure on an underlying plan, less complicated but more subtle than in any of its predecessors.

Persuasion is a very short novel; as the reader is surprised on turning again to *Pride and Prejudice*, to realize in how few words the personalities of the novel have been created: so he returns to those spheres of Kellynch, Uppercross, Lyme Regis and Bath, present to his mind

228

with a fullness of reality which it must, he feels, require a novel on the scale of *War and Peace* to have built up; only to find that the work which contains them all is little longer than a long short-story. The rapidity and sureness with which Jane Austen evolves the scene are centred of course in her creation of character; the opening chapters of *Persuasion* do not differ markedly in this respect from those of any of its predecessors; in each the materials for her characters are quickly assembled, she breathes the breath of life between their lips, and there they stand for ever. The technical process is in each case the same, at once visible but incommunicable.

Nevertheless there is something about *Persuasion* very different from anything in her other five novels.

Professor Bradley discussed the rival merits of *Pride and Prejudice* and *Mansfield Park*, as the two leading candidates for the distinction of Jane Austen's best-loved novel; one believes that there would be a party, albeit a smaller one than either of the other two, to urge the claims of *Persuasion*; and that this party would make up for its lack of members by the almost religious character of its enthusiasm.

Anne Elliot is the maturest of all the heroines; not only is she older than any of them (she is twenty-seven), but whereas they all make some error of greater or less importance which it is the story's province to correct, her mistake has been made eight years before the story opens; and having made the initial blunder of allowing herself to be over-powered by Lady Russell's judgement into breaking off an engagement with the man she truly loved, she never afterwards makes a single error in morality, judgement or taste. It is not the least remarkable achievement of the work that with so much perfection her character is neither priggish nor unreal. Her involuntarily clear-sighted perception of the faults of her father and sister and the enigmatic Mr. Elliot, and her humbleness, which through the changes of hopeless resignation, trembling hope, and 'senseless joy' becomes a triumphant certainty of happiness, keep her altogether vulnerable and human.

The atmosphere of each of Jane Austen's novels is determined by the character of its heroine, but nowhere is this harmony so striking as in *Persuasion*. Anne Elliot believes herself to be looking back to a bright, irrecoverable past, from a present that is like a landscape from which the light has been withdrawn. The preliminary stages of the story occupy the months of late summer, but its first important event, the removal of Sir Walter Elliot to Bath, is accomplished in September, to leave Kellynch Hall free for the reception of Admiral and Mrs. Croft, whom his extravagances have obliged him to accept as tenants in October. Anne does not wish to accompany her unsympathetic father and sister; she dreads 'the possible heats of September in all the white glare of Bath' and grieves to forgo 'all the influence so sweet and so sad of the autumnal months in the country.' But it so happens that her married sister Mary insists on her coming to make herself useful at the neighbourhood village of Uppercross. She is thus settled there for the autumn months when the completely estranged Captain Wentworth comes to spend his shore leave at Kellynch Hall, and consequently she is a spectator of his flirtatious friendship with the two Musgrove girls, who, young, energetic and untried by care, have the very attractions she cannot hope to possess. The walk the whole party takes from Uppercross to Winthrop, where lives the young cousin to whom Henrietta Musgrove is tacitly understood to be engaged, is taken through the landscape of Somerset on an autumn day. 'Anne's object was, not to be in the way of anybody; and where the narrow paths across the fields made many separations necessary, to keep her with brother and sister. Her *pleasure* in the walk must arise from the exercise and the day, from the view of the last smiles of the fading year upon the tawny leaves and withered hedges, and from repeating to herself some few of the thousand poetical descriptions extant of autumn, that season of peculiar and inexhaustible influence on the mind of taste and tenderness.' The fateful expedition to Lyme Regis is undertaken in November; the weather is fine; still it is late autumn, and it gets dark so early they cannot go out again after dinner. The atmosphere of Lyme, under the short-lived brightness of a November day, and empty of its summer company, is a setting of the strangest aptness for the events which there take place.

This interpretation of the beauty of autumn is particularly interesting, both from the period at which *Persuasion* was written and from the additional light it throws upon Jane Austen's sensitiveness to natural beauty. It was not until the eighteenth century had achieved a comparative immunity from the winter's discomforts, that people were at leisure to see beauty in late autumn, as apart from the season of fruit and harvest, and in approaching darkness as well as in moon and starlight. When these seasons of the day and year had once begun to be appreciated they made a triumphant entry into poetry and art.

Although the autumnal atmosphere of *Persuasion* is true to a prevalent literary fashion it is so exquisitely natural that it seems no more influenced by that fashion than is the season itself. The sad beauty of autumn heightens, like music, the emotional interest of the opening of the story. Jane Austen was sensitive to the beauty, even of winter, when autumn was over, and there was no hint of spring. When Catherine Morland stepped out on to the lawn for an outside view of

230

Northanger Abbey we are told that 'the steep woody hills rising behind to give it shelter were beautiful even in the leafless month of March'; but passages of *Persuasion* are charged with a feeling for natural beauty even where it is not a point to create a harmonious background; for instance, Jane Austen cannot even say that the party walked down to the sea without adding that they lingered to gaze at it 'as all must linger and gaze on a first return to the sea who ever deserve to look on it at all.' But the progress of the lovers' reconciliation, the theme of the book, soon leaves the sad beauty of the dying year behind it. *Persuasion* is the tenderest and most romantic of all Jane Austen's creations; but even in this story of ideal emotions the workings of probability, as viewed moreover by a mind singularly disillusioned and penetrating, are never subordinated to the claims of romantic beauty. Captain Wentworth's love was not dead : that warmth lingered in its embers is proved by his behaviour to her even in the terrible stiffness and estrangement of the opening chapters; but it required the admiration of another man to make him see the beauty which he had previously declared to have vanished; and jealousy of that other man to revive his love to a white heat. The profoundness of the character-drawing of this group of people has scarcely been equalled in English fiction.

It is not that Jane Austen possessed a more interesting mind or a more varied imagination that her successors; it is a foolish method of appreciation that exalts *Persuasion* at the expense of *Middlemarch* or of *Jane Eyre*. A supernatural power of creating character is not the only attraction of a novelist; it is not indisputably the first. The capacity violently to stir emotion, by what machinery soever, will always be valued by certain readers beyond any other; a novel of which the chief interest is the philosophical one of seeing its characters as puppets in the workings of fate will always, to some people, have an interest superior to that whose first achievement is that it gives the sensation of contact with an actual being; but in the power to work this miracle of bestowing life, Jane Austen stands supreme. Her method has this virtue, that whatever the restrictions of type and circumstance under which she practises it, when she has waved her hand and thrown her spell, it seems that the greater is, after all, included in the less; that limited as the circumstances are in which she shows her characters, for the time at which we read about them, their vicissitudes seem to cover a vast range of human experience. This is especially true of *Persuasion*; the story of Anne Elliot and Captain Wentworth, so simply related, but so profoundly felt, sinks into the consciousness like a stone dropped into water, and spreads about itself widening and ever-widening rings of association, of imagination, of intuition. The remark that Jane Austen placed all her principal characters in one walk of life, that of the upper-middle-class, is always meaningless when offered as a criticism; but its futility is never more apparent than to the reader who has just turned the last pages of *Persuasion*.

The climax of the reconciliation is the most exciting passage in any of her works. In Mrs. Musgrove's sitting-room at the White Hart, Anne and Captain Harville enter upon their argument as to the relative constancy of men and women. Each of them is speaking with an earnestness that makes them oblivious of their surroundings. Captain Harville because of his dead sister, and Anne from the knowledge of her own heart. ' "We shall never agree upon this question," Captain Harville was beginning to say, when a slight noise called their attention to Captain Wentworth's hitherto perfectly quiet division of the room. It was nothing more than that his pen had fallen down; but Anne was startled at finding him nearer than she had supposed——' The scene that follows is very short, but it is weighted so deep with emotion, it seems as though poetry must start from it; but the characters are not figures seen through the enlarging mists of the Elizabethan stage. They are a man and woman meeting in the crowded sitting-room of an hotel. This agonizing bliss finds no relief in a flood of blank verse; it merely lays waste the powers of an ordinary human being.

'Before she was beyond the first stage of full sensation, Charles, Mary and Henrietta all came in. The absolute necessity of seeming like herself produced then an immediate struggle; but after a while she could do no more. She began not to understand a word they said.'

As one would expect from the fact that so profound an effect is achieved in so little space, the structure of *Persuasion* is flawless. It illustrates, for the last time, Jane Austen's own method of interaction of character (if she excused a desultory novel in other people on the grounds of spirit, she never permitted a desultory course to herself); but it shows this method developed to a further degree; *Persuasion*— and it is perhaps this that accounts for the singular intensity of its effect—not only shows a group of people who all react upon each other; but a group of people who are all, from the angle at which their lives are viewed, illustrations of one theme, that of love. The variety of character interest is so great that it distracts attention from the structure, so that the heightening effect of that structure is felt before it is analysed. The daily life, too, of the characters is conveyed with such variety of surface, such economy and brilliance, that in the case of many of them it is the surface which catches the eye rather than the underlying significance; the latter makes its contribution, unthought

232

of and unseen, to the profoundly moving achievement of the whole. Nevertheless, it will be realized that every one of the important characters, either singly or in pairs, though we see them as naval officers or country squires or adroit adventurers, the daughters of an aristocratic house or of a delightful, homely circle, each illustrates in his or her different manner some aspect of the central theme. We have the central story of Anne and Captain Wentworth, which is not only pre-eminent in romantic beauty, but is the connecting link of all the other stories; the courageous happy life of his sister and brother-in-law, the Crofts; the flirtation of Captain Wentworth with the lively, healthy, excitable Louisa Musgrove; the shy, uncertain, courtship of Henrietta Musgrove and Charles Hayter; the typical cat-and-dog marriage of Charles and Mary Musgrove, where selfishness and stupidity and good humour are so wonderfully blended; the self-centred, frigid matrimonial ambition of Elizabeth Elliot, the bereavement and desolation of Captain Benwick, which makes him, all unknown to himself, ready to fall in love again with the first sympathetic girl he meets; the domestic contentment of dear, good-natured old Mr. and Mrs. Musgrove; the unscrupulous, cold-blooded passion of Mr. Elliot, the well-meaning but mistaken interference in Anne Elliot's love affair by Lady Russell; the ridiculous vanity of Sir Walter Elliot which nearly makes him the victim of the odious Mrs. Clay. All these separate trains of interest converge upon the central love story, and the sum of the book is that we are enriched in our perception of the beauty of true and single-hearted love.

Variety of character is an essential feature of Jane Austen's art, but in Persuasion the characters strike one as being in stronger contrast than in any of the other novels. The characters of the hero and heroine are, it is true, always the complement of each other; there is not more difference between the sensitive, enduring Ann and the practical, impetuous Captain Wentworth than between Elizabeth and Mr. Darcy, or Emma and Mr. Knightley; but of the other characters one may say that the harmony produced from them is the harmony of strongest contrast. There is the brilliant audacity of combining Louisa Musgrove with Captain Benwick, and the contrast of Anne's unsatisfactory home life with the glowing picture of the Musgroves' domestic circle. Jane Austen had drawn no family like the Musgroves before, and though her satiric spirit never sleeps, they bloom under its rigours. There is the scene at Uppercross into which Louisa walks before dinner, explaining that she has come on foot to leave room in the carriage for the harp. ' "And I will tell you our reason," she added, "and all about it. I am come on to give you notice that papa and mama are out of spirits, especially mama; she is thinking so much of poor Richard! And we agreed it would be best to have the harp, for it seems to amuse her more than the pianoforte." ' There is Mrs. Musgrove's constant, homely kindness to Anne, her sympathy with the happiness of young people, and the noble set piece on the occasion of Lady Russell's call in the Christmas holidays, when Mr. Musgrove talked in a raised voice, 'but from the clamour of the children on his knees, generally in vain,' while Mrs. Musgrove observed 'with a happy glance round the room, that after all she had gone through, nothing was so likely to do her good as a little quiet cheerfulness at home.' *Persuasion* contains the last addition to that gallery of portraits in which a commonplace woman is revealed in a satiric masterpiece. Mary Musgrove's portrayal has not the vivacity of Mrs. Bennet's or Mrs. Norris's or Mrs. Elton's, but its comedy, though more subdued, is as marked; in photographic realism it equals theirs if it does not excel them, and the type of folly and disagreeableness it represents is that most commonly to be found among any that Jane Austen has displayed. On meeting so perverse, egotistical and silly a woman, one is puzzled to know how she ever attracted a good-natured man. The reply invariably is, when one is faced with an example of this temperament, exactly in the form of the explanation supplied by Jane Austen: that when such women are the centre of attention, they are, or can be, exceedingly amiable. During an engagement or a honeymoon they have their lapses, but as the exclusive object of their lovers' and their friends' attention, they manage to behave themselves very well. It is not until the ordinary wear and tear of married life begins that they show themselves in their true colours. Their outstanding characteristic is that they can never be brought to understand their own unreasonableness, and they manage to put aside all proofs of it without the smallest difficulty. When Anne goes to stay with Mary, the latter is lying on the sofa and complaining of ill-health.

' "Oh! Anne, I am so very unwell. It was quite unkind of you not to come on Thursday."

' "My dear Mary, recollect what a comfortable account you sent me of yourself! You wrote in the cheerfullest manner, and said you were perfectly well, and in no hurry for me; and that being the case, you must be aware that my wish would be to remain with Lady Russell to the last, and besides what I felt on her account, I have really been so busy, have had so much to do, that I could not very conveniently have left Kellynch sooner."

' "Dear me! what can *you* possibly have had to do?"

' "A great many things, I assure you. More than I can recollect in a

234

moment, but I can tell you some. I have been making a duplicate of the catalogue of my father's books and pictures. I have been several times in the garden with Mackenzie, trying to understand, and make him understand, which of Elizabeth's plants are for Lady Russell. I have had all my own little concerns to arrange, books and music to divide, and all my trunks to repack, from not having understood in time what was intended as to the waggons; and one thing I have had to do, Mary, of a more trying nature; going to almost every house in the parish, as a sort of take-leave. I was told that they wished it; but all these things took up a great deal of time."

' "Oh well!" and after a moment's pause, "but you have never asked me one word about our dinner at the Pooles yesterday." '

In her serious conversation, Jane Austen sometimes departs from the exact intonation of daily speech to give that utterance of the soul which daily speech does not give. But in her comic utterances she does not vary an iota from the standard of absolute realism.

Admiral and Mrs. Croft strike, as it were, a major chord in the harmony of *Persuasion*. The Admiral himself, whom one always thinks of as standing at the window of the print shop in Milsom Street gazing in fascinated wonder at the artist's idea of the construction of a boat, is a figure so lovable that, with the Musgroves, he does much to create the domestic warmth of the story, that contrasts so effectively with the atmosphere of Sir Walter, Mrs. Clay and Mr. Elliot. One of his most heart-warming remarks is delivered apropos of his settling in at Kellynch; it depends of course for its peculiar felicity on the previous account of how Sir Walter, impoverished but haughty, arrogant and foolish, thought it the utmost condescension on his own part to let his house at all, and that any tenant was far too fortunate in being allowed to rent it on any terms. The Admiral, once he has taken away the number of full-length looking-glasses out of Sir Walter's dressing-room, finds himself very comfortable at Kellynch and says to Anne: 'Take it altogether, now that we have been into most of the houses hereabouts and can judge, there is not one that we like better than this. Pray say so, with my compliments. He will be glad to hear it.'

It is Mrs. Croft, however, who is really the more interesting of the two. Her devotion to her husband is complete, and she had the strength of mind and body to be able to enter actively into the way of life his profession imposed upon her. In drawing-room at the Great House at Uppercross when Louisa and Henrietta are poring over the Navy List, hunting up the various ships in which Captain Wentworth had served, and Anne sits by, disregarded, Mrs. Croft vigorously repels her brother's statement that women had much better not be taken on

235

board a man-of-war because it is impossible to have them looked after properly, unless at the expense of the ship's efficiency. She details her experiences on board to the placid, wondering Mrs Musgrove. 'I do assure you, ma'am, that nothing can exceed the accommodations of a man-of-war; I speak, you know, of the higher rates. When you come to a frigate, of course, you are more confined, though any reasonable woman may be perfectly happy in one of them; and I can safely say, that the happiest part of my life has been spent on board a ship. While we were together, you know, there was nothing to be feared.'

... One of Jane Austen's means of enhancing probability is the extraordinary care—or perhaps the spontaneous insight—with which she manages a family relationship. This is one of the rarest attributes among novelists, but she has it in perfection. The Bennet family provide an excellent example of her skill in this respect; Jane Bennet inherits the mother's beauty and the mother's disposition towards good humour, which in Mrs. Bennet had been soured by her having no strength of mind to act as a preservative; but Jane combines this good humour with the father's strong cast of mind, though that particular mind in Mr. Bennet had deteriorated into selfishness and cynicism. Elizabeth, so far as she can be defined at all, is a bewitching combination in which the intellectualism of the father has a much greater part than in her sister, tempered by the volatile femininity which she inherited through the mother. Mary has the father's leaning towards academic interests, but the mother's folly has turned it in her case into vanity and pedantry. Kitty is a feeble edition of her mother, but without the health or beauty Mrs. Bennet had originally possessed. Lydia, bouncing and forward, self-centred and brainless, appears to be all the mother, but the father's capacity has made her a much more determined edition of Mrs. Bennet. Isabella Knightley, with her valetudinarianism and her anxious affection, and her fondness for gruel, is as much Mr. Woodhouse's daughter as Emma was the child of Mrs. Woodhouse, of whom Mr. Knightley said that in her mother Emma had lost the only person able to cope with her. One of the most striking cases of family likeness is that between Mrs. Croft and Captain Wentworth. There is the same capacity for affection, the same practical ability, amounting in the brother's case almost to genius. He was a man born to succeed in his profession; but the essential likeness is modified by the difference of sex. Mrs. Croft is calmer, though not less penetrating. When the Admiral said that one of the Musgrove girls would make a good wife for Frederic because they were so agreeable: ' "Very good-humoured, unaffected girls indeed," said Mrs. Croft in a tone of calmer praise, such as made Anne suspect that her keener powers might not consider either of them as quite worthy of her brother.' But Captain Wentworth's criticisms, though not expressed, showed themselves in a satirical eye and a curling mouth; and capable of strong feeling as Mrs. Croft was, and excellent as she would have been in giving practical assistance, she could scarcely have felt the impetuous, devoted sympathy showed by Captain Wentworth to poor Captain Benwick when he had to be told that the girl he was coming home to marry had died in the course of his voyage. Captain Harville told Anne: ' "I was at Plymouth, dreading to hear of him; he sent in letters, but the *Grappler* was under orders for Portsmouth. Then the news must follow him; but who was to tell it? Not I. I would as soon have been run up to the yard arm. Nobody could do it but that good fellow" (pointing to Captain Wentworth). "The *Laconia* had come into Plymouth the week before; no danger of her being sent to sea again. He stood his chance for the rest; wrote up for leave of absence, but without waiting the return, travelled night and day till he got to Portsmouth, rowed off to the *Grappler* that instant, and never left the poor fellow for a week. That's what he did, and nobody else could have saved poor James. You may think, Miss Elliot, whether he is dear to us!" ' People with relations in the Royal Navy plume themselves a little on the idea that they can realize better than others the verisimilitude of this description of Captain Wentworth's behaviour. The sympathy of men on active service for each other has been always celebrated; but the bond uniting men at sea together is often something unique in human experience. Captain Wentworth had done his best with the peculiarly unprofitable Dick Musgrove; and the story is the same today, when officers apply themselves with energy to straightening out the matrimonial and other entanglements of their crew, sometimes having to help and advise men actually older than themselves; while it is a thing often said that no one can be kinder and more comforting to a bereaved man than his shipmates.

Persuasion is, with all its naturalness and strength, so finished a work of art, that though Jane Austen never gave it the revision she was keeping it by her to perform, it seems at first blush as if even she could have done nothing more to it; but there are two passages in the work, nevertheless, which arouse criticism, and the reply to that criticism is, not that it is unfounded, but that the book is not before us in the form in which Jane Austen intended us to see it.

One of these concerns the narrative of Mrs. Smith, which, by contrast with the rest, is undeniably bald and flat. It is a piece of machinery which has not been softened and illuminated into life. The brilliantly spirited character of her writing as a whole impresses the reader irresistibly with the conviction that it came in all the first glow of creative energy and that its correctness of expression was due to the highly trained mind that formed a correct sentence involuntarily. That she did, of course, make minor corrections very frequently in a first draft is proved for instance by the edition of *Sanditon* which the Clarendon Press published in 1925, and which shows, roughly, an average of half a dozen corrections to every page of manuscript; but in almost every case they are corrections which are made upon a sentence already complete. Even in a first draft, Jane Austen does not appear to have begun a paragraph, halted in it and then crossed it out to begin afresh. Her changes are in the nature of giving the final lustre to what is already there. It would require alterations of a much more radical nature than these to bring up the story of Mrs. Smith to the level of Jane Austen's characteristic writing; and the improvements which we feel that she would almost certainly have made in it would have been obliged to have taken the form, not of a word scratched out here and another inserted there, but a taking of material into the crucible of imagination, and bringing it out again as a living substance; nor, though the powers behind the operation were great, and the matured product of a lifetime, would the changes themselves have occupied much space; they might all have been accomplished within that occupied by the episode in its present form.

Jane told Cassandra that she had lopped and cropped *Pride and Prejudice* successfully; she said she hoped that when a great deal more of *Which is the Heroine?* had been written down, Anna would feel equal to scratching out some of what had already been done; and it seems likely that the revision of her work which occupied so much of her time was principally concerned, in the later works at least, in taking out rather than in putting in: for one thing, Henry Austen said of her—and if his testimony is to be disregarded, there seems no reason why anybody else's should be believed—that 'in composition she was equally rapid and correct,' but that she *did* rely very much on the impression she gained of her work when she read it over some time after it had been written, when 'the charm of recent composition was dissolved.' In his estimate of his sister's character as an author, he contrasted, as two opposing features of it, her 'invincible distrust of her own judgement' which made her unwilling to let anything be seen by the public until she had come to a settled conclusion about it herself, with the unhampered brilliance and rapidity with which she actually wrote. Now *Persuasion* was finished in the July of 1816; and even in March of the next year Jane was writing of the book to Fanny Knight as of 'something ready for publication which may perhaps appear about a twelvemonth hence.' Had it been 'ready for publication' in the true sense of the word, as apart from being merely finished, she would not have envisaged a space of twenty months between its being finished and being offered to a publisher.

So much recollection is necessary before one comes to a consideration of the startling passage about Dick Musgrove. Many years before, Jane Austen had been annoyed by the parade the Debaries made about the death of their uncle, 'of whom they *now* say' that they saw a great deal while they were in London; the attitude of Mrs. Musgrove to her son, who was 'poor Richard' now that he was dead, but who had never been anything but 'a thick-headed, unfeeling, unprofitable Dick Musgrove' while he was living, struck her in the same way. Mrs. Musgrove's grief when she was reminded, by the introduction of Captain Wentworth to Uppercross, of the whole episode, 'her poor son gone for ever and all the strength of his faults forgotten,' had been greater 'than what she had known on first hearing of his death.' And on the evening of the famous party when the girls are scanning the Navy List, Mrs. Musgrove speaks to Captain Wentworth of Dick in such terms that Captain Wentworth's face assumes momentarily an expression which is too transient for anyone but Anne to catch; but 'in another moment he was perfectly collected and serious, and almost instantly afterwards coming up to the sofa, on which she and Mrs. Musgrove were sitting, took a place by the latter and entered into conversation with her, in a low voice, about her son, doing it with so much sympathy and natural grace, as showed the kindest consideration for all that was real and unabsurd in the parent's feelings.' The behaviour of Captain Wentworth is perfectly natural; he, in fact, appears in a much better light than Jane Austen on this occasion, who says that he should be 'allowed some credit for the self-command with which he listened to her large fat sighings over the destiny of a son, whom alive nobody had cared for.' She goes on to say that 'a large, bulky figure has as good a right to be in deep affliction as the most graceful set of limbs in the world. But, fair or not fair, there are unbecoming conjunctions which reason will patronize in vain—which taste cannot tolerate—which ridicule will seize.' We are not disposed to be nearly so ruthless in our dissection of Mrs. Musgrove's reasons for grief; nor does it seem to us that affliction is more moving in a graceful person than in one of exceedingly comfortable appearance; on the contrary, it seems to most people more harrowing in someone of normally hearty and cheerful exterior; that comment is, we feel, inadmissible in any case and the whole episode forms admirable material to the people who feel uncomfortable in the

239

presence of Jane Austen's skill. To those people such a passage can never be explained away; nor is it reasonable to expect that it should, for with the notorious remark about Mrs. Hall of Sherborne, it is all they have to go upon; but to those who are interested in trying to reconcile its distastefulness with the general impression of Jane Austen's kindliness, sympathy, and good taste, it must be recalled that what threw her out at the start was the fact, which always upset her, of someone's affecting a serious sensation which they did not genuinely feel. She abhorred rhapsodizing on religious topics; she consistently under-rated her own feeling for music because she so much disliked an affection of musical taste; her very strong feeling against hypocrisy and deceit (the suspicion of which damned Mr. Elliot long before his real unscrupulousness had been revealed) was another manifestation of the same instinct; and though Mrs. Musgrove is not charged with a shadow of either, she was indulging in sentimentality under the guise of a sacred feeling which, by the very nature of the case, she had never known; she was, in fact, feeling 'luxuriously low,' as people sometimes incline to be tearful after a heavy meal. It was all perfectly natural; and such of it as could be respected by even the keenest observer, was done full justice to by Captain Wentworth; but such striking clarity of vision exercised on a situation of which the component parts—poor old mother, son lost at sea—are enough to make most of us respond immediately without enquiring into the merits of the case, comes as a shock, particularly in a book so marked by tenderness of feeling. One cannot but remember how Mrs. Musgrove is treated when she really is in anguish over the accident to Louisa. Henrietta was brought back from Lyme in a state of collapse, and Captain Wentworth left her in the carriage while he went in and broke the news to Mr. and Mrs. Musgrove, and did not go back to Lyme till 'he had seen the father and mother quite as composed as could be hoped, and the daughter all the better for being with them.'

When we realize that none of the other novels contains an angularity like the treatment of Dick Musgrove, we feel that what is alarming in it as it now stands, not only ought to have come out, but would have come out if death had allowed the time.

At the time of the actual composition of *Persuasion* she felt the strain that ill-health put upon her powers, and it led her to do something which, from the impression it made on her immediate family, shows that it was altogether unusual with her. When she had come to the crisis of the lovers' reconciliation, she felt that she had handled it in a manner that was not sufficiently at concert pitch; she finished the last chapter on July 18th, but in the days that followed she was weighed

240

down by the sense that the climax was not fitted to crown the intensity of what led up to it. It was 'tame and flat,' she thought. One night she went to bed in such a state of depression as was altogether unusual to her; but the depth of her gloom was the turning point, for the next day she re-wrote the whole episode, bringing the Musgroves to Bath, and creating the two chapters in the course of which she gives that unequalled picture of the ecstasy of relief, and of happiness that is too acute to be felt at first except as pain.

Fortunately the cancelled chapter has survived, and to read it after one has read *Persuasion* is to gain some of the interest and pleasure which the more fortunate were able to enjoy in persuading Jane Austen to tell them other things about the characters of her novels. It does not, indeed, bear comparison with the *tour de force* with which it was replaced. It is conceived on a much simpler scale, and the acute moment takes place when Anne and Captain Wentworth are by themselves in the drawing-room of the Admiral's lodgings in Gay Street, so that the brilliantly varied comic background, which throws the state of their feelings into such relief, is absent; as also is the discussion on constancy between Anne and Captain Harville, which leads up to the climax with such effectiveness, but a good deal of the earlier version was incorporated into the latter, and the original contains one descriptive touch upon Captain Wentworth which the reader would be sorry to miss. 'His colour was changing and he was looking at her with all the power and keenness which she believed no other eyes than his possessed.'

The autobiographical significance of *Persuasion* is frequently debated, and one can but record the opinion once again that in essentials it has been very much overstressed. On the surface, it appears a matter for fruitful exploration. There is, for one thing, the fact of Jane Austen's own visit to Lyme twelve years before; the depth and vividness of her impression of its loveliness, as mirrored in her recollection. So present were her memories to her as she wrote, that she did not even view the beauties of the coast and sea through the eyes of the characters; she uttered her praise of them in her own person. Then there is the famous conversation in which Anne claimed for women the privilege 'of loving longest, when existence or when hope is gone!' The words would stand for a dead lover as well as for a faithless one. The impression that when Jane Austen wrote of Anne Elliot she was writing of herself, has been much strengthened by the unnamed lady who was acquainted with her, and who said that Jane Austen *was* Anne Elliot, in her quietness, elegance and sweetness.

But directly we approach the idea of trying to identify the characters of the novel with those of real life, including Jane Austen herself, we receive a very different impression. Captain Harville, for example, was understood to have been in part a picture of Frank Austen. Captain Frank Austen said many years afterward: 'I believe that part of Captain Harville's character was suggested by my own,' and it is easy to see what that part was, from the description of Captain Harville's domestic habits. He had immensely increased the accommodation of the little house at Lyme by his 'ingenious contrivances,' and made the doors and windows proof against the roughest weather. 'He drew, he varnished, he carpentered, he glued; he made toys for the children; he fashioned new netting needles and pins with improvements, and if everything else was done, sat down to his large fishing net at the corner of the room.' The warm family affection of Captain Harville was certainly to be found in Captain Austen, but would the self-contained, undemonstrative Captain Austen have made one in that conversation with Anne Elliot? Would he have been so profoundly moved by Captain Benwick's falling in love again after the death of Fanny Harville? How exceedingly different Frank Austen's temperament was from that of the emotional, eloquent Captain Harville, may be judged from the anecdotes given by Lord Brabourne. Sir Francis Austen was once on board, watching one of his officers taking a swim, when he saw that the bather was being pursued by a shark, and ejaculated with his usual precision: 'Mr. Pakenham, you are in danger of a shark—a shark of the blue species!' From the Admiral's measured utterance, Mr. Pakenham thought he must be joking, and was only induced to come on board in the nick of time. On another occasion Sir Francis Austen took a chronometer back for inspection to the maker from whom he had had it five years before. 'Well, Sir Francis,' said the maker complacently, 'it seems to have varied none at all!' 'Yes,' said Sir Francis, 'it *has* varied —*eight seconds!*'

On the question of Jane Austen's being identified with Anne Elliot, we need only ask, could Anne Elliot have written *Pride and Prejudice*? Anne Elliot's charms did not include vivacity and brilliance; she was clear-sighted and sensible, but her powers of judgement did not take the form of a startling insight into other people's characters; she could never have maintained a conversation such as Emma had with Mr. Knightley, or laughed at and with Captain Wentworth as Elizabeth's liveliness played over Mr. Darcy. Then we have a glimpse of what Anne Elliot had been at school; when Mrs. Smith first knew her she was a 'blooming, silent, unformed girl of fifteen.' Jane Austen, as a child, was blooming, indeed; but neither silent nor unformed. At twelve she was annoying Phila Walter with her airs; at fourteen she was writing *Love and Friendship*. But, at the same time, Jane Austen's own experience has left its mark on the book, though not through the method of being transferred to it. If she had never known what it was to love, she could not have known what love meant to Anne Elliot, and the effort she had once been obliged to make so that no one but Cassandra should know how desperately unhappy she was, had told her what fortitude meant, in a daily round that was lived through at home, in close family intercourse, without the relief of outside employment. But she had recovered in a way that was not possible to such a nature as Anne Elliot's; it was true that she had refused Mr. Bigg Wither, as Anne had refused Charles Musgrove. But whereas Anne could never have loved again, Jane Austen in her own person boldly rebutted the idea that one could be blighted for life by such an incident. As she said to Fanny Knight: 'It is no creed of mine, as you must be well aware, that such sort of disappointments kill anybody.' She said of Anne Elliot that the 'only thoroughly natural, happy and sufficient cure,' a second attachment, had not been possible to her, because the limited society in which she moved did not provide anybody whom she could love. The author therefore was prepared to believe that *circumstances* made a second attachment impossible to Anne Elliot; but Anne herself did not believe that her actual marriage with Captain Wentworth would have cut her off from other men more decidedly than her own feelings for him; and the differentiation between the character of the author and the creature of the author's mind is sealed by what Jane Austen said to Fanny about the novel: 'You may *perhaps* like the heroine, as she is almost too good for me.'

CHAPTER NINETEEN

Mr. John Murray owned the *Quarterly Review*. He had founded it in 1809, partly in opposition to the spirit of the *Edinburgh Review*, which to the list of its victims and opponents had added Sir Walter Scott. The fact that John Murray had published *Emma* was no doubt responsible for the novel's being reviewed by Scott in the *Quarterly*, but Scott's own appreciation of Jane Austen made his tribute a willing one. The actual review of *Emma*, however, is not so enthusiastic but that one believes that Mr. Jeffreys, who had been kept up by the novel for three nights, might have treated it rather better in the *Edinburgh*. Scott's review took the form of a discussion of Jane Austen's work as a whole; he celebrated the fact that she had developed and crystallized by her art that form of fiction which, he said, 'has arisen almost in our own time, and which draws the character and incidents introduced more immediately from the current of ordinary life than was permitted by the former rules of the novel.' Speaking particularly of *Emma*, he said that the novel showed the fault to which this form of fiction was liable: that though Mr. Woodhouse and Miss Bates were admirably presented, we saw too much of them, and therefore they were apt to become as tedious as they would have been in real life. But though we may think the review deficient in appreciation, Jane Austen did not. For the first years of its appearance, Mr. Murray found it very difficult to produce the *Quarterly* at the date on which it should properly have appeared; and therefore, though Scott's review had been written in 1815, it did not appear till March of 1816. Murray sent Jane Austen a copy of the review, and on April 1st she returned it with her thanks, saying: 'The authoress of *Emma* has no reason, I think, to complain of her treatment in it'; but she was distressed that Scott, in referring as he did to *Sense and Sensibility*, *Pride and Prejudice*, and *Emma*, had omitted all mention of *Mansfield Park*. 'I cannot but be sorry,' she said, 'that so clever a man as the reviewer of *Emma* should consider it unworthy of being noticed.' But she leaves the topic immediately 'You will be pleased to hear,' she goes on, 'that I have received the Prince's thanks for the *handsome* copy I sent him of *Emma*. Whatever he may think of *my* share of the work, yours seems to have been quite right.'

But, as not infrequently happens, the judgement of the critic when privately expressed is a good deal warmer than that which he permits himself to print. Nine years after Jane Austen's death Scott wrote in

244

his diary the appreciative comment of her work which, rather than the *Quarterly* article, has become the accepted expression of his opinion. On March 14th, 1826, he recorded: 'Read again for the third time at least, Miss Austen's finely written novel of *Pride and Prejudice*. That young lady had a talent for describing the involvements and feelings and characters of ordinary life which is to me the most wonderful I ever met with. The big Bow-Wow strain I can do myself like any now going; but the exquisite touch which renders ordinary common-place things and characters interesting from the truth of the description and the sentiment, is denied to me. What a pity such a gifted creature died so early!' When Mr. Edward Austen Leigh visited Abbotsford after Scott's death, he was shown Scott's own edition of Jane Austen's works; he noticed how well-worn the volumes were; as 'an unusual favour' he was allowed to take one of them into his hands.

When Scott referred to 'that exquisite touch which renders ordinary common-place things and characters interesting,' he laid his finger on one of the most integral aspects of Jane Austen's art, and that one in relation to which the story of her life is the most important.

The occult power of creating human personality—the rarest form of literary genius—which invests Jane Austen's work with its extraordinary nature, was a part of her with which, so to speak, she had nothing to do. Her conscious effort was merely directed to the exercising of it to what seemed to her the best advantage. The genius seems, in most cases, to be born with some self-protective consciousness, which enables him to adopt the conditions necessary to the producing of his work. It may be that those conditions involve a complete overthrowing of the conventional régime of existence; or it may be that, as in Jane Austen's case, he escapes the interference of the world by so identifying himself with ordinary life that he avoids its observation altogether. However much the methods differ, the end is always the same. To keep yourself unspotted from the world is not only true religion before God; it is also one of the first necessities of art. The injunction does not imply a separation of the artist from the world, but quite the contrary; in fact it may be doubted whether those great souls who are obliged to retreat to uninhabited localities and shake off the restraints of civilization before they can put pen to paper have very much strength of creative impulse behind their work. But it does imply that he must have the strength of mind and the desire to work irrespective of the intoxication of popular success. It would scarcely be denied that the majority of successful writers have not this strength and this desire, and the popular writers of to-day are more severely handicapped than those of fifty years ago, because the machinery of publicity has become so highly organized. Of publicity, we might say, what Burns said of adultery, that:

'It hardens all within, and petrifies the feeling.'

The method of expression imposed upon Jane Austen, by circumstances and personal choice, was one particularly liable to injury from the distortion of existence incurred by becoming a celebrity. If she had not been a genius, but merely a very talented writer, she would not, could not, have withstood the poison of success. Her persistent refusal to be known as an authoress, her anonymous publications, her distress at Henry Austen's revealing her identity, her gratitude to Captain Frank Austen for keeping it a secret, seem incomprehensible to many people of to-day. There was, it is true, an inducement to a woman writer then to preserve her anonymity which now barely exists. The female novelist and poet and writer of *belles lettres* was not then the accepted creature that she is to-day. In 1820 the gentle Charles Lamb was expressing the following views: he spoke of Mrs. Inchbald, the translator of *Lover's Vows*, as 'the only endurable clever woman he had ever known; called them impudent, forward, unfeminine, and unhealthy in their minds.' Of Letitia Landon he said: 'If she belonged to me, I would lock her up and feed her on bread and water till she left off writing poetry. A female poet, or female author of any kind, ranks below an actress, I think.'

At the same time, the prejudice against women writers was not universal, as may be seen by the brilliant success of Fanny Burney, and the praise which Jane Austen received from men even during her life-time. Had she wished to appear before the world as a novelist, and to taste in her own person the pleasures of celebrity, she could have done it. Not only could she have developed her acquaintance with Mr. Clarke, whom she had completely fascinated, and through him made her *entrée* into a very distinguished circle of literary society; it was her own positive refusal that prevented her doing so as it was. While she was with Henry in London on the occasion of her visit to Carlton House, Henry was approached by 'a nobleman' whose name, in repeating the anecdote, he did not give. This gentleman was giving a party at his town house, at which Madame de Staël was to be present. Madame de Staël had said that she would very much like the opportunity of meeting Miss Jane Austen. The host was very anxious to meet her also. Would she therefore come to the party? She refused to do so without a moment's hesitation. Considering Jane's fondness for parties and social amusements, and how gladly she would have gone in the

246

ordinary way with Henry to escort her, her refusal is significant. It was not the company she demurred at; she would have been quite at ease, in her unassuming way; she would have been interested enough to see Madame de Staël if she could have done so as an onlooker. It was the fact of having to appear as an author that made her reject the idea instinctively; and the incident suggests how mistaken those writers are who, in deploring her early death, say that had she lived longer she would have been able to emerge from her obscurity into a round of lunching and dining with the great.

Her immediate sensation in recoiling from the position she would naturally have held was no doubt one of unaffected modesty; she delighted to hear of praise, but she did not want to receive it in person; but whatever the conscious motive which led her to refuse to enter society as an authoress, she was actually obeying a profound instinct of self-preservation. The resolute determination never to relinquish the vantage ground of the ordinary human being had always possessed her. It accounted for her otherwise extraordinary attitude to Cassandra. Caroline Austen remembered that when she asked her Aunt Jane to tell her anything or explain anything to her, her Aunt Jane, in giving the required explanation, always said that Aunt Cassandra knew much more about the matter than she did, or could have explained it better. She invariably represented her sister as wiser, better informed, more important in every respect than she was herself; nor can one doubt that she really thought so. Affectation was as foreign to her as conceit. But it was not love and admiration only which guided her opinion; it was the need to take shelter behind another person, so that undue prominence and attention should not have to be supported by herself. Henry Austen said that *nothing* would have persuaded his sister, had she lived, to allow any of her novels to be published under her own name, and similarly, one feels nothing would have induced her to accept a position, even in her family, in which she had to support a well-defined attitude, or to be anything but the most natural and simple of human beings; such a position would have been abhorrent to her conscious mind, and it would have threatened that capacity of vision that was the inspiration of her art.

That, as a private individual, she was not of a retiring nature, is shown by the keen pleasure she took in social events, in the daily intercourse of family and friends. Her life and her work cannot really be described as in accord, because no external mode of life could suggest that extraordinary method which she practised of selecting from a range of imaginative experience those details which are so profoundly significant that they carry with them depth

247

upon depth of implication, and are yet displayed so artlessly that it is only the impact of the whole which leads one gradually to apprehend the adamantine solidity and strength of its construction. But from a superficial point of view her experience of life may be recognized as providing the texture of the backgrounds of her stories, and her acutely sensitive reactions to the social scene about her were what she guarded by her humility. She had the love of the children; her presence at Godmersham and Steventon could not but make a joyful stir; but, generally speaking, the scene did not alter because she came upon it; that was why she could see it with such undisturbed clarity. It is a favourite pastime to try to establish how much of it in actual detail she converted to her own use. The scarlet strawberries discovered at Chawton perhaps gave the idea of Mrs. Elton's strawberry party; the apricot detected on one of the trees, that of Mrs. Norris's acrimonious discussion with Dr. Grant. The fact that she thought Charles Austen's children not in such 'good order' as they ought to be and easily might be, is perhaps reflected in the behaviour of little Walter Musgrove, who would climb on to his Aunt's back as she was kneeling by his sick brother; an accident to the Austen's connection, Fanny Cage, who was taken to the White Hart and suffered dreadfully from the noise, may have had some share in the description of Louisa Musgrove's convalescence, in which she could not bear even the sudden shutting of a door. Jane Austen's desire to drive out in the phaeton of the somewhat disreputable gentleman at Bath may have had some bearing on Catherine Morland's adventures with John Thorpe. The topaze cross, and the delights of having home a young midshipman brother who was vigorously fond of dancing, had indubitably made their contribution to her work. But, in general, it was not the actual scene, just as it was not the precise locality, which informed her work; it was the distillation of it produced by her imagination; and though it is fascinating to stand in Leatherhead church and read that Mr. Knightley rebuilt the pulpit, it is a kind of amusement to which it is easy to attach too much value and which is apt to obstruct the approach to a true understanding of Jane Austen's genius. The attempt to reconstruct something of biographical significance from those characters who form the chief part of each novel not only under-rates the power of Jane Austen's achievement, it also overlooks the tendency in the mind of the imaginative person to create a compensation for what is not there; not in the crude sense of what is described as 'wish fulfilment,' by which Jane Austen would be presumed to be writing a story of successful love because her own had been unsuccessful; but in the sense that the eye, where it has been dazzled by a primary colour, on being turned away from it, sees the complementary colour for a moment. People who pride themselves upon a knowledge of psychological matters are frequently very eager to infer from the presence of certain types in a novel the presence of those types in the author's experience. They would show themselves better informed if they argued from it a condition exactly the reverse.

The idea that Jane Austen preyed, as it were, upon society to find material for her books, was not only repudiated by herself, when she said she was too proud of her gentlemen to admit that they were only Mr. A. or Captain B.—it was strenuously denied by her relations. Caroline Austen said there was no one of whom it was so little reasonable to be afraid as of her Aunt Jane; and the stillness she often maintained in her latest years, though it was sometimes ascribed by people who had, against her will, heard that she was a novelist, to a taking of mental notes, was owing, said her family, to the fact that, with all her pleasantness, she was a little reserved and shy before strangers.

But Miss Mitford, in her *Recollections of a Literary Life*, expressed a different view. Miss Mitford said, that her mother had said, that when *she* had lived in the neighbourhood of Steventon before her marriage, Jane Austen had been 'the prettiest, silliest, most affected, husband-hunting butterfly' Mrs. Mitford ever remembered. The portrait, allowing for Miss Mitford's spite, is an attractive one, though some doubts are cast upon its reliability by Mr. Edward Austen Leigh where he says in his memoir that Mrs. Mitford had married in 1785, when Jane was ten years old, and that Mrs. Mitford had actually left Ashe, of which parish her father Dr. Russell was the Rector, in 1783, and therefore her acquaintance with the Austen family had ceased when Jane was seven. But Miss Mitford went on to say; 'A friend of mine who visits her now, says that she has stiffened into the most perpendicular, precise, taciturn piece of "single blessedness" that ever existed and that, till *Pride and Prejudice* showed what a precious gem was hidden in that unbending case, she was no more regarded in society than a poker or a fire-screen. The case is very different now. She is still a poker, but a poker of whom everybody is afraid. It must be confessed that this silent observation from such an observer is rather formidable . . . a wit, a delineator of character who does not talk, is terrific indeed!'

The latter description of Jane Austen, she said, it is true, might not be correct, because though the lady from whom she had it was 'truth itself,' she was a relation of the gentleman who was suing Edward Knight for the Chawton property, and as such would be disagreeable to Jane Austen's family and probably treated by them with reserve; but Miss Mitford goes on to say, in explaining the legal complication which had given rise to the suit—'You must have remarked how much her stories hinge upon entailed estates—doubtless she had learned to dislike entails.' Miss Mitford is not to be blamed for not knowing that *Pride and Prejudice* as a story was composed in 1797; or even for not realizing that it was published in 1813, a year before the lawsuit in question arose. It is the statement that Jane Austen's stories 'hinge so much upon entails' that, coming from someone who professed to know something of what she was talking about, and having, moreover, a respectable literary reputation to support, causes some degree of astonishment. In *Sense and Sensibility* the inheriting of a property by the male descendants, to the exclusion of the female, is the only apology for an entail in the story; and of all her six novels, *Pride and Prejudice* is the only one which mentions an entail or could be said to 'hinge upon it.'

This portion of Miss Mitford's comment may be judged by ourselves; the other was not only indignantly denied by her relations, but the editor of Miss Mitford's *Recollections* felt obliged to enter his protest against it. The Rev. G. L. L'Estrange added a footnote to this anecdote, saying it was only fair to add that every other account of Jane Austen, from any source whatever, spoke of her as being graceful, elegant and shy. Miss Mitford says a few lines further on: 'I do not think Walter Scott did write *Guy Mannering*.'

The fact that Jane's nieces and nephews, whose dearest recollections of her dated from the last years of her life, suggested that she was, though pleasantly ready to talk, somewhat shy before strangers, and that the lady who was truth itself, meeting her after 1814, saw something in her manner which she was able to describe as stiffness and taciturnity, suggests at least that a change had come over her, that she was not well. By the end of 1815 she knew that she was not, though no one outside Chawton Cottage knew it.

That she was not a satiric poker, if it were worth while seriously to debate the question, would, one feels, be sufficiently shown by a consideration of her work. Her style, and most especially that of the four latest works, has the liveliness and spontaneity of conversation. It is strikingly correct though not invariably so. On the first page of *Emma* we read that Emma was the youngest of Mr. Woodhouse's two daughters; we quite frequently meet with a clause followed by a subject not its own; as in the end of the tenth chapter of *Persuasion*, where we read of Mrs. Croft, that 'by coolly giving the reins a better direction herself, *they* happily passed the danger,' but the errors are few, and they are all the faults of conversation; apart from its evocative power, which can scarcely be appreciated unless the work be read as a whole, her writing is a remarkable blend of correctness with the spontaneous intimate tone of conversation. In one sense her task was easier than it would be now. The novelist of to-day, even when writing of the educated class, runs a great risk, if he makes his characters speak correctly, of making them sound unnatural; in 1815, incorrect speech in a novel as supposed to be uttered by educated people would have drawn a broadside of contumely and derision from every reviewer. At the same time, Jane Austen was faced with an obstacle which we do not meet, and she surmounted it. Without the aid of bad grammar, she managed, for example, exactly to convey the mentality of Harriet Smith, of Mrs. Price and Isabella Thorpe; and if one considers how eagerly the writer of to-day would fly to the aid of exclamation and characteristic faults of speech to express the personalities of Harriet and Isabella, and Mrs. Price, and what his feelings would be if he were told that he must discard them all and create the impact of those personalities in English language that was perfectly correct, we gain some idea once again of the strength of intellectual achievement behind the placing of those simple words. The conversational emphasis of such a style could never have been formed by someone who was not socially-minded, drawn to gatherings of people, accustomed to converse. It is no more the style of a recluse than that of a scholar.

The late Alice Meynell, who spoke of 'the essential meanness of Jane Austen's art,' said that her style was 'a mouthful of thick words.' As Jane herself said of a malapropos remark of Mrs. Digweed's:* 'What she meant, poor woman, who shall say?'

* Letter 75.

251

CHAPTER TWENTY

In December of 1816 Henry Austen was ordained and received the curacy of Bentley, near Alton, but before the transformation of the London banker into the country clergyman was complete, he performed a last office for his sister in his former capacity. He visited the offices of Messrs. Crosby and, for the sum of £10, regained possession of *Northanger Abbey*. The family tradition says that when the transaction was concluded, and not till then, he told the firm that the manuscript they had had in their possession for the past thirteen years, and had just parted with, was by the author of *Pride and Prejudice*, *Mansfield Park* and *Emma*.

It was a pleasant thing to Jane to have Henry so near at hand, and another member of the immediate circle had begun to take a more important part in it. Edward Austen (Mr. Austen Leigh) was in his last year at Winchester. Like all of James Austen's children, Edward was writing a novel. His Aunt Jane read it as a matter of course; she thought it very spirited, which was what she always required of a novel, and it interested her because, after Anna's work, it was so masculine. She thoroughly enjoyed Edward's novel, Edward's society and Edward's letters. On his coming home for his last summer holiday, he had written to her to announce his arrival, with the address of Steventon Rectory at the top of his letter. She replied to this: 'I am glad you recollected to mention your being come home. My heart began to sink within me when I had got so far through your letter without its being mentioned. I was dreadfully afraid that you might be detained at Winchester by severe illness, confined to your bed perhaps, and quite unable to hold a pen, and only dating from Steventon in order, with a mistaken sort of tenderness, to deceive me. But now, I have no doubt of your being at home. I am sure you would not say it so seriously unless it actually were so.' The party in Chawton Cottage, she said, had been amused by watching the procession of countless post chaises coming down the Winchester road as a result of the school's breaking up, 'full of future heroes, legislators, fools and villains.' She hoped that Edward was going to pay them a visit, but she knew it could not be yet, because his mother had been ill; but after she should be recovered, Jane said: 'A little change of scene may be good for you, and your physician, I hope, will order you to the sea, or to a house by the side of a very considerable pond.' When Mary was well enough she went to

Cheltenham to complete her cure and Cassandra went with her; meanwhile Edward came, as his aunt had hoped, to Chawton Cottage. When Jane wrote to Cassandra, she said they had all heard as much of Edward's novel as had been written. She added: 'It is extremely clever; written with great ease and spirit;—if he can carry it on, in the same way, it will be a first rate work, and in a style, I think, to be popular. Pray tell Mary how much I admire it; and tell Caroline that I think it is hardly fair upon her and myself, to have him take up the novel line.'

In December, Edward left Winchester for good, and his Aunt Jane wrote to him saying: 'One reason for my writing to you now, is that I may have the pleasure of directing to you *Esqre*. I give you joy of having left Winchester. Now you may own how miserable you were there; now, it will gradually all come out—your crimes and your miseries—how often you went up by the mail to London and threw away fifty guineas at a tavern, and how often you were on the point of hanging yourself.' Henry Austen had not yet preached his first sermon in the neighbourhood, but he had written some, and Jane had read them. She said to Edward: 'Uncle Henry writes very superior sermons.—You and I must try and get hold of one or two, and put them into our works;—it would be a fine help to a volume; and we could make our heroine read it aloud of a Sunday evening, just as well as Isabella Wardour in the *Antiquary* is made to read the history of the Hartz Demon in the ruins of St. Ruth—though I believe, upon recollection, Lovell is the reader.' And speaking of novels, she remembered Mary's telling them that some of Edward's manuscript had become mislaid. 'By the by, my dear Edward, I am quite concerned for the loss your mother mentions in her letter, two chapters and a half to be missing is monstrous! It is well that *I* have not been at Steventon lately, and therefore cannot be suspected of purloining them;—two strong twigs and a half towards a nest of my own, would have been something—I do not think however that any theft of that sort would be really very useful to me. What should I do with your strong, manly, spirited sketches, full of variety and glow? How could I possibly join them on to the little bit (two inches wide) of Ivory on which I work with so fine a brush, as produced little effect after much labour?' This famous description of her own work, tossed off in a letter that appears to consider her nephew's writing on the same level of importance as her own, has been frequently applied by other people as an objective criticism of Jane Austen's writing. When one remembers that brilliantly rapid opening of *Pride and Prejudice*, that sets its characters moving almost as soon as we hear their names; the vigorous delineation of Mr. Price and his family; the sense of space she conveys in the drawing of

253

her great houses—Northanger, Pemberley and Mansfield; to say nothing of her wide range of characters, none of whom ever repeats another, the universal nature of her comic vision, the depth of the emotional passages in *Persuasion*, to name but a few of the aspects of her work, 'the little bit (two inches wide) of Ivory,' and, above all, the brush, so fine that it produces little effect after much labour, seem altogether inappropriate as images of her workmanship. The passage requires the context of the letter in which it was written to set it in correct proportion; it was a figure conceived to form a complete contrast to the scale of Edward's work, rather than a considered impartial definition of her own. The 'little result' attained after 'much labour' is characteristic, not perhaps of her own genuine estimation of her work, but of the way she chose to speak of it to anyone but Cassandra. Though we know that she thought Elizabeth Bennet as delightful a creature as had ever appeared in print, no one but Cassandra knew it at the time.

In the January of 1817 Jane felt better than she had done for some months and able to undertake a wider correspondence. She wrote to Alethea Bigg, who was staying with relations-in-law at Streatham, saying: 'I think it time there should be a little writing between us.' She began by speaking of the floods and hoping nobody at Streatham had become rheumatic in the damp. As for the rain, she said: 'Though we have a great many ponds and a fine running stream through the meadows, on the other side of the road, it is nothing but what beautifies us and does to talk of.' She then went on to say that she had become stronger during the winter. She had come to the conclusion that bile was the cause of her trouble, which, she said, 'makes it easy to know how to treat myself.' She gave Miss Bigg news of the Steventon family. Edward was more and more a favourite with both his aunts; while Anna, whose second baby had been born the previous October, was looking better than she had done since her marriage; they could not see her often, however; her grandmother, who was so very fond of her, could not move from the cottage, and the roads had been so wet and dirty, Anna had not been able to get over to them. The donkey carriage was not in use either, and both donkeys were out at grass, so altogether communication was hardly possible at present. Henry was to preach for the first time at Chawton the next Sunday. His sister said: 'I shall be very glad when the first hearing is over. It will be a nervous hour for our pew, though we hear that he acquits himself with as much ease and collectedness as if he had been used to it all his life.'

The illness from which she thought she was recovering pursued its insidious course. In the March of 1817 the future, as it is for most people, was cut off from the family as by a wall; they were anxious about

254

her, but if they had been told it, they could not have grasped the idea that she had only four more months in which to live. But when the train of events is reviewed from the other end, it casts an impressive shade over the last letters which she wrote immediately before she realized that she was very ill; such are the two letters to Fanny Knight, written in March, and though they are lively as ever, they are more tender than before, and they contain advice which must have made Fanny thankful that she had brought on the correspondence, when by the margin of a few weeks she might have lost the chance of doing it for ever.

Fanny was again in a perplexity about getting married. She was now being pursued by Mr. Wildman of Chilham Castle, a seat in the neighbourhood of Godmersham. When her aunt received the letters telling her everything about the affair, she wrote in reply: 'My dearest Fanny, You are inimitable, irresistible. You are the delight of my life. Such letters, such entertaining letters as you have lately sent! Such a description of your queer little heart! Oh, what a loss it will be when you are married. You are too agreeable in your single state, too agreeable as a niece—I shall hate you when your delicious play of mind is all settled down into conjugal and maternal affections.' She felt sure from what Fanny had said, that Mr. Wildman was determined to be a successful lover. 'Do not imagine that I have any real objection. I have rather taken a fancy to him than not, and I like Chilham Castle for you;—only I do not like you should marry anybody. And yet I do wish you to marry very much, because I know you will never be happy till you are.' Then, besides being in doubt over Mr. Wildman, Fanny was agitated because Mr. Plumtree, whom she had obliged to think that he had been deceiving himself two years ago, now showed signs of being about to marry somebody else. Her Aunt Jane tried to brace her. 'Why should you be living in dread of his marrying somebody else? (yet, how natural!) You did not choose to have him yourself; why not allow him to take comfort where he can?'

Fanny sent a very long and full letter in reply, and its contents caused Jane to alter her opinion of Mr. Wildman's eligibility. 'I have pretty well done with Mr. Wildman. By your description, he cannot be in love with you, however he may try at it, and I could not wish the match unless there were a great deal of love on his side.' She discussed the question of marriage for women in general. 'Single women have a dreadful propensity for being poor,—which is one very strong argument in favour of matrimony.' (But it had not prevailed on her to marry Mr. Bigg Wither.) 'Well,' she said, 'I shall say as I have often said before, Do not be in a hurry; depend upon it, the right man will

255

come at last; you will in the course of the next two or three years meet with somebody more generally unexceptionable than anyone you have yet known, who will love you as warmly as ever *he* did, and who will so completely attach you that you will feel you never really loved before.' Within three years of her death, Jane's words came true; in 1820 Fanny made her happy marriage with Sir Edward Knatchbull. She must often have thought of her aunt's prophecy.

Jane Austen advanced another reason why postponing marriage for a year or two would be all to the advantage of her favourite niece. Anna Lefroy had had two children in less than two years, and now it seemed that she was to have another. Cassandra had been over to Wyards the day before, and Jane said: 'Anna has a bad cold, looks pale, and we fear something else.' Ten days later her aunt's fears were confirmed. Jane wrote to Fanny: 'Anna has not a chance of escape; her husband called here the other day, and said she was *pretty* well but not equal to so long a walk; she must come in her donkey carriage.—Poor animal, she will be worn out before she is thirty.—I am very sorry for her.' But Fanny, said her Aunt Jane, by not 'beginning the business of mothering quite so early in life,' would keep her youthfulness of face and figure while her contemporaries, who were married already, were growing old by confinements and nursing.

Fanny had not at all broken off acquaintance with Mr. Wildman; on the contrary, she had obliged him to read one of Jane Austen's novels and had then extracted his opinion of it without telling him her relationship to the author. Her father had told her this was unfair, particularly as the opinion expressed by Mr. Wildman had not been favourable. Fanny sent an account of the whole to her Aunt Jane, who was interested to hear it all, but had to agree with 'your Papa' that it was *not* fair. 'You are the oddest creature! Nervous enough in some respects, but in others perfectly without nerves!—Quite unrepulsable, hardened and impudent. Do not oblige him to read any more.—Have mercy on him, tell him the truth and make him an apology.' She was much interested none the less to hear what Mr. Wildman's views had been, she said: 'I *hope* I am not affronted, and do not think the worse of him for having a brain so very different from mine.' Mr. Wildman had clearly thought that the heroine of whichever novel he had been obliged to read was deficient in propriety. Jane Austen said: 'He and I should not in the least agree of course in our ideas of novels and heroines:—pictures of perfection, as you know, make me sick and wicked,—but there is some very good sense in what he says, . . . and he deserves better treatment than to be obliged to read any more of my works.'

256

She spoke now of *Persuasion*: 'You will not like it, so you need not be impatient,' and added her remark about Fanny's *perhaps* liking the heroine, as she was almost too good for herself.

'Many thanks,' she said, 'for your kindness of my health. I certainly have not been well for many weeks, and about a week ago I was very poorly, I have had a good deal of fever at times and indifferent nights, but am considerably better now, and recovering my looks a little, which have been bad enough, black and white and every wrong colour. I must not depend upon being ever very blooming again. Sickness is a dangerous indulgence at my time of life.' In a small letter to Caroline she said: 'I am a poor honey at present. I will be better when you can come and see us.'

They had had a saddle made for her to ride on one of the donkeys, as she was longing for fresh air and could not walk without becoming so very much tired. She told Fanny on March 23rd that she had been for her first ride the day before and liked it very much. Edward had come over from Steventon, and he walked on one side of her and Cassandra on the other. They went up Mounters Lane and round by where some new cottages were to be, and Jane enjoyed it all—air, exercise and agreeable companions. 'Aunt Cass is such an excellent nurse,' she said, 'so assiduous and unwearied! But you know that already.'

Though by the middle of March she was feeling too weak to walk, for the previous three months she had thought herself so much better as to be able to begin another novel. To the thirteen-year-old manuscript of *Northanger Abbey*, when it was once more in her hands, she did nothing, except to write a preface, in which she apologized for such parts of the story as should have become obsolete during the time which had elapsed since its composition, and in which she could not forbear to say: 'That any bookseller should think it worth while to purchase what he did not think worth while to publish, seems extraordinary.' But she had by no means determined the book should be published now. On March 17th, 1817, she wrote to Fanny—'*Miss Catherine* is put upon the shelf for the present, and I do not know that she will ever come out.' But she had begun a work in January, and continued it for three months, till she was obliged to put it by. This fragment, to which her family attached the name of *Sanditon*, was referred to at length by Mr. Edward Austen Leigh in the memoirs, but not published in full till 1925. Few people, probably, would see in *Sanditon* the promise of a novel such as we see promised by *The Watsons*. There is no character in *Sanditon*, although the first twelve chapters introduce two heroines, in whom we feel such a degree of interest as we feel for Emma Watson.

But the work is precious and important, because of its character as a whole, coming as it does immediately after the composition of *Persuasion*. People who are fond of deducing a novelist's experience from the characters of his work have always, in the case of Jane Austen, pinned their theories upon *Persuasion*. Coming, as was supposed, at the end of Jane Austen's career as a writer, *Persuasion* offered a ground for theorizing too tempting to be ignored. The fact that it showed, besides its new, pensive sensibility, a fuller use of the adornment of landscape, and that landscape under the sweet sadness of autumn, and a tendency to dwell on scenes she herself had visited in the past, seemed to make the book a most appropriate close to the full and brilliant period of her novel-writing, and people said confidently that had she lived, her next novels would have showed a marked change from those written before 1816, and been altogether more on the lines suggested by *Persuasion*. With regard to the probable character of the final fragment, such critics had not only *Persuasion* from which to argue, but the undoubted fact that when she wrote it, Jane Austen was not ill only, but dying. It was most disconcerting of her to have written *Sanditon*.

For *Sanditon* is so brilliantly comic that were it not for the fact that, as ever, her characters are real men and women inhabiting a real world, one would describe it as a farce. Its mainspring, so far as the twelve chapters allow one to judge, is a case of *idée fixe*, dominating two members of the Parker family, Mr. Parker, a married man with four children, and his sistser Diana. In Mr. Parker's case the ruling passion has found an outlet in the projection of a small watering-place on the immediate coast-line, in front of the old village of Sanditon, which is to perpetuate the name, and to be a rival not only to every other speculator's mushroom of the kind, but to the established Sussex watering-places of Brighton and Eastbourne. The scheme had become the motive for Mr. Parker's existence; he saw everything in terms of Sanditon, and the opening of the story establishes, not only the connection of one of the heroines with Sanditon, but the whole bent of Mr. Parker's mentality.

He and Mrs. Parker invite the eldest Miss Heywood to visit them at their house in Sanditon. In this young lady Jane Austen redeemed the promise she had lightly made to Cassandra, when she heard how thorough-going Miss Charlotte Williams had been in her admiration of Chawton Cottage, of calling a heroine after her. Charlotte Heywood, a sensible, attractive girl of twenty-two, is the character through whose eyes we have the first view of Sanditon and its inhabitants.

On the way thither the carriage passes the old home of the Parkers, now let to another family, while the Parkers have established themselves right up on the cliff in a new house, called Trafalgar House, 'which by the by,' said Mrs. Parker, 'I almost wish I had not named Trafalgar—for Waterloo is more the thing now. However, Waterloo is in reserve—and if we have enough encouragement this year for a little crescent to be ventured on—(as I trust we shall) then we shall be able to call it Waterloo Crescent—and the name joined to the form of the buildings which always takes, will give us the command of lodgers.— In a good season, we should have more applications than we could attend to.'

Mr. Parker looks now with scorn on the old house, surrounded by trees and sheltered by a hill. 'Our ancestors, you know, always built in a hole,' he said; and when Mrs. Parker says wistfully that all the same they had been exceedingly happy there, and had never felt the high winds which in their new house almost rock their beds, her husband replies eagerly: '*We* have all the grandeur of the storm, with less real danger, because the wind, meeting with nothing to oppose or confine it around our house, simply rages and passes on,—while down in this gutter—nothing is known of the state of the air below the tops of the trees,—and the inhabitants may be taken totally unawares by one of those dreadful currents, which do more mischief in a valley when they *do* arise than an open country ever experiences in the heaviest gale.'

The scene of Sanditon itself is more fully described than most of Jane Austen's localities. The old village stood at the foot of a hill, 'whose side was covered with the woods and enclosures of Sanditon House and whose height ended in an open down where the new buildings might soon be looked for.' The village 'contained little more than cottages, but the spirit of the day had been caught, as Mr. Parker observed with delight to Charlotte, and two or three of the best of them were smartened up with white curtains and "Lodgings to Let"—and farther on, in the little green court of an old farm house, two females in elegant white were actually to be seen with their books and camp stools—and in turning the corner of the baker's shop, the sound of a harp might be heard through the upper casement.'

Mr. Parker was delighted by all this, because if the village were attracting holiday-makers, what might not be expected from the hill? 'He anticipated an amazing season. At the same time last year (late in July), there had not been a single lodger in the village!—nor did he remember any during the whole summer, excepting one family of children who came from London for sea air after the whooping cough, and whose mother would not let them be nearer the shore for fear of their tumbling in.' As they ascend the hill, Jane Austen's curious aptitude for suggesting the atmosphere of the sea, which she had displayed

259

in *Mansfield Park* and *Persuasion*, is exercised again. When they reached the top of the down, there appeared Trafalgar House, 'a light, elegant building, standing on a small lawn with a very young plantation round it, about an hundred yards from the brow of a steep, but not very lofty cliff, and the nearest to it of every building, excepting one short row of smart-looking houses, called the Terrace, with a broad walk in front, aspiring to be the mall of the place. In this row were the best milliner's shop and the library—a little detached from it, the hotel and billiard-room.—Here began the descent to the beach, and to the bathing machines'; and when the travellers had been set down at Trafalgar House, and Mr. and Mrs. Parker were being welcomed by their children, Charlotte, having been shown to her room, 'found amusement enough in standing at her ample, Venetian window, and looking over the miscellaneous foreground of unfinished buildings, waving linen, and tops of houses, to the sea, dancing and sparkling in sunshine and freshness.' There are many short passages where, with a sentence here and a reference there, Jane Austen calls up a vision of the concrete scene: the Devonshire valley of Barton, the Park at Rosings, the villages of Highbury and Uppercross, the bare fields about Winthrop: but nowhere, not even in her descriptions of Portsmouth and Lyme Regis, has she given so full-length a picture of visible surroundings. This one is of particular interest historically, because, composed in 1817, it was an utterance of the time which regarded even Brighthelmstone as of comparatively recent origin, and to those who know the olive-grey turf that is meant by Sussex downs and who, from the Regency buildings of Brighton, white or butter-yellow, or the colour of clotted cream, can visualize Trafalgar House and its neighbouring terrace above that dancing, sparkling sea, the description calls up a view startling in its bare elegance and fresh clarity.

It may have been that Jane Austen's correspondence with Mr. Clarke, the last of whose letters had been addressed to her from the Pavilion, had turned her thoughts towards Brighton and the speculating in seaside resorts. There is no actual record of her having been to one of the new watering-places, or even to Brighton, Folkestone or Eastbourne; she was of course familiar with Ramsgate, which, prospering definitely as a seaside resort, would have been much nearer to the character at which Sanditon aimed than either Southampton or Lyme Regis; it may be that the conception of 'projecting' a sea-side resort had its origin in something she heard or saw between the years 1806 and 1809, when she was living at Southampton.

The enthusiasm which made the really pleasant, guileless Mr. Parker transfer his house, his family, his custom and all his interests to

Sanditon, in the attempt to nourish and force the plan into success, shows itself in the great Lady of the neighbourhood, Lady Denham, 'born to wealth but not to education.' She is the patron of a young niece and nephew, Sir Edward and Miss Denham, who live near her at Denham House, and has living with her on a visit of undefined length the girl whom we recognize as the other heroine, an exceedingly impoverished but reserved and beautiful creature, tall, elegant and blue-eyed, called Clara Brereton. Lady Denham is far from being without goodness; she was, apparently, very kind to Clara; but with a mixture of vulgarity and shrewdness, she entirely saw through every attempt to court her because of her money, and at the same time enjoyed the power and influence her money enabled her to exert. She takes an immediate fancy to Charlotte, and after the latter has had a slight introduction to Lady Denham's nephew and niece, Lady Denham, walking about the Terrace with her, begins to relate family matters to her, 'with the excuse of one who felt that any notice from her was an honour, and communicative from the influence of the same conscious importance or a natural love of talking.' Among other instances of her own sagacity and benevolence, she told Charlotte that when her husband had died, she had given Sir Edward his gold watch. 'She said this with a look at her companion which implied its right to produce a great impression, and seeing no rapturous astonishment in Charlotte's countenance, added quickly: "He did not bequeath it to his nephew, my dear—It was no bequest. It was not in the will. He only told me, and *that* once, that he should wish his nephew to have his watch; but it need not have been binding if I had not chose it."' Lady Denham's designs were of a much more personal nature than Mr. Parker's, and when it was understood that two parties of visitors, a boarding-school from Camberwell and a lady with a West Indian heiress under her care, were expected in Sanditon, she at once designed the heiress for her impecunious nephew, and for the pupils of the former she said: 'Out of such a number, who knows but some may be consumptive and want asses' milk—and I have two milch asses at this present time.' When the West Indian young lady arrived, Lady Denham 'made the acquaintance for Sir Edward's sake and the sake of her milch asses. How it might answer with regard to the baronet remained to be proved, but as to the animals, she soon found that all her calculations of profit would be vain.' The young lady's guardian, Mrs. Griffiths, 'would not allow Miss Lambe to have the smallest symptom of a decline, or any complaint which asses' milk could possibly relieve. "Miss Lambe was under the constant care of an experienced physician; and his prescriptions must be their rule."—and except in favour of some tonic pills,

261

which a cousin of her own had a property in, Mrs. Griffiths did never deviate from the strict medicinal page.'

The expected arrival of the two families and its outcome forms the climax of the novel in so far as it has progressed. Mr. Parker's sister Diana, of whom, with her sister Susan, it was said that they must either be very ill or very busy, had heard, through a chain of intelligence, of Mrs. Griffith's desire for a seaside resort ('You must have heard me mention Miss Capper, the particular friend of my very particular friend, Fanny Noyce—now Miss Capper is extremely intimate with a Mrs. Darling, who is on terms of constant correspondence with Mrs. Griffiths herself'); and with her brother's own zeal, though in a more feminine and intensified form, she had insisted on Sanditon's being recommended to Mrs. Griffiths. At the same time she had heard that the lady in charge of the Camberwell seminary was also proposing to move to the sea-side, and Diana Parker got her friend Mrs. Charles Dupuis to recommend Sanditon to *her*. This lady was strong-minded and capable and able to choose lodgings for herself, but Mrs. Griffiths, Miss Diana Parker believed, was enervated and undecided and quite at a loss, and consequently, although she had been in the throes of severe illness, and her sister Susan equally so, they both, accompanied by their brother Arthur, appeared suddenly at Sanditon, and while Susan and Arthur remained and settled the question of lodging, Diana ran about, hiring a house at eight guineas a week for Mrs. Griffiths, and opening preliminary negotiations with cooks, house-maids, washer-women and bathing-women from whom Mrs. Griffiths was to take her choice; and then wrote a letter to Mrs. Griffiths, to whom she was entirely unknown, telling her that everything was ready for her reception. The note that had been sounded in the opening pages of Mr. Parker's obsession, swells to a crescendo when it is realized that Mrs. Griffiths' party and the Camberwell seminary are one and the same: 'The Mrs. Griffiths who in her friend Mrs. Darling's hands, had wavered as to coming, and been quite unequal to the journey, was the very same Mrs. Griffiths whose plans were at the same period (under another representation), perfectly decided, and who was without fears or difficulties.— All that had had the appearance of incongruity in the reports of the two, might very fairly be placed to the account of the vanity, the ignorance or the blunders of the many engaged in the cause by the vigilance and caution of Miss Diana Parker. *Her* intimate friends must be officious like herself, and the subject had supplied letters and extracts and messages enough to make everything appear what it was not.' The *dénouement*, the resolving of the family party and the girls' boarding-school into one party consisting of Mrs. Griffiths and three young

262

ladies, occurs in a scene which is the height of the whole comic achievement.

There are two aspects of the work which are altogether new in Jane Austen's writing, the first concerning her treatment of Sir Edward Denham. The character breaks new ground; because though Willoughby had a very ugly story in his past, and Wickham thought nothing of eloping with a girl who threw herself at his head, and Henry Crawford was so loose-living that he couldn't resist an affair even in circumstances when it was bound to cost him the engagement he was really anxious to secure; Edward Denham, the young man who had read too many novels and fancied himself as a Lovelace, approached the matter from a different angle, and his attitude is defined with an outspokenness unprecedented even in Jane Austen's workmanlike frankness, and with an almost weary cynicism. 'It was Clara whom he meant to seduce. Her seduction was quite determined on. Her situation in every way called for it. She was his rival in Lady Denham's favours, she was young, lovely and dependent.—He had very early seen the necessity of the case, and now been long trying with cautious assiduity to make an impression on her heart, and to undermine her principles—Clara saw through him and had not the least intention of being seduced—but she bore with him patiently enough to confirm the sort of attachment which her personal charms had raised. A greater degree of discouragement indeed would not have effected Sir Edward:—he was armed against the highest pitch of disdain or aversion.—If she could not be won by affection he must carry her off. He knew his business.—Already he had had many musings on the subject. If he *were* constrained so to act, he must naturally wish to strike out something new, to exceed those who had gone before him—and he felt a strong curiosity to ascertain whether the neighbourhood of Timbuctoo might not afford some solitary house adapted for Clara's reception;—but the expense, alas! of measures in that masterly style was ill-suited to his purse, and prudence obliged him to prefer the quietest sort of ruin and disgrace for the object of his affections, to the more renowned.'

The second consideration is that of a use of scenery—not so beautiful as that in *Persuasion*, or even that in *Mansfield Park* and in *Emma*, but of an eerie sensibility, quite unlike anything she had touched before, and oddly in keeping with the story. One morning Charlotte goes with the simple, pleasant, somewhat wistful Mrs. Parker to pay a call on Lady Denham at Sanditon House. It is a close morning in late July, and the sea mist is so dense that when, on their way, they unexpectedly meet with Mr. Parker's brother, the dashing, flippant Sydney, driving himself in his carriage, and taking Sanditon in his way from

263

Eastbourne, they are almost upon him before they can make out what the vehicle is, and whether it is drawn by one horse, two, three or four. The ladies turn into the road to Sanditon House, 'a broad, handsome planted approach between fields,' and presently come to the park paling, 'with clusters of fine elms and rows of old thorns, following its line almost everywhere.' But some gaps were left, and as they walked along, 'through one of them, Charlotte . . . caught a glimpse over the pales of something white and womanish in the field on the other side; it was a something which immediately brought Miss Brereton into her head— and, stepping to the pales, she saw indeed and very decidedly in spite of the mist, Miss Brereton seated, not far before her, at the foot of the bank. . . . Miss Brereton seated very composedly, and Sir Edward Denham by her side. They were sitting so near each other and appeared so closely engaged in gentle conversation that Charlotte instantly felt she had nothing to do but step back again and say not a word.' The 'something white and womanish' appearing in the mist strikes a note quite different from any she had sounded before, but it follows more naturally upon *Persuasion* than it would have followed upon any of the other novels. At the same time, enough of *Sanditon* remains to show that the remarkable alternation of shadow and light in *Sense and Sensibility, Pride and Prejudice, Mansfield Park, Emma* and *Persuasion* would have been maintained by *Sanditon*'s returning to vivid brightness after the pensive sweetness of *Persuasion*.

The dates attached to the manuscript are January 27th on the first quire, and March 18th on the last.

264

CHAPTER TWENTY-ONE

On March 28th occurred the death of Mr. Leigh Perrot. As he was a man of great wealth, childless, and Mrs. Austen his only surviving sister, it was generally expected that he would leave Mrs. Austen and her children provided for in his will. But when the will was read it was found that he had left everything to his wife, except a considerable sum to James Austen, and a provision that £1,000 should be inherited by each of his nephews and nieces who outlived his wife. Mrs. Austen was not mentioned at all, and despite the very disagreeable shock, it was her common sense which supplied the explanation, namely, that her brother had always expected to outlive her.

The will came hard to the Austen family. The Chawton lawsuit was settled in this year by Edward Knight's retaining possession of the estate but paying down a large sum for it, but he was the only member of the family in a position to do anything substantial towards helping the rest, and he had eleven children. Still, they were not as a whole unduly cast down by the matter, awkward and somewhat painful as it was; but Jane was now so weak in nerves and health that it did come as a severe shock to her. She would have faced poverty courageously, but she was none the less afraid of it. She had always taken a refreshing satisfaction in her own gains. 'Though I like praise as well as anybody, I like what Edward calls Pewter too,' she had said, apropos of *Mansfield Park*.* 'Single women have a dreadful propensity for being poor,' she had said to Fanny. She was now in a state in which she felt everything with almost unbearable intensity, and the sensation which the others were able to throw off remained with her. Cassandra had gone with James and Mary to help and console Mrs. Leigh Perrot at Scarlets; but when the will became known at Chawton, Jane felt an alarming increase of illness; she thought she was going to be quite helpless, and she implored Cassandra to come back.

Almost as soon as her sister was in the house once more, Jane began to feel better. On April 6th she wrote to Keppel Street, to Charles, a letter long overdue, but, she said, 'I am ashamed to say that the shock of my uncle's will brought on a relapse and I was so ill on Friday and thought myself so likely to be worse, that I could but press for Cassandra's returning with Frank after the funeral last night, which of course she did, and either her return or my having seen Mr. Curtis, or my

* Letter 106

265

disorder choosing to go away, have made me better this morning. I live upstairs however for the present and am coddled. I am the only one of the legatees who has been so silly, but a weak body must excuse weak nerves.' Charles' second child Harriet had been causing great anxiety by an affection of the head which they thought might be water on the brain; but she seemed now to be a little better. Jane sent her a message at the end of the letter to her father. 'Tell dear Harriet that whenever she wants me in her service again, she must send a hackney chariot all the way for me, for I am not strong enough to travel any other way, and I hope Cassy will take care that it is a green one.' On the outside of this letter is written in Captain Charles Austen's handwriting: 'My last letter from dearest Jane.' The circumstance of Mr. Leigh Perrot's will, or perhaps a feeling that her own death might be nearer than she knew, caused her to make her own will in this month. In it she left all the money she possessed at the time of her death, and any which might afterwards accrue through the sale of her works, to Cassandra, except that she left £50 to Henry, and £50 to poor Madame Bigeon.

But on May 22nd she wrote cheerfully to Miss Anne Sharp, who had at one time been a governess at Godmersham. In this letter she said that she had had another relapse, and been in bed since April 15th, only moving from there to the sofa; but now she was getting better once more, and would have got up, had she been left to herself. As it was, she could employ herself perfectly well in bed, of which her writing the letter was a proof. She had had many things, she said, for which to be thankful; she had never been delirious, and she seemed very much to value that: and she had had, on the whole, very little pain. She had had a discharge which the Alton apothecary did not pretend to be able to cope with, and so a Mr. Lyford from Winchester had been called in, and his applications had been very successful, and the consequence was, she said, 'that instead of going to town to put myself into the hands of some physician, as I should otherwise have done, I am going to Winchester instead for some weeks, to see what Mr. Lyford can do farther towards re-establishing me in tolerable health.' Cassandra was going to take her there on Saturday, 'and as that is only two days off, you will be convinced that I am now really a very genteel, portable sort of invalid.' Mrs. Heathcote had engaged lodgings for them already, and James was sending the carriage from Steventon to take them. Jane mentioned, as ever, the unspeakable kindness and comfort she had had from Cassandra; but everyone, she said, had shown her such kindness. She said: 'In short, if I live to be an old woman, I must expect to wish I had died now; blessed in the tenderness of such a family, and before I had survived either them or their affection.' In

266

a letter posthumously published in the form of an extract by Henry, she showed the state of her nerves and how agonizingly acute every feeling and emotion had become: 'as to . . . the anxious affection of all my beloved family on this occasion, I can only cry over it, and pray to God to bless them more and more.'

She ended gaily to Anne Sharp, saying what a comfort it would be to have Elizabeth Heathcote in Winchester; but Alethea Bigg would not be with them: 'she being frisked off, like half England, into Switzerland.'

It had been arranged that while James and Mary Austen were at Scarlets, Caroline should come to Chawton, but when it came to the point, Jane was found to be too ill for them to have such a young visitor in the house, and Caroline went to her sister at Wyards instead. One morning at the beginning of April they both walked over to see her. She was upstairs, but they were allowed to go up to her, and found her sitting in a chair in her dressing-gown. She was cheerful and like her usual self, except that she looked pale and weak; she got up when they came in, and pointed to two seats by the fire, saying: 'There is a chair for the married lady, and a little stool for you, Caroline.' On looking back, those were the last words of her Aunt Jane's that Caroline could remember; she retained nothing else of what was said: nor was there time for much conversation; in less than a quarter of an hour, their aunt Cassandra came and fetched them away, and in Caroline's words: 'I never saw Aunt Jane again.'

On May 24th Jane said good-bye to Chawton Cottage and got into James's carriage for the drive to Winchester; with Cassandra beside her, she was perfectly comfortable, except that, as it was raining, she was constantly worried by the thought that Henry, who rode at one side of the carriage, and young William Knight on the other, would be getting wet.

The lodging taken by Mrs. Heathcote was one of a small lane of houses, which terminated in the buildings of the school. Its little bow-windowed drawing-room overlooked the headmaster's garden on the opposite side of the lane. In summer, the height of May, there could hardly be a pleasanter situation. Jane was very hopeful of getting better. Three days after her arrival she wrote to Steventon to thank Edward for the loving anxiety he had shown for her during her illness; she could only repay it by telling him much much she was improving. 'I will not boast of my hand-writing; neither that nor my face have yet recovered their proper beauty, but in other respects I am gaining strength very fast. I am *now* out of bed from nine in the morning till ten at night—upon the sofa, 'tis true,—but I eat my meals with Aunt Cass

267

in a rational way, and can employ myself and walk from one room to another.' She added: 'Mr. Lyford says he will cure me, and if he fails, I shall draw up a memorial and lay it before the Dean and Chapter, and have no doubt of redress from that pious, learned and disinterested body.' As Mr. Austen Leigh said on Mr. Lyford's behalf, it was not his business to discourage his patient; but from the first moment of his seeing her in Winchester, he thought there was no hope. The fourteen-year-old Charles Knight was still at Winchester, and his Aunt Jane said they were to have him in to breakfast the next day, which was a holiday. 'We have had but one visit yet from *him*, poor fellow, as he is in the sick room, but he hopes to be out to-night.'

Old Mrs. Austen wrote notes to Anna, saying that though Jane's state was very precarious, there had been some good news of better nights; but James, who had come over from Steventon, wrote to Edward and said he must be prepared for any letter now to contain the worst news.

June passed into July, and James and Henry felt that it was their duty as clergymen to tell her she must face the fact that she might be going to die. She realized the significance of what they said, but she was 'not appalled' by it. She was thankful that she had been able to remain in her right mind throughout the illness, and now she asked them to administer the communion service to her, before she might become too weak and wandering to follow it with all her faculties. All her life she had said so little about religion, and shrunk so much from people who talked a great deal about their religious feelings, that Henry thought it impossible that ordinary acquaintances could have had any idea of how settled and devout her convictions were.

Mary Austen was with them now; she had promised Cassandra she would come if she could be of any use, and as a nurse who had been got in did not quite please Cassandra, Mary had come to take her place. Jane had often in a private letter expressed herself as harassed by the peculiarities of Mary's temperament, but she did not find them trying now. On one occasion when Mary was doing something for her she turned to her and said: 'You have always been a kind sister to me, Mary.' One of the links with the outer world which lasted longest was the pleasure she got from reading Fanny's letters. They were as full, as loving, as amusing and enlivening as ever. Cassandra blessed her niece; she knew the effort it must have cost her to write in such a strain, but the pleasure it gave to Jane was inexpressible.

On Thursday evening, July 17th, Cassandra went into the town to fulfil something Jane was anxious to have done; and when she got back a little before six o'clock, she found that Jane had had an attack of faintness. She was recovered enough to tell Cassandra about it, and was quietly talking to her as the clock struck six; but very soon afterwards the faintness came back again, and for half an hour she felt the actual pangs of death; she had no fixed pain, but she said she could not tell them what she suffered. 'God, grant me patience!' she gasped. Such it was to die in pain without the alleviation of injections or drugs. Cassandra, waiting for Mr. Lyford, who had been sent for, tried to discover if there were anything she could do for her. Jane's voice was altered, but it was intelligible to the last. When Cassandra asked if she wanted anything, she replied: 'Nothing but death.'

When Mr. Lyford came, he did something to relieve her, and by seven o'clock she was in a state of quiet unconsciousness. She lay perfectly still except that every breath caused a slight motion of her head. For six hours Cassandra sat beside the bed with a pillow on her lap because Jane's head was nearly off the bed. Then Mary took her place for two hours and a half. At half-past three Cassandra came back again, and Jane died in her arms at half-past four on the morning of the 18th of July.

CHAPTER TWENTY-TWO

The funeral was conducted in Winchester Cathedral; it had to be very early because the morning service began at ten. Cassandra did not go to it. Fanny had written a long letter full of anguish and distress; she could not imagine how Cassandra would bear it. Cassandra wrote back, comforting her: 'I am perfectly conscious of the extent of my irreparable loss, but I am not at all overpowered.' 'You know me too well,' she said, 'to be at all afraid that I should suffer materially from my feelings.' Poor Cassandra's was not a nature that could find relief in an attack of nervous prostration; the only relief in her power was to give the details of the last night to Fanny. 'My dearest Fanny, doubly dear to me now for her dear sake whom we have lost.' She gave the account, of which she said: 'I could not write so to anybody else.' There had been nothing in Jane's last appearance, she said, which gave the look of pain; 'but for the continued motion of the head, she gave me the idea of a beautiful statue.' Cassandra thanked God that she had been able to do everything for her at the end. Fatigue and grief had not impaired her faculties at all so long as she could be of any use; even when the funeral procession left the house for the cathedral, she did not break down. 'I watched the little mournful procession the length of the street; and when it turned from my sight and I had lost her for ever, even then I was not overpowered, nor so much agitated as I am now in writing of it.'

They left Winchester the day after the funeral and went back to Chawton, to Steventon, to Bentley, to a family life that had lost its brightest ornament. Writing in middle life, one of the nieces said:

'It comes back to me now, how strangely I missed her. It had become so much a habit with me to put things by in my mind with a reference to her, and to say to myself, I shall keep this for Aunt Jane'; and one of the Godmersham nephews used to say that after the death of his Aunt Jane, his visits to Chawton were always a disappointment to him. 'He could not help expecting to be particularly happy in that house; and never till he got there could he realize to himself how all its peculiar charm was gone.'

Henry undertook the publication of her two remaining works: *Miss Catherine*, on whose publication Jane Austen had not actually decided, he called *Northanger Abbey*, and to the last one he gave the title of *Persuasion*. The works were published in one set of volumes by Mur-

270

ray in 1818, and Henry prefixed to them the biographical notice of his sister which was the first account of any kind to be written of her.

Henry Austen's temperament made such an impression on the people who came in contact with him, that he is almost never mentioned without some exclamation on his charm and wit; but his liveliness did not transfer itself to the written word, and the essay on Jane Austen, though of unique value, is something of a disappointment.

His naturally solemn manner of writing, the fact that the essay was itself an elegy, and that the convention of the time prevented his putting before the public that sort of intimate portrait which, in conversation, no one could have given so well as he, have made his description of so dated a nature, that only the extreme interest of its subject makes it possible for us to read it with any degree of intelligent participation. Its expression is as foreign to us as a marble monument of a veiled urn, or a memorial ring, showing a weeping willow made of the departed's hair.

The memoir of Mr. Edward Austen Leigh will always remain, after her own writings, the reader's most thrilling contact with Jane Austen. In certain aspects it is as eloquent of the 1870's as his Uncle Henry's is of 1818; but Mr. Austen Leigh had two points in his favour: he knew that there was a public anxious to hear anything which he could tell, and had Henry Austen felt sure of this, it would have altered the scope of his work considerably; secondly, the Edward Austen who had been writing a novel that had pleased his aunt had something of the novelist's capacity to present a human being, and the little anecdotes and remarks he collected from his own remembrance and that of his sisters, though they are so few in number, give one occasionally a sense almost of clairvoyance. He opens his memoirs at the point at which the ordinary biography of Jane Austen must naturally close, and when one has read the account of Cassandra Austen's vigil until half-past four of a summer's morning, in the house opposite the headmaster's garden, and her saying that they took the coffin away so quietly that had she not been 'upon the listen', she would not have heard them, it is then that Mr. Austen's opening words take on their true perspective. 'More than half a century has passed away, since I, the youngest of the mourners, attended the funeral of my dear Aunt Jane in Winchester Cathedral.' After the ceremony, he said: 'Her brothers went back sorrowing to their several homes. They were very fond and very proud of her . . . and each loved afterwards to fancy a resemblance in some niece or daughter of his own to the dear sister Jane, whose perfect equal they never yet expected to see.'

Cassandra Austen returned to Chawton Cottage, where for ten years

271

she lived looking after her mother. When it had become known that Jane's recovery was impossible, the family, in the midst of their own grief, had turned their thoughts to Cassandra with a dreadful presentiment of horror; but, as Cassandra had said to Fanny Knight, she was not one to be overborne; she could suffer and go on living as before. As a very old lady, she was once seen at a family wedding, pale, with black eyes and a kind smile. Once when she was visited by a relation whose seventeen-year-old daughter had never seen Jane Austen they were struck, when Cassandra spoke of her sister, by 'the accent of *living* love' in her voice.

There never was a time when Jane Austen's work was altogether unrecognized. The appreciation that began in the mind of an older sister and extended to a family circle has spread through the channel of a small and cultivated group until the ordinary reader has become sufficiently familiar with the names of the books she wrote to be able to lay his hand on them naturally, and to feel on opening them that it was for him, after all, that they were originally written. Her fame has not only grown with immense rapidity in the last fifty years, but it is of such a nature as must increase and become more deeply founded as the number increases of people who have not time only but mental energy to read. Another circumstance which makes for the growth of her popularity is that her language offers no difficulty: for she possessed, through a happy combination of art and chance, a style composed of those elements of language which do not date. One may say with tolerable certainty that in fifty year's time the work of those writers of to-day who make use of such expressions as 'plutocrat-flattering bunk' and 'he thought he would go bug-house,' will sound old-fashioned beside the conversation of Emma Woodhouse and Mr. Knightley.

Another aspect of her work which, though an external one, has considerable influence in keeping a writer's work free from the accretions of decay, is that it is notably unhampered by detail. Her characters reveal the fact that they were born in the first decades of the nineteenth century by some of the reasons they supply for the things they do, and by the fact that they call each other Mr. and Miss instead of using the Christian name: but these things are no more important in the reader's comprehension of them, than the fact that they ride in carriages instead of cars and aeroplanes. Actually they seem to meet, not in time, but space.

This is not an age favourable to the development of aesthetic genius; it may be that for a time all forms of art will pass into the domination of those who think that a good picture can be painted only if the artist's political views accord with theirs, and that it is only possible to write a good novel provided the author follows the rules they have laid down.

But such a state of things would not endure in a race with such powers of imagination, so vigorous and independent as our own. If and when that period should arrive, we must remind ourselves:

This is no common waste, no common gloom,
But nature in due course of time, once more
Shall here put on her beauty and her bloom.

Then the great writers of the past will come into their own more fully than before. So far from belonging to an outworn past, their work belongs to a future which will reveal more fully the beauty and the wonder of human nature, by recognizing more completely the rights of human existence.

BIBLIOGRAPHY

The Letters of Jane Austen, Oxford Edition, ed. R. W. Chapman.

A Memoir of Jane Austen, J. E. Austen Leigh.

Northanger Abbey and *Persuasion*, with a biographical notice of the author.

Letters of Jane Austen, edited by Edward Lord Brabourne.

Life and Letters of Jane Austen, W. and R. A. Austen Leigh.

Personal Aspects of Jane Austen, M. A. Austen Leigh.

Jane Austen and her Sailor Brothers, J. H. Hubback.

'Pen Portraits in Jane Austen's Novels', J. H. Hubback, *Cornhill Magazine*, May 1928.

Jane Austen, her Home and Friends, Constance Hill.

Jane Austen, Lord David Cecil.

Grand Larceny, Sir F. D. Mackinnon.

The Picturesque, Christopher Hussey.

The Rule of Taste, John Steegman.

La Belle Assemblée, 1800–1810.

Charades, etc., written a hundred years ago by Jane Austen and her family.

SOURCES OF ILLUSTRATIONS

Colour plates

I Portrait of Jane Austen by Cassandra (National Portrait Gallery)

II Portrait of Cassandra Austen by John Miers (Hickman Collection; Photo: Cooper-Bridgeman Library)

III Rowlandson's cartoon of undergraduates (Victoria and Albert Museum; Photo: R. Todd-White)

IV and V Illustrations from Humphrey Repton's *Fragments of Theory and Practice of Landscape Gardening* (Victoria and Albert Museum; Photo: R. Todd-White)

VI and VII Thirteen water-colour sketches of Kings and Queens of England by Cassandra Austen (By courtesy of Colonel E. J. C. Spanton, a great-great nephew of Jane Austen; Photo: Jeremy Whitaker)

VIII–XI Aquatints of Bath by J. C. Nattes (Victoria Art Gallery, Bath)

XII Two young ladies in a phaeton (Victoria and Albert Museum; Photo: R. Todd-White)

XIII Water-colour of Fanny Knight by Cassandra Austen (Jane Austen House, Chawton; bequeathed by Sir Hugh Knatchbull-Huggeson, K.G.M.G.; Photo: Jeremy Whitaker)

XIV Gouache of Chawton House (Collection of Edward Knight, Esq., Chawton House; Photo: Jeremy Whitaker)

XV Oil painting of the church and house at Chawton (Jane Austen House, Chawton; presented by Miss Beryl Bradford; Photo: J. Butler-Kearney)

XVI Detail of a patchwork quilt worked by Mrs. Austen with the help of Jane and Cassandra (Jane Austen House, Chawton; lent by Mrs. Christopher Knight. Photo: Jeremy Whitaker)

XVII Needlecase made by Jane Austen (Jane Austen House, Chawton; Photo: J. Butler-Kearney)

XVIII and XIX Illustrations from Ackermann's *Microcosm of London* (Victoria and Albert Museum; Photo: R. Todd-White)

XX Wedgwood and Byerley's warehouse at York Street, St James's Square, from *Repository of Arts* (Mansell Collection)

XXI Water-colour by Cassandra Austen of Lawrence Sterne's *Maria* (Jane Austen House, Chawton; from the collection of T. E. Carpenter; Photo: Jeremy Whitaker)

XXII and XXIII Coloured engravings of Carlton House from W. H. Pyne's *The History of Royal Residences* (Mansell Collection)

XXIV The Old Wells and Pump Room at Cheltenham, an engraving by H. Merke (Victoria and Albert Museum; Photo: B.P.C. Picture Library)

Black and white illustrations

1 Drawing of the rear of Steventon Rectory by Anna Lefroy (Jane Austen House, Chawton; presented by Dr R. W. Chapman; Photo: J. Butler-Kearney)

2 Map of the grounds of Steventon Rectory (Jane Austen House, Chawton; Photo: Jeremy Whitaker)

3 Miniature of the Reverend George Austen (Jane Austen House, Chawton; Photo: Jeremy Whitaker)

4 Silhouette of Mrs George Austen (Jane Austen House, Chawton; Photo: J. Butler-Kearney)

5 Silhouette of the Reverend George Austen presenting his son Edward to Mr and Mrs Thomas Knight (Collection of Edward Knight, Chawton House; Photo: Jeremy Whitaker)

6 Portrait of Edward Austen on the Grand Tour (By kind permission of Alton Urban District Council; Photo: Jeremy Whitaker)

7 Miniature of the Reverend James Austen (Jane Austen House, Chawton; Photo: Jeremy Whitaker)

8 Portrait of the Matthew family (Jane Austen House, Chawton; Photo: Jeremy Whitaker)

9 Miniature of Henry Thomas Austen (Jane Austen House, Chawton; Photo: Jeremy Whitaker)

10 Miniature of Francis William Austen (Jane Austen House, Chawton; Photo: Jeremy Whitaker)

11 Miniature of Charles Austen (Jane Austen House, Chawton; Photo: Jeremy Whitaker)

12 Miniature of Mrs Philadelphia Hancock (Jane Austen Museum, Chawton; presented by Mrs M. Purvis; Photo: Jeremy Whitaker)

13 Miniature of Eliza Hancock, Comtesse de Feuillide, from M. C. Hill, *Jane Austen, her homes and her friends*, 1902

14 Portrait of Warren Hastings by T. Kettle (National Portrait Gallery)

15 Detail from an engraving of the siege of the Bastille (B.P.C. Picture Library)

16 Fanny Burney, Madame d'Arblay, by E. F. Burney (National Portrait Gallery)

17 Hall's Circulating Library (Radio Times Hulton Picture Library)

18 Miniature of Tom Lefroy (By courtesy of Major J. G. Lefroy, Royal Irish Rangers)

19 Supplement to the Ladies Diary for 1794 (Victoria and Albert Museum; Photo: R. Todd-White)

20 Miniature of Elizabeth Bridges (Collection of Edward Knight, Esq., Chawton House; Photo: Jeremy Whitaker)

21 Portrait of Edward Knight (Collection of Edward Knight, Esq., Chawton House; Photo: Jeremy Whitaker)

22 Engraving of Godmersham Park, from J. P. Neale's *Views of Seats*, 1826 (Victoria and Albert Museum)

23 Engraving of Strawberry Hill, from a *Description of the villa of Mr Horace Walpole at Strawberry Hill, near Twickenham, Middlesex* (Victoria and Albert Museum)

24 Illustration from *The Old English Baron* (Mary Evans Picture Library)

25 Aquatint of Bath by J. C. Nattes (Victoria Art Gallery, Bath)

26 The Royal Crescent, Bath, from Woodruffe's *Views of Bath* (Victoria and Albert Museum; Photo: R. Todd-White)

27 Aquatint of the Sydney Hotel, Bath, by J. C. Nattes (Victoria Art Gallery, Bath)

28 The Circus, Bath, from Woodruffe's *Views of Bath* (Victoria and Albert Museum; Photo: R. Todd-White)

29 Aquatint of the exterior of the Pump Room, Bath, by J. C. Nattes (Victoria Art Gallery, Bath)

30 Rowlandson's cartoon of a subscription concert in Bath (Radio Times Hulton Picture Library)

31 and 32 Rowlandson's cartoons of the 'Comforts of Bath' (Radio Times Hulton Picture Library)

33 and 34 Silhouettes of Mr and Mrs James Leigh Perrot (Jane Austen House, Chawton; Photo: J. Butler-Kearney)

35 King's Bench Prison, from Ackermann's *Microcosm of London* (Radio Times Hulton Picture Library)

36 Portrait of Nelson by Charles Grignon (Radio Times Hulton Picture Library)

277

37 Mameluke Cap from *Fashions of London and Paris*, February 1804

38 Nelson's ships by Nicholas Pocock (Radio Times Hulton Picture Library)

39 and 40 Views of Lyme Regis (British Museum)

41 Handkerchief worked by Jane Austen (Jane Austen House, Chawton; presented by Miss Mowl; Photo: J. Butler-Kearney)

42 Title-page of Jane Austen's music book (Jane Austen House, Chawton; Photo: Jeremy Whitaker)

43 Title-page of the first edition of *Sense and Sensibility* (Jane Austen House, Chawton; presented by T. Edward Carpenter; Photo: J. Butler-Kearney)

44 Playbill of *Lovers' Vows* (Jane Austen House, Chawton; presented by George Chadwick; Photo: J. Butler-Kearney)

45 Edward Kean as Shylock (Victoria and Albert Museum; Photo: R. Todd-White)

46 Eliza O'Neal as Mrs Beverley (Victoria and Albert Museum; Photo: R. Todd-White)

47 Title-page of the first edition of *Pride and Prejudice* (Jane Austen House, Chawton; presented by T. Edward Carpenter; Photo: J. Butler-Kearney)

48 Dedication to the Prince Regent in *Emma* (Jane Austen House, Chawton; presented by T. Edward Carpenter; Photo: J. Butler-Kearney)

49 Drawing in pencil and chalk of John Murray by W. Brockedon (National Portrait Gallery)

50 Engraving of the nave of Winchester Cathedral from John Britton's *History of Winchester Cathedral* (British Museum)

Picture research by Philippa Lewis and Annette Brown

INDEX

283

286